Contents

Part 3   Researching Intercultural Interaction

Part 4   Resources

List of Figures

General Editors' Preface

Research and Practice in Applied Linguistics is an international book series from Palgrave Macmillan which brings together leading researchers and teachers in Applied Linguistics to provide readers with the knowledge and tools they need to undertake their own practice related research. Books in the series are designed for students and researchers in Applied Linguistics, TESOL, Language Education and related subject areas, and for language professionals keen to extend their research experience.

Every book in this innovative series is designed to be user-friendly, with clear illustrations and accessible style. The quotations and definitions of key concepts that punctuate the main text are intended to ensure that many, often competing, voices are heard. Each book presents a concise historical and conceptual overview of its chosen field, identifying many lines of enquiry and findings, but also gaps and disagreements. It provides readers with an overall framework for further examination of how research and practice inform each other, and how practitioners can develop their own problem-based research.

The focus throughout is on exploring the relationship between research and practice in Applied Linguistics. How far can research provide answers to the questions and issues that arise in practice? Can research questions that arise and are examined in very specific circumstances be informed by, and inform, the global body of research and practice? What different kinds of information can be obtained from different research methodologies? How should we make a selection between the options available, and how far are different methods compatible with each other? How can the results of research be turned into practical action?

The books in this series identify some of the key researchable areas in the field and provide workable examples of research projects, backed up by details of appropriate research tools and resources. Case studies and exemplars of research and practice are drawn on throughout the books. References to key institutions, individual research lists, journals and professional organizations provide starting points for gathering information and embarking on research. The books also include annotated lists of key works in the field for further study.

The overall objective of the series is to illustrate the message that in Applied linguistics there can be no good professional practice that isn't based on good research, and there can be no good research that isn't informed by practice.

Christopher N. Candlin and David R. Hall
Macquarie University, Sydney

Acknowledgements

Numerous people have helped to make this book possible and we would like to acknowledge with gratitude their contribution. Firstly, we express our thanks to all those colleagues, writers, researchers and scholars – known to us personally or through their published work – whose insights we have benefited from. Many of these feature in the book itself and their names, of course, appear in the text. We are also very grateful to the countless participants in our courses, workshops and conference presentations who over the years have greatly enriched our thinking. Without the stimulation of their experiences and insights, this book would have been very much poorer.

We are particularly indebted to a number of people and would like to mention them by name: Chris Candlin, for inviting us to write the book and for his insightful comments on the chapters as they were written and re-written; Klaus Dinkelaker, Stephanie Frei and Stefanie Stadler for reading the manuscript and for their helpful feedback comments; Stephanie Frei and Markus Haag for their contributions to Chapter 12; Annette Becker, Stephanie Frei, Sarah Hanisch, Martin Pehlke, Julia Reinacher and Judith Schade for obtaining and archiving literature, managing a database of references, and handling many of the references. We would also like to thank Priyanka Pathak at Palgrave for her patience and encouragement as we endeavoured to finish the manuscript amidst our very busy schedules.

We are also very grateful to each other for the countless stimulating discussions that we have enjoyed; for each other's detailed feedback on initial drafts; and for the other's patience and understanding when pressures of other work prevented us from responding quickly to each other.

Finally, we are both very thankful to our families (Andrew, Jonathan and Daniel for Helen, and Antje, Kim, Eva and Tom for Peter) for putting up with our numerous absences from family life during the writing of the book – and for the many intercultural interactions we have shared and discussed with them.

We and the publishers wish to thank the following for permission to use copyright material:

Mouton de Gruyter for the table reproduced in Concept 3.6, which was originally published as Table 1 in Prechtl, E. and Davidson Lund, A. (2007)

Intercultural competence and assessment: perspectives from the INCA project. In H. Kotthoff and H. Spencer-Oatey (eds) *Handbook of Intercultural Communication*. Berlin: de Gruyter, p. 472.

Cambridge University Press for extracts reproduced in Experiential Example 4.1 which were originally published in Tyler, A. (1995) The coconstruction of cross-cultural miscommunication. *Studies in Second Language Acquisition*, 17 (2): 129–52. Also, Andrea Tyler for her personal permission to reproduce these extracts.

WorldWork Ltd. for allowing us to use their company's unpublished material which is reproduced in Concept 3.9, Instrument 8.3 and Sample 9.3.

The Directorate General for Education, Training, Culture and Multilingualism of the European Commission for permission to incorporate in Research Reports 9.2, 9.3, 9.5 and 9.6 material from the LACE (Languages and Cultures in Europe) 2007 Report: The Intercultural Competences Developed in Compulsory Foreign Languages Education in the European Union. The European Commission: DG Education, Training, Culture and Multilingualism.

David Marsh and Andrzej Kurtyka for permission to quote from their unpublished country reports which formed source data for the LACE (2007) study.

1
Introduction

Becoming intercultural [...] a personal journey.

Kim 2001: 194–5

Chapter outline

1.1   Aim and readership of the book

This book has grown out of our personal experiences of living and working in different countries, in different contexts and with people from different professions or backgrounds. Many of the intercultural episodes that we have experienced have been salient to us in some way – sometimes amusing, sometimes upsetting, sometimes confusing or difficult to understand and sometimes challenging to handle (e.g., see Experiential Examples 1.1 and 1.2). We have also been deeply enriched by the experiences, especially as we have reflected on them over time. We are gradually 'becoming intercultural' (Kim 2001).

Our aim in this book is to help others explore this exciting field of intercultural interaction for themselves, and to pursue with us this same journey towards greater intercultural competence. Some may want to do this for academic reasons; for example, they may be taking postgraduate courses in the field or undertaking (postgraduate) research. Some may want to do it for professional development purposes; for example, they may already be working as intercultural developers, but

1

want to update their understanding of the field and learn about recent research. Some may have little 'academic' background in intercultural interaction, but participate regularly in intercultural encounters in their jobs and thus want to gain a greater conceptual understanding of the field for professional reasons. Yet others may have a personal interest; for instance, they may have neighbours, friends and/or family members who are from different cultural backgrounds, or they may have lived in or travelled to many different types of societies, and thus have a general interest in the field. For all these different types of readers, we believe that this book will provide a very helpful 'mapping of the field', accessible analyses of the processes of intercultural interaction, and pointers for the journey towards greater intercultural competence.

Experiential Example 1:1   A puzzling request

One year I got to know the Chinese students on our MA course fairly well, and kept in touch with several of them after they returned to China. I met up with them occasionally when I visited Beijing, but then I gradually lost contact. Several years later, one of them was posted to the Embassy in London, and his daughter was accepted onto a pre-degree English language training course at my university. He got back in touch and came to the university to visit me. During the conversation, he said, 'You were my teacher in England; you are still my teacher and you will be my teacher for life. Now, here is my daughter, please take her as your daughter.' I was shocked. What did he mean? Was he just being polite, or did he expect me to do something concrete? Was he asking us to invite her to stay in our home, or was he just asking me to keep an eye on her and befriend her? I had no idea and didn't know how to reply.

Helen Spencer-Oatey

Experiential Example 1:2   A puzzling reaction

Early on in my stay in Germany I bought a pair of shoes and was disappointed after a week or so when one of the shoelaces broke. Expecting them to be replaced free of charge, I returned to the shop to complain. When I had done so, the shopkeeper produced a pair of shoelaces from the shelf behind him and said, '2 deutschmarks 50'. I was astonished: he actually expected me to pay for the replacement shoelaces. He obviously hadn't understood my far from perfect German. So I repeated the story of the unsatisfactory lace. The shopkeeper listened somewhat impatiently, and when I was finished nodded and repeated the price of the laces – rather more loudly and clearly. Despairing of my German and the shopkeeper, I then said very clearly that I was making a complaint and that I expected the laces to be replaced free of charge because of their poor quality. Only then did the shopkeeper with a sarcastic remark agree not to charge me for them. What an odd person, I thought leaving the shop. So slow in the uptake. It was only some time later that I realised that complaints in Germany had to be handled rather more assertively than back home.

Peter Franklin

1.2 Title of the book

We have chosen the title of the book, *Intercultural Interaction: A Multidisciplinary Approach to Intercultural Communication*, with care. There are four key elements to this title (intercultural, interaction, communication, and multidisciplinary); we discuss each of them in turn.

Intercultural

The term 'intercultural' literally means 'between cultures', and so a fundamental question is how can 'culture' be defined and hence what is meant by '*intercultural* interaction/communication'? Chapter 2 explores the concept of culture in detail, so here we will just focus on the term 'intercultural'. At one level, this could refer to all interaction/communication between members of two social/cultural groups, but since we are all simultaneously members of numerous social/cultural groups, virtually all interaction/communication would then be defined as intercultural. Žegarac (2007: 41) distinguishes intracultural from intercultural communication from a cognitive point of view, and identifies an intercultural situation as one in which 'the cultural distance between the participants is significant enough to have an adverse effect on communicative success, unless it is appropriately accommodated by the participants.' In this book, we follow Žegarac's cognitive perspective to a large extent, but revise it slightly as follows:

> An intercultural situation is one in which the cultural distance between the participants is significant enough to have an effect on interaction/communication that is noticeable to at least one of the parties.

Interaction

We have chosen the word 'interaction' for our main title for two reasons. Firstly, it draws attention to the activity of people talking to each other, and thus helps distinguish it from cross-cultural or culture-comparative studies, that is studies in which the language and/or behaviour of two different groups is compared for its similarities and differences. We distinguish repeatedly in the book between culture-comparative studies and culture-interactional studies. Comparative studies are extremely important in that they provide culture-interactional studies with very valuable baseline data for interpretation purposes. However, it cannot be assumed that people's behaviour in intercultural encounters will necessarily be the same as in intracultural encounters because people often automatically make adjustments.

This leads us to our second main reason for choosing the word 'interaction' – it helps draw attention to the dynamic nature of behaviour and language use. As Arundale (2006: 194) points out: 'Social interaction is remarkable for its emergent properties which transcend the characteristics of the individuals that jointly produce it.' This natural feature of all communicative interaction poses us with a range of challenges for the study of intercultural interaction; for example:

- How do we identify 'cultural behaviour' in intercultural interaction, and distinguish it from idiosyncratic behaviour?
- How can we help people manage intercultural encounters more effectively, when it is impossible to predict whether/to what extent cultural behaviour will occur?

There are no easy answers to these questions, but we attempt to address them in this book.

Communication

Linguists typically distinguish between signals that are communicative and those that are informative, depending on whether the information is conveyed intentionally or not. For example, a deliberate wink is distinguished from an involuntary blink by the communicative intention that lies behind it. Yet in intercultural interaction, information conveyed unintentionally may actually be interpreted as intentional; for instance, in some cultures showing the soles of one's shoes can communicate an insult and when somebody does that, it is typically assumed to have communicative intent. However, for someone from a cultural group where that convention does not exist, such behaviour would be unintentional and hence would not be communicative. In other words, a given piece of behaviour may be communicative to some of the participants and only informative to others. This is another reason, therefore, why we prefer the term 'interaction' to 'communication' – it is broader in scope.

Nevertheless, the phrase 'intercultural communication' is used very extensively across a wide range of disciplines and is now regarded by many as a field in its own right. The father of the field is widely acknowledged to be the anthropologist E. T. Hall. He published a large number of books from the late 1950s to the mid-1980s and his influence on the study of intercultural communication was far-reaching. The 1970s witnessed a rapid increase in publications by other authors and disciplines, yet they were primarily published in the United States, and were confined mostly to the fields of communication studies and anthropology. Geert Hofstede, a Dutch social psychologist, published his classic work, *Culture's Consequences*, in 1980, and he quickly became one of the most quoted writers in the field. A very large amount of research which draws on his work is now conducted by psychologists around the world. The international management context of his data prompted management specialists to conduct further research, and as a result, anthropologists and social psychologists, as well as management specialists, have had a considerable impact on management thinking and practice. Linguists have a very long tradition of contrastive analysis, but until relatively recently the application was almost exclusively to second/foreign language acquisition. In the 1980s, cross-cultural pragmatics emerged as a growing area of study, with an emphasis primarily on the investigation of speech acts such as requests, apologies and so on. Since then, interlanguage and intercultural pragmatics have developed as important areas of pragmatics, and the focus has broadened. In addition, discourse analysts have also focused on intercultural discourse. As a result, the field of intercultural communication today is studied by specialists in a wide range of disciplines.

Multidisciplinary

As the previous paragraph indicates, intercultural communication is a focus of interest in many different subject areas, and especially in anthropology, communication studies, social and organizational psychology, sociology, marketing, management studies, foreign languages and foreign language education, applied linguistics, pragmatics and discourse analysis. Blommaert (1991: 13), a specialist in pragmatics, maintains that 'intercultural communication is the locus par excellence for interdisciplinary analysis'. However, up to now, both multidisciplinary and interdisciplinary theorizing and research has been patchy. There is a fair amount of cross-referencing and some multidisciplinary investigations within communication studies, psychology, and business/management studies, but significantly less in the other disciplines. For example, few publications in applied linguistics, pragmatics and discourse analysis refer regularly to studies in the other subject areas, and similarly, few publications in the other subjects include any detailed accounts of studies from applied linguistics, pragmatics or discourse analysis. We believe that this is a major drawback for the growth and development of the field, and so a key aim of this book is to take a multidisciplinary approach. We are especially keen to demonstrate how applied linguistics, pragmatics and discourse analysis can offer the field of intercultural communication many helpful insights that are frequently overlooked and also how applied linguistics can profit from other fields. We thus draw on studies from a very wide range of subjects. Which disciplines predominate depends very much on the topic under consideration. In addition, we aspire to an interdisciplinary stance, whereby we incorporate insights from different disciplines into the conceptual frameworks we present.

1.3 Authors' subjectivity

We are very aware that our own values, experiences, interests, beliefs, social identities and so on have shaped the writing of this book and the perspectives that we have taken. We have been working primarily in an Anglo-Saxon tradition, drawing mainly on research literature and insights published in English by colleagues who, even if not Anglo-Saxon in origin, are mostly writing in that tradition as well. The fact that we have only occasionally referred to publications in languages other than English may also make the book Anglo-centric in the eyes, for example, of continental Europeans and Asians with their own research insights and scholarly traditions, largely inaccessible to us for linguistic reasons. This culture-centredness also applies to the style in which the book is written, which for a German researcher, for example, might be regarded as refreshingly accessible, or unduly simplified, according to taste.

As we discuss in Chapter 11, cultural decentring is vital for effective culture-comparative and culture-interactional research, but complete cultural neutrality is an impossibility. The content, foci, orientations and so on of this book, therefore, are very much a product of our own interests, experiences, priorities and so on. To help people interpret our book in this light, we share something of our own personal backgrounds (see Profiles 1.1 and 1.2).

Profile 1.1   Helen Spencer-Oatey

Professor and Director of the Centre for Applied Linguistics, University of Warwick, UK.
http://www.warwick.ac.uk/al
Disciplinary background: BA Hons in Psychology; MEd with specialisms in Teaching English as a Foreign Language and Educational Psychology; interdisciplinary PhD – pragmatics and social psychology.
Research interests: language and intercultural relations, politeness theory and rapport management; working collaboratively across cultures.
Inspired by: the teacher–student relationship I experienced in China; my Christian faith; challenging questions from students and colleagues.
Life: grew up in monocultural Cornwall where 'foreigners' were those in the next county; experienced my first main culture shock when living with Americans in Austria, shortly after completing my undergraduate degree; started reflecting more seriously on culture when I began learning Chinese in Hong Kong, and later when I lived and taught in Shanghai for seven years; started researching intercultural interaction when students asked me probing questions; was challenged to put 'theory into practice' and to reflect more on collaborative working across cultures when managing a set of Sino-UK collaborative projects (http://www.echinauk.org/ and http://www.globalpeople.org.uk/).

Profile 1.2   Peter Franklin

Professor at the HTWG Konstanz University of Applied Sciences, Germany. Co-founder of the KIeM Institute for Intercultural Management, Values and Communication, Konstanz, and originator of dialogin The Delta Intercultural Academy.
Disciplinary background: BA in Modern and Medieval Languages. After discovering professionally and personally that there was more to successful intercultural communication than communicative competence in a shared language, I found insights from translation studies, communication studies, social psychology, anthropology and management essential for answering the questions and solving the problems I was dealing with.
Research interests: language, communication and culture in international business and management; intercultural management; intercultural competence; developing intercultural competence.
Inspired by: a belief in the supreme value of not merely accepting but also benefiting from difference; the people I encounter in development interventions who have to master intercultural situations far more complex than my own.
Driven by: quite a few 'wasted' years and a desire to make at least a small difference.
Life: upbringing in East Kent with first experiences of the nearby Continent. After a university education enlivened by periods in Germany, Sweden and Austria, I left Britain for a two-year stay in Germany, which hasn't ended

after more than thirty years. Teaching English as a foreign language in teacher education made me interested in intercultural communication, not least also to explain the process of acculturation I was engaged in. Interested by life outside schools and universities, I turned to business and management to apply and extend my newly acquired knowledge. 'Going native' in Germany with a bilingual and bicultural family, and participating since the early nineties in international projects, have given me the opportunity to put what I have learned to the test.

From these diverse but also overlapping backgrounds and experiences, there emerged a shared set of beliefs that have motivated and guided the writing of this book. We acknowledge these in Profile 1.3.

Profile 1.3   Values underpinning our work

We value:

- working with researchers from different disciplines and with practitioners
- conducting research that can be useful to practitioners
- an openness to different types of research methods
- a multidisciplinary and culture-interactional approach as a way to move intercultural communication studies forward

We reject:

- the ideological dismissal of different approaches, without exploring them or trying to understand them
- the belief that the study of intercultural communication is properly the business of only one lead discipline
- data interpretation that ignores the potential influence of contextual factors

1.4   Overview of the book

As with all books in this series, the book is divided into four main parts. These are: Conceptualizing intercultural interaction (Chapters 2–7), Promoting competence in intercultural interaction (Chapters 8 and 9), Researching intercultural interaction (Chapters 10 and 11), and Resources (Chapter 12). The aim is to move from theory through practice to research, and to indicate what resources are available for each of these aspects. Throughout the book, and especially in Parts I and II, there are frequent authentic examples of intercultural interactions to illustrate the issues being discussed.

Part I, Conceptualizing intercultural interaction, aims to provide the theoretical foundation to the book. Chapter 2 takes a multidisciplinary approach to exploring the notion of culture – how it has been defined, the frameworks that have been used for describing it, and cultural group membership. It concludes with a brief discussion of the dangers of over-generalization, stereotyping and essentialism/reductionism when investigating intercultural interaction – topics we return to later in the book. Chapter 3 focuses on the conceptualization of intercultural interaction competence. Drawing on research from a range of disciplines, including psychology, communication studies, applied linguistics, language education and management studies, it considers the various competencies that have been identified and the frameworks that have been developed for summarizing them.

Chapters 4 and 5 are devoted to the processes of intercultural interaction. Chapter 4 explores how understanding is achieved in interaction and how cultural factors may affect this process. It concentrates on the construction of message meaning, and discusses the competencies that are needed to achieve this effectively. Chapter 5 focuses on the management of rapport. It examines the factors that influence people's perceptions of (dis)harmony in interpersonal relations, and discusses the competencies that are needed for managing rapport effectively in intercultural contexts. In both these chapters we use authentic intercultural interaction data to illustrate the discussion.

The final two chapters of Part I deal with two important outcomes that may result from encounters with cultural difference. Chapter 6 first considers impression management and perception from an intercultural perspective, and then demonstrates how in situations of power difference, disadvantage and domination may be the undesirable results. Chapter 7 examines the necessary and at least to some degree almost inevitable consequence of intercultural interaction – namely the changes that occur in the cognition, affect and also behaviour of those involved. It considers not only culture shock and its management, but also personal growth and changed identities.

Part II, Promoting competence in intercultural interaction, is the practice-oriented part of the book. Chapter 8 provides an overview of the instruments available for assessment purposes, including the assessment of people's culture-related value orientations and their intercultural interaction competence. Development is the theme of the following chapter, which describes the goals and methods of intercultural development interventions, often referred to as intercultural training. It also brings together recent research into intercultural development in school education and in particular the language classroom.

Part III, Researching intercultural interaction, comprises two chapters which are designed to stimulate and support those interested in conducting research projects in the area of intercultural interaction. Chapter 10 outlines some key research topics and numerous sample studies associated with the various issues explored in Chapters 3 to 8. Priority is given to describing culture-interactional studies and special attention is paid to the varying methods that can be used to research these issues. Chapter 11 deals with the various steps that are involved in carrying out a research project, and for each of these steps considers the ways in which cultural factors need to be taken into consideration.

The final part, Resources, provides a rich list of different types of resources that may be useful to those considering research into intercultural interaction. They are drawn from a wide range of disciplines and include books, journals, professional associations and their related conferences and congresses, internet resources, assessment instruments and resources for developing intercultural competence.

Each of the chapters ends with some suggestions for further reading, and we hope that the book as a whole will stimulate readers to engage more deeply with intercultural interaction both conceptually and experientially.

Part 1

Conceptualizing Intercultural Interaction

2
Unpacking Culture

All people are the same [...] It's only their habits that are different.

Confucius

Chapter outline

Jan Blommaert (1991), a specialist in pragmatics, has asked a key question for the study of intercultural interaction: 'How much culture is there in intercultural communication?'. Even though it is impossible to answer the question definitively, it is clearly essential to consider first what culture is. This chapter explores this issue from a multidisciplinary perspective.

2.1 Defining culture

Culture is notoriously difficult to define. In 1952, the American anthropologists, Alfred Kroeber and Clyde Kluckhohn, critically reviewed concepts and definitions of culture, and compiled a list of 164 different definitions. Apte (1994: 2001), writing in the ten-volume

Encyclopedia of Language and Linguistics, summarizes the problem as follows: 'Despite a century of efforts to define culture adequately, there was in the early 1990s no agreement among anthropologists regarding its nature.' This is a view which is still widely shared at the time of writing. Concept 2.1 illustrates some different definitions that have been proposed.

Concept 2.1   Definitions of Culture

Culture consists of patterns, explicit and implicit, of and for behavior acquired and transmitted by symbols, constituting the distinctive achievements of human groups, including their embodiment in artifacts; the essential core of culture consists of traditional (i.e. historically derived and selected) ideas and especially their attached values; cultural systems may on the one hand be considered as products of action, on the other, as conditional elements of further action.

(Kroeber and Kluckhohn 1952: 181; cited by Berry 2004: 168)

Culture consists of the derivatives of experience, more or less organised, learned or created by the individuals of a population, including those images or encodements and their interpretations (meanings) transmitted from past generations, from contemporaries, or formed by individuals themselves.

(T. Schwartz 1992; cited by Avruch 1998: 17)

Man is an animal suspended in webs of significance he himself has spun. I take culture to be those webs, and the analysis of it to be therefore not an experimental science in search of law, but an interpretive one in search of meaning.

(Geertz 1973: 5)

[...] the set of attitudes, values, beliefs, and behaviors shared by a group of people, but different for each individual, communicated from one generation to the next.

(Matsumoto 1996: 16)

Culture is to society what memory is to the person. It specifies designs for living that have proven effective in the past, ways of dealing with social situations, and ways to think about the self and social behavior that have been reinforced in the past. It includes systems of symbols that facilitate interaction (Geertz 1973), rules of the game of life that have been shown to 'work' in the past. When a person is socialized in a given culture, the person can use custom as a substitute for thought, and save time.

(Triandis 1989: 511–12)

Culture is a fuzzy set of basic assumptions and values, orientations to life, beliefs, policies, procedures and behavioural conventions that are shared by a group of people, and that influence (but do not determine) each member's behaviour and his/her interpretations of the 'meaning' of other people's behaviour.

(Spencer-Oatey 2008b: 3)

Culture is a universal orientation system very typical of a society, organization or group. [...] It influences the perceiving, thinking, evaluating and acting of all its members and thus defines their affiliation to the culture. Culture as an orientation system structures a specific field of action for those who feel affiliated to this culture and thus creates the prerequisites for developing its own ways of coping with its environment.

(Thomas 1996a: 112; translated by Franklin)

To study culture is to study ideas, experiences, feelings, as well as the external forms that such internalities take as they are made public, available to the senses and thus truly social. For culture, in the anthropological view, is the meanings which people create, and which create people, as members of societies. [...] On the one hand, culture resides in a set of public meaningful forms [...]. On the other hand, these overt forms are only rendered meaningful because human minds contain the instruments for their interpretation. The cultural flow thus consists of the externalizations of meaning which individuals produce through arrangements of overt forms, and the interpretations which individuals make of such displays – those of others as well as their own.

(Hannerz 1992: 3–4)

The definitions in Concept 2.1 draw attention to a number of important characteristics of culture:

- Culture is manifested through different types of regularities, some of which are more explicit than others.
- Culture is associated with social groups, but no two individuals within a group share exactly the same cultural characteristics.
- Culture affects people's behaviour and interpretations of behaviour.
- Culture is acquired and/or constructed through interaction with others.

In this chapter we focus on the first two points: that culture is manifested through different types of regularities and that it is associated with social groups. We deal with the other two points in subsequent chapters. First, we consider some of the key frameworks that have been developed in different disciplines for studying and comparing the regularities of culture.

2.2   Etic frameworks for comparing cultures: multidisciplinary perspectives

A fundamental issue in the analysis of culture is the question of universalism. Are some aspects of behaviour universal and other aspects culturally relative? Are there pan-cultural frameworks that can be used for studying and comparing cultures, or should each cultural group be studied from within and in its own right? The *etic-emic* distinction underlies such questions. The terms *etic* and *emic*, which were originally coined by the linguist and anthropologist Kenneth Pike (1954), are derived from the linguistic distinction between phon*etics* and phon*emics*. As Concept 2.2 explains, they refer to two different approaches to analysing culture, but these approaches need to be seen as complementary rather than contradictory.

Concept 2.2   Etics and emics

Emics, roughly speaking, are ideas, behaviours, items, and concepts that are culture-specific. Etics, roughly speaking, are ideas, behaviours, items, and concepts that are culture general – i.e., universal. [...] Emic concepts are essential for understanding a culture. However, since they are unique to the particular culture, they are not useful for cross-cultural comparisons. [...] More formally, emics are studied *within* the system in one culture, and their structure is discovered within the system. Etics are studies *outside* the system in more than one culture, and their structure is theoretical. To develop 'scientific' generalizations about relationships among variables, we must use etics. However, if we are going to understand a culture, we must use emics.

(Triandis 1994: 67–8)

One fundamental and important point to remember when studying cultural differences in people and across cultural groups is that there are both etics and emics in the world.

(Matsumoto 1996: 21)

Compilations of emic observations can help create etic frameworks that in turn can be used to discover and compare emic differences and similarities across cultures. Thus, emic-level findings can help to expand and refine etic knowledge, and etic frameworks can help to discover and enlighten emic concepts.

(Hall 2002: 67)

In this section, we present some well known etic frameworks for comparing cultures that have been developed in different disciplines: psychology, anthropology, international business/management, and linguistics. Needless to say, the field is vast, and we have had to be highly selective in our reporting. In Section 2.3 we consider some emic research.

2.2.1 Frameworks in psychology

Research within social psychology and cross-cultural psychology has mainly concentrated on fundamental values (see Concept 2.3), and has aimed to identify a number of key dimensions on which different cultural groups can be compared. Here we present the dimensions identified by two influential social psychologists: Geert Hofstede and Shalom Schwartz.

Concept 2.3   What are values?

A broad tendency to prefer certain states of affairs over others.

(Hofstede 2001: 5)

I define values as conceptions of the desirable that guide the way social actors (e.g., organisational leaders, policy-makers, individual persons) select actions, evaluate people and events, and explain their actions and evaluations [...] In this view, values are trans-situational criteria or goals [...], ordered by importance as guiding principles in life. Cultural values represent the implicitly or explicitly shared abstract ideas about what is good, right, and desirable in a society.

(Schwartz 1999: 24–5)

During the late 1960s and early 1970s, Hofstede was a researcher at the large multinational firm, IBM, and conducted surveys of the attitudes and work-related values of IBM employees around the world. He accumulated a databank of around 116,000 responses from employees in more than 70 different countries and regions, which he then analysed. He aimed to characterize whole countries rather than individuals, so for each specific question, he averaged the scores of all the respondents from a particular country. He then used a number of other statistical techniques to identify fundamental dimensions of country-level variation, and four emerged: high–low power distance, individualism–collectivism, masculinity–femininity, high–low uncertainty avoidance. Later, a fifth dimension, long-term–short-term orientation, was added. (See Concept 2.4.)

Concept 2.4   Geert Hofstede's (1980/2001, 1991) Five dimensions of country-level cultural variation

Individualism (loose ties between individuals who give priority to their own needs and preferences) – **Collectivism** (strong ties within cohesive in-groups who give priority to the goals and needs of the group)

High Power Distance – **Low Power Distance** (the extent to which less powerful members of a cultural group expect and accept that power is distributed unequally)

Masculinity (clearly differentiated social gender roles) – **Femininity** (overlapping social gender roles)

High Uncertainty Avoidance – **Low Uncertainty Avoidance** (the extent to which members of a cultural group feel threatened by uncertain or unknown circumstances)

Long-term – **Short-tem Orientation** (whether the focus of people's efforts is on the future or the present)

Hofstede (1980/2001, 1991) published the scores and rank orderings of all of the countries on each of the dimensions, and listed the key behavioural differences between each dimension's polarities (e.g., Quote 2.1). His work has had a massive impact on the study of cultural groups and the differences between them and, to a lesser extent, on the study of intercultural interaction. He is exceptionally widely quoted, not only in psychological publications but also in many other fields such as business and management. His dimensions have been adopted in numerous empirical studies, and they are frequently used to explain behavioural differences. These explanations have been regarded by many in the international management field as especially convincing (e.g., Quote 2.2).

Quote 2.1   Key differences between low- and high-power distance societies in the work organization (Extracts from Hofstede 2001: 107)

Low power distance	High power distance
Decentralized decision structures; less concentration of authority	More centralized decision structures; more concentration of authority
Flat organization pyramids	Tall organization pyramids
The ideal boss is a resourceful democrat	The ideal boss is a well-meaning autocrat
Subordinates expect to be consulted	Subordinates expect to be told

> ## Quote 2.2   Lane, Distefano and Maznevski (2006: 41–2) on power distance
>
> One US company we worked with was extremely low on hierarchy. The headquarters managers of this company had a very difficult time with its subsidiary in India, which had a relatively high preference for hierarchy [...]. The American managers were frustrated that their Indian subordinates would not embrace empowerment and make decisions. The Indian subordinates were frustrated that their American bosses were so inefficient and were taking so much time to discuss simple decisions with everyone, when just telling everyone what to do and then letting them go about their business would be much faster.

Nevertheless, there has been much criticism of Hofstede's work, including the generalizability of his data and the methodology that he used (e.g., McSweeney 2002). Conceptually, there is also a fundamental concern in applying his findings to intercultural interaction: how can scores that are country-level averages be used to explain the influence of culture on individual behaviour? In fact, Hofstede himself (1991: 112) warns that this should not be done, explaining that if the individual level is confused with the societal level, an error known in the social sciences as the ecological fallacy is committed. He points out that his figures reflect central tendencies for the national group as a whole, and that any single individual may well be significantly different from the group average. He maintains that 'the usefulness of the country scores is not for describing individuals, but for describing the social systems these individuals are likely to have built. Social systems are not made for the exceptional individual, but they have to take account of the dominant values of the majority from the people involved' (Hofstede 1991: 253–4). Gudykunst (2004) takes up this issue, and argues that national level values have an indirect effect on individual behaviour in two ways: they influence societal norms and rules, and they influence some of the socialization processes that individuals experience, which in turn can influence (along with many other factors) people's behaviour.

Another social psychologist, Shalom Schwartz, has developed a conceptual framework for comparing cultures that provides measures not only at the country level but also at the individual level. Schwartz's approach is conceptually driven. Unlike Hofstede whose starting point was the IBM questionnaire on attitudes towards preferred states and behaviours in the workplace, Schwarz began by reviewing earlier theory and studies of values, from both Western and non-Western sources, and used them to draw up a list of values and a research questionnaire. He has collected large amounts of empirical data from over 63 different national groups, and has used smallest space analysis – a procedure which changes associations among variables into distances – to represent his findings in multi-dimensional space. He distinguishes between the value priorities of individuals and of social groups, and has found that the structure of group-level and individual-level values is similar but not identical. He has found that at the individual level, ten different value constructs emerge consistently, and that at the group level, seven different value constructs emerge. The individual-level constructs are shown in Figure 2.1 and Concept 2.5, and as Figure 2.1 shows, they can be summarized as two bi-polar dimensions: Openness to Change versus Conservation, and Self-Enhancement versus Self-Transcendence.

Schwartz's framework is very well known to psychologists, but as yet is less familiar to people in other disciplines. Only a minority of books on intercultural communication (e.g., Fitzgerald 2003) and international business (e.g., Comfort and Franklin 2008; Hofstede 2001; House et al. 2004; Jackson 2002) include mention of his work. However, a number of studies (e.g., Schwartz 1999; Smith, Peterson and Schwartz 2002) have found links between Schwartz's values and work-related issues, such as the importance of work in people's lives, the rewards people seek through their work, and the sources of guidance on which managers rely. Chan and colleagues (2004) found significant correlations between some of the values and people's concern for rapport promotion in service encounters, and Spencer-Oatey (2007a) suggests that the framework could be useful for conceptualizing the different types of self-attributes that people may be sensitive to in interaction.

Asking about values rather than preferred behaviours and states may reduce the likelihood of situational factors impacting on answers; nevertheless, Schwartz's work has also been criticized precisely for asking explicit questions about values, as this may result in respondents giving answers which are socially acceptable rather than those which are shown in their behaviour. Schwartz's Portrait Values Questionnaire (PVQ) (cf. Section 11.1.2) is a further development of his original questionnaire and attempts to meet this criticism by formulating the questions more indirectly. It offers a reliable, easy-to-administer instrument for measuring people's individually-held values.

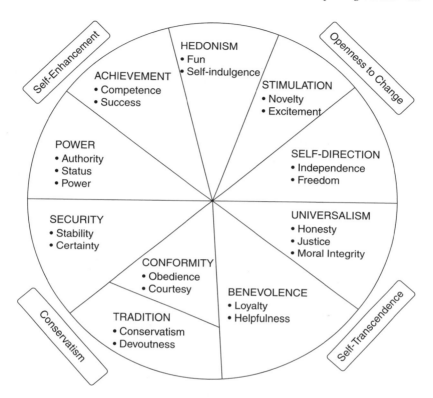

Figure 2.1 Schwartz's value constructs and their structured relationship (based on Schwartz 1992: 44 and originally published in Spencer-Oatey 2007a: 650).

Concept 2.5   Schwartz's value constructs and their associated qualities (based on Schwartz and Bardi 2001: 270 and originally published in Spencer-Oatey 2007a: 651)

Value construct	Explanation	Illustrative component values
Power	Social status and prestige, control or dominance over people and resources	Social power, authority, wealth, preservation of public image
Achievement	Personal success through demonstrating competence according to social standards	Success, competence, ambition

Hedonism	Pleasure and sensuous gratification for oneself	Pleasure, self-indulgence, enjoyment of life
Stimulation	Excitement, novelty and challenge in life	Variety, daring, excitement
Self-direction	Independent thought and action-choosing, creating, exploring	Freedom, independent, curiosity, creativity
Universalism	Understanding, appreciation, tolerance and protection for the welfare of all people and for nature	Equality, harmony, justice, care for the environment, broadmindedness
Benevolence	Preservation and enhancement of the welfare of people with whom one is in frequent personal contact	Helpfulness, loyalty, responsibility, forgiveness, honesty
Tradition	Respect, commitment and acceptance of the customs and ideas that traditional culture or religion provide the self	Humility, respect for tradition, devoutness
Conformity	Restraint of actions, inclinations and impulses likely to upset or harm others and violate social expectations or norms	Obedience, self-discipline, proper behaviour, respect for elders
Security	Safety, harmony and stability of society, relationships, and of self	Health and security for the family and the nation

2.2.2   Frameworks in anthropology

Anthropologists have also developed a number of frameworks for comparing cultural groups. Two that are particularly well known in the intercultural field are those proposed by Edward T. Hall and by Florence Kluckhohn and Fred Strodtbeck.

Hall has written a number of classic books and articles (e.g., Hall 1959, 1966, 1976) in which he describes dimensions of cultural difference. Instead of focusing on fundamental values, as so many cross-cultural psychology researchers have done, Hall has concentrated on dimensions of behavioural difference. Three of his dimensions of behavioural difference are extremely widely quoted: monochronic–polychronic time, high and low context communication, and use of personal space (Concept 2.6). For the former two, Hall argues that the behavioural patterns of different cultural groups give emphasis to different ends of the dimension. With regard to personal space, he maintains that people's conceptions as to what constitutes a 'suitable distance' varies across cultural groups.

Unlike psychological researchers, Hall does not provide quantitative data on how different cultural groups are 'located' on these dimensions.

Concept 2.6 Three dimensions of cultural difference according to Hall (1976)

Monochronic time (M-time) (characterized by doing one thing at a time, emphasis on schedules and promptness; activities are compartmentalized and treated in a linear fashion)	**Polychronic time (P-time)** (characterized by doing many things at a time; emphasis on involvement with people and completion of transactions rather than adherence to preset schedules)
Low-context Communication (patterns of communication that use explicit verbal messages to convey meaning)	**High-Context Communication** (patterns of communication that draw heavily on context such as social roles and positions, shared knowledge and experience, and on non-verbal channels such as pauses, silence and tone of voice, to convey meaning)

Use of Personal Space

Intimate distance (a suitable distance for lovemaking, comforting, whispering secrets)	**Personal distance** (a suitable distance for casual conversations, a person's invisible 'space bubble')	**Social distance** (a suitable distance for formal business transactions or formal interaction)	**Public distance** (a suitable distance for public lectures or performances)

Rather, he presents ethnographic – some would say anecdotal – descriptions of differences, such as the following:

> Americans overseas are psychologically stressed in many ways when confronted by P-time systems such as those in Latin America and the Middle East. In the markets and stores of Mediterranean countries, one is surrounded by other customers vying for the attention of a clerk. There is no order as to who is served next, and to the northern European or American, confusion and clamor abound. [...] In contrast, within the Western world, man finds little in life that is exempt from the iron hand of M-time. In fact, his social and business life, even his sex life, are apt to be completely time-dominated. Time is so thoroughly woven into the fabric of existence that we are hardly aware of the degree to which it determines and co-ordinates everything we do, including the modelling of relations with others in many subtle ways.
>
> (Hall 1976: 17–18)

Nevertheless, there have been a number of studies that have explored Hall's concepts empirically. For example, Watson and Graves (1966) investigated North American and Arab students' use of space. They found that the Arab students not only stood closer to one another than did the North Americans but that they also talked more loudly, touched each other more often, maintained a higher degree of eye contact, and faced each other more directly.

Hall's *descriptions of behaviours* in the workplace, such as in Hall and Hall (1990) which was written almost 20 years ago and in other earlier works, frequently appear obsolete, or at least obsolescent, and sometimes evaluative. Nevertheless, Hall's *framework* continues to be referred to regularly in the intercultural development field (cf. Section 9.3), perhaps because it is straightforward and plausible, resonating as it does with many people's experiences of cultural differences.

Another important anthropological framework for considering cultural differences is the *Cultural Orientation Framework (COF)* developed by Kluckhohn and Strodtbeck (1961). These anthropologists analysed hundreds of ethnographic studies of cultures throughout the world that were conducted by researchers from many different disciplinary backgrounds. They identified five areas of life which pose problems that all societies have to cope with: relationship to the environment, relationships among people, mode of human activity, belief about basic human nature, orientation to time. The solutions to these problems chosen by

Concept 2.7 Kluckhohn and Strodtbeck's (1961) Cultural orientation framework	
Orientations	**Cultural responses**
Relationship to the Environment	*Subjugation to Nature – Harmony with Nature – Mastery over Nature*
Relationships among People	*Lineality* (preference for hierarchical relations) – *Collectivism* (preference for group identification) – *Individualism* (preference of individual autonomy)
Mode of Human Activity	*Being* (acceptance of the status quo) – *Being-in-Becoming* (preference for transformation) – *Doing* (preference for direction intervention)
Belief about Basic Human Nature	*Evil – Mixture of Good and Evil – Good*
Orientation to Time	*Past – Present – Future*

a group, depend on cultural orientations. For each of these orientations, they identified the various different responses that different societies have developed for coping with these problems (see Concept 2.7).

As with Hall's dimensions, Kluckhohn and Strodtbeck's framework has often been applied to intercultural interaction, especially in the business field. Lane, Distefano and Maznevski (2006), for example, describe it in detail, and discuss the 'management impact' for each of the orientations. For instance, they argue that variations in orientation to the environment can affect goal-setting, and that variations in beliefs about human nature can affect management style and levels of workplace control (Quote 2.3).

Quote 2.3   Lane, Distefano and Maznevski on the management impact of cultural orientations

Harmony cultures tend to identify system-wide goals, and to link sets of goals to each other. Goals are seen as a way of articulating the ideal system. Mastery cultures tend to identify specific achievements as goals, and see goals as intentions of control over a situation. If the team has subjugation-oriented members, they may have taken either set of goals, but the meaning of 'goal' would have been different. In a subjugation culture, if the goals are not achieved after a good attempt then they might be recognized as the wrong goals, or it might be decided that production improvement is not the right thing to do at this point.

> Flexible work arrangements – in which people can come and go from the office as they wish provided they achieve work goals – are more predominant in organizational cultures characterized by a dominant goal orientation. Cultural orientations dominated by a neutral or mixed value produce moderately tight controls, with modifications based on managers' experience with the people involved.
>
> (Lane, Distefano and Maznevski 2006: 36 and 46)

More modern anthropologists and other interculturalists would regard Hall's and Kluckhohn and Strodtbeck's approach to the description of culture as no longer in tune with the more heterogeneous and dynamic nature of many national and ethnolinguistic cultures. The social anthropologist Hannerz, for example, talks of culture as a 'flow' (see Concept 2.1 above) and describes how some cultures undergo a process of 'creolization' in which they emerge out of 'multidimensional cultural encounters. [...] Meanings established in the past change as they are drawn into classificatory systems brought in from afar' (1992: 265). In such approaches, culture is perceived not as a static and stable system, as the frameworks described above and in Section 2.2.3 do, which is useful for the interaction scholar interested in capturing cultural differences, but as a current of meanings that continually dissolves old relationships while establishing new ones (Breidenbach and Zukrigl 1998). The challenge posed by the changing nature of national and ethnolinguistic culture in particular is one yet to be met satisfactorily in the investigation of intercultural interaction.

2.2.3   Frameworks in international business

As we have indicated above, much work in international business and management draws on the frameworks developed by psychologists and anthropologists. However, there are two 'business' frameworks that are particularly well known in this sector – one developed by Fons Trompenaars (later in collaboration with Charles Hampden-Turner), and the other developed by a team of people in the *Globe Study of 62 Societies*.

Trompenaars (1993) and Trompenaars and Hampden-Turner (1997), drawing on the work of the anthropologists, Kluckhohn and Strodtbeck (1961), and the sociologists, Parsons and Shils (1951), identify seven dimensions of cultural variability (Concept 2.8). To investigate the impact of each of these dimensions on people's behavioural choices, they devised, amongst other tasks, sets of 'dilemma scenarios', each with a limited number of options for handling the problem. The options reflect a range of preferences associated with that particular

Concept 2.8 Trompenaars and Hampden-Turner's fundamental dimensions of culture

Dimension	Explanatory quotations
Universalism – Particularism	The universalist approach is roughly: 'What is good and right can be defined and always applies.' In particularist cultures far greater attention is given to the obligations of relationships and unique circumstances. (p. 8)
Individualism – Communitarianism	Do people regard themselves primarily as individuals or primarily as part of a group? (p. 8)
Neutral – Emotional	Should the nature of our interactions be objective and detached, or is expressing emotion acceptable? (p. 9)
Specific – Diffuse	In specific-oriented cultures a manager segregates out the task relationship she or he has with a subordinate and insulates this from other dealings. [...] However, in some [diffuse-oriented] countries every life space and every level of personality tends to permeate all others. (p. 81)
Achievement – Ascription	Achievement means that you are judged on what you have recently accomplished and on your record. Ascription means that status is attributed to you, by birth, kinship, gender or age, but also by your connections (who you know) and your educational record. (p. 9)
Attitudes to Time	In some societies what somebody has achieved in the past is not that important. It is more important to know what plan they have developed for the future. In other societies you can make more of an impression with your past accomplishments than those of today. (p. 10)
Attitudes to the Environment	Some cultures see the major focus affecting their lives and the origins of vice and virtue as residing within the person. Here, motivations and values are derived from within. Other cultures see the world as more powerful than individuals. They see nature as something to be feared or emulated. (p. 10)

(Trompenaars and Hampden-Turner 1997: 8–10)

dimension, and respondents are asked to choose one of the options. Trompenaars and Hampden-Turner (1997) obtained responses to their dilemmas from about 15,000 informants in 50 different countries, and in their book they show the percentage of respondents per country who answered a given question in a particular way. (See Quote 2.8.)

Quote 2.4   A problematic scenario from Trompenaars and Hampden-Turner

A defect is discovered in one of the installations. It was caused by negligence of one of the members of a team. Responsibility for this mistake can be carried in various ways.

A: The person causing the defect by negligence is the one responsible.
B: Because he or she happens to work in a team the responsibility should be carried by the group.

Which one of these two ways of taking responsibility do you think is usually the case in your society, A or B?
The percentage of respondents opting for individual responsibility (Option A) ranged as follows: 16% in Indonesia; 37% in China; 48% in the UK; 58% in Australia; 69% in Cuba.

(Trompenaars and Hampden-Turner 1997: 54, 56)

Trompenaars and Hampden-Turner's (1997; first edition published in 1993) framework has been sharply criticized by Hofstede (1996), especially from a research methodology perspective. However, Hampden-Turner and Trompenaars (1997) argue that they do not attempt to represent nations as being at particular points on each axis, as Hofstede does, because they want to acknowledge the impact of contextual variability. Rather, they prefer to focus on the dilemmas that people face, and they argue that the key to success in intercultural interaction is in finding creative, synergistic solutions that can satisfactorily reconcile conflicting values and preferences (Hampden-Turner and Trompenaars 2000). Much of their current consultancy work is directed at helping companies achieve such synergistic reconciliation.

Recently a major study has been published on the relationship among culture, leadership and societal effectiveness. It is known as the GLOBE Study and has involved 170 investigators from 62 different countries/ regions (House et al. 2004). In their conceptualization of culture, the team build heavily on previous work, especially by Hofstede (2001; first edition published in 1980) and by Kluckhohn and Strodtbeck (1961).

Concept 2.9 Dimensions of cultural variability used in the Globe Study	
Dimension	**Definition**
Power Distance	The degree to which members of a collective expect power to be distributed equally.
Uncertainty Avoidance	The extent to which a society, organization or group relies on social norms, rules, and procedures to alleviate the unpredictability of future events.
Humane Orientation	The degree to which a collective encourages and rewards individuals for being fair, altruistic, generous, caring, and kind to others.
Collectivism I (Institutional Collectivism)	The degree to which organizational and societal institutional practices encourage and reward collective distribution of resources and collective action.
Collectivism II (In-group Collectivism)	The degree to which individuals express pride, loyalty, and cohesiveness in their organizations or families
Assertiveness	The degree to which individuals are assertive, confrontational, and aggressive in their relationships with others.
Gender Egalitarianism	The degree to which a collective minimizes gender equality.
Future Orientation	The extent to which individuals engage in future-oriented behaviours such as delaying gratification, planning, and investing in the future.
Performance Orientation	The degree to which a collective encourages and rewards group members for performance improvement and excellence.
(House et al. 2004: 30)	

This can be seen from the nine dimensions of cultural variability they used (see Concept 2.9). The study collected measures of these dimensions at societal levels of analysis, both in terms of practices (the way things are) and as values (the way things should be).

2.2.4   Frameworks in applied linguistics and discourse studies

Linguistic frameworks for studying culture take two complementary perspectives: one focuses on the maxims or principles that underlie language use (and that may be valued differently in different cultural groups), and the other analyses the patterns or styles of language use (and that may show different mean frequencies across different cultural groups).

The best known framework in relation to maxims or principles is Leech's (1983) Politeness Principle. Originally conceptualized as comprising six maxims, Leech (2005, 2007) has recently revised it slightly, replacing the term 'maxim' with 'constraint' and identifying a single super-constraint labelled the Grand Strategy of Politeness (GSP). Leech explains the GSP as follows:

> In order to be polite, S expresses or implies meanings which place a high value on what pertains to O or place a low value on what pertains to S. (S = self, speaker; O = other person[s], [mainly the addressee])
>
> (Leech 2007: 181)

Leech identifies a number of constraints (Concept 2.10) that unpack the GSP, and he argues that the hearer-oriented constraints are generally more powerful than the speaker-oriented ones. He implies that these constraints are universal, although their relative strength may vary across cultures. Moreover, he identifies a number of contextual factors (labelled rather confusingly as 'scales of value') that also are subject to different interpretation from society to society. Leech argues that all of this provides a basis on which well-founded culture-comparative pragmatic research can proceed.

Leech's framework, and in particular the relative weighting of the different constraints in different cultures, provides a very helpful tool for comparing language use across cultures. For example, the relative weighting given to Modesty can affect (along with other factors) how people respond to compliments, and the relative weighting given to Agreement can affect (along with other factors) how freely people feel able to disagree with others. This may lead to different styles of interaction, as we explain below.

Leech's framework is mostly unknown outside the field of linguistics, yet the social psychologist Mark Leary reports an interesting debate in the psychological literature about culture and self-enhancement (Quote 2.5). From Leech's point of view, he would not concern himself with people's inner motives for being modest or self-enhancing; he would concentrate on the social constraints influencing 'external' behaviour.

Concept 2.10 Interactional constraints and scales of value associated with Leech's (2005, 2007) Grand Strategy of Politeness

	Hearer-orientation		Speaker-orientation		
	Constraints	Typical speech act(s)		Constraints	Typical speech act(s)
Generosity	Place high value on O's wants	Commissives	Tact	Place low value on S's wants	Directives
Approbation	Place high value on O's qualities	Directives	Modesty	Place low value on S's qualities	Self-devaluation
Obligation (of S to O)	Place high value on S's obligation to O	Apology, Thanks	Obligation (of O to S)	Place low value on O's obligation to S	Responses to thanks and apologies
Agreement	Place a high value on O's opinions	Agreeing/ disagreeing	Opinion –reticence	Place a low value on S's opinions	Giving opinions
Sympathy	Place high value on O's feelings	Expressing feelings	Feeling – reticence	Place a low value on S's feelings	Suppressing feelings

Scales of value that influence interpretation of the constraints

1. Vertical distance between S and O (in terms of status, power, role, age, etc.).
2. Horizontal distance between S and O (intimate, familiar, acquaintance, stranger, etc.).
3. Weight of value: how large is the benefit, the cost, the favour, the obligation, etc.
4. Strength of socially-defined rights and obligations (e.g., a teacher's obligations to a student; a host's obligations to a guest; service providers' obligations to their clients or customers.
5. 'Self-territory' and 'other-territory' (in-group membership vs. out-group). There are degrees of membership of 'self-territory' and 'other-territory'.

Quote 2.5   Are there cultural differences in self-enhancement?

Most studies of self-enhancement have been conducted in the United States, Europe, and Australia, leaving open the question of whether people in other cultures, particularly in east Asia, also self-enhance [...]. On one side of the debate, researchers have suggested that people in certain cultures, such as Japan, do not show the same self-enhancing tendencies as people in the United States (e.g., Heine et al. 1999; Markus and Kitayama 1991). [...]

Other researchers have argued that all people [...] behave in self-enhancing ways that promote self-esteem. However, because different characteristics are valued in different cultures, people promote their self-esteem in culturally defined ways. [...] In support of this hypothesis, Sedikides Gaertner and Toguchi (2003) found that both American and Japanese participants self-enhanced but used different tactics to do so.

(Leary 2007: 322–3)

Spencer-Oatey and Jiang (2003) have built on Leech's notion of maxims/constraints to develop the concept of sociopragmatic inter-actional principles (SIPs). They define these as 'socioculturally-based principles, scalar in nature, that guide or influence people's productive and interpretive use of language' (2003: 1635). They point out that the principles are typically value-linked, so that in a given culture and/or situational context, there are norms or preferences regarding the implementation of the principles, and any failure to implement the principles as expected may result in mild to strong evaluative judgements. This suggests that there are likely to be connections (although not necessarily direct ones) between the value dimensions that psychologists have identified (especially the individual-level ones, such as those identified by Schwartz 1992) and the interactional principles that linguists can identify in discourse. More research is needed in this area to find out whether this is the case or not.

A second approach to culture-comparative research that has been particularly common in pragmatics (a branch of linguistics that focuses on the construction of meaning in social interaction) and in discourse analysis is to compare the ways in which speech acts (e.g., requests, apologies) and communicative events (e.g., business meetings, lectures) are carried out. There are no universal frameworks that can be used for this purpose, although the notions of semantic components and directness–indirectness have been extremely useful for studying speech acts (see Spencer-Oatey 2008c: 22–5 for more details). Some linguists (e.g., House 2003) have argued that there are dimensions of communication style, such as directness–indirectness, orientation towards self – orientation towards other, on which speakers from different cultural groups can be compared. We discuss this further in Chapters 4 and 5.

2.3   Emic perspectives on culture

At the beginning of Section 2.2, we noted that culture can be studied from two perspectives: from an etic perspective which entails comparisons across cultures, and from an emic perspective which entails culture-internal research. We also noted that these are not contradictory approaches, but that each complements the other in important ways.

The frameworks presented in the last section were all attempts to provide valid tools for exploring the similarities and differences between cultures. In fact, such tools need preliminary emic research to help develop them, and ongoing emic research to help refine them. This is particularly reflected in the work of the German psychologist Alexander Thomas (1996a, 2003b). Thomas aims to determine *Kulturstandards* (*culture standards*) for national groups by starting with behavioural experiences. Focusing on a particular culture, he first conducts semi-structured interviews with people who have moved into this new cultural context, and who have a high degree of interaction with the new host culture. He asks them to describe frequently occurring, task-related encounters in which their interaction partner reacted in a way that they had not expected. Then, on the basis of an extensive set of such critical incidents (both positive and negative), he derives a set of what he describes as 'behaviour-relevant characteristics' or culture standards of the group under investigation. Thomas and others claim that this kind of analysis of critical incidents can lead them to a set of recurring culture standards for a given culture, regardless of the culture of the informant. He describes culture standards as the central orienting characteristics of culture; examples of the culture standards that Thomas derives for German culture are task-orientation, rule-orientation, directness/honesty (2003b: 26).

According to Brueck and Kainzbauer (2003), the *Kulturstandards* have a clearly relative and bilateral character, and cannot be used more generally to compare one particular national group to a variety of others. So, for example, the *Kulturstandards* identified for Austria and Hungary cannot be taken as representing universally valid sets of Austrian standards and Hungarian standards. Nor can they be taken as a universal framework for comparing cultures, as the frameworks discussed in Section 2.2 aim to do. However, Brueck and Kainzbauer argue that far from being a weakness, this relativity is what makes *Kulturstandards* particularly valuable for intercultural development programmes, because it is the most problematic aspects of specific interactions that people most want to address in training. Franklin (2007) takes the argument one step further by pointing out that the culture standards approach allows training to concentrate not merely on what is different in a culture and therefore potentially difficult to cope with, but to focus on those areas of interaction where culture standards in two cultures are not merely different but are actually contradictory. Like Brueck and Kainzbauer (2003), he argues that the emic nature of the culture standards approach allows much greater differentiation than the application of etically derived, universal dimensions of difference.

2.4   Culture and regularity

2.4.1   Types of cultural regularity

An important theme underlying our discussion of etic and emic conceptualizations of culture is the notion of regularity. There has been a tendency for theorists in different disciplines to focus on different types of regularities in their unpacking of culture; for example, fundamental values in cross-cultural psychology, orientations to life in anthropology, and communicative principles and conventions in linguistics. In our view, however, it is important to attempt to incorporate *all* forms of regularity that are characteristic of a given cultural group when analysing intercultural interaction.

Blommaert (1998a) contrasts a conceptualization of culture that focuses on values and norms with the conceptualization provided by the sociolinguist John Gumperz, who has worked extensively in the field of intercultural communication. He argues as follows:

> A first point he [Gumperz] underscores is the fact that 'culture' in the sense of a transcendent identity composed of values and norms and linearly related to forms of behaviour is not necessarily there. What can be observed and analyzed in intercultural communication are different conventions of communication, different speech styles, narrative patterns, in short the deployment of different communicative repertoires. [...] But in actual fact, not 'culture' is deployed, but communicative repertoires.
>
> (Blommaert 1998a: online)

Although we agree with Blommaert that there is certainly no linear relationship between values and behaviour, we believe it would be strange to assume that values are held isolated in one's mind and heart and remain behaviourally unexpressed in interaction with others. We also believe it is a mistake to draw a contrast between culture and conventions of communication. In fact, Gumperz himself (e.g., Gumperz and Roberts 1991) links differences in conventions of language use with the notion of culture. In our view, the culture of a given group is best seen as a complex web of different types of regularities which can include one or more of the following interconnected key elements:

- Orientations to life and beliefs
- Values and principles
- Perceptions of role relationships, including rights and obligations associated with them
- Behavioural rituals, conventions and routines (linguistic and non-linguistic)
- Artefacts and products, including laws, regulations, policies and procedures

Members of some types of cultural groups (see Section 2.5 for a discussion of different types of cultural groups) share a larger range of types of regularity than others, and in fact this could be one way of assessing the relative ease with which new or non-members are likely to be able to integrate into a group. Instruments which have this purpose are discussed in Chapter 8.

2.4.2 Culture, regularity and variability

Kecskes in an interview with Spencer-Oatey questions the validity of a 'regularity' approach to culture, arguing as follows:

Kecskes: Your definition of culture [...] seems to put emphasis on regularity rather than variability, although it does not deny the importance of the latter. Currently, however, there has emerged a constructivist *approach* that focuses on variability, arguing that cross-cultural encounters create an entirely new context in which the rules that will govern the relations between cultures do not yet exist and hence must be constructed. Norms in this view arise directly out of the communicative process, occasioned by the need of individuals to coordinate their actions with others. Several researchers (e.g., Bulcean and Blommaert 1997; Blommaert 2001;

Rampton 1995) argued that 'culture' is situational in all its meanings and with all its affiliated concepts and depends on the context in which concrete interactions occur. Culture cannot be seen as something that is 'carved' in every member of a particular society or community. It can be made, changed, manipulated and dropped on the spot. What do you think about this approach? How do you think regularity and variability relate to each other in culture?

(Spencer-Oatey 2005: 338)

In our view, regularity and variability go hand in hand. We believe that a social constructionist perspective (see Quote 2.6) can be fully compatible with a view of culture that emphasizes regularities. This is in line with Bourdieu's concept of 'the habitus', which he defines as 'the durably installed generative principle of regulated improvisations [... which produces] practices' (1977: 78). In other words, people incorporate into their habitus the regularities they experience over time both in and across given contexts, yet their actual practices emerge from a dynamic interaction of these regularities with improvisation and creativity.

Quote 2.6   Social constructionism

The ways in which we commonly understand the world, the categories and concepts we use, are historically and culturally specific [...] If our knowledge of the world, our common ways of understanding it, is not derived from the nature of the world as it really is, where does it come from? The social constructionist answer is that people construct it between them. It is through the daily interactions between people in the course of social life that our versions of knowledge become fabricated.

(Burr 1996: 3)

In relation to regularities, it is important to remember that a given social group does not necessarily manifest regularities in each of the elements discussed above in order for it to be regarded as having its own culture. For example, members of a work-based community of practice (Wenger 1998) may share various regularities that are associated with their specific practice (including, for example, work-related behavioural conventions and routines, artefacts, assumptions about role rights and obligations, and so on). However, those same members may simultaneously hold very different beliefs about life (e.g., religious beliefs) from each other, or may each make very different assumptions about the rights and obligations of family members. So, in other words, the group may show features of a culture in those aspects which are pertinent to the particular nature of the group in question but variability in others which are not.

There is also a contextual basis to the manifestation of regularities and variation. For example, if a group develops an informal, 'personalized' style of interaction, in which joking and teasing is common and in which personal self-disclosure is valued, this does not mean that these group members will necessarily interact in the same way with other people or in other groups. It is possible that they may, but it is equally possible that they may regard that as inappropriate and hence show very different behaviour in different contexts. On the other hand, it is equally possible that certain very deep-seated cultural features will *not* be contextually based. For example, members of social groups who uphold the value of hierarchy in the management of relationships may apply that value in a range of contexts (e.g., at work, in the family, in the community), even though it may be operationalized differently in each of these contexts. Similarly, members of social groups who stress the fundamental equality of relationships may uphold this across a range of communicative situations, although again it may be operationalized differently in different contexts.

So whilst we would agree that it is vital to study and analyse culture in specific situations, we would not agree with Blommaert (1998a) that culture, in all its meanings and with all its affiliated concepts, is *always* situational. Even though behavioural and communicative conventions are typically situationally dependent, very fundamental assumptions and values can be pan-situational (despite being operationalized differently in different contexts). For example, acceptance (or rejection) of high power distance in relations may apply across a range of contexts, such as in the workplace, in the home, in the community and so on.

Thirdly, variation can occur among the members of a given social group. When social psychologists refer to cultural norms, they are not in fact implying uniformity. On the contrary, they regard them as kinds of behavioural/attitudinal 'means', which by definition entail distributional variability. Žegarac (2007: 39–40) provides a helpful analogy between culture and epidemics to illustrate this point (Quote 2.7) and Wenger's (1998) explication of core and peripheral membership of communities of practice adds further insights (Quote 2.8).

Quote 2.7   Žegarac on the analogy between culture and epidemics

Just as there is no epidemic without individual organisms being infected by particular viruses or bacteria, there is no culture without representations being distributed in the brains/minds of individuals. [...] There is no epidemic without diseased individuals, but the study of epidemics cannot be reduced to the study of individual pathology. From this perspective, the boundaries of a given culture are not any sharper than those of a given epidemic. An epidemic involves a population with many individuals being afflicted to varying degrees by a particular strain of micro-organisms over a continuous time span on a territory with fuzzy and unstable boundaries. And a culture involves a social group (such as a nation, ethnic group, profession, generation, etc.) defined in terms of similar cultural representations held by a significant proportion of the group's members. In other words, people are said to belong in the same culture to the extent that the set of their shared cultural representations is large.

(Žegarac 2007: 39–40)

Quote 2.8   Wenger on core and peripheral membership

The ability to have multiple levels of involvement is an important characteristic of communities of practice [...] Indeed, because it is defined by engagement rather than a reification of membership, a community of practice can offer multiple, more or less peripheral forms of participation. From this perspective, a community of practice is a node of mutual engagement that becomes progressively looser at the periphery, with layers going from core membership to extreme peripherality.

(Wenger 1998: 117–18)

As Corder and Meyerhoff (2007) point out, people may be peripheral members of a community of practice (and, in our view, of any cultural group) either because they choose (for whatever reason) not to adopt all the practices associated with core membership, or else because they are novices in that community. This leads us to another aspect of variability in culture: the variability that occurs over time. When a new social group forms, its group-specific practices emerge over time; in other words, its culture gradually develops. However, sooner or later the cultural manifestations of the group stabilize, and so new members of the group have to be inducted into/learn the culture through socialization, training and so on. Meanwhile, (some of) the cultural manifestations of the group can themselves change over time, either through innovation or else through diffusion. In other words, the variability of culture is also reflected in the changes that can occur over time.

How then do these understandings of regularity and variability in culture affect our approach to intercultural interaction? Wenger's (1998) comments (Quote 2.9) on repertoires closely reflect our views.

Quote 2.9   Wenger on shared repertoires

I call a community's set of shared resources a *repertoire* to emphasise both its rehearsed character and its availability for further engagement in practice. [...] Histories of interpretation create shared points of reference, but they do not impose meaning. Things like words, artifacts, gestures, and routines are useful not only because they are recognizable in their relation to a history of mutual engagement, but also because they can be re-engaged in new situations. [...] All have well-established interpretations, which can be re-utilized to new effects, whether these new effects simply continue an established trajectory of interpretation or take it in unexpected directions.

(Wenger 1998: 83)

In specific encounters, people can uphold, manipulate or drop cultural practices, according to their goals, preferences and so on. They have the freedom to make those individual choices, and they can convey interactional 'meanings' through those choices. (See Chapters 4 to 6 for a more detailed discussion of intercultural communication processes.) However, unlike Blommaert (1998a), we do not believe that they 'make culture' in a single encounter; culture only emerges when patterns start to develop or sometimes when they are consciously created through espoused values and so on, as in organizational cultures. In fact, Blommaert (1998b), in his review of Rampton (1995), reports use of 'crossing' (the use of Panjabi, Caribbean creole and stylized Asian English within adolescent peer-groups by speakers who cannot claim 'ownership rights' to these language varieties) in terms of patterns, albeit very complex ones; for example:

Crossing into SAE [stylized Asian English] and Panjabi seems to occur mostly in situations in which 'normal' ways or conduct or rules of behaviour could not be taken for granted and needed to be transgressed: risky situations, self-talk, cross-sex talk, impropriety. [...] crossing does not abolish or eliminate the existing ethnic stratifications in society, but manipulates them situationally.

(Blommaert 1998b: 121)

In other words, the strategic use of language depends on both regularity and variability; variability often only takes on strategic meaning against the backdrop of regularity. However, we do not believe that the variability itself can be regarded as culture; at least, not until (or not unless) the variability itself becomes patterned in its occurrence!

2.5   Culture and social groups

Throughout this chapter, we have indicated that culture, by its very nature, is associated with social groups. Within the intercultural field, there is often an implicit assumption that cultural group is equivalent to national or ethnic group, and much of the research has been conducted on that basis. Yet as Avruch (1998) explains (Quote 2.10), this is far too limited a view.

Quote 2.10   Avruch on multi-group membership

Individuals are organized in many potentially different ways in a population, by many different (and cross-cutting) criteria: for example, by kinship into families or clans; by language, race, or creed into ethnic groups; by socio-economic characteristics into social classes; by geographical region into political interest groups; and by occupation or institutional memberships into unions, bureaucracies, industries, political parties, and militaries. The more complex and differentiated the social system, the more potential groups and institutions there are. And because each group or institution places individuals in different experiential worlds, and because culture derives in part from this experience, *each of these groups and institutions can be a potential container for culture.* Thus no population can be adequately characterized as a single culture or by a single cultural descriptor. As a corollary, the more complexly organized a population is on sociological grounds (class, region, ethnicity, and so on), the more complex will its cultural mappings appear.

(Avruch 1998: 17–18; emphasis in the original)

The fact is that there are many different types of social groups, and where members of any group share patterns of regularity in some way (as discussed in Section 2.4.1), they can be regarded as belonging to a cultural group. Up to now the field of intercultural interaction has mainly focused on national groups and organizational groups; however, it needs to incorporate these different types of group within its remit because any kind of inter-group interaction has the potential to be intercultural. In this section, we examine some different types of social groups, apart from nationality, that can be regarded as having their own cultures. For reasons of space, we can only discuss a few of them relatively briefly.

2.5.1 Culture and religious groups

'Religion is inextricably woven into the cloth of cultural life' (Tarakeshwar, Stanton and Pargament 2003: 377). The culture of a religious (sub-)group can be manifested in a variety of ways, including in members' values, beliefs and orientations to life, in their communicative conventions, in their policies and procedures, and in their buildings, rituals and behaviour. These cultural manifestations can have a major impact across a wide range of contexts and at different levels – personal (see Experiential Example 2.1), organizational, and regional/national.

Experiential Example 2.1   How can I be both a Christian and Japanese?

Teased and rejected at school for embracing a Western religion, he wondered how it was possible to be Christian and Japanese at the same time, when the two cultures had such different values. He described his religion as a suit of Western clothes that did not fit his Japanese body, and which he wished to exchange for a kimono. It seemed that Christianity was despised in Japan and he longed to visit the West [...] After the Second World War, Endo travelled to France to study, hoping to find some answers in the heartland of Catholicism; but here he simply suffered further rejection in a climate of anti-Japanese hostility. [...] Unable to find answers in Asia or Europe, and suffering from tuberculosis, Endo slipped into a dark depression. Before returning home, however, he visited the Holy Land in order to research the life of Jesus, and he discovered something he had never realized before. Jesus, too, had been rejected by those around him. [...] On his return to Japan, Endo resolved to re-tailor his ill-fitting clothes, to make them Japanese and find a Christian message that would make sense in Japanese terms. He did so in a series of novels that explored themes of rejection and salvation, focusing in particular on the choices facing those trying to reconcile Japanese culture with Christian faith. [...] And Endo must have struck a chord. By the time of his death in 1966, he was regarded as one of Japan's greatest novelists of modern times.

(Hill 2005: 53–4)

There are comparatively few culture-comparative and culture-interactional studies that focus on religious groups, so Tarakeshwar, Stanton and Pargament (2003: 390) argue that more research is needed in this area for the following reasons:

- Religion is important in the lives of people across cultural groups.
- Religion has been found to be a significant predictor of salient variables (e.g., physical and mental well-being) across cultural groups.
- Religion is associated with critical culturally-related value dimensions.
- The cultures of other social groups shape religious beliefs and practices.

2.5.2   Culture and organizations

Organizations can be said to have their own culture in that they can have espoused or assumed values, established practices and procedures, behavioural conventions and so on. Hofstede's (1980/2001, 1991) and Schwartz's (1992) frameworks for characterizing national cultures cannot necessarily be applied to organizations, although Hofstede lists features of the workplace and management characteristic of the value orientations he describes. By contrasting the four end points of the uncertainty avoidance and power distance dimensions, he also generates four implicit models of organization (something very similar to organizational cultures, although he avoids the term) likely to be encountered in particular national cultures (Hofstede 1991: 151–2). Other specifications may be needed and have been proposed (Concept 2.11). On the other hand, Schneider and Barsoux (2003) and others maintain there are causal connections between features of national cultures and organizational cultures; Lane, Distefano and Maznevski (2006), for example, imply that Kluckhohn and Strodtbeck's orientations to life are applicable to organizational cultures.

When two organizations, such as Daimler-Benz and Chrysler or Rover and BMW, merge, clashes of culture are commonplace and it is not always clear to those involved whether it is a matter of national culture clash or organizational culture clash. Whatever their roots, such clashes may soon lead to discomfort and conflicts when, for example, the employees of the newly acquired or merged company are expected to adhere to the standardized procedures and processes or to the code

Concept 2.11   Frameworks for characterizing organizational cultures

Hofstede (2001: 398)	Handy (1976: 188–96)	Trompenaars (1993: 139)
Process oriented – Results oriented	Power	Egalitarian – hierarchical
Employee oriented – Job oriented	Role	Orientation to the person – orientation to the task
Parochial – Professional	Task	
Open system – Closed system	Person	
Loose control – Tight control		
Normative – Pragmatic		

of conduct and values statement of the new parent company. In the same way, when individuals move from one organization to another, they may well experience acculturative stress or 'culture shock', especially if the organizations differ significantly in values as well as practices, procedures and behavioural conventions. This can be particularly noticeable if someone moves from a public sector organization (such as education) to a private sector one (such as a company). (See Chapter 7 for a detailed discussion of adaptation to different cultures.)

2.5.3   Culture and professional groups

Wang (2001) describes professional cultures as follows:

> Professions create and sustain relatively unique work cultures referred to as professional cultures. [...] A professional culture binds members of a profession to form a professional community, ensures the continuance of a profession as a group collectivity, and guides the members to think and behave as the profession requires. Because a profession is not limited to the framework of a given organization or even a given industry or nation, its professional culture exists across the boundaries of organizations, industries or nations.
>
> (Wang 2001: 4)

There has been relatively little research which has attempted to characterize the cultures of different professions from an interactional perspective, yet during the last few years there has been a marked increase in demand for inter-professional working. For example, in the health care sector in the United Kingdom there has been a major call for integrated community care, which requires social workers and district nurses to work together; in the education sector, the development of e-learning materials requires academics, instructional designers and technical staff to work closely together. In international business, in areas such as in product development, work in inter-professional and cross-functional teams, which frequently also bring together members of different national and organizational cultures, has been common for a long time.

A growing number of books (e.g., Freeth et al. 2005; Malin 2000) and articles are now being published which explore the issues at stake in inter-professional working. Most of them acknowledge that such ways of working are not always easy. For example, Freeman, Miller and Ross (2000) researched a number of different teams within the UK health sector, and argue that multi-professional teamwork is challenging (Research Report 2.1).

Research Report 2.1   How effective are multi-professional teams in the UK National Health Service?

Multi-professional 'teamwork' has become the preferred model of practice promoted for many areas of health care by policy makers, professional bodies, and [...] management. Based on an assumption of beneficial outcomes for patients, the requirement of professionals to communicate 'effectively', to understand each other's contribution to the care process and to be prepared to blur the boundaries of their roles has been proposed in much recent research as the most effective form of managing patient care [...] The evidence [...] from a funded [research] project [...] showed that achieving patterns of professional interaction identified above would appear to be fraught with difficulties; the 'ideal' of effective team-working as defined in the prescriptive literature is apparently rarely realised.

(Freeman, Miller and Ross 2000: 237–8)

They found that philosophies of team-working (which were related to but not synonymous with professional divisions) influenced people's perceptions of what constituted effective communication and role understanding, how role contribution was valued, and the degree of perceived need for a shared vision within the team.

Moore and Dainty (2001) report comparable findings in the UK engineering sector. They investigated design and build project teams and report as follows.

Research Report 2.2   How effective are multi-professional teams in the UK engineering sector?

There was evidence that professional divisions between team members had led to discontinuities and ineffective responses to unexpected variations that had occurred during the construction phase. [...] Professional priorities within the workgroup were based around traditional project-based responsibilities. The design team had a clear emphasis on design quality, whereas the commercial team on delivering the project to programme. This division emphasized the lack of a single focus for the project team, and led to an emphasis on reactive problem solving as opposed to proactive problem avoidance, and on 'best-fit' approaches rather than innovative solutions.

(Moore and Dainty 2001: 560)

Research into the cultural bases of such professional differences has been extremely limited. Wang (2001: 16) found that 'project management professionals have common work-related values and beliefs that bind them to form a professional community across organizational and industrial boundaries and make them think and behave as the profession requires.' Ziegenfuss and Singhapakdi (1994), in a study of internal auditors, found that members were more influenced by the official standards of conduct of their professional group than by any employer requirements/threats. This suggests that policies and procedures, often based on internationally enforceable law, are an important unifying factor for some professional groups, which interestingly are then able to transcend the borders of national and organizational cultures. Health and safety at work is another area in which professional culture shaped by legal or official requirements typically exerts a stronger influence on behaviour than, for example, organizational culture. There is clearly a need for much more research in this area.

2.5.4   Culture and communities of practice

Another type of social group that applied linguists and discourse analysts increasingly refer to when discussing culture is 'community of practice'. According to Wenger (1998), who is the key proponent of this concept, there are three criteria for defining a community of practice: mutual engagement of members, members' jointly negotiated enterprise, and members' shared repertoire. All three criteria need to be in place for a group to be identified as a community of practice.

Holmes and Stubbe (2003), in reporting their research into different work teams (which can be regarded as communities of practice), demonstrate how both small talk and humour varied among teams. For example, they found that in one team, humour was predominantly supportive and had a positive pragmatic effect; in a second team, jocular abuse was common; and in a third team, where status and power distinctions were strong, subversive humour was characteristic.

Holmes and Stubbe also illustrate the differences that can occur in small talk.

Experiential Example 2.2   Small talk in the workplace

One of our informants reported feeling quite uncomfortable initially when she began work in a new organisation where people routinely shared quite intimate details of their personal lives to an extent that would have been deemed 'unprofessional' in her previous workplace. She eventually became accustomed to this practice, and in fact valued it as an important way in which members of the group provided support to one another, but she remained aware that it presented a potential barrier to the integration of new team members.

(Holmes and Stubbe 2003: 168)

The types of cultural regularities of a community of practice are likely to be much more limited in scope than those of some other types of groups, and are less likely to include the 'deeper' manifestations of values, beliefs and ideologies. So newcomers to a community of practice may have less difficulty integrating in the 'different culture' because the range of types of cultural differences that they need to adjust to will probably be smaller. Nevertheless, differences in practice can still be a source of discomfort and misunderstanding, and should not be ignored by interculturalists.

2.5.5   Culture and multi-group membership

It is generally accepted that everyone is simultaneously a member of many different cultural groups and that if intercultural researchers focus on only one type of cultural group (such as country-level culture), they are ignoring the potential impact of other types of cultures (such as regional culture, ethnic culture, professional culture, organizational culture and/or religious culture). Nevertheless, in practice, there is little understanding of how these different 'cultures' impact on each other or how multi-group membership affects interaction. This is a major set of issues which the field of intercultural interaction has yet to grapple with in depth.

2.6   Culture and representation

It is clearly very complex to 'unpack' culture:

- the regularities of culture are manifested in numerous different but interrelated ways;
- these regularities go hand in hand with variability;
- culture is associated with infinite types of social groups that can vary in size and complexity;
- people are simultaneously members of many different cultural groups.

How then can we meaningfully describe cultural groups?

There are three particularly prevalent, interrelated dangers that we need to be aware of. First, there is the risk of over-generalizing about groups on the basis of minimal evidence. This is a common occurrence, but can be very problematic. Experiential Example 2.3 illustrates such an invalid over-generalization.

Experiential Example 2.3 Are the English really a 'civilized people'?

I once went to see a friend. I had to take a taxi since his house is somewhat remote. The taxi driver was an English man in his fifties. He mistook our destination because of my poor English pronunciation, and drove me to a street that I had never been to. After explaining laboriously where I would like to go, he finally understood me and drove me correctly to my friend's house. He just charged me for the right route and kept saying sorry to me. Although it was my fault that led to the trouble, the driver time and again said that he should take the blame and he charged me fairly. The incident has convinced me that the English are civilized people; it reflects the degree of civilization of a nation.

(Overseas student's description of an interaction in the UK, Spencer-Oatey's research data)

Secondly, there is the risk of inappropriate stereotyping. Hinton (2000) explains that stereotyping has three important components: (1) a group of people is identified by a specific label, which can refer to any characteristic whatsoever, such as nationality (e.g., German), religious belief (e.g., fundamentalist Christian), occupation (e.g., traffic warden) or colour of hair (e.g., redhead); (2) a set of additional characteristics is attributed to the group as a whole, such as fundamentalist Christians are intolerant, or redheads are quick-tempered; (3) on identifying a person as belonging to the group (e.g., that s/he is German or a fundamentalist Christian), we attribute to him/her the additional characteristics that we associate with the group as a whole. This can result in all kinds of problems, including prejudice and discrimination. Chapter 6 explores this complex, important area in more detail.

Thirdly, it is important to avoid excessive essentialism and reductionism. When people take an essentialist approach, they assume or assert that a cultural group has certain 'essential' properties that make them one group rather than another. This, in effect, is a classic view of categories, which assumes that all category members share certain important defining features. For most social categories, categorization does not work in this way, although rather ironically group members may sometimes try to represent themselves like this.

Both the second and third risks need to be considered in the light of psychological research into categorization. In addition to the classic view of categories, two other important approaches are the prototype view and the exemplar view. In an influential series of studies, Rosch (1978) developed the idea that most category boundaries are essentially fuzzy, and that within any given category, certain members are regarded as more prototypic or representative of the entire category than others are. The members do not all share the same attributes, but rather display 'family resemblances' in relation to a much wider set of features. The prototype of the category may not be an actual category member but may just be an abstract representation. Other theorists (e.g., Smith and Zarate 1992) who support an exemplar view of categorization argue that people's representations are not abstract in this way, but rather are based on salient or particularly memorable exemplars.

Whichever view is taken, it is clear that the cognitive representation of categories (such as cultural groups) naturally entails a certain amount of reductionism. In intercultural interaction, there is a genuine practical need to help people interact more effectively with others from different social groups, for both social reasons and task-based reasons. So can 'reductionist' descriptions of other groups ever be helpful for such purposes, and if so, what kinds of descriptions are likely to be most helpful? We touch on these crucial questions in Chapter 9.

Finally, it is important to remember that the members of a cultural group may have a strong sense of in-group identity, and may want to project that identity clearly too. Such identity concerns can play a crucial role in intercultural interaction, and we discuss these in Chapter 7.

2.7   Concluding comments

In this chapter we have explored a number of key aspects of culture that are relevant to our study of intercultural interaction, including: frameworks for comparing how culture is manifested in different societies, ways in which cultural groups can be conceptualized, and the challenge of representing cultural groups. The chapter provides a foundation for the rest of the book, and subsequent chapters follow up on many of the points. However, we have paid relatively little explicit attention to the impact of culture on interpersonal interaction. The next chapter turns to this issue, and explores the competencies that have been identified as most valuable for this.

Suggestions for further reading

Ferraro, G. P. (2005) *The Cultural Dimension of International Business*, 5th edn. Upper Saddle River, NJ: Prentice Hall. This book takes an anthropological approach. It provides excellent descriptions of ways in which cultures may differ, drawing particularly on the frameworks of Hall and of Kluckhohn and Strodtbeck, and explains their relevance for working internationally, especially in business.

Holliday, A., Hyde, M. and Kullman, J. (2004) *Intercultural Communication: An Advanced Resource Book*. London: Routledge. This book takes a constructionist approach to culture, and focuses on three key themes: identity, otherization and representation.

Lane, H. W., Distefano, J. J. and Maznevski, M. L. (2006) *International Management Behavior: Text, Readings and Cases*, 5th edn. Malden, MA: Blackwell. Part 1 of this book deals with many of the issues covered in this chapter. It describes Kluckhohn and Strodtbeck's orientations and discusses their implications for international management. It includes a reading by Hofstede and another reading on the dangers of stereotyping.

3
Intercultural Interaction Competence (ICIC)

Competence, like truth, beauty and contact lenses, is in the eye of the beholder.

Peter 1969: 43

Chapter outline

3.1 Introduction: terminology and definitions
3.2 The contribution of psychology and communication studies
3.3 The contribution of applied linguistics and foreign language education
3.4 The contribution of international business and management studies
3.5 Concluding comments
    Suggestions for further reading

Interaction between members of different cultural groups can be challenging in many different ways, as the experiential examples throughout this book illustrate. In Chapter 2 we explored the many different ways in which cultural groups can differ – values, orientations to life, beliefs, attitudes to time, communicative conventions and styles, and so on. Yet it is these elements that provide us with our reference and orientation system – a cockpit of instruments that guide our behaviour. So when we engage in intercultural interaction, we are faced with a range of challenges – our 'instruments' function less well or not at all, and in order to handle the uncertainties we face, we need to master sophisticated skills in managing 'cultural complexity' (Hannerz 1992).

Much effort has been expended in trying to discover what it takes to communicate and interact successfully at the interface of different cultures. In this chapter we turn to this complex question. We focus on the conceptual frameworks that have been proposed, drawing on the research and theorizing that have taken place in a number of different academic fields. In Section 8.3 and Section 11.2.2, we explore the instruments developed to assess this competence and how they can be used.

Experts in psychology, communication studies, international business/management studies, and foreign language education have all attempted to conceptualize intercultural interaction competence (ICIC). Yet, as will become apparent from this chapter, much of the work on ICIC is limited to identifying lists of characteristics, with few authentic examples that explain or illustrate what is really meant. Other research, including applied linguistic research (which has made little contribution to such ICIC frameworks) can provide insights into many of these features, and we report and discuss these in Chapters 4 to 7. Such research helps explain and illustrate many of the characteristics of ICIC referred to in this chapter, but unfortunately, the literature has rarely established any explicit links between the two. We hope to rectify this, at least partially.

3.1 Introduction: terminology and definitions

Ruben (1989), in a widely quoted overview article, begins with the words, 'Much of the impetus for the study of *cross-cultural communication competence* [...]' (our italics), and in the next paragraph refers to '*intercultural competence*' (our italics). This terminological inconsistency in the space of a few lines is characteristic of scholars' attempts to name and describe proficiency at dealing with intercultural interaction. A plethora of terms is used with little semantic rigour. Sometimes one term is used to refer to different conceptualizations and sometimes a different term is chosen for the same conceptualization (Concept 3.1). This is confusing and makes discussion of the concept and research into it difficult to handle.

In this book we use the rather unwieldy term 'intercultural interaction competence' (ICIC). We use it partly as an umbrella term for reporting the work of different theorists on this issue, and partly to emphasize our focus on interaction; in other words, we use it to refer to the competence not only to communicate (verbally and non-verbally) and behave effectively and appropriately with people from other cultural groups, but also to handle the psychological demands and dynamic outcomes that result from such interchanges.

Concept 3.1   Labelling and defining intercultural interaction competence

Terms used	Example
Intercultural competence	Intercultural competence shows itself in the ability to recognise, respect, value and use productively – in oneself and others – cultural conditions and determinants in perceiving, judging, feeling and acting with the aim of creating mutual adaptation, tolerance of incompatibilities and a development towards synergistic forms of cooperation, living together and effective orientation patterns with respect to interpreting and shaping the world. (Thomas 2003a: 143; translated by Franklin)
Intercultural effectiveness	Cui (1989) defined intercultural effectiveness as the general assessment of a sojourner's ability for effective intercultural communication. He proposed an integrative approach to intercultural effectiveness by combining the existing perspectives – interpersonal skills, social interaction, cultural empathy, and personality traits – and the above dimensions were reproduced in his factor analysis. (Cui and van den Berg 1991: 228)
Intercultural communication competence	[...] the ability to negotiate cultural meanings and to execute appropriately effective communication behaviours that recognise the interactants' multiple identities in a specific environment. This definition emphasizes that competent persons must know not only how to interact effectively and appropriately with people and environment, but also how to fulfil their own communication goals by respecting and affirming the multilevel cultural identities of those with whom they interact. (Chen and Starosta 1996: 358–9) [...] defined as the overall internal capability of an individual to manage key challenging features of intercultural communication: namely, cultural differences and unfamiliarity, intergroup posture, and the accompanying experience of stress. [... It] is explained not as communication competence in dealing with a specific culture but as the cognitive, affective, and operational adaptability of an individual's internal system in all intercultural communication contexts. (Kim and Korzenny 1991: 259)

Transcultural communication competence	Transcultural communication competence (TCC) refers to an integrative theory-practice approach enabling us to mindfully apply the intercultural knowledge we have learned in a sensitive manner. Specifically, it refers to a transformation process connecting intercultural knowledge with competent practice. [...] Culture-specific and ethnic-specific knowledge, in conjunction with a TCC approach, will yield a wealth of interaction skills that permit individuals to cross cultural boundaries flexibly and adaptively. (Ting-Toomey 1999: 261)
Intercultural action competence	[...] from the comparison of the recognisably too one-sided personality-oriented and situation-oriented concepts of intercultural competence it is possible to derive an interactionist concept of intercultural competence in which intercultural action competence is regarded as the result of the interaction of the individual and the situation. (Thomas 2003a: 143; translated by Franklin)

3.2 The contribution of psychology and communication studies

As we noted in Chapter 1, a very large proportion of work on intercultural interaction has been carried out by social psychologists or cross-cultural psychologists, and by US-based scholars of communication studies. We report here on their contribution to our understanding of ICIC.

3.2.1 Goals of ICIC identified by psychologists and communication scholars

As indicated by the quotations in Concept 3.1, numerous definitions of ICIC have mentioned the ability to interact effectively and appropriately, thus picking up on Spitzberg's general definition:

> Competent communication is interaction that is perceived as effective in fulfilling certain rewarding objectives in a way that is also appropriate to the context in which the interaction occurs.
>
> (Spitzberg 1988: 68)

The appropriateness criterion draws attention to the importance of context, and people's capacity to be contextually flexible in their behaviour, as Kim indicates in her explanation of ICIC:

> Intercultural communication competence (ICC) must be [...] anchored within a person as his or her capacity to manage the varied contexts of the intercultural encounter regardless of the specific cultures involved.
>
> (Kim 1991: 265)

The appropriateness criterion also draws attention to another issue: that there is no absolute criterion of appropriateness, because assessments always entail subjective judgements by the participants concerned. This has important consequences for those interested in assessing ICIC (see Sections 8.3 and 11.2.2); it means that, although self-report data and/or observation data generated by an outsider are vital for assessing ICIC, they are insufficient on their own. They need to be complemented, as Hammer explains, by:

> competence judgements from significant others. These may include, for instance, the host country national who is a sojourner's boss in a multinational organisation; the host country national with whom the tourist-sojourner typically interacts on a regular basis; and teachers or dormitory counsellors of foreign-student sojourners.
>
> (1989: 254)

In the light of this, recent attempts to introduce 360 degree assessment, a procedure which gathers perceptions and judgements from a number of interactants (see Chapter 8), seem to be promising.

A shortcoming of the appropriateness criterion as commonly conceptualized is that it is often interpreted as the creation of *cultural* appropriateness with respect to the other *interactant(s)*, rather than as *communicative* appropriateness with respect to the *communication situation* in which the interactants find themselves. There is often an implicit assumption that the interaction of the parties to the communication must be modified, primarily to take account of cultural differences between the interactants, for example, in communication style. Another implicit assumption is that the other interactant is a prototypical member of the other or 'host' culture towards whose culturally based expectations the first interactant has to adjust, rather than a person possessing intercultural experience and/or competence *also* able to adjust in order to create interactional appropriateness. The appropriateness criterion does not recognize that interaction also needs to be modified to take account of the possibly problematical nature of the communication situation and that therefore interactants need to create *communicative* appropriateness by employing communication skills, usually expressed in language. This kind of appropriateness thus implies the ability, for example, to negotiate meaning, create understanding and repair misunderstanding.

The effectiveness criterion draws attention to the complex layers involved in successfully conveying meaning and achieving both transactional and relational goals. It hints at the complex negotiation and co-construction of meaning that takes place during the dynamics of interaction, and the crucial importance of understanding and managing these processes.

Ting-Toomey and Chung (2005) propose two additional criteria, adaptability and creativity, and argue that the overall goal is behavioural flexibility (Concept 3.2). Applied linguistic research has major insights to offer in relation to all of these criteria, and this is reported and discussed in the next three chapters.

Concept 3.2   On flexibility in intercultural interaction

The criteria of communication appropriateness, effectiveness, adaptability, and creativity can serve as evaluative yardsticks of whether an intercultural communicator has been perceived as behaving flexibly or inflexibly [...] in an interaction episode. A dynamic, competent intercultural communicator is one who manages multiple meanings in the communication exchange process – appropriately, effectively, adaptively, and creatively. [...] Communication adaptability refers to our ability to change our interaction behaviours and goals to meet the specific needs of the situation. [...] Communication creativity [...] is to produce something inventive through an imaginative lens and flexible skills.

(Ting-Toomey and Chung 2005: 17–19)

3.2.2   Components of ICIC identified by psychologists and communication scholars

In numerous empirical studies, psychologists and communication scholars have focused their attention on identifying the nature of intercultural interaction competence. In a six-page overview table, Dinges and Baldwin (1996) list the purpose, design, method, subjects and results of 22 such studies published from 1985 to 1993. Other review-type articles or articles which contain a review, such as Arasaratnam and Doerfel (2005), Hammer (1989) and Spitzberg (1989), attempt to undertake similar, more or less comprehensive summaries. A few examples of such studies, among them some of the most frequently cited and some more recent ones not included in the Dinges and Baldwin review, are described in Research Report 3.1.

Research Report 3.1   Research into the components of ICIC

Dimensions of intercultural effectiveness: an exploratory study
Subjects: US students, N = 53
(The study) investigated some of the major dimensions of intercultural effectiveness. Based upon a review of the literature, 23 'abilities' thought to be important for intercultural effectiveness were generated. Fifty-three subjects who had reported functioning effectively in other cultures rated these abilities in terms of their importance in facilitating intercultural effectiveness. Factor analysis of the data yielded three dimensions of intercultural effectiveness: (1) the ability to deal with psychological stress; (2) the ability to communicate effectively; and (3) the ability to establish interpersonal relationships.

(Hammer, Gudykunst and Wiseman 1978: 382–9)

A cross-cultural confirmation of the dimensions of intercultural effectiveness
Subjects: Japanese students, N = 57
This study compared the dimensions of intercultural effectiveness found in Hammer, Gudykunst and Wiseman (1978) using American sojourners with the dimensions found using Japanese sojourners. The results revealed five dimensions for the Japanese sample: (1) the ability to communicate interpersonally; (2) the ability to adjust to different cultures; (3) the ability to deal with different societal systems; (4) the ability to establish interpersonal relationships; and (5) the ability to understand each other. Both similarities and differences were found between the American perceptions and the Japanese perceptions of intercultural effectiveness.

(Abe and Wiseman 1983: 53)

Measuring intercultural effectiveness: an integrative approach
Subjects: US business people living in China, N = 74
The results show that cross-cultural adjustment and effective job performance are correlated to a significant degree. This finding suggests that intercultural effectiveness should be studied as two related processes – adjustment to the cultural environment and to the work place. [...] The study also suggests that cross-cultural adjustment and effective job performance have different requirements and priorities. For cross-cultural adjustment, the order is as follows: personality traits, interpersonal skills, social interaction, managerial ability, and cultural empathy; for effective job performance, the

order is interpersonal skills, cultural empathy, managerial ability, and personality traits.

(Cui and Awa 1992: 324)

The relationship between intercultural competence and expatriate success: a structural equation model
Subjects: German students after completing an assignment abroad, N = 323
As hypothesized, intercultural competence positively influences success overseas. Empathy, open-mindedness, realistic expectations, communication skills, and self-confidence explain each of the success measures by more than 40 per cent, indicating evidence of concurrent validity.

(Gelbrich 2004: 274)

Intercultural communication competence in the healthcare context
Subjects: Culturally diverse sample of medical care providers and patients.
N = 45 and N = 91
This study examined the intercultural communication competence of medical providers at a healthcare organisation, including patient perceptions of the medical provider's ability to communicate to a diverse patient population. [...] One survey asked medical providers to rate their own ability to communicate across cultures, and the other survey instructed patients to rate the intercultural competence of their medical providers. Analysis of variance and Pearson correlation coefficients were used to analyse the data from 45 medical providers and 91 patients. The findings demonstrate that empathy, bilingualism, and intercultural experience are related to intercultural communication competence.

(Gibson and Zhong 2005: 621)

The various lists of such empirically derived factors yield a somewhat diffuse but intuitively plausible picture of the components of ICIC. Open-mindedness, non-judgementalness (sometimes referred to as interaction posture), empathy, tolerance for ambiguity, flexibility in thinking and behaviour, self-awareness, knowledge of one's own and other cultures, resilience to stress, and communication or message skills (including foreign language proficiency, although this is less frequently mentioned) are among the components which are identified as playing an important role in the creation of appropriateness and effectiveness in intercultural interaction.

Nevertheless, the usefulness of these studies can be questioned for a number of reasons. Terminology seems to be used inconsistently. For example, Chen and Starosta (1996: 369) describe empathy as a behavioural feature whereas Gelbrich (2004: 263) sees it as an affective one. Many of the studies have a small number of respondents, and these respondents have been drawn from a relatively restricted range of populations. In fact, these and stronger reservations have been voiced by psychologists and communication studies scholars themselves. In addition to criticizing the area as a whole for its terminological and conceptual confusion, Spitzberg (1989) levels particular criticism at the empirical studies for their lack of theoretical integration and their lack of methodological rigour in measurement. The outwardly convincing lists of features and factors regarded as contributing to ICIC, especially those which result from overview surveys of the studies, suggest an empirical robustness which does not exist (Quote 3.1).

Quote 3.1   Spitzberg's criticisms of empirical studies

Any list is intended to be an abstraction, and any responsible user is intended to inspect the original sources of such lists. However, such abstractions vary in their degree of slippage from the data, and the levels of subjectivity are easily multiplied in the process of interpretation and transmission. Furthermore, such lists provide the 'illusion of validity' implying that the characteristics have passed some 'test' of inclusion and recommendation. [...] In fact, most of the characteristics listed represent high-level inferences from unreliable data-reduction techniques performed with relatively small samples of unknown comparability.

Additionally, the illusion of validity is strengthened when there is apparent consistency across lists of characteristics. [...] the lists may imply a conceptual consensus that does not exist.

(Spitzberg 1989: 245)

Items generated for measuring intercultural competence are too often reminiscent of the 'list technique'. The literature generally is not critically reviewed to exclude poorly done, overly anecdotal, or overly ambiguous research, or even to define clearly the domain-relevant characteristics of the concept of 'effectiveness'. The instruments being used in current research are not necessarily invalid. The problem is that their validity is simply unknown, given their developmental histories and construct validity evidence to date. The search for conceptual and measurement directions appears justified.

(Spitzberg 1989: 249)

Despite these criticisms, there have been a number of attempts to synthesize the research findings into conceptual frameworks, as we report in the next sections.

3.2.3   ICIC conceptual frameworks developed by psychologists and communication scholars

Concept 3.3 identifies the key components and attributes of three conceptual frameworks, all of which have important implications for the

Concept 3.3 ICIC conceptual frameworks developed within psychology and communication studies

Source	Components	Description	Attributes
Chen and Starosta (2005)	Personal attributes	The traits that constitute an individual's personality. These traits stem from our unique experiences within a culture and reflect, in part, our heredity.	Self-disclosure
			Self-awareness
			Self-concept
			Social relaxation
	Communication skills	The verbal and nonverbal behaviours and other skills that enable us to be effective in interactions with others	Message skills
			Social skills
			Flexibility
			Interaction management
	Psychological adaptation	Our ability to adjust to a new culture. It entails a complex process through which we acquire the ability to fit in the new cultural environment.	Frustration
			Stress
			Alienation
			Ambiguity
	Cultural awareness	Our understanding of the conventions of the host culture that affect how people think and behave.	Social values
			Social customs
			Social norms
			Social systems
Ting-Toomey (1999)	Knowledge blocks	Without culture-sensitive knowledge, communicators cannot become aware of the implicit 'ethnocentric lenses' they use to evaluate behaviours in an intercultural situation. Without accurate knowledge, communicators cannot accurately reframe their interpretation from the other's cultural standpoint. Knowledge here refers to the process of in-depth understanding of important intercultural communication concepts that 'really make a difference'.	

	Mindfulness	Mindfulness means attending to one's internal assumptions, cognitions, and emotions, and simultaneously attuning to the other's assumptions, cognitions, and emotions. Mindful reflexivity requires us to tune in to our cultural and personal habitual assumptions in viewing an interaction scene.	
	Communication skills	Communication skills refers to our operational abilities to interact appropriately, effectively, and satisfactorily in a given situation. Many communication skills are useful in enhancing TCC. Four core communication skills are mindful observation, mindful listening, identity confirmation, and collaborative dialogue.	
Gudykunst (2004)	Motivation	Our desire to communicate appropriately and effectively with strangers	Need for predictability
			Need to avoid diffuse anxiety
			Need to sustain our self-conceptions
			Approach–avoidance tendencies
	Knowledge	Our awareness or understanding of what needs to be done in order to communicate appropriately and effectively	Knowledge of how to gather information
			Knowledge of group differences
			Knowledge of personal similarities
			Knowledge of alternative interpretations

Skills	Our abilities to engage in the behaviours necessary to communicate appropriately and effectively	Ability to be mindful
		Ability to tolerate ambiguity
		Ability to manage anxiety
		Ability to empathise
		Ability to adapt our communication
		Ability to make accurate predictions and explanations

assessment and development of ICIC, the subjects of Chapters 8 and 9. A summary table like this can obviously only convey an overall picture of the frameworks, and readers need to go to the original sources for more details. Here we highlight a few points that are particularly relevant for assessing and developing ICIC.

Firstly, it is important to note that all three frameworks attach great importance to communication skills and to knowledge (labelled as cultural awareness in Chen and Starosta's framework). These are both elements that we explore further in subsequent chapters.

Secondly, Ting-Toomey and Gudykunst both refer to the importance of mindfulness, a concept promoted by Langer (1989). As the quotations in Concept 3.4 indicate, mindfulness entails openness and a focused attention on process. Sometimes this can seem a little abstract, so Chapters 4 and 5 explain and illustrate with authentic examples ways in which this can be operationalized.

Concept 3.4   Langer, Gudykunst and Ting-Toomey on Mindfulness

The key qualities of a mindful state of being [are]: (1) creation of new categories; (2) openness to new information; and (3) awareness of more than one perspective. [...]

Creating new categories
Just as mindlessness is the rigid reliance on old categories, mindfulness means the continual creation of new ones. Categorizing and recategorizing, labelling and relabelling as one masters the world are processes natural to children. They are an adaptive and inevitable part of surviving in the world. [...] As adults, however, we become reluctant to create new categories. [...] our outcome orientation tends to deaden a playful approach. [...] When we make new categories in a mindful way, we pay attention to the situation and the context. [...]

Welcoming new information
A mindful state also implies openness to new information. Like category making, the receiving of new information is a basic function of living creatures. [...] Our minds, however, have a tendency to block out small, inconsistent signals. For example, if a familiar quotation is altered so that it is made nonsensical (but retains sufficient structural familiarity), someone reading it out loud is likely to read the original quote. [...] In contrast, mindfully engaged individuals will actively attend to changed signals [...].

More than one view
Openness, not only to new information, but to different points of view is also an important feature of mindfulness. [...] Once we become mindfully

aware of views other than our own, we start to realize that there are as many different views as there are different observers. [...] imagine that someone has just told you that you are rude. You thought you were being frank. If there is only one perspective, you can't both be right. But with an awareness of many perspectives, you could accept that you are both right and concentrate on whether your remarks had the effect that you actually wanted to produce.

(Extracts from Langer 1989: 62–9)

We must be cognitively aware of our communication if we are to overcome our tendency to interpret strangers' behaviour based on our own frames of reference. When we interact with strangers, we become mindful of our communication. Our focus, however, is usually on the outcome [...] rather than the process of communication. For effective communication to occur, we must focus on the process of our communication with strangers. [...] When we are mindful, we can make conscious choices as to what we need to do in the particular situation in order to communicate effectively.

(Gudykunst 2004: 253–5)

Mindfulness means being aware of our own and others' behaviour in the situation, and paying focused attention to the process of communication taking place between us and dissimilar others.

(Ting-Toomey 1999: 16)

Thirdly, Chen and Starosta include psychological adaptation and personal attributes. We explore psychological adaptation in Chapter 7. The inclusion of personal attributes raises an important issue in relation to the development and acquisition of ICIC as the objective of education and training. It is reasonable to assume that it is probably not possible to develop the personality-related components of ICIC among adults in the short-term, if at all (although the long-term nature of school education and the youth of the students make this a more realistic goal in the school setting). This means that all elements of ICIC probably cannot be fostered/developed equally well in all adults, and that some personality traits militate against the achievement of ICIC. In this case, the components of ICIC which are more susceptible to development and which fall into the category of learnable knowledge and trainable skills assume a particular importance. We return to this topic in Chapter 9.

3.3 The contribution of applied linguistics and foreign language education

Somewhat surprisingly, the fields of applied linguistics and foreign language education have paid relatively little attention to researching and conceptualizing ICIC, despite their intrinsic concern for communication, their major focus on second/foreign language acquisition, and their interest in communicative competence. Roberts and her colleagues argue that this is because communicative language teaching, which has been the dominant teaching approach for several decades in many 'Western' countries, has been so influenced by speech act theory and discourse analysis that its links with the cultural sphere have been lost.

> Hymes' notion of communicative competence stresses the cultural in the development of communicative competence. [...] However, despite its roots in Hymes' work, [...] communicative competence has come to be interpreted somewhat narrowly and prescriptively, as appropriate language use rather than competence in the social and cultural practices of a community of which language is a large part.
>
> (Roberts, Byram, Barro, Jordan and Street 2001: 26)

Even though there has been an attempt in Europe, since the late 1980s, to incorporate intercultural skills into the foreign language curriculum (see Chapter 9, Section 9.4), there has still been comparatively little work on the nature of ICIC itself. Michael Byram is one of the few scholars working in language education who has specifically focused on this issue, and so much of this section deals with his work.

3.3.1   Applied linguists' concerns about criteria of ICIC

As indicated above, Hymes's notion of communicative competence is linked with the notion of appropriateness, and in foreign language teaching there was a tendency, for many years, to take the native speaker as the model for judging appropriateness. More recently, though, this has been challenged, in that using the native speaker as a model not only sets an impossible target for learners but may also be psychologically undesirable (Byram 1997: 11, 32). In particular, it is often an inaccurate representation of reality because in much intercultural interaction, no native speakers are involved at all, and even when they are, 'both interlocutors have different social identities and therefore a different kind of interaction than they would have with someone from their own country speaking the same language' (Byram 1997: 32).

In place of the native speaker model, linguists have suggested the following:

> The characteristic of a 'competent language user' [is] not the ability to speak and write according to the rules of the academy and the

social etiquette of one social group, but the adaptability to select those forms of accuracy and those forms of appropriateness that are called for in a given social context of use.

(Kramsch 1998: 27)

The [...] desirable outcome is a learner with the ability to see and manage the relationships between themselves and their own cultural beliefs, behaviours and meanings, as expressed in a foreign language, and those of their interlocutors, expressed in the same language – or even a combination of languages – which may be the interlocutors' native language, or not.

(Byram 1997: 12)

3.3.2 ICIC conceptual frameworks developed by applied linguists and foreign language education specialists

Linguists have conducted little explicit research into the components or characteristics of ICIC. Nevertheless, there have been numerous studies within various branches of linguistics such as pragmatics, interactional sociolinguistics, and discourse studies, where attention has been focused on problematic communication. We report on some of these studies in subsequent chapters, because they provide us with a different and richer demonstration of the issues at stake in authentic interaction than lists of categories and labels can.

However, despite this paucity of research into the components of ICIC, Byram (1997), and more recently the INCA Project team, have each developed a conceptual framework. Byram's framework (Concept 3.5) is primarily derived not from empirical studies but from conceptual thinking on communicative competence/communicative ability in foreign language education, drawing on the work of earlier theorists such as Canale and Swain (1980) and van Ek (1986).

Byram's model draws heavily on van Ek's (1986) model of 'communicative ability', utilizing his concepts of linguistic competence, sociolinguistic competence and discourse competence. However, Byram modifies these concepts somewhat in order to give greater weight to 'discovery', 'interpretation' and 'establishing a relationship', which he regards as being of crucial importance for intercultural speakers (Byram 1997: 48).

Byram's description of the 'skill of interaction' has resonances with the concept of mindfulness that we discussed in Section 3.2.3, and

Concept 3.5 Byram's (1997) conceptualization of intercultural communicative competence		
Components		**Description**
Linguistic competence		The ability to apply knowledge of the rules of a standard version of the language to produce and interpret spoken and written language.
Sociolinguistic competence		The ability to give to the language produced by an interlocutor – whether native speaker or not – meanings which are taken for granted by the interlocutor or which are negotiated and made explicit with the interlocutor.
Discourse competence		The ability to use, discover and negotiate strategies for the production and interpretation of monologue or dialogue texts which follow the conventions of the culture of an interlocutor or are negotiated as intercultural texts for particular purposes.
Intercultural competence	Attitudes	Curiosity and openness, readiness to suspend disbelief about other cultures and belief about one's own.
	Knowledge	Knowledge of social groups and their products and practices in one's own and in one's interlocutor's country, and of the general processes of societal and individual interaction.
	Skills of interpreting and relating	Ability to interpret a document or event from another culture, to explain it and relate it to documents from one's own.
	Skills of discovering and interacting	Ability to acquire new knowledge of a culture and cultural practices and the ability to operate knowledge, attitudes and skills under the constraints of real-time communication and interaction.
	Critical cultural awareness/ political education	An ability to evaluate critically and on the basis of explicit criteria perspectives, practices and products in one's own and other cultures and countries.

perhaps goes a little further in explaining how mindfulness may function in intercultural interaction to facilitate communication skills:

> The skill of interaction is above all the ability to manage these constraints [of time and mutual perceptions and attitudes] in particular circumstances with specific interlocutors. The individual needs to draw upon their existing knowledge, have attitudes which sustain sensitivity to others with sometimes radically different origins and identities, and operate the skills of discovery and interpretation. In particular, the individual needs to manage dysfunctions which arise in the course of interaction, drawing upon knowledge and skills. They may also be called upon not only to establish a relationship between their own social identities and those of their interlocutor, but also to act as mediator between people of different origins and identities. It is this function of establishing relationships, managing dysfunctions and mediating which distinguishes an 'intercultural speaker', and makes them different from a native speaker.
>
> (Byram 1997: 38)

He elaborates on this skill of interaction in a way reminiscent of Stahl's empirically derived 'metacommunication skills' (see Section 3.4.1 below) and is also to be found in our framework of message communication competencies (see Section 4.1):

> [...] intercultural and native speakers – or intercultural speakers of different languages and culture origins need to negotiate their own modes of interaction, their own kinds of text, to accommodate the specific nature of intercultural communication. This might involve, for example, negotiated agreements on meta-commentary, on when and how to ensure that each interlocutor is able to interrupt the normal flow of interaction to ask for explanations of differences and dysfunctions, or to give a richer account of the pre-suppositions of a statement than would usually be necessary.
>
> (Byram 1997: 49)

However, one key difference between Byram's model and others presented in this chapter is that his model is located firmly in the context of the teaching and learning of foreign languages in schools. The detailed objectives that he identifies (and which space limitations prevent us from presenting here) represent broad educational goals, many of which require long-term exposure for their development. In this

Concept 3.6 Framework of intercultural competence developed by the INCA Project

	(A) Motivation	(B) Skill/Knowledge	(C) Behaviour
1. Tolerance for ambiguity (TA)	Readiness to embrace and work with ambiguity.	Ability to handle stress consequent on ambiguity.	Managing ambiguous situations.
2. Behavioural flexibility (BF)	Readiness to apply and augment the full range of one's existing repertoire of behaviour.	Having a broad repertoire and the knowledge of one's repertoire.	Adapting one's behaviour to the specific situation.
3. Communicative awareness (CA)	Willingness to modify existing communicative conventions.	Ability to identify different communicative conventions, levels of foreign language competencies and their impact on intercultural communication.	Negotiating appropriate communicative conventions for intercultural communication and coping with different foreign language skills.
4. Knowledge discovery (KD)	Curiosity about other cultures in themselves and in order to be able to interact better with people.	Skills of ethnographic discovery of situation-relevant cultural knowledge (including technical knowledge) before, during and after intercultural encounters.	Seeking information to discover culture-related knowledge.
5. Respect for otherness (RO)	Willingness to respect the diversity and coherence of behaviour, value and belief systems.	Critical knowledge of such systems (including one's own when making judgements).	Treating equally different behaviour, value and convention systems experienced in intercultural encounters.
6. Empathy (E)	Willingness to take the other's perspectives.	Skills of role-taking de-centring; awareness of different perspectives.	Making explicit and relating culture-specific perspectives to each other.

(Prechtl and Davidson Lund 2007: 472)

sense, some of the details of his model are less applicable to non-school contexts, where more immediate results are desired.

Nevertheless, Byram's model influenced the thinking of the INCA Project team (of which he was a member). This project involved academic experts (mostly linguists) and engineering employers from Austria, the Czech Republic, Germany and the United Kingdom, and its aim was practical: 'to develop a valid framework of intercultural competence and robust instruments for assessing intercultural competence to meet the needs of employers' (Prechtl and Davidson Lund 2007) (Concept 3.6). Their framework is a hybrid of the components identified by Kühlmann and Stahl (see Research Results 3.5 in Section 3.3.1) and by Gudykunst (see Concept 3.3 in Section 3.2.3), with the addition of Byram's emphasis on knowledge discovery.

Using the notion of 'can do' statements, which are widely used in foreign language assessment, the team attempted to operationalize each of the components of the grid with a series of 'can do' descriptors. They also developed a number of instruments for probing each of the components. We discuss these further in Chapter 8.

3.4   The contribution of international business and management studies

Management scholars began to show interest in ICIC in the 1970s and 1980s when reports of expatriate failure among US managers became more frequent and were taken more seriously. Researchers attempted to find reasons for the failure to adjust to the new environment, and Tung (1987: 117) reported the following reasons (in descending order of importance) in a much-quoted survey:

1. Inability of the manager's spouse to adjust to a different physical or cultural environment.
2. The manager's inability to adjust to a different physical or cultural environment.
3. Other family-related problems.
4. The manager's personality or emotional immaturity.
5. The manager's inability to cope with responsibilities posed by overseas work.
6. The manager's lack of technical competence.
7. The manager's lack of motivation to work overseas.

The results of this kind of questionnaire survey led to work being done on the profile of the successful expatriate or international manager, and

Research Report 3.2   Components of intercultural interaction competence identified in management studies

Desirable characteristics named by personnel managers in 83 companies in Germany in descending order of importance (Marx 1999: 152)	Desirable characteristics named by approximately 50 U.S., British and Japanese companies in descending order of importance (Barham and Devine 1991: 21)
Social competence	Strategic awareness
Openness to other ways of thinking	Adaptability in new situations
Cultural adaptation	Sensitivity to different cultures
Professional excellence	Ability to work in international teams
Language skills	Language skills
Flexibility	Understanding international marketing
Ability to manage/work in a team	Relationship skills
Self-reliance/independence	International negotiating skills
Mobility	Self-reliance
Ability to deal with stress	High task-orientation
Adaptability of the family	Open, non-judgemental personality
Patience	Understanding of international finance
Sensitivity	Awareness of own cultural background

his/her implicit ICIC, with the aim of improving selection and training procedures. There is little or no explicit discussion of ICIC criteria, but the dominant concern is clearly effectiveness.

3.4.1   Components of ICIC identified by international business and management scholars

An approach used frequently in international management studies for identifying the nature of ICIC is to ask representatives of companies (e.g., human resource specialists) to describe the characteristics of their successful international managers. Here too, the dominant criterion for the respondents is clearly effectiveness rather than appropriateness. The result is a series of lists of more or less intuitively convincing features (see Research Report 3.2). To what extent they genuinely reflect success factors or features of effectiveness in intercultural business and management interaction is, of course, unknown. Similarly, whether or not the failure to take appropriateness into account is significant is equally unknown. What is striking, though, is that many of the features identified recur across similar studies and that many are familiar from the studies by psychologists and communication scholars discussed earlier in the chapter.

Another approach has been to generate characteristics on the basis of a selective reading of the management literature, surveys, and anecdotal and experiential evidence derived from the business press. This impressionistic method leads to lists of features, for example, those compiled by Schneider and Barsoux (2003), summarized in Concept 3.7, which are no less convincing for the way in which they have been generated, and which indeed again show remarkable similarities with other taxonomies of ICIC.

A final approach, but one which is relatively rare in the literature, is to question international managers themselves. Hampden-Turner and Trompenaars (2000) report briefly on a survey conducted among an unspecified number of managers from various cultures (Research Report 3.3).

Concept 3.7 Competencies for managing internationally identified by Schneider and Barsoux	
Managing differences abroad	**Additional competencies for managing differences at home**
Interpersonal (relationship) skills	Understand business interdependencies
Linguistic ability	Respond to multiple cultures simultaneously
Motivation to work and live abroad (cultural curiosity)	Recognise the influence of culture 'at home'
Ability to tolerate and cope with uncertainty and ambiguity	Be willing to share power
Flexibility	Demonstrate cognitive complexity
Patience and respect	Adopt a 'culture-general' approach
Cultural empathy	Rapidly learn and unlearn
Strong sense of self/ego strength	
Sense of humour	
(Schneider and Barsoux 2003: 190–8)	

Research Report 3.3   Hampden-Turner and Trompenaars on cross-cultural competence

Cross-cultural competence, as measured by our questionnaire, correlates strongly, consistently and significantly with:

1. Extent of experience with international assignments
2. Rating by superiors on 'suitability for' and 'success in' overseas postings and partnerships
3. High positive evaluations via '360-degree feedback'
4. Success in a strategy evaluation exercise [...]
5. Interestingly, there is a negative correlation with assessed technical competence [...].

(Hampden-Turner and Trompenaars 2000: 357)

Their conclusions are perhaps surprisingly unhelpful and indeed the first one contradicts a counter-intuitive insight derived from a number of studies (e.g. Kealey 1989; Leslie et al. 2002) that international experience does not in fact co-occur significantly with ICIC. However, the second finding they list adds support to the 'suitability' approach to describing the nature of ICIC.

In an exhaustive study of 211 managers from 41 countries using a series of psychological tests as well as assessments by others, Leslie and colleagues (2002) studied their managerial effectiveness, distinguishing between those managers with jobs of 'high global complexity' and those with jobs of 'low global complexity' (Research Report 3.4). Again we recognize some aspects of their picture of effectiveness in work of high global complexity, such as the ability to cope with stress, adaptability and empathy, from other descriptions we have encountered in this chapter.

Research Report 3.4   On competencies for management of low and high global complexity

The patterns of traits, role skills, and capabilities global managers need to be effective is similar to that of domestic managers. The bosses of global managers say emotional stability, skill in the roles of leader and decision maker, and the ability to cope with stress are key components to managerial effectiveness regardless of the job's global complexity. In addition, bosses look to conscientiousness, skill in the role of negotiator and innovator, business knowledge, international business knowledge, cultural adaptability, and the ability to take the perspective of others as significant to the effectiveness of global managers. [...] It appears that the action roles (decision maker and negotiator) are relatively more critical to the global manager than to the domestic manager. The learning capabilities were also significantly more critical to effectiveness ratings for the global manager. [...] Neither early exposure to other languages and cultures, experience living in other countries, multilingualism at work, nor past experience working with heterogeneous workgroups predicted effectiveness ratings in a global or domestic context.

(Leslie et al. 2002: 63)

The two empirical studies reported on here fail to bring out the more overtly communicative and relational characteristics which feature in the results of the 'suitability' approach and the 'impressionistic' approach described in this section and which also occur in the studies conducted by psychologists and communication scholars. However, Kühlmann and Stahl's (1998) large-scale study using qualitative methods draws attention to these aspects, but leaves questions unanswered which could provide fruitful fields of activity for applied linguists.

Kühlmann and Stahl (1998: 216) criticize the majority of studies of ICIC for their conceptual and methodological shortcomings. They believe that the components of ICIC that are listed are badly operationalized, so that what the behaviours really mean remains unclear. They argue that the studies frequently do not explore the actual determinants of success of intercultural encounters, but rather simply record the respondents' personal theories of suitability. Kühlmann and Stahl (1998) themselves employ the critical incident method (see Concept 9.1 and Section 11.2.2 for more details). Drawing on the experiences of more than 300 German managers who had just returned from an expatriate assignment, they list a number of characteristics of the successful expatriate (see Research Report 3.5). They regard these characteristics as necessary, but not sufficient for success on assignments abroad: task-, company- or culture-related factors lead to additional requirements or shifts in weighting. (Interestingly they remark that both too high and too low goal-orientation can endanger the success of an expatriate assignment.)

Stahl (2001), who reports (in English) on the same study, attempts to unpack what these characteristics mean in practice by listing behavioural indicators for each of the categories, which make clear how the competence is exhibited in behaviour.

Research Report 3.5   Characteristics of the successful expatriate manager identified by Kühlmann and Stahl

Characteristic	Description
Tolerance for ambiguity	The tendency to feel comfortable in uncertain, ambiguous and complex situations or at least not to feel impeded.
Behavioural flexibility	The ability to adjust very quickly to changed situations and in those situations to fall back on a broad repertoire of behaviours.
Goal orientation	The ability to strive towards the achievement of goals which have been set even in difficult circumstances.
Sociability	The tendency actively to establish social contacts and to maintain existing relationships.
Empathy	The ability to recognize the needs and intentions of interactants and to react to them in a situationally appropriate fashion.
Polycentrism (non-judgementalness)	Free of prejudice concerning other opinions, attitudes and behavioural patterns, in particular those typical of other cultures.
Meta-communicative competence	The ability to intervene and control in difficult communication situations and to repair disturbances in the communication.

(Kühlmann and Stahl 1998: 217–18; translated by Franklin)

These indicators are derived presumably from the critical incident research, that is are reports of the interactants themselves on their experiences. How accurate the descriptions of the indicators are, and how exactly these things are done in intercultural interaction in various languages used for lingua franca purposes by interculturally competent interactants, remains largely a matter for conjecture. Such a body of knowledge would, however, be important for the more accurate assessment of intercultural interaction competence (the subject of Chapter 8) and for the more effective development of intercultural competence (the subject of Chapter 9). Generating such knowledge would also be a promising research activity for applied linguists.

Moreover, as we mentioned in Section 3.3, Kühlmann and Stahl's framework has greatly informed the work of the INCA Project in conceptualizing and operationalizing ICIC.

Concept 3.8 Behavioural indicators of ICIC as described by Stahl	
Competence	**Behaviour**
Sociability	Initiates contact with foreign partner; makes new appointments; asks about the partner's personal background; is talkative; smiles at partner; exchanges 'conversational currency'.
Empathy	Considers the local partner's situation; shows appropriate discretion; argues from the position of the host national; picks up on the partner's contribution sympathetically.
Non-judgementalness	Expresses approval of the host culture; avoids stereotypes; avoids making jokes about host nationals; discusses the uniqueness of the host country in a factual manner.
Meta-communication skills	Tries to dissolve ambiguities and misunderstandings; provides appropriate feedback; asks if he or she has been understood; negotiates rules of play for the conversation; summarizes contributions.
(Stahl 2001: 202)	

3.4.2 ICIC conceptual frameworks developed by international business and management scholars

A conceptual framework which has been derived from research in a variety of disciplines, including much that has been referred to in this chapter, and which is used increasingly widely in international business and management, is that developed by the company WorldWork Ltd., London (Concept 3.9). They explain on their website that:

> based on current research and the practical experience of people operating internationally, WorldWork has identified 10 key competencies covering 22 different factors which enable people to become rapidly effective in unfamiliar cultural settings.
>
> (WorldWork, n.d.; see Concept 3.9)

They have developed a number of instruments to assess ICIC, which we explain and discuss in Chapter 8.

Concept 3.9	WorldWork's framework of international competencies	
Key competencies	**Component factors**	**Description**
1. Openness	1.1 New thinking	Receptive to new ideas, and typically seeks to extend understanding into new and unfamiliar fields. Likes to work internationally as they are exposed to ideas and approaches with which they are unfamiliar.
	1.2 Welcoming strangers	Keen to initiate contact and build relationships with new people, including those who have different experiences, perceptions, and values to themselves. Often takes a particular interest in strangers from different and unfamiliar cultural backgrounds.
	1.3 Acceptance	Not only tolerates but also positively accepts behaviour that is very different from their own. In an international context they rarely feel threatened by, or intolerant of, working practices that conflict with their own sense of best practice.
2. Flexibility	2.1 Flexible behaviour	Adapt easily to a range of different social and cultural situations. Have either learned or are willing to learn a wider range of behaviour patterns. Ready to experiment with different ways of behaving to find those that are most acceptable and most successful.
	2.2 Flexible judgement	Avoid coming to quick and definitive conclusions about the new people and situations they encounter. Can also use each experience of people from a different culture to question assumptions and modify stereotypes about how such people operate.
	2.3 Learning languages	Motivated to learn and use the specific languages of important business contacts, over and beyond the lingua franca in which they conduct their everyday business activities. Ready to draw on key expressions and words from the languages of these international contacts to build trust and show respect.

3. Personal autonomy	3.1 Inner purpose	To hold strong personal values and beliefs that provide consistency or balance when dealing with unfamiliar circumstances, or when facing pressures that question judgement of challenge sense of worth. Such values also give importance and credibility to the tasks that they have to perform.
	3.2 Focus on goals	Set specific goals and tasks in international projects, combined with a high degree of persistence in achieving them regardless of pressures to compromise, and distractions on the way. Believe they have a strong element of control over their own destiny, and can makes things happen in the world around them.
4. Emotional strength	4.1 Resilience	Usually tough enough to risk making mistakes as a way of learning. Able to overcome any embarrassment, criticism or negative feedback they may encounter. Have an optimistic approach to life and tend to 'bounce back' when things go wrong.
	4.2 Coping	Able to deal with change and high levels of pressure even in unfamiliar situations. They remain calm under pressure, and have well-developed means of coping even without their normal support networks. Have the personal resources necessary to deal effectively with the stress from culture shock.
	4.3 Spirit of adventure	Ready to seek out variety, change and stimulation in life, and avoid safe and predictable environments. Push themselves into uncomfortable and ambiguous situations, often unsure whether they have the skills required to be successful.
5. Perceptiveness	5.1 Attuned	Highly focused on picking up meaning from indirect signals such as intonation, eye contact and body language. Adept at observing these signals of meaning and reading them correctly in different contexts – almost like learning a new language.
	5.2 Reflected awareness	Very conscious of how they come across to others; in an intercultural context particularly sensitive to how their own 'normal' patterns of communication and behaviour are interpreted in the minds of international partners.
6. Listening orientation	6.1 Active listening	Check and clarify, rather than assume understanding of others, by paraphrasing and exploring the words that they use and the meaning they attach to them.

7. Transparency	7.1 Clarity of communication	Conscious of the need for a 'low-risk' style that minimized the potential for misunderstandings in an international context. Able to adapt to 'how a message is delivered' (rather than just 'what is said') to be more clearly understood by an international audience.
	7.2 Exposing intentions	Able to build and maintain trust in an international context by signalling positive intentions, and putting needs into a clear and explicit context.
8. Cultural knowledge	8.1 Information gathering	Take time and interest to learn about unfamiliar cultures, and deepen their understanding of those they already know. Employ various information-gathering strategies for understanding the specific context they require.
	8.2 Valuing differences	Like to work with colleagues and partners from diverse backgrounds, and are sensitive to how people see the world differently. Keen not only to explore and understand others' values and beliefs, but also communicate respect for them.
9. Influencing	9.1 Rapport	Exhibit warmth and attentiveness when building relationships in a variety of contexts. Put a premium on choosing verbal and non-verbal behaviours that are comfortable for international counterparts, thus building a sense of 'we'/ Able in the longer-term to meet the criteria for trust required by their international partners.
	9.2 Range of styles	Have a variety of means for influencing people across a range of international contexts. This gives greater capacity to 'lead' an international partner in a style with which he or she feels comfortable.
	9.3 Sensitivity to context	Good at understanding where political power lies in organizations and keen to figure out how best to play to this. Put energy into understanding the different cultural contexts in which messages are sent and decisions are made.
10. Synergy	10.1 Creating new alternatives	Sensitive to the need for a careful and systematic approach to facilitating group and team work to ensure that different cultural perspectives are not suppressed, but are properly understood and used in the problem-solving process.

(WorldWork, n.d.)

Once again, we see yet more different categories and labels, but with many of the same themes emerging, including mindfulness, contextual appropriateness, communication skills, knowledge, psychological adaptation and the management of social relations. Spencer-Oatey and Stadler (2009) have drawn on the WorldWork framework to develop a competency framework for intercultural effectiveness in international project work, and we also build on it in the next few chapters, using it as a springboard for identifying and discussing the competencies needed for handling a range of aspects of intercultural interaction.

3.5   Concluding comments

The multidisciplinary work presented in this chapter provides us with a somewhat bewildering array of models of ICIC and of their components. Nevertheless, all of the frameworks recognize that ICIC is a multi-faceted phenomenon and they all draw, at least in part, on the distinction between **a**ffective, **b**ehavioural and **c**ognitive components – the ABCs of ICIC. Sometimes this distinction is operationalized under the headings of attitudes (**a**ffective components), skills (**b**ehavioural components) and knowledge or awareness (**c**ognitive components), as in Gudykunst's conceptualization (see Concept 3.3) or Byram's (see Concept 3.5). Sometimes other concepts, such as motivation (e.g., Concept 3.3 and 3.6), are used to capture those factors which are clearly not primarily behavioural or cognitive in nature. Others do not distinguish between skill and knowledge (see Concept 3.6), and yet others make no distinctions at all and simply refer to them all as competencies or factors (see Concept 3.9).

Most of the models are presented in rather abstract terms, with little unpacking of what the concepts mean in practice, let alone any detailed descriptions or analyses of authentic intercultural interaction that can illustrate them. In the next four chapters, we aim to rectify this and to 'put flesh on the bones' by examining in detail key areas of intercultural interaction and the component competencies that are needed to handle them appropriately and effectively. We pay particular attention to the data and insights that applied linguistic research can offer. In Chapter 9 we return to the ABC distinction, which is widely used by intercultural developers and which can be very useful for such contexts.

Suggestions for further reading

Byram, M. (1997) *Teaching and Assessing Intercultural Communicative Competence.* Clevedon: Multilingual Matters. An approach to the subject from the perspective of language education in school settings.

Gudykunst, William B. (2004) *Bridging Differences: Effective Intergroup Communication*, 4th edn. Thousand Oaks: Sage. A classic US textbook introduction to the subject from the communication studies/psychology perspective.

Thomas, A. (2003) Interkulturelle Kompetenz. Grundlagen, Probleme, Konzepte. *Erwägen, Wissen, Ethik*, 14(1): 137–50. A very useful text for readers of German.

Ting-Toomey, S. (1999) *Communicating across Cultures*. New York: The Guilford Press. The chapters on mindfulness and transcultural communication competence are particularly interesting.

4
Achieving Understanding in Intercultural Interaction

People do not always or even usually say what they mean.

Thomas 1995: 1

Chapter outline

4.1 The communication process and message communication competencies
4.2 An authentic example: misconstruals of meaning
4.3 Effective use of message communication competencies
4.4 Ineffective use of message communication competencies
4.5 Non-verbal behaviour
4.6 The communication process revisited
4.7 Achieving understanding through an interpreter
4.8 Concluding comments
    Suggestions for further reading

In the last chapter we noted that competence in communication is an important component of intercultural competence. In this chapter we explore this aspect in greater depth, focusing on the impact of culture on the process of achieving understanding, and the competencies that are needed for handling this. We concentrate on the 'content' aspect of understanding; in other words, on the construction of 'message' meaning. The next chapter, Chapter 5, explores another important aspect of communication – 'relational' meaning – how people's use of language may lead to judgements such as polite, offensive, encouraging, annoying and so on, and thus how interpersonal rapport can be managed in intercultural interaction.

4.1   The communication process and message communication competencies

A number of factors influence how well participants of an intercultural interaction understand each other's messages. One of the most fundamental of these is use of the linguistic code. If people cannot speak a given language fluently, and/or if proficient speakers use it in 'unhelpful' ways, it will be very difficult for them to understand each other. However, even when there are no problems of this kind, achieving understanding can still be extremely difficult.

An early model of communication, the 'code-model', assumed that language could provide an automatic pairing of messages and signals (i.e. that language could pair exactly the meanings that people send and receive with what is physically transmitted, such as sound or writing), and that communication was thus successful to the extent that senders and receivers each paired signals and messages in the same way. Modern theories of communication, on the other hand, especially in branches of linguistics such as pragmatics, realize that this is incorrect. Although human communication to a large extent exploits a language code (such as English, Chinese or German), it is not feasible for everything to be conveyed explicitly in the code. Much has to be left for the interlocutors to work out, and in intercultural interaction this can be particularly problematic because people may focus on different clues when inferring meanings, and/or they may arrive at different meanings from the same clues. As a result, mismatches may occur in the messages that people think have been communicated.

Bearing this in mind, and building on the ICIC frameworks presented in Chapter 3, especially the competencies identified by WorldWork and by Spencer-Oatey and Stadler (2009) (see Section 3.4.2), we suggest that there are a number of different competencies associated with communicating messages, especially in intercultural contexts (see Concept 4.1). We explore them in this chapter, illustrating why they are so important. We start with an authentic example.

4.2   An authentic example: misconstruals of meaning

This example, which is from Tyler (1995), concerns a tutoring session that took place in the United States between a Korean tutor and an American student.

Concept 4.1	Message communication competencies
Message attuning	Picks up meaning from indirect signals such as paralanguage (e.g., intonation, speaking volume and speed, pausing) and non-verbal communication (e.g., eye contact and other elements of body language), and uses these signals to draw inferences about people's message meanings.
Active listening	Does not assume understanding – checks and clarifies the meaning of words and phrases, and tests own understanding.
Building of shared knowledge	Discloses and elicits key information, including the intentions and broader context as to why something is said or requested, in order to help build trust and mutual understanding and to reduce uncertainty.
Linguistic accommodation	Adapts use of language (e.g., choice of words, speed of delivery, clarity of pronunciation, use of colloquial expressions) to the proficiency level of the recipient(s).
Information structuring and highlighting	Structures and highlights information by using discourse markers to 'label' language, by using visual or written aids, and by paying attention to the sequencing of information.
Stylistic flexibility	Uses different language styles and conventions flexibly to suit different purposes, contexts and audiences.

The tutor was a male, Korean graduate in Computer and Information Science who had been in the United States for over 2 years. His English was generally comprehensible, although he had some problems with grammar and pronunciation. He was a member of an advanced, elective English oral skills course, and as a regular part of this course, he offered free tutoring in his area of expertise to US undergraduates so as to improve his English communication skills. The student was a female, native speaker of American English. She was taking an introductory computer programming course and needed help with a programming assignment: to write a computer program for keeping score in bowling. The first part of the interaction proceeded as follows:

1   S: we have to write a program that scores bowling right?
2   T: mhm
3   S: the game of bowling and he want us to be able to put in like how many pins well do you know how to score the game?

4	T:	yeah approximately
5	S:	OK cause he he has a little thing that tells you how (shows pages on handout) See I don't know how to score
6	T:	Oh you don't know how to score the bowling game?
7	S:	unhuh I'm like just I've played like I've scored a couple times but I'm not too good on it
		(Then the student asks the tutor to read the assignment to himself)
8	T:	uhmm open, spare, strike
9	S:	OK that has to do with the bowling game
10	T:	OK can you guess the amount you have to figure out?
11	S:	that's what I need to know OK we're going to start from the beginning
12	T:	OK
13	S:	I'm going to tell you what I think the inputs are OK and you tell me whatever I need
14	T:	mhm
15	S:	OK first thing I need to input in the computer is like the number of pins that get knocked down by the ball?
16	T:	mhm
17	S:	OK is that correct?
18	T:	mhm
19	S:	OK next I need to input I guess I get 2 balls per game
20	T:	2 balls per frame
21	S:	balls per frame OK let me write these down
		(Student writes. Then the student maintains that there are always two balls per frame; the tutor explains the rules differently. The interaction continues as below)
35	S:	OK let me ask you a question let's say you and I are playing right?
36	T:	mhm
37	S:	and I rolled a strike
38	T:	mhm
39	S:	on the first ball
40	T:	right
41	S:	first ball rolled I get them all down
42	T:	mhm
43	S:	would I go again or would you go?
44	T:	doesn't matter in in in this in this a program
45	S:	no but I just need to know that
46	T:	I don't know exactly how how real play is played I think the
47	S:	oh OK then don't worry about it
48	T:	real pl aa real bowling game is played like this you have 10 frames and in each frame you you are entitled 2 shots
49	S:	right
50	T:	OK 2 shots and if you knock down all the pins in the first shot
51	S:	mhm

52	T:	you don't have to use the second shot
53	S:	OK
54	T:	OK so you move
55	S:	OK
56	T:	if you knock down all the all the pins you have to move on to the next frame

(The tutor continues to explain the scoring in detail, including that there are three possibilities in each frame)

| 70 | S: | is this for this? do I need to know this? OK do I input date [hits assignment sheet which is in front of the tutor with a pencil] inside of here? |

(Tyler 1995: 133, 149)

At the end of the tutoring session, both the tutor and the student identified the tutorial as problematic, and each independently approached the supervisor to complain about the other's uncooperative attitude. Tyler conducted playback sessions with the participants in order to explore how they each interpreted the various parts of the interaction. On the basis of this evidence, she argues that the two misunderstood each other in these initial exchanges, and that as the interaction continued, the problem was exacerbated by further mismatches of interpretation. Let us consider why the clash took place and how this relates to the competencies for communicating messages identified in Concept 4.1.

4.3 Effective use of message communication competencies

There are a number of features of effective use of message communication (MC) competencies, especially by the American student. Although Tyler (1995) does not provide any information on speed of delivery, pausing, pronunciation and so on, the transcript does suggest that the student was accommodating linguistically in terms of vocabulary. For example, she is aware that the terminology associated with bowling may be unfamiliar to the tutor, so in turn 9 she comments on the terminology and in turn 41 she rephrases turn 39 in simpler English. Linguistic accommodation of the kind found in investigations of native-speaker adjustments to non-native speakers (e.g., Long 1983) is extremely important for achieving understanding, and Concept 4.2 lists a range of ways in which native speakers and advanced speakers of a foreign language can do this. Of course, it is important to remember that over-accommodation (e.g., simplifying too much) is as problematic – albeit in different ways – as under-accommodation, so another MC competency, message attuning, is needed in order to ensure an appropriate degree of accommodation. Spencer-Oatey and Xing (2005) discuss an authentic intercultural visit where linguistic accommodation was used very effectively.

Concept 4.2   Linguistic accommodation that is helpful from fluent/native speakers when interacting with less proficient speakers

Speak more clearly and slowly than usual
Pause and emphasize key words
Increase redundancy; i.e. repeat and paraphrase
Avoid unnecessarily technical words, slang, idioms
Restrict the range of your vocabulary
Use short sentences
Use transparent sentence structure; e.g., *He asked if he could leave,* not *He asked to leave*
Avoid contractions, e.g., *I'll, shouldn't've*
[...]
Use more yes/no questions
Provide answers for the interlocutor to choose from, e.g., *We can set up the equipment in two ways: like this [...] and like that [...] Which do you prefer?*

(Comfort and Franklin 2008: 93)

Another MC competency that the American student uses very effectively is the structuring and highlighting of information. She regularly 'labels' her own communication (cf. research on effective native-speaker business negotiators by Rackham and Carlisle 1978), commenting on what she is 'doing' with what she says; see, for example, turns 11 (second phrase), 13 and 35 (first phrase). She also uses discourse markers (e.g., *first* in turn 15 and *next* in turn 19) to label it. The tutor, on the other hand, does not do this at all (or at least, not in the extract that Tyler provides). From turn 70 we see clearly that the student did not understand why the tutor was explaining in detail the three possibilities for scoring a frame, and an initial 'packaging' comment (more technically known in linguistics as a meta-communicative comment), which explained why he was giving this information, would probably have been very helpful.

A third MC competency that the tutor and student use (although to a much lesser extent in the extract Tyler provides) is active listening. This includes:

- showing you are listening and following by using backchannelling (e.g., mhm, uhuh, yes, etc.);

- asking for clarification;
- checking whether you have understood something correctly (e.g., by summarizing what the other person has said) (cf. 'testing understanding' in Rackham and Carlisle, 1978);
- repairing misunderstandings.

Such behaviour is extremely important for achieving mutual understanding. When something is unclear, there is often a strong temptation to 'let it pass'; however, if this is done too frequently or at too critical points, serious problems in achieving mutual understanding can result.

4.4　Ineffective use of message communication competencies

A key MC competency that underpins the achievement of understanding is the building of shared knowledge. This refers to the disclosure and elicitation of key information that is fundamental to the current interaction or to future interaction. In the case of Tyler's intercultural tutoring session, it was vital for the tutor and the student to establish right at the beginning how familiar they each were with bowling and how it is scored, because that would affect how easily the tutor could help the student with the required task of writing a computer program. The student seemed well aware of this, and so at the very beginning of the exchange she asked the tutor directly whether he knew how to score bowling. However, despite this, the two failed to build mutual awareness. What then went wrong?

The tutor responded to the student's direct question with 'Yeah approximately'. To the student, it sounded as though he was only roughly familiar with bowling, but Tyler reports that the tutor was unaware that the student interpreted him in this way. In fact, he often bowled and was quite knowledgeable about how to score the game, but he did not feel he could say so directly. In the playback session, he explained to Tyler (1995: 136) that in Korean it would be considered rude to state explicitly that one is an expert in an area. If asked directly about it, the 'polite' way to claim expertise and yet not sound arrogant is to use a formulaic conventionalized hedge that translates roughly as 'approximately'. The tutor maintained that any Korean would recognize this tag as polite self-effacement and would interpret him as saying, 'Yes, I know how to score bowling.'

Shortly after his 'polite' response, the student admitted that she herself was not too good at scoring. The tutor said nothing in response, and in the playback session the student reported that she took this as an indication that he had no bowling experience. She assumed that if he had had relevant experience, he would have mentioned it at this point. However, Tyler reports the tutor's interpretation as follows:

> In the playback session, when asked why he did not mention his bowling experience when the student revealed her lack of knowledge, the Korean tutor noted that it might be embarrassing to the student for a foreigner to openly say he knows more about a game from her own culture than she did. Because the tutor already believes that he has asserted his expertise, he does not feel required to respond [...] with an account of his own bowling experience. In fact, to say that he is quite familiar with the game might be considered as 'one-upping' the student. [...] The tutor's silence at this point is a second self-defined attempt to be polite.
>
> (Tyler 1995: 138)

The tutor and the student thus failed to build mutually shared knowledge in relation to this crucial piece of information, and one of the main reasons underlying this was the lack of flexibility in style that they both showed. The student was using a direct style of speech and was expecting the tutor also to be direct; the tutor was using a more indirect style of speech and assumed that the student would know how to interpret indirect ways of claiming competence. Neither seemed aware that they were using different styles, nor of the impact this was having on how they were interpreting each other. Moreover, neither was flexible in the use or interpretation of communication styles.

The notion of communication style is widely referred to in anthropology, communication studies and applied linguistics. Concept 4.3 provides some applied linguistic explanations of the notion. All of the applied linguistic explanations assume that communication style is a resource for conveying and/or negotiating an identity, and Eggins and Slade (1997) associate it with subcultural groups. However, there is less acknowledgement in applied linguistics, compared with anthropology and communication studies, that people may be unaware of their often culturally-based communication styles and that in intercultural interaction, it can be helpful to sensitize people to potentially different styles. This is often a key goal of intercultural development interventions.

Concept 4.3   Communication style

We are defining style as a clustering of linguistic resources, and an association of the clustering with an identifiable aspect of social practice.

(California Style Collective 1993; cited by Auer 2007: 12)

Style [...] is how speakers construct a 'way to be' or identity by combining the social and linguistic resources available in a community in a salient way. [...] Speakers choose the manner in which to manipulate the resources to which they have access, and carve out particular representations of self by exploiting the meanings assigned and assignable to recognisable styles.

(Moore 2004: 379–80)

Analysis of conversational style reveals that we are not talking about individual speakers so much as groups of speakers sharing common styles. Interactive styles provide recognition criteria for subcultural groups, and indicate dimensions of difference that are significant for cultural members.

(Eggins and Slade 1997: 36)

One of the best known dimensions of communication style in the field of intercultural communication, proposed by the anthropologist Edward Hall (see Section 2.2.2), is that of high-context – low-context (see Concepts 2.6 and 4.4).

Concept 4.4   High-context – low-context communication style

Low-context communication (LCC) refers to communication patterns of direct verbal mode: straight talk, nonverbal immediacy, and sender-oriented values (i.e. the sender assumes the responsibility to communication clearly). In the LCC system, the speaker is expected to be responsible for constructing a clear, persuasive message that the listener can decode easily. In comparison, high-context communication (HCC) refers to communication patterns of indirect verbal mode: self-humbling talk, nonverbal subtleties, and interpreter-sensitive values (i.e. the receiver or interpreter of the message assumes the responsibility to inter the hidden or contextual meanings of the message) [...] In the HCC system, the listener or interpreter of the message is expected to 'read between the lines', to accurately infer the implicit intent of the verbal message, and to decode the nonverbal subtleties that accompany the verbal message.

(Ting-Toomey and Chung 2005: 172)

In the interaction reported by Tyler (1995), the tutor used a high-context communication style: he was indirect and self-humbling, and assumed that the student would be able to infer that he was competent at bowling. For example, he stated 'I don't know exactly how real play is played' prior to asserting his expertise. He did not expect the self-effacing comment to be taken literally, but assumed it would be interpreted as a politeness remark (cf. English native speakers' use of face-giving phrases like 'That's an excellent point, but [...]' prior to a potentially face-threatening disagreement, when they too do not expect it to be taken literally). The student, however, interpreted it literally. The style that she was used to was a low-context one: she was direct and straightforward in her questions and comments, and she assumed that the tutor would interact with her in a similar style. (For further information on directness–indirectness, see Spencer-Oatey 2008c: 28–31; and Comfort and Franklin 2008: 35–6; 106–7.)

When people are used to a low-context, direct style of communication, they tend to have difficulty working out the intended meaning of other people's indirect language, either because they are not aware of the possible need to do so or because they do not notice the cues or because they do not know how to interpret them. Experiential Example 4.2 provides another example of this. Moreover, direct communicators may attach negative judgements to indirect speakers, regarding them as unnecessarily – and perhaps even sarcastically – polite, indecisive, lacking in openness or even dishonest. If people are used to an indirect style of communication, on the other hand, they may make negative judgements about people who speak directly, regarding them as rude, unnecessarily assertive, imposing and so on. It seems that these types of attributions occurred in the interaction reported by Tyler (1995). (See Chapters 5 and 6 for a fuller discussion of evaluative judgements, where we consider the management of intercultural relations and impression management.)

Experiential Example 4.1   A conceptual misunderstanding in the workplace

At a meeting recently held in Japan, an American was discussing two alternative proposals with his colleagues, all of whom were native speakers of Japanese. The American was well schooled in the Japanese language and was, indeed, often called 'fluent' by those around him. At this meeting, proposal A was contrasted to proposal B, and a consensus was reached about future action, and the meeting then dismissed. Upon leaving the room the American commented, 'I think the group made a wise choice in accepting proposal A'. A Japanese colleague, however, noted, 'But proposal B was the group's choice.' The American continued: 'But I heard people say that proposal A was better'. The Japanese colleague concluded, 'Ah, you listened to the words but not to the pauses between the words.'

(Brislin 1978: 205; quoted in Gutt 2000: 78)

In terms of MC competencies, both low-context and high-context communicators not only need to become more flexible in their styles, but also to become more attuned (which tends to be more difficult for low-context than high-context communicators because of their reliance on explicit verbal messages). Gumperz (1982, 1992; Gumperz and Roberts 1991), a renowned sociolinguist who has studied intercultural encounters in the workplace very extensively, argues that people use a range of cues to help them interpret meaning. He calls these 'contextualization cues' (See Concept 4.5), and points out that communication is likely to be problematic if the participants of an interaction pay attention to different cues. So, for instance, with regard to the workplace misunderstanding described in Experiential Example 4.1, Gumperz would argue that the American did not use the cue of paralinguistic pausing during the discussion of the proposal, and because he did not, he drew the wrong conclusion regarding the decision that had been reached.

Concept 4.5 Gumperz on contextualization and contextualization cues

I use the term 'contextualization' to refer to speakers' and listeners' use of verbal and nonverbal signs to relate what is said at any one time and in any one place to knowledge acquired through past experience, in order to retrieve the presuppositions they must rely on to maintain conversational involvement and assess what is intended. [...] Contextualization relies on cues which operate primarily at the following levels of speech production:

1. Prosody, which I take to include intonation, stress or accenting and pitch register shifts.
2. Paralinguistic signs of tempo, pausing and hesitation, conversational synchrony, including latching or overlapping of speaking turns, and other 'tone of voice' expressive cues.
3. Code choice, [...] as for example in code or style switching [...]
4. Choice of lexical forms or formulaic expressions, as for example opening or closing routines or metaphoric expressions [...]

How do contextualization cues work communicatively? They serve to highlight, foreground or make salient certain phonological or lexical strings *vis-à-vis* other similar units, that is, they function relationally and cannot be assigned context-independent, stable, core lexical meanings. Foregrounding processes, moreover, do not rest on any one single cue. Rather, assessments depend on co-occurrence judgements [...] that simultaneously evaluate a variety of different cues. [...] Moreover, inferences are subconsciously made so that [...] they are not readily accessible to recall. It is therefore difficult to

> elicit information about the grounds upon which particular inferences are made through direct questioning. The relevant interpretive processes are best studied through in-depth, turn-by-turn analysis of form and content.
>
> (Gumperz 1992: 230–2)

This raises an important question for intercultural development interventions: can people who participate in intercultural interactions be helped to notice and produce contextualization cues that were originally unfamiliar to them? If people are being trained for a very specific context, Gumperz's (1982) research suggests that they can be. However, it is obviously impossible for people to become familiar with all the contextualization cues of all cultural groups in all communicative contexts, and so the generic MC competency of attuning is of the utmost importance. WorldWork's coaching manual makes a number of suggestions for increasing people's ability to be attuned, including:

- Identify and become mindful of the key components of non-verbal communication such as stance, gesture, eye movement and voice quality.
- Find examples of each of the above components that are used by any of your international partners, and that you perceive to be less common in your own culture.

It is of course also important for people to be mindful of the fact that the meaning given to a particular non-verbal behaviour may be different from culture to culture, as we discuss in Section '4.5.

4.5 Non-verbal behaviour

As the discussion in the last section has indicated, non-verbal behaviour is an integral part of the communication process. Participants make extensive use of this mode, in combination with verbal signals and features of the physical context, to construct meaning (Goodwin 2000).

In intercultural interaction, not only may the relative importance of non-verbal behaviour be different (i.e. it usually plays a more significant role in high-context than low-context communication); the conventions associated with non-verbal behaviour may also be very different. In parts of Greece and Turkey, for example, forcefully tossing the head upwards and returning it more gently to the neutral position, and simultaneously raising the eyebrows typically means 'no', but for English speakers it could easily be taken for 'yes'. Morris and colleagues (1979) identify 38 different conventional meanings for the head toss. Further examples of the potential impact of differences in non-verbal conventions on the construction of message and/or interpersonal meaning are given in Experiential Examples 4.2.

Experiential Examples 4.2 Non-verbal behaviour and the construction of meaning

Type of non-verbal behaviour	Example of a critical issue	Experiential example
1. Kinesics (movement)	Who is it appropriate to smile at?	[When the first McDonald's store opened in Moscow] the training of employees hit a real glitch when they tried to teach them to smile at customers. The problem was resolved when the automatic social behaviour was identified. 'The Russians insisted they were a very friendly people; the problem was friendliness didn't include smiling at strangers. In Russia you only smile at people you know.' (Decker 1990; cited by Victor 1992: 197)
2. Oculesics (eye behaviour)	What does avoidance of eye contact indicate during a reprimand?	I made a major cultural error. While disciplining an American Indian student for skipping school, he took his eyes off me and put his head down. I said, 'When I'm talking to you, pick up your head and look me straight in the eye.' Later, from the father, I discovered it was a sign of respect when an American Indian responds by lowering his eyes. It meant he was accepting this responsibility in this situation. When I forced him to look me in the eye, it went against his cultural and historical customs. I created a situation of confusion and probably hostility. (Doyle 1989, cited by Victor 1992: 207)
3. Haptics (touching)	What does touching 'mean'?	When I first came to the UK as a student, I was struck by the lack of human interaction. I did some part-time work in a shop in Guildford.

One day the female manager had a visit from another woman. Afterwards, she said the woman was her aunt. I found it hard to believe. No hugs, no kisses, nothing.

Where I come from, there's so much touching. As a child, you are handed from one lap to another. As a boy, you often carry one of your cousins or relatives around with you. You see Arab children whose cheeks are covered in red marks; they come from kissing. From the moment you are born, you're taught to express yourself physically as much as verbally. And it doesn't stop when you grow up. When you meet someone you have not seen for a while, you kiss – even one man to another.

During my first year at college in the UK, my Arab friends and I enjoyed shocking the British. We would kiss each other on both cheeks – just to see their reaction. It took some time for the joke to wear off. After I had lived in the UK for several years, I visited Jordan. I was walking along the street with one of my male cousins when he held my hand. My reflex action was to withdraw my hand immediately. I had not realized how British I had become! It took me a few minutes to remember that I was now at home and that it was perfectly normal for two men to hold hands. I took hold of my cousin's hand again. This was my first lesson in learning how to be at ease with both cultures.

(Dr Jehad al Omari, reported by Carté and Fox 2004: 72–3)

| 4. Proxemics (use of personal space) | When can you enter 'my space'? | I myself remember that, after having spent several years in the United States, I was shocked when a new colleague, who had just arrived from France, knocked and 'barged into' my office. Everyone else waited for a 'come in', including French people who had been living in the United States for a longer period of time.

(Reported by a French anthropologist, Carroll 1987: 18) |

4.6   The communication process revisited

The discussion so far in this chapter has indicated that people use two main sources of knowledge to construct meaning in interaction: linguistic knowledge (i.e. knowledge of the language code) and 'world' knowledge (i.e. experiential and theoretical knowledge of social processes, facts, concepts, etc.). Both types of knowledge are always involved in the making of meaning, although their relative impact on the achievement of understanding can vary. Sometimes linguistic factors can be paramount, such as when the proficiency level of one of the speakers is low, or when someone is using an unfamiliar regional variety of the language. At other times, knowledge factors can be paramount; for instance, lack of knowledge of computing can hamper people's understanding of a presentation on e-learning. Lack of familiarity with the terminology may be part of the problem (i.e. a linguistic knowledge problem), but the lack of background conceptual knowledge is often even more significant.

Between these two extremes lie most of the communication difficulties discussed in this chapter. They require not only linguistic and 'world' knowledge for the successful construction of meaning, but also sociocultural or pragmatic knowledge. Sociocultural or pragmatic knowledge refers to the conventions and principles that underlie language use in a given sociocultural group. Some aspects of such pragmatic knowledge are more linguistic in nature while others are more social in nature, and Leech (1983: 10–11) uses the terms 'pragmalinguistics' and 'sociopragmatics' to distinguish between these aspects. Pragmalinguistics is at the linguistic end, and is concerned with the linguistic resources available and conventionally used for conveying a given pragmatic meaning in a given context. Sociopragmatics is at the social end, and is concerned with social appropriateness in language use. Thomas (1983) uses the terms pragmalinguistic failure and sociopragmatic failure to refer to the mismatches that may occur between a speaker's intended meaning and the hearer's constructed meaning.

The tutor's use of the word 'approximately' in Tyler's (1995) data is an example of pragmalinguistic failure. For the Korean tutor, 'approximately' was a direct translation of the Korean word 'com', which is a conventional term for acknowledging competence in a non-arrogant manner; it hence indicated in a polite manner a high level of competence in bowling. For the American student, on the other hand, it was a straightforward response to her direct question about competence, which was to be taken literally. She had no idea about its conventional use in Korean, and so to her it indicated a minimal level of competence in bowling on the tutor's part. (See White 1993 and 1997 for more examples of pragmalinguistic failure; his 1997 article also deals with sociopragmatic failure.)

However, sociopragmatic knowledge is often closely linked with pragmalinguistic knowledge, and typically needs to be combined with it for effective interpretation. People's use of language is closely associated with the values and principles that they hold, including issues such as the relative importance of showing concern for the other (compared with self), and the relative importance of conveying modesty, deference and so on. As we have noted above, the Korean tutor was concerned not to appear arrogant and hence wanted to use modest forms of speech; moreover, when he became aware that the American student did not know how to score bowling, he wanted to avoid embarrassing her by stating clearly his own competence at a game that was from her own rather than his culture. Here we can clearly see how sociopragmatic factors combined with pragmalinguistic ones can lead to a significant communication failure.

Thomas (1983) points out that sociopragmatic aspects of communication are more complex to deal with than pragmalinguistic ones because they entail value-laden social judgements, while pragmalinguistic aspects are mainly only matters of the linguistic code. This raises an important question for developing ICIC: to what extent should participants of intercultural interactions be expected to adjust their language/ behaviour from a social point of view, especially when it goes against their values and interactional principles? There are no easy answers to this question, which is discussed in greater detail in Chapter 9. We discuss sociopragmatic issues further in the next two chapters.

4.7   Achieving understanding through an interpreter

Up to now, we have assumed that communication takes place directly between the participants of an intercultural interaction. Sometimes, however, it takes place indirectly via an interpreter, and in this final section we consider how understanding is achieved when an interpreter is involved.

In interpreter-mediated intercultural interactions, there are at least three parties: the two or more (groups of) primary interlocutors who want to communicate with each other but who cannot converse in a language that is mutually intelligible to everyone, and the interpreter(s). The primary interlocutors need to manage their communication in very similar ways to those discussed in the earlier sections of this chapter. As can be seen from Concept 4.6, many of the characteristics of effective communicative behaviour with an interpreter correspond to the MC competencies discussed so far.

Concept 4.6 Guidelines for using interpreters

1. Speak clearly and directly to the client as if s/he understands.
2. Pause frequently so the interpreter can remember and interpret what is being said.
3. Use plain English and avoid jargon.
4. Observe facial expressions, body language, tone of voice and gestures to gain clues to the client's emotional state.
5. Clarify with the client any verbal or non-verbal behaviour that is not understood. Be aware that cultural differences in body language may lead to misunderstanding.
6. Give the client the opportunity to ask for clarification of anything that has not been understood or add any other information that is relevant.
7. Do not rush the interaction. Interpreting accurately everything that has been said takes time.
8. Be aware that the client may understand some English and therefore speak as if the client does understand.
9. Avoid discussions with the interpreter.
10. Ask what the interpreter is doing if there are discussions between the client and the interpreter.
11. Be aware that in some situations the client may be emotional; s/he may talk at length or break down.
12. Agree to the interpreter taking notes to aid his/her memory.
13. Ensure the interpreter gets adequate breaks.

(Office of Ethnic Affairs, New Zealand)

Needless to say, it is not just the behaviour of the primary interlocutors that affect the outcome of an intercultural interaction via an interpreter; the interpreter can have a very major impact on the construction of meaning. Sometimes the interpreter, and particularly the conference interpreter in the cabin, is regarded as a 'non-person'; in other words, as an 'invisible translating machine' (Pöchhacker 2004: 147) who should contribute nothing to the substance of the interaction. For example, Spencer-Oatey and Xing (2007: 229) report the following comment made about an (untrained) interpreter by a participant of a Chinese-British business meeting (which we discuss in the next chapter): 'In fact, let me say something not so pleasant, [interpreter's name] was just a translator, nothing more [...] he shouldn't have taken part in anything else.' His colleagues chorused agreement with him. However, as

Wadensjö (1998: 67) points out, there are aspects of an interpreter's role that do not fit this role as a non-person, because in many interpreting contexts 'the interpreter's talk conditions the talk of others (and vice versa)'. The California Healthcare Interpreter's Association (2002) identifies four main roles for interpreters: message converter, message clarifier, cultural clarifier and patient advocate. In each of these roles, the interpreter has the potential to influence dynamically the ways in which the discourse develops and meanings are constructed, and cultural factors can have a major impact on this process (see Spencer-Oatey and Xing 2007, for further details).

When interpreters 'convert messages', culture can impact on the process in two main ways: how explicitly or implicitly the message is converted, and whether the message is actually converted or not. In relation to the former, suppose a Western company makes a proposal to a Chinese company and receives the response *kaolu kaolu*. This literally means 'I/we (implied) will (implied) think it over', but in this context it is generally understood as signifying a polite refusal (Kondo et al. 1997). How should this be interpreted? Rendering it as, 'we'll think it over' could give the wrong impression, and lead the Western representative to expect a response later. On the other hand, saying 'I'm afraid we cannot agree at this time' might be too specific, especially if the Chinese company wanted to be deliberately ambiguous. Clearly, the interpreter's decisions on such matters can have a major impact on the meanings the participants construct, as well as on the way the interaction develops.

Sometimes, an interpreter may feel unable, for cultural convention reasons, to 'convert the message' at all, as Experiential Example 4.3 illustrates.

Experiential example 4.3   An interpreting dilemma

Kaufert researched the experiences of Aboriginal health interpreters in Canada, and one of the examples he reports is as follows. A 72-year-old Aboriginal man was admitted to hospital for diagnostic evaluation of urinary tract problems. He spoke only Ojibway, and on his admission, his son acted as interpreter. The next day he was scheduled for a cystoscopic examination, and so arrangements were made for a male interpreter to come to help explain the procedure and get the patient's signature of consent. Unfortunately the male interpreter was called away, and the only interpreter available was a 28-year-old woman. The urologist started his explanation, but soon became frustrated because he felt the interpreter was hesitating too much and seemed unable to get his message across. After several unsatisfactory exchanges, he drew a sketch of the male urinary system, and eventually the patient agreed to the procedure, saying that although he didn't understand everything, he would sign because he trusted them to do the best for him. Why was the interpreter so hesitant and seemingly incompetent? Kaufert explains it as follows:

> After the consent agreement was signed, the interpreter returned to her office and discussed the encounter with her supervisor. She explained how the direct translation of the physician's explanation of the procedure would have forced her to violate fundamental cultural prohibitions against references to urinary and reproductive anatomy in cross-gender communication. She added that her reluctance in this case was strongly influenced by the patient's age and by his status as a respected elder. The Director of the Aboriginal Services Program told her that professional medical interpreters must translate stigmatised concepts objectively and accurately. The interpreter agreed, but said that the elder would not have understood that her role as an interpreter had given her the privilege of using words which he saw as disrespectful in a conversation between a male elder and a young woman. The program Director conceded the validity of her point and agreed that the interview should have been delayed until a male interpreter was available.
>
> (Kaufert 1999: 415–17)

This example illustrates the kind of dilemmas that interpreters may face because of cultural factors (see Hale 2007 for more examples). In such situations it is often not clear what interpreters should do, and Hale simply recommends that they 'use their best professional judgement'.

Interpreters' performance, therefore, can have a major impact on the achievement of understanding in intercultural interaction, and their effectiveness is not just dependent on their level of linguistic proficiency in the languages concerned. Interpreting is a professional skill in its own right, which requires specialist training, and using untrained individuals who simply speak the other language can run many risks (Knapp-Potthoff and Knapp 1987a, 1987b; Spencer-Oatey and Xing 2007). We argue, therefore, that competence in the communication elements of intercultural interaction includes understanding how to arrange for quality interpreting when interpreting is needed.

4.8   Concluding comments

In this chapter we have demonstrated how meaning does not lie simply in the verbal and non-verbal elements used, such as words, phrases and emblems; rather, the participants of an interaction actively construct and negotiate the meanings of the behaviour. In this process, they draw on a variety of knowledge, in addition to their familiarity with the linguistic and paralinguistic codes. This includes their awareness of the verbal and non-verbal behavioural conventions of their social group, their assumptions about appropriate styles of interaction, and their background knowledge about a topic. Culture can impact on this meaning-making process in that members of different social groups may draw on different knowledge and assumptions. As the experiential examples in this chapter have illustrated, this can lead to misunderstandings, although it need not necessarily do so.

We have focused in this chapter on the achievement of 'message' understanding. However, we have also noted that difficulties in developing this kind of mutual understanding can also affect interpersonal relations and the rapport that people feel towards each other. We turn to this important issue in the next chapter.

Suggestions for further reading

Thomas, J. (1995) *Meaning in Interaction: An Introduction to Pragmatics*. London: Longman. This book provides an excellent introduction to meaning, and the ways in which both speaker and hearer construct it in interaction. It is extremely readable, and has a large number of authentic examples which bring the theory to life.

Spencer-Oatey, H. (ed.) (2008) *Culturally Speaking: Culture, Communication and Politeness Theory*, 2nd edn. London: Continuum. The chapters in Part 1 of this book provide a clear explanation of the factors that affect the communication process, and discuss the interrelationship between culture and communication. The chapters in Part 2 report empirical studies of cross-national differences in language use.

House, J., Kasper, G. and Ross, S. (eds) (2003) *Misunderstanding in Social Life: Discourse Approaches to Problematic Talk*. London: Longman. The chapters in this edited volume each deal with misunderstanding. They cover a number of different sectors (e.g., the legal system and education) and of activity types (e.g., employment interviews, political interviews and oral proficiency interviews), and include discussion of misunderstanding as a phenomenon. Although intercultural issues are not the primary focus of the book, many of the studies entail intercultural interaction.

5
Promoting Rapport in Intercultural Interaction

> Reckless words pierce like a sword, but the tongue of the wise brings healing.
>
> The Bible, Proverbs 12: 18

Chapter outline

5.1   Rapport and rapport management competencies
5.2   An authentic example: a problematic business meeting
5.3   Contextual awareness
5.4   Interpersonal attentiveness
5.5   Information gathering
5.6   Social attuning
5.7   Emotion regulation
5.8   Strategies for managing rapport
5.9   Strategies for managing conflict
5.10   Concluding comments
        Suggestions for further reading

In the last chapter, we saw from Tyler's (1995) data that when people differ in the meanings that they construct and attribute to each other, a sense of hurt and offence can result. Such problems of rapport are widely reported in the intercultural literature, and this chapter focuses on reasons for their occurrence and ways in which they can be reduced or managed. In fact, problems of rapport are common in *intra*cultural interaction as well as *inter*cultural interaction, and much of the material in this chapter is relevant to both types. However, we pay special attention to intercultural perspectives. With the help of a number of authentic experiential examples, we explore the factors that dynamically influence people's perceptions of rapport and the competencies that are needed to handle them. We also consider strategies for managing rapport in intercultural encounters, and ways of dealing with conflict.

5.1 Rapport and rapport management competencies

We use the term 'rapport' to refer to people's subjective perceptions of (dis)harmony, smoothness–turbulence and warmth–antagonism in interpersonal relations, and we use the term 'rapport management' to refer to the ways in which this (dis)harmony is (mis)managed. Building on the ICIC frameworks presented in Chapter 3, and applying the concepts developed in 'Politeness Theory', we suggest that there are a number of competencies associated with the management of rapport (see Concept 5.1). We examine them one by one in this chapter, illustrating why they are important.

Concept 5.1	Rapport management competencies
Contextual awareness	Sensitive to key features of the interaction, including participant relations (equality/inequality and distance/closeness), the rights and obligations of people's roles, and the nature of the communicative activity.
Interpersonal attentiveness	Pays focused attention to people's face sensitivities (e.g., their status, competence, social identity), behavioural expectations and interactional goals, and manage them effectively.
Social information gathering	Gathers information about the interactional context (e.g., people's roles and positions in a hierarchy) by asking relevant others or by careful observation.
Social attuning	Uses indirect signals such as paralanguage (e.g., intonation, speaking volume and speed, pausing) and non-verbal communication (e.g., eye contact and other elements of body language) to infer social meaning – how s/he is coming across to others (how his/her behaviour is being evaluated from a relational point of view) and what the emotional state (e.g., offended, annoyed) of the other person is.
Emotion regulation	Resilient – is able to handle criticism or embarrassment when things go wrong. Accepts and feels at ease with people who are different (e.g., who hold different views or values).
Stylistic flexibility	Uses a range of strategies flexibly so that they are congruent with people's rapport sensitivities.

First, though, we describe an interaction during which the rapport was mismanaged, to help show the kinds of problems that can occur and to help illustrate our subsequent theoretical discussion.

5.2 An authentic example: a problematic business meeting

This example, which is from Spencer-Oatey and Xing (2004, 2008), concerns the visit of a Chinese business delegation to a British engineering company with whom they had recently signed a deal. The visit turned out to be highly problematic from a relationship point of view. The Chinese cancelled all the training sessions that had been arranged for them, and insisted on shopping and sightseeing for the whole of the ten-day trip. Both parties were unhappy. The Chinese complained that the British were 'commanding, in control, contemptuous' and the British maintained that the Chinese had 'no ethics and no due respect for their hosts'. Experiential Example 5.1 describes some of the things that happened, and how the participants reacted. (Data on people's reactions were gathered through post-event interviews and video playback sessions.)

Experiential Example 5.1   Problematic incidents

1. Seating arrangements for the welcome meeting

The welcome meeting took place in the company's conference room which had a large oblong table placed in the middle of the room. The British chairman sat at one end of the table, and the Chinese visitors sat round the rest of the table. Five other British staff either sat or stood behind the Chinese visitors because there was not enough room for them at the table. The British chairman was aware that the room was too small, and was embarrassed about this, but the company did not have a larger room on its premises as it was primarily a factory building. He sat at the 'head' of the table for practical reasons – so that he could see and hear the guests more easily. However, in the follow-up interviews, the Chinese delegation leader complained as follows:

> *It shouldn't have been that he sat in the chair position and we were seated along the sides of the table. With equal status, they should sit along this side and we should sit along that side, shouldn't we? That would have been the right way. You see, they were chairing, and we were audience, which naturally means that you do what you are told to. [His colleagues chorus agreement] They were, right from the start, they were commanding, in control, contemptuous. In actual fact we should have been given equal status [...]*

2. Team introductions and a return speech

The British chairman started the meeting by welcoming the visitors, and then asked the British staff to introduce themselves in turn. When they had done this, he invited each of the Chinese visitors to introduce themselves, but this immediately caused confusion. The delegation leader turned to consult the others, and one of them requested in Chinese that he do it on their behalf. It was almost a minute before the delegation leader responded to the chairman's request, and at this point he began reading out a speech. Immediately the interpreter interrupted him saying, in Chinese, that they should first introduce themselves. This resulted in further worried faces and discussion in Chinese, before the visitors started introducing themselves individually. In the follow-up interview and video playback session, the Chinese visitors all argued that it was normal and polite for the head of the delegation to 'say a few words of appreciation', and then introduce himself and each member of the delegation. They were clearly offended that he had not been given this opportunity. They discussed whether the interpreter was to blame for this, but concluded that he must have known British customs and that the British chairman cannot have wanted them to give a return speech. The head of the Chinese delegation argued as follows:

> *According to our home customs and protocol, speech is delivered on the basis of reciprocity. He has made his speech and I am expected to say something. [...] In fact I was reluctant to speak, and I had nothing to say. But I had to, to say a few words. Right for the occasion, right? But he had finished his speech, and he didn't give me the opportunity, and they each introduced themselves, wasn't this clearly implied that they do look down on us Chinese.*

In the follow-up interview with the British chairman, he explained that current delegations are very different from earlier ones, and that neither the Chinese nor the British expect too much formality.

3. Business Relationships

The Sales Manager for China was away on an overseas trip when the visitors arrived; he was due back during the middle of their visit. The Chinese visitors expected that, since he was their 'old friend', he would make contact with them immediately after he returned, either officially in the office, or unofficially at their hotel, or at least telephone them. However, when he made no contact with them on the day of his return, they were annoyed. They repeatedly asked, and at one stage even demanded, the accompanying British staff to contact him, and then asked for his home telephone number. This continued for the next few days, including the weekend.

The Sales Manager eventually arranged a meeting with them the following Monday, one day before their departure. In the follow-up interview, he explained that he needed to spend time with his family, since he had been away on a long trip. However, from the Chinese visitors' point of view, he had failed to act as a genuine friend.

(Adapted from Spencer-Oatey and Xing, 2004 and 2008)

In the following sections, we draw on these incidents, and others, to explore the rapport management competencies we outlined in Concept 5.1.

5.3   Contextual awareness

Research within pragmatics has demonstrated that a range of contextual factors influence people's behaviour and use of language, and that people's behaviour and use of language in turn influences interpersonal rapport. Three of the most important contextual factors are participant relations, role rights and obligations, and the nature of the communicative activity. In intercultural interaction, participants may assess these contextual variables in different ways and this may lead to problems of rapport, so a good grasp of the context is absolutely essential.

5.3.1   Participant relations

Participant relations are usually conceptualized in terms of power and distance–closeness. Several classic studies (e.g., Brown and Gilman 1960; Brown and Levinson (1987) have helped to establish these two variables, although as Spencer-Oatey (1996) explains, people sometimes conceptualize and operationalize them slightly differently and use a range of different terms to label them (e.g., power, social power, status, authority, dominance; distance, social distance, solidarity, closeness, familiarity, relational intimacy). Concept 5.2 quotes Brown and Gilman's (1960/1972) classic conceptualization.

Concept 5.2   Brown and Gilman on power and distance

Power

One person may be said to have power over another in the degree that he is able to control the behavior of the other. Power is a relationship between at least two persons, and it is nonreciprocal in the sense that both cannot have power in the same area of behavior.

(Brown and Gilman 1972: 225)

Distance

Now we are concerned with a [...] set of relations which are symmetrical [...] Not every personal attribute counts in determining whether two people are solidary enough to use the mutual T [T refers to the familiar version of the pronoun 'you', after the French 'tu']. Eye color does not ordinarily matter nor

> does shoe size. The similarities that matter seem to be those that make for like-mindedness or similar behavior dispositions. [...] The T of solidarity can be produced by frequency of contact as well as by objective similarities. However, frequent contact does not necessarily lead to the mutual T. It depends on whether contact results in the discovery or creation of the like-mindedness that seems to be the core of the solidarity semantic.
>
> (Brown and Gilman 1972: 258)

In applied linguistic research, power is typically operationalized in terms of unequal role relations, such as teacher–student, employer–employee. Distance–closeness is operationalized in more variable ways, but typically includes one or more of the following: length of acquaintance, degree of familiarity, sense of like-mindedness, frequency of contact, positive/negative affect and social similarity/difference.

As we noted in Chapter 2 (see Concept 2.4), Hofstede (1980/2001, 1991) provides evidence that there is variability across countries in the importance attached to power and in the extent to which people regard power differences as usual and acceptable. Such differences also exist across organizations, across sections within organizations, and across individuals. As we shall see in Section 5.4, power is a highly face-sensitive variable, so it is particularly important that people pay close attention to this contextual variable.

5.3.2   Role rights and obligations

Social/interactional role is a second contextual factor that needs to be considered. When people interact with each other, they often take up clearly defined social roles, such as teacher–student, employer–employee, friend–friend, sales assistant–customer, chairperson–committee member. These role relationships not only partially influence the power and distance of the relationship, but also help specify the rights and obligations of each role member. People have the right to expect certain things of the other member and an obligation to carry out certain other things. For example, a teacher has an obligation to handle classroom management issues, and a right to expect the students to comply with classroom management directives. Similarly, a sales assistant has an obligation to serve a customer helpfully, and a right to expect the customer to pay for the goods or service and not to be abusive or offensive. However, there are limits to the scope of the rights and obligations of any given role, and so if people go beyond that scope and assume rights that they are not entitled to, or fail to uphold the rights and obligations that are perceived as within that role, then offence may occur. In intercultural interaction, this can be problematic because there can be differences across cultures in the nature and scope of the rights and obligations associated with a given role. Quote 5.1 illustrates this in the healthcare sector.

Quote 5.1   Differing perspectives on the rights and obligations of patients and healthcare professionals in the UK

In Britain, competent adults have a right to full information about their condition and about their treatment and care options. They also have the right to refuse examination, diagnostic procedures and treatment. [...] In some cultures, major decisions are normally taken by senior family members or by the whole family. Patients who are used to this may find it hard to take decisions on their own behalf and may not want to. They may delegate authority and decisions, explicitly or implicitly, to other people. They may not expect to deal with distressing information or difficult choices and may be ill-equipped to do so. [...]

An elderly Asian woman was due to see me following a hysterectomy. I planned to discuss management options with her as the histology confirmed an aggressive malignancy. I was surprised when her husband and sons appeared instead. They said they had come for the results and that the patient was at home. I had to explain gently but firmly that I could not discuss any medical details or treatment options with them and that I needed to see the patient herself. (British Asian consultant gynaecologist)

(Henley and Schott 1999: 147–8, 159)

5.3.3   Type of communicative activity

A third important contextual variable that needs to be considered is the type of communicative activity that is taking place; for example, a lecture, a job interview, or a court trial. The notion of activity type was proposed by Levinson (1979: 368) and his definition is given in Concept 5.3.

Concept 5.3   Levinson on activity types

[...] a fuzzy category whose focal members are goal-defined, socially constituted, bounded, events with *constraints* on participants, setting, and so on, but above all on the kinds of allowable contributions. Paradigm examples would be teaching, a job interview, a jural interrogation, a football game, a task in a workshop, a dinner party and so on.

(Levinson 1979: 369)

Communicative activities often have *communicative genres* associated with them: 'historically and culturally specific conventions and ideals according to which speakers compose talk or texts and recipients interpret it' (Günthner 2007: 129). For instance, obtaining an appropriate balance between modesty and boasting is a recurrent communicative problem, but what counts as appropriate can vary from one activity type to another. For example, in job interviews in Britain, candidates are typically expected to 'sell' themselves, but not to appear 'too' proud; yet at an awards ceremony, the person receiving the award (e.g., the actor, writer, etc.) is supposed to minimize his/her achievements and to give credit to others (e.g., the director, fellow actors, supportive wife, etc.).

Similarly, speaking rights and turn-taking can vary from one activity type to another. For example, in an interview in Britain, it is normally only the panel members who can ask questions, until they pass that right to the interviewee; on the other hand, at a dinner party there is much greater freedom over who can speak when, yet there are still conventions over the fine-tuning of turn-taking (e.g., the acceptability of overlaps).

5.3.4   Contextual awareness and Experiential Example 5.1

In Experiential Example 5.1, power, role rights and obligations, and communicative genres were all important contextual variables that, in the Chinese visitors' eyes, were not handled appropriately by the British. Spencer-Oatey and Xing (2008: 267) report, in relation to this visit, that the British had difficulty identifying the roles and positions of the visitors and in assessing their relative importance. They thought they were engineers who were 'not much higher ranking' than other visitors, while in the Chinese eyes they were sales managers with significant power and status.

The British also showed lack of awareness of the Chinese conventions associated with various aspects of the communicative activity 'business meeting', including how rank affects seating positions, and how introductions and welcome speeches are handled.

Moreover, their interpretation of the rights and obligations associated with a salesman–customer role relationship was very different from that of the Chinese visitors, as was the distance–closeness that they attributed to the relationship. The Chinese regarded the British sales manager as an 'old friend', yet the manager had in fact only met two of the people once before in China, and none of them was sure whether they would actually recognize each other. In British terms, such a level of acquaintance would not count as an 'old friend', yet in Chinese contexts it would not be uncommon.

This weak contextual awareness by both parties, and lack of congruity in contextual assessments that was associated with this, was a key factor influencing the rapport management problems that occurred.

5.4   Interpersonal attentiveness

A second RM competency, which is closely related to contextual awareness, is interpersonal attentiveness. If rapport is to be managed effectively, it is vital for the participants of an interaction to pay close attention to people's face, their behavioural expectations and their interactional goals. These three elements form the bases of rapport, as shown in Figure 5.1.

5.4.1   Face

'Face' is a key concept that is integral to rapport. It is a concept that is intuitively meaningful to most people, but one that is difficult to define precisely. It is concerned with people's sense of worth, dignity and identity, and is associated with issues such as respect, honour, status, reputation and competence (Concept 5.4) (cf. Ting-Toomey and Kurogi 1998).

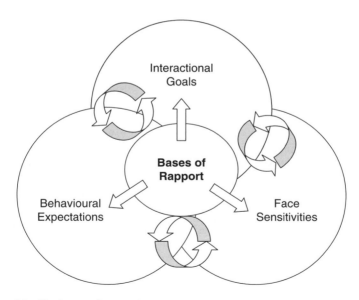

Figure 5.1   The bases of rapport.

Concept 5.4   Definitions of face

[...] the positive social value a person effectively claims for himself by the line others assume he has taken during a particular contact.

(Goffman 1967: 5)

The concept of face is about identity respect and other-identity consideration issues within and beyond the actual encounter episode. Face is tied to the emotional significance and estimated calculations that we attach to our own social self-worth and the social self-worth of others.

(Ting-Toomey and Chung 2005: 73)

The claim for face is the claim that the other should acknowledge, whether explicitly or implicitly, that one possesses the claimed virtues.

(Lim 1994: 210)

Face is the negotiated public image, mutually granted each other by participants in a communicative event.

(Scollon and Scollon 1995: 35)

We all evaluate our personal attributes or characteristics in some way: we view some of them positively (e.g., clever, musical), some of them negatively (e.g., overweight, unartistic), and others neutrally. We have a fundamental desire for others to evaluate us positively, and so we typically want others to acknowledge (explicitly or implicitly) our positive qualities, and *not* to acknowledge our negative qualities. Face is associated with these affectively sensitive attributes; however, exactly which attributes are face-sensitive can vary from person to person and from context to context. Nevertheless, people seem to be particularly sensitive to issues of status and competence. (See Spencer-Oatey 2007a for a more detailed discussion of the interconnection between face and identity.)

As the popular phrase 'lose face' conveys, we do not always receive the respect from others that we would like. People may criticize us or boss us around, insult us and call us names; and when they do, we typically feel embarrassed or uncomfortable. Brown and Levinson (1987), in their very well known model of politeness (see Section 5.8.2 below), propose the notion of *face-threatening acts* to explain this phenomenon. They claim that certain communicative acts (e.g., criticism, disagreement, apologies, requests) inherently threaten the face needs of the hearer, and they label these *face-threatening acts* (FTAs). Others maintain that almost any behaviour has the potential to be face-threatening, if the hearer interprets it as impacting on a sensitive attribute.

Face can be threatened or lost, but it can also be maintained or enhanced. It is extremely valuable to remember this, because it can often be very important to 'give people face' by publicly drawing attention to their positive qualities.

The attributes that people are face-sensitive about can apply not only to the person as an individual but also to the group or community that the person belongs to and/or identifies with. For example, with regard to the attribute 'talented', a person could regard him/herself as a talented individual (e.g., a talented artist), and s/he could regard the small group or community that s/he belongs to as being talented (e.g., a talented family or a talented work team or sports team). So face threat, face loss, face maintenance and face gain can apply both to individuals and to groups.

5.4.2   Behavioural expectations

Rapport can also be influenced by behavioural expectations. People typically form expectations (conscious or unconscious) as to the behaviour that will occur in a given context, based on the norms, conventions, principles, legal agreements and protocols that are associated with that context. They may then develop a sense that others should or should not perform that behaviour, and prescriptive and proscriptive overtones become associated with that behaviour. As a result, people start perceiving sociality rights and obligations in relation to them, and may feel annoyed if the expected behaviour does not occur.

In fact, behavioural norms and conventions are often not arbitrary. They may reflect efficient strategies for handling practical demands, and they may also be manifestations of more deeply held values. For example, conventions in relation to turn-taking and rights to talk at business meetings are partly a reflection of the need to deal effectively with the matters at hand, but they are also likely to reflect more deeply held beliefs about hierarchy and what is socially appropriate behaviour for given role relationships. There seem to be two fundamental principles that underlie interaction: equity and association (see Concept 5.5). On different occasions, and for contextual and goal-related reasons, people may give greater weight to equity than association, or vice versa. However, this may also be influenced by their personal values (which in turn may be influenced by the communities that they are members of). Equity can be linked with (but of course is not identical to) individualism and to an independent construal of self, and association can be linked with collectivism and to an interdependent construal of self (cf. Concept 2.4 and Concept 5.8).

Concept 5.5   Value-laden principles of interaction

Equity: We have a fundamental belief that we are entitled to personal consideration from others, so that we are treated fairly: that we are not unduly imposed upon, that we are not unfairly ordered about, and that we are not taken advantage of or exploited. There seem to be two components to this equity entitlement: the notion of *cost–benefit* (the extent to which we are exploited or disadvantaged, and the belief that costs and benefits should be kept roughly in balance through the principle of reciprocity), and the related issue of *autonomy–imposition* (the extent to which people control us or impose on us).

Association: We have a fundamental belief that we are entitled to social involvement with others, in keeping with the type of relationship that we have with them. These association rights relate partly to *interactional involvement – detachment* (the extent to which we associate with people, or dissociate ourselves from them), so that we feel, for example, that we are entitled to an appropriate amount of conversational interaction and social chit-chat with others (e.g., not ignored on the one hand, but not overwhelmed on the other). They also relate to *affective involvement – detachment* (the extent to which we share concerns, feelings and interests). Naturally, what counts as 'an appropriate amount' varies according to the nature of the relationship, as well as sociocultural norms and personal preferences.

(Spencer-Oatey 2008c: 16)

Another important distinction for smooth intercultural interaction is that between normative conventions (which are treated as flexible) and prescriptive/proscriptive conventions (which are treated as compulsory). Although the distinction is often fuzzy and subject to much individual variation, it is an extremely important one. If normative conventions are broken, people may feel surprised or uncertain what to do or how to behave, but they do not usually feel too offended by the breach. This is because they do not attach sociality rights and obligations to these conventions. However, if prescriptive/proscriptive conventions are broken, they can often regard it as a serious breach and may be genuinely annoyed or offended by it. We return to this topic in the context of intercultural development in Section 9.3.2.

5.4.3   Interactional goals

A third factor that can influence interpersonal rapport is interactional goals. People often (although not always) have specific goals when they interact with others. These can be interpersonal (i.e. relational) as well as transactional (i.e. task-focused) in nature, or most commonly both. These 'wants' can significantly affect people's perceptions of rapport because any failure to achieve them can cause frustration and annoyance.

It is widely claimed in the international business literature (e.g., Adler 2001; Schneider and Barsoux 2003) that some social groups are more task-oriented in their interaction whilst others are more relationship-oriented (Research Report 5.1). It may be that this is partly a question of timing – that some social groups move more quickly to task-oriented issues than others. Yet some linguistic studies, especially those that have analysed small talk, have also mentioned this. Chiles (2007), for example, in a preliminary study of workplace mentoring, reports that the amount of non-work talk in mentor–mentee meetings varied across workplaces, and was influenced by the degree of structure and formality with which an organization ran its mentoring programme.

Research Report 5.1   Relationship-building in China

A recent study of Hong Kong business people negotiating in China confirmed the role relationships play in successful negotiation. 'Good personal relationships' was the only factor rated of 'high importance' by the 168 business people who responded to the survey. 73% said they had social meetings in restaurants, and 68% sent gifts to their Chinese counterparts (Leung and Yeung 1995). Another indicator of the role banquets play in influencing opportunities in Chinese business life is that officials (who control approvals) spent more than 100 billion yuan in 1993 on food and drink, more than the central government spent on health, education, science and welfare combined (Pye 1995).

(Blackman 1997: 47)

Perhaps even more important for intercultural interaction and rapport management is mutual understanding of each other's goals and the congruence of them. For example, Marriott (1990) analysed an initial business negotiation meeting between an Australian and a Japanese business person, and found that the participants' goals for the initial meeting were quite different. Neither was aware of the other's goals, and each was frustrated by the meeting (see Research Report 5.2).

Research Report 5.2   Mismatching goals

An Australian businessman, working in the cheese industry, was interested in selling his products in Japan. He made contact with an appropriate Japanese company in Melbourne, and arranged a meeting. The meeting lasted for 40 minutes, and at the end of it, both had a negative impression of the other. One of the main reasons for this was the participants' differing goals for the initial meeting. The Australian wanted to assess the level of interest the Japanese businessman had in his product so that he could decide whether the negotiations should be pursued or whether they should be dropped. Yet at the end of the meeting, he was unclear whether he was interested or not. The Japanese, on the other hand, wanted to gather background information on the Australian company, its plans and so forth. When he was provided with little information of this nature, and was instead pressed to accept some sample products, he felt both irritated and unimpressed.

(Marriott 1990)

5.4.4 Interpersonal attentiveness and Experiential Example 5.1

Now let us think back to Experiential Example 5.1. All three of those incidents were face-threatening to the Chinese visitors. The seating arrangements and the lack of opportunity to give a return speech were perceived by the Chinese as undermining their claim to status, and the Sales Manager's lack of response to their requests to meet him undermined their claim to importance. Rapport was damaged, therefore, because the visitors' face sensitivities (to status and importance) were not attended to adequately by the British (from the Chinese visitors' point of view) and their face was thus threatened.

Face was not the only factor, however, in the rapport issues that arose; behavioural expectations also played a role. All three problematic incidents demonstrate that a key source of annoyance was one or more of the participants failing to do something that others felt *should* have been done, or in them doing something that the others thought *should not* have been done (note how such obligations are mentioned in the post-event comments). In other words, the participants not only had expectations as to what was likely to occur, but they also felt they had the *right* to expect such behaviour, and others had the *obligation* to perform it. Failure to fulfil these expectations then resulted in offence.

On closer examination, the second problematic instance in Experiential Example 5.1 illustrates the difference between flexible conventions and those that are treated as compulsory. Both the invitation to give self-introductions and the failure to request a return speech were breaches of behavioural expectations. The Chinese visitors were taken by surprise that they were each asked to introduce themselves, so they needed to discuss among themselves how they should handle this. Yet they did not seem to be offended by the request. On the other hand, they perceived the lack of opportunity to give a return speech as a serious breach, because this delegation regarded reciprocal speech giving as a prescriptive convention. For the British, however, individual introductions and speech giving (reciprocal or not) were both flexible conventions. When the British chairman was told afterwards that the Chinese delegation leader had wanted to give a return speech and that the interpreter had interrupted him, he commented, 'if the interpreter had said to me that they are just making a return speech, then it would have been fine'. So when the interpreter interrupted the start of the return speech, and insisted on individual introductions, he created a problem that would not otherwise have occurred.

The third problematic instance in Experiential Example 5.1, in which the Sales Manager delayed making contact with the Chinese visitors, illustrates the different value-laden interactional principles that people may hold and how this can affect rapport. The British team (as well as the Sales Manager himself) placed emphasis on the manager's personal equity rights – his right to some rest and refreshment after a long trip; the Chinese visitors, on the other hand, placed emphasis on their association rights – their right to expect the manager to show concern for his 'old friends' who are in a foreign land and need/want his help. This mismatch in the relative importance attributed to the two interactional principles by the Chinese and British participants, along with the differing assessments they made of their 'friendship', was a key factor in causing the problems of rapport, irritating the British staff (by repeatedly asking them to phone the Sales Manager, even at the weekend) and upsetting the Chinese visitors (by the Manager failing to give priority to them).

Rapport was also damaged by factors associated with interactional goals. The official purpose of the visit was to inspect the goods, but the visit had been delayed and the goods had already been despatched. The British assumed, however, that the visitors would still like to receive a certain amount of product training (especially as they thought they were engineers) and regarded this as an important goal for the visit. They were then very offended when the visitors cancelled all the training sessions and insisted on spending the full ten days sight-seeing and shopping.

5.5   Information gathering

As the last section has illustrated, people's claims to face and sociality rights, as well as their interactional goal aspirations, all need to be attended to carefully if rapport is to be managed effectively. Sometimes important contextual information, such as the hierarchy of staff in an organization and their respective roles needs to be sought actively, with conscious efforts made to gather such information. Spencer-Oatey and Tang (2008: 168), for example, report that one senior Chinese member of staff involved in a major Chinese-British collaborative programme commented as follows: 'The British might think that the Chinese were working inefficiently, but it was because they didn't understand our organizational structure. Particularly after the restructuring of the school, they should know who was responsible for what and whom they should go to for certain issues.' Similarly, Spencer-Oatey and Xing (2008: 267) report in relation to Experiential Example 5.1 that the British hosts were only given partial information about the roles of the Chinese visitors – they were only given their 'expertise' titles, not their 'position' titles, and that this influenced their understanding of the visitors' roles (and hence what they would be interested in doing and seeing during their visit) and the importance of the visitors in business terms (and hence what their status was and how face-sensitive they were likely to be to status).

One way of gathering useful contextual information is by asking relevant people or 'cultural mediators' – people who are sensitive to the perspectives of members of both cultures and able to explain them. Another is by observing interactions very carefully, such as noticing who sits where, who talks when, how introductions are made, how meetings are closed, and so on. Often a large amount of very relevant information can be gathered in this way.

5.6 Social attuning

Another important competency for managing rapport in intercultural interaction is social attuning. As Scollon and Scollon (1995) explain, although much relevant information can be derived from an awareness of the context (e.g., the relative status of the individuals), a significant amount needs to be perceived as the interaction unfolds. The competency of social attuning is necessary for this.

Social attuning competency is very similar in nature to the message attuning competency discussed in Chapter 4. It entails the ability to pick up meaning from indirect signals such as paralanguage (e.g., intonation, speaking volume and speed, pausing) and non-verbal communication (e.g., eye contact and other elements of body language), and the ability to draw inferences from these indirect signals. These include inferences about the other person's preferences and intentions and how the other person is feeling (e.g., offended, annoyed, anxious), and how one's own behaviour is being evaluated. The cues are frequently extremely subtle and very difficult for a cultural outsider to interpret. So for ongoing interactions of this kind, one way of addressing the difficulty is to use the cultural mediator, or broker, mentioned above, who can help 'interpret' the behaviour and emotional reactions of each party to the other.

5.7   Emotion regulation

Matsumoto and his colleagues (2007) maintain that emotion regulation is the most critical ingredient for intercultural adaptation and adjustment, and we suggest that it is also vital for developing and maintaining rapport. For the latter it entails two main components: resilience and acceptance.

In intercultural interaction, people need to be able to handle criticism or embarrassment when things go wrong, and to bounce back if they have lost face or been thwarted in what they want to achieve. In other words, they need to be resilient. In addition, they need to have an accepting orientation, which is not too critical or demanding of others. For example, when we have shown the video recording of Experiential Example 5.1 to other Chinese people, many of them have commented that this particular group of visitors were unusually sensitive to status, and that others would not have reacted so negatively. Whether this is true or not is hard to say, but there are definitely differences between individuals in the degree to which they are sensitive to face threats, to infringements of their sociality rights and to thwarts to their interactional goals.

5.8   Strategies for managing rapport

So far in this chapter, we have concentrated primarily on the potential sources of turbulence or conflict in interpersonal relations, because sensitivity to these can be extremely helpful in preventing problems arising. In this section, we turn to people's orientations towards rapport, and the strategies they can use for managing rapport.

5.8.1   Orientations towards rapport

Spencer-Oatey (2008c: 31–2) proposes that there are four main orientations to rapport:

- **Rapport enhancement orientation**: a desire to strengthen or enhance harmonious relations between the interlocutors.

- **Rapport maintenance orientation**: a desire to maintain or protect harmonious relations between the interlocutors.
- **Rapport neglect orientation**: a lack of concern or interest in the quality of relations between the interlocutors (perhaps because of a focus on self).
- **Rapport challenge orientation**: a desire to challenge or impair harmonious relations between the interlocutors.

People's reasons or motives for holding a given orientation can be various, and can result from a very complex interplay of a wide range of factors. Moreover, their orientations are very dynamic, and likely to vary both within and across interactions.

According to Communication Accommodation Theory (e.g., Gallois, Ogay and Giles 2005), people tend to reflect their rapport orientations in the extent to which they make their (linguistic) behaviour more or less similar to that of the other participants in the interaction. Ylänne explains it as follows:

> There is a general propensity for communicators to converge along salient dimensions of speech and nonverbal behaviour in cooperative social encounters. The psychological process at the heart of convergence and of 'being accommodative' is 'similarity attraction' [...] Speakers who want to cooperate and who want to be approved of will tend to converge. Correspondingly, when a speaker becomes more similar to a listener, it is generally more likely that the listener will in fact approve of him or her more strongly. These tendencies give Accommodation Theory some power to explain the *strategic* use of language codes and communication styles. Codes and styles do not merely co-vary with social groups and social situations. Rather, we can begin to see code- and style-choice as sociolinguistic strategies which individuals and groups will employ – again, whether consciously or sub-consciously – to achieve the social and relational results they want. [...] *Maintenance* and *divergence* of codes and styles are obvious further possibilities.
>
> (Ylänne 2008: 166)

Of course, the extent to which people are able to converge or diverge is partly dependent on the range of their communicative repertoires, and partly on the degree of mindfulness that they employ in their interactions. These are both elements that intercultural development can address.

5.8.2 Rapport management strategies

Work in linguistics has focused to a large extent on directness–indirectness as a strategy for managing rapport. One of the most influential works is Brown and Levinson's (1978/1987) face model of politeness. They propose that people (unconsciously) weigh up the seriousness or weightiness of their message, by considering three factors: the power difference between the participants, the distance–closeness of the participants, and the degree of imposition or relational impact of the message content. They then choose an appropriate strategy, working on the basis that the more an act threatens the speaker's or hearer's face, the more appropriate it will be to choose a higher-numbered strategy, that is a more indirect strategy (Figure 5.2).

In Brown and Levinson's (1978/1987) framework, the most direct strategy entails 'bald' language in which the meaning is conveyed explicitly through the grammar or vocabulary, such as using an imperative or a word like 'order' to express a directive. The most indirect strategy is a hint which requires a large amount of inferential work in order to interpret the meaning. Between these two extremes are 'positively polite' language and 'negatively polite' language. Many people find this terminology confusing, and have used alternative labels. For example, Scollon and Scollon (1995) refer to 'strategies of involvement' and 'strategies of independence'. However, this wording could imply that people who use strategies of independence are not substantively involved with others, which of course is patently false, as the difference is one of strategic preference not interactional substance. So we suggest the terms 'expressiveness' and 'restraint' instead, and Concept 5.6 provides examples of each type of strategy.

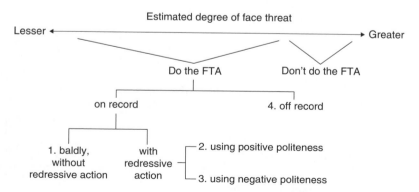

Figure 5.2 Brown and Levinson's superstrategies for performing FTAs (based on Brown and Levinson 1987: 60).

Concept 5.6   Linguistic strategies of expressiveness-restraint

Linguistic strategies of expressiveness: Some examples	Linguistic strategies of restraint: Some examples
1. Notice or attend to hearer: *I like your sweater. Are you feeling better today?*	1. Make minimal assumptions about hearer's wants: *I don't know if you will want to send this by airmail or by courier.*
2. Exaggerate (interest, approval, sympathy with hearer): *Do be careful cycling home, it's getting dark. You always do so well in sport.*	2. Give hearer the option not to do the act: *It would be nice to have dinner together, but I am sure you are very busy.*
3. Claim in-group membership with hearer: *All of us here at the University of Warwick [...]*	3. Minimize threat: *I just need to borrow a little piece of paper, any scrap will do.*
4. Claim common point of view, opinions, attitudes, knowledge, empathy: *I know just how you feel. I had a virus like that last month.*	4. Apologize: *I'm sorry to trouble you, could you tell me the time?*
5. Be optimistic: *I think we should be able to finish that annual report very quickly.*	5. Be pessimistic: *I don't suppose you'd know the time, would you?*
6. Indicate speaker knows hearer's wants and is taking them into account: *I'm sure you will all want to know when this meeting will be over.*	6. Dissociate speaker, hearer from the discourse: *This is to inform our employees that [...]*
7. Assume or assert reciprocity: *I know you want to reach your targets this year as much as I want you to do well.*	7. State a general rule: *Company regulations require an examination [...]*
8. Use given names and nicknames: *Jenny, can you get that report to me by tomorrow?*	8. Use family name and titles: *Mr Roberts, there's a phone call for you.*
9. Be voluble.	9. Be taciturn.
10. Use hearer's language or dialect.	10. Use own language or dialect.

(Adapted from Scollon and Scollon 1995: 40–1)

Brown and Levinson's (1978/1987) model for predicting people's choice of different strategies (Figure 5.2) is controversial, yet the impact of using restrained or expressive strategies is supported by many studies. For example, Bailey (1997, 2000) analysed interactions between Immigrant Korean retail merchants and their African-American customers and report on their importance. He found that differences in preference for use of restrained or expressive strategies were a key factor underlying people's perceptions of lack of respect (see Research Report 5.3). He argues that this difference was a significant contributing factor to the conflict that took place between the two groups.

Research Report 5.3 Bailey on communicative behaviour and conflict in interethnic service encounters

Face-to-face interaction between Korean immigrant retailers and African-American customers in Los Angeles often leaves members of each group feeling as if the other has behaved in insultingly inappropriate ways. Twenty-five service encounters involving both African-American and immigrant Korean customers were video-recorded in a liquor store and transcribed for analysis. These encounters reveal divergent communicative patterns between immigrant Koreans and African-Americans. [...] Interviews with retailers and customers reveal a distinctive pattern of divergent perceptions regarding behaviour in stores: while African-American customers focus complaints on the relative *lack of interpersonal engagement and involvement* of Korean immigrant retailers, the retailers emphasize the relative *lack of restraint on the part of customers.*

African-Americans [...] described to me how they were disrespected in immigrant Korean stores by emphasizing perceptions of what the store-owners do *not* do, e.g. greet with a smile, maintain eye contact, and make small talk, i.e. personally engage the customer. The relative taciturnity and restraint of immigrant Koreans is not seen as polite, but as rude. [...]

Most storekeepers framed criticisms of customer behaviour not in terms of 'respect', but in terms of the 'self-centeredness' and, more frequently, lack of 'education' of the individuals involved. [...] Behaviours that many African-Americans might interpret as signs of sociable involvement in service encounters, e.g. unsolicited small-talk about the weather or jokes about current events, are considered an imposition and a sign of poor manners by many Korean immigrants. The relatively forceful and dramatic interactional style displayed by many young African-American male customers in low-income neighborhoods seems to retailers to be particularly self-centred and recklessly inconsiderate of others.

(Bailey 2000: 86, 90–1, 93; italics in original)

Another example is to be found in Franklin's work on Anglo-German management interaction (2006, 2007). He found that British managers perceived the restraint strategy of using family names and titles employed by their German colleagues as a substantive barrier to cooperation. In other societies, use of expressive strategies, such as calling everyone at work by their personal name, may make others feel uncomfortable.

Brown and Levinson's (1987) framework assumes that there is a universal procedure for managing rapport, as illustrated in Figure 5.2. However, many people have argued that directness–indirectness should not be linked with impoliteness–politeness in a simplistic way, and that there are substantial cultural and contextual variations in how directness–indirectness is perceived.

Another main way in which rapport can be managed is by using a communicative style of interaction that is congruent with the interactional principles or values that the participants hold. For example, modesty or self-effacement is an important interactional principle in some societies and to some individuals, and when this is the case, a self-effacing communication style is likely to help keep relations smoother than when a self-enhancement style is used (see Concept 5.7). Similarly, in high power distance societies and when people are very status oriented, a formal status-oriented style of interaction is likely to be received more positively than an informal, person-oriented style (see Concept 5.8).

Concept 5.7   Ting-Toomey on self-enhancement and self-effacement communication styles

The self-enhancement verbal style emphasizes the importance of boasting about one's accomplishments and abilities. The self-effacement verbal style, on the other hand, emphasizes the importance of humbling oneself via verbal restraints, hesitations, modest talk, and the use of self-deprecation concerning one's effort or performance.

[...] Condon (1984) observes that in Japan, when one offers something to another person such as a gift or a meal that one has prepared, verbal self-deprecation is expected. There are set expressions for verbal humility such as *It's not very tasty* and *It's nothing special*. The hostess who apologizes to her guests that *There is nothing special to offer you* has probably 'spent the better part of two days planning and preparing the meal. Of course the guest should protest such [a] disclaimer' (Condon 1984: 52) and re-emphasize her or his gratitude. Self-effacement is a necessary part of Japanese politeness rituals.

[...] In the U.S. culture, we encourage individuals to 'sell and boast about themselves'. For example, [...] an American ad [in a personal column of a magazine] might begin, *a handsome, athletic male with a good sense of humor seeks a fun-loving partner [...]*; the comparable Japanese ad might read, *Although I am not very good looking, I'm willing to try my best to work hard [...]*

(Ting-Toomey 1999: 107–8)

> ## Concept 5.8   Ting-Toomey on person-oriented and status-oriented communication styles
>
> The person-oriented verbal style is an individual-centred verbal mode that emphasizes the importance of informality and role suspension. The status-oriented verbal style is a role-centred verbal mode that emphasizes formality and large power distance. The former emphasizes the importance of symmetrical interaction, whereas the latter stresses asymmetrical interaction.
>
> [...] Those who engage in status-oriented verbal interaction use specific vocabularies and paralinguistic features to accentuate the status distance of the role relationship (e.g., in parent-child interaction, superior-subordinate relations [...]) [...] Yum (1988) notes that the Korean language [...] has special vocabularies for each sex, for different degrees of social status and intimacy, and for different levels of formality depending on the occasion. The use of proper verbal styles for the proper types of relationships and in the proper contexts are sure signs that one is an 'educated' person in the Korean culture. [...]
>
> Okabe (1983) observes that U.S. Americans tend to [...] 'shun the formal codes of conduct, titles, honorifics, and ritualistic manners in their interaction with others. They instead prefer a first-name basis and direct address. They also strive to equalize the language style between the sexes.'
>
> (Ting-Toomey 1999: 106–7)

As Concept 5.8 indicates (and as Brown and Gilman's 1960 classic study found), forms of address are an extremely important feature of language use that affects rapport management. This is because they indicate both the power and the distance–closeness of the participants, and if these relational indicators are not in accordance with the assumed or desired relationship, rapport is likely to be affected (either positively or negatively).

5.9   Strategies for managing conflict

In this final section of the chapter, we turn to the reverse of rapport – the management of conflict.

In business and management studies, it is argued that people may hold different orientations towards a conflict, depending on the degree to which they want to satisfy their own concerns and the degree to which they want to satisfy the other's concerns. For example, Kenneth Thomas (1976), in a classic paper which takes no account of possible cultural variables, proposed five orientations: neglect, appeasement, domination, compromise and integration (see Figure 5.3).

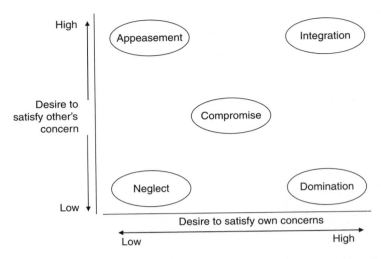

Figure 5.3 Thomas's 'grid' framework of conflict management orientations (based on Thomas 1976: 900).

Neglect reflects avoidance or indifference, in that no attention is paid to the concerns of either self or other. Appeasement reflects a lack of concern for self, but a high concern for the other, whilst domination represents a desire to win at the other's expense. Compromise is intermediate between appeasement and domination, and is often the least satisfactory for the two parties. Integration represents a problem-solving orientation where there is a desire to integrate both parties' concerns.

Thomas (1976) maintains that people's response styles are hierarchically ordered, in that they have a dominant style, a back-up style, a least-preferred style and so on. He suggests that this hierarchy could be influenced by factors such as personality, motives and abilities. Could culture, therefore, influence this hierarchy, with some orientations being more prevalent in certain societies than in others? Many cross-cultural studies have explored this question, and a widespread finding (e.g., Bond and Hwang 1986; Morris et al. 1998; Ohbuchi and Takahashi 1994; Trubinsky et al. 1991) is that a neglect style (that is also labelled 'avoidance') is more common among East Asians than among Americans. From a Western management perspective, this could suggest that East Asians are less effective at handling conflict, because there is an assumption that avoidance of a problem is equivalent to covering it up or 'burying your head in the sand'. However, Friedman, Chi and Liu (2006) collected qualitative data and found that their Chinese respondents often displayed a long-term orientation, reporting tactics such as 'do nothing right now, but draw a lesson for future actions' and 'say nothing but collect more data on my own'. In other words, they found that avoidance was a technique for achieving a satisfactory resolution of the conflict in the longer term. It is important, therefore, to distinguish between people's orientations (i.e. the degree to which they want to satisfy their own desires and those of the opposing party) and the tactics they use to pursue them.

In social psychology and communication studies, it is common to link people's conflict-handling preferences with individualist and collectivist values. Ting-Toomey (1999: 211–12), for example, argues that individualist and collectivist values (which link with independent and interdependent self-construals respectively) can impact significantly on people's handling of conflict (see Concept 5.9).

Bennett (1995) also assumes that culturally-based preferences in conflict resolution exist. Modifying a US-centric set of conflict management

---

Concept 5.9   Ting-Toomey on cultural values, self-construals and the conflict process

Individualist values and independent self-construals	Collectivist values and interdependent self-construals
1. Conflict is perceived as closely related to the goals or outcomes that are salient to the respective individual conflict parties in a given conflict situation.	1. Conflict is weighted against the face threat incurred in the conflict negotiation process; it is also interpreted in the web of in-group/out-group relationships.
2. Communication in the conflict process is viewed as dissatisfying when the conflict parties are not willing to deal with the conflict openly and honestly.	2. Communication in the conflict process is perceived as threatening when the conflict parties push for substantive discussion before proper facework management.
3. Conversely, communication in the conflict process is viewed as satisfying when the conflict parties are willing to confront the conflict issues openly and share their feelings honestly (i.e. assertively but not aggressively).	3. Communication in the conflict interaction is viewed as satisfying when the conflict parties engage in *mutual* face-saving and face-giving behaviour and attend to both verbal and non-verbal signals.
4. The conflict outcome is perceived as unproductive when no tangible outcomes are reached or no plan of action is developed.	4. The conflict process or outcome is perceived as unproductive when face issues are not addressed and relational/group feelings are not attended to properly.

5. The conflict outcome is perceived as productive when tangible solutions are reached and objective criteria are met.	5. The conflict process or outcome is defined as productive when both conflict parties can claim win–win results on the facework front in addition to substantive agreement.
6. Effective and appropriate management of conflict means individual goals are addressed and differences are dealt with openly, honestly, and properly in relation to timing and situational context.	6. Appropriate and effective management of conflict means that the mutual 'faces' of the conflict parties are saved or even upgraded in the interaction and they have dealt with the conflict episode strategically in conjunction with substantive gains or losses.

(Derived from Ting-Toomey 1999: 211–12)

styles proposed by Simpson (1977a, 1977b), he describes a set of 'cross-cultural styles of conflict resolution' (1995: 150) which takes account of culture-specific preferences: Denial or Suppression; Power or Authority; Third-person Intermediary; Group Consensus; and Direct Discussion. These preferred styles can be related to regions, as Bennett does, or to value- or interactional-based orientations, as we show in Concept 5.10.

Concept 5.10   Orientations for managing conflict

Style (Bennett 1995)	Geographical region (Bennett)	Value- or interactional-based orientations
Denial or suppression		higher context, more collectivist, more face-saving, lower uncertainty avoidance
Third-person intermediary	Asian-Pacific, African, Arab	higher context, more face-saving
Group consensus	Asian, Hispanic, African-American	more collectivist, smaller power distance, higher uncertainty avoidance
Direct discussion	European-American	lower context, more individualist, lower power distance, higher uncertainty avoidance
Power or authority		larger power distance, higher uncertainty avoidance

This macro-level research and theorizing can help people gain a useful generalized picture of a cultural group's preferred approach. However, its weakness is that it ignores the very important context-ual variation that we considered in Section 5.3. For even though there may be cross-cultural differences in preferred styles for managing con-flict, generalizations can gloss over the rich complexity and variation that exists in real-life situations and may mislead people into ignor-ing important contextual differences. Davidheiser's (2005) study of mediation practices in south-western Gambia illustrates this point very vividly. He observed and recorded 121 live conflict mediation events, conducted 54 ethnographic interviews and 39 semi-structured inter-views, and held panel sessions with Gambian mediation experts. He draws the following conclusions:

> Shared values have a profound effect both on how mediation is prac-ticed and on the nature of the process itself. However, this impact is multi-dimensional and resists easy generalization. [...] Whilst it is true that there appear to be meta-level normative differences in orientations to mediation in the West and elsewhere, there is also great heterogeneity in both of these areas. Dichotomizing mediation praxis according to whether the practitioners are Western or non-Western, traditional or modern, high- or low-context communica-tors, glosses over the multiplicity of practice found outside the realm of theory and dramatically over-simplifies a complex picture.
>
> Mediation practices can be described as 'embedded', or linked to macro- and micro-level influences and varying according to the spe-cific context and characteristics of each case. Peacemaker behaviour was influenced by numerous factors, including the sociocultural per-spectives of the participants and situational variables such as the type of dispute in question, the nature of the social relations between the parties, and the participants' personalities.
>
> (Davidheiser 2005: 736–7)

If we are to gain an in-depth understanding, therefore, of intercultural conflict in real-life situations, it is vital to consider contextual and indi-vidual variability.

5.10   Concluding comments

In this chapter we have explained that a wide range of competen-cies are needed in order to manage interpersonal rapport: contextual awareness, interpersonal attentiveness, information gathering, social attuning, emotion regulation, and rapport management strategies. We have also demonstrated how rapport is influenced by a number of factors, and that there can be cultural differences in the perception and impact of these factors. However, it is important to remember that whilst such differences may be important underlying sources of divergent interpretations and reactions, they do not inevitably 'cause' or lead to such outcomes. For example, Spencer-Oatey and Xing (2003) compare the delegation visit described in Experiential Example 5.1 with an earlier delegation visit where the seating arrangements were almost identical and where the British also did not invite the visitors to give a return speech. That visit was very successful, and there were no problematic outcomes. So Spencer-Oatey and Xing argue that it is the compounding effect of a range of variables, including individual- and cultural-level factors, that result in one set of outcomes rather than another.

The ideas in this chapter present a number of challenges for intercultural developers and researchers. For example, how can people be helped to nurture the competencies that are needed for effective rapport management in intercultural interaction, and what type of research data is needed to underpin such development activities? We return to these questions in Parts 2 and 3 of the book. In the next chapter, we turn to another important issue in intercultural interaction – the risk of disadvantage and domination.

Suggestions for further reading

Günthner, S. (2008) Argumentation and resulting problems in the negotiation of rapport in a German–Chinese conversation. In H. Spencer-Oatey (ed.) *Culturally Speaking: Culture, Communication and Politeness Theory*, 2nd edn, pp. 207–26. London: Continuum. This chapter provides an in-depth analysis of a social conversation between Chinese and German students who were studying at a German university, and explores how culturally specific expectations of communicative situations and different communicative conventions can give rise to problems of rapport.

Lindsley, S. and Braithwaite, C. (1996) 'You should "wear a mask"': Facework norms in cultural and intercultural conflict in maquiladoras. *International Journal of Intercultural Relations*, 20(2): 199–225. This article reports an ethnographic study of conflict communication among Mexicans and US Americans working in US American-owned assembly plants in Mexico.

Spencer-Oatey, H. (2008) Face, (im)politeness and rapport. In H. Spencer-Oatey (ed.) *Culturally Speaking: Culture, Communication and Politeness Theory*, 2nd edn, pp. 11–47. London: Continuum. This book chapter provides a readable and more detailed account of most of the concepts presented in this chapter.

Van Meurs, N. and Spencer-Oatey, H. (2007) Multidisciplinary perspectives on intercultural conflict: The 'Bermuda Triangle' of conflict, culture and communication. In H. Kotthoff and H. Spencer-Oatey (eds) *Handbook of Intercultural Communication*, pp. 99–120. Berlin: Mouton de Gruyter. This chapter provides a multidisciplinary overview of theories and research findings on conflict, culture and communication, and their interconnections.

6
Confronting Disadvantage and Domination in Intercultural Interaction

> Cultural diversity is as necessary for humankind as biodiversity is for nature.
>
> UNESCO

Chapter outline

6.1 Impression management and disadvantage
6.2 Stereotypes and disadvantage
6.3 Prejudice, conscious discrimination and deliberate domination
6.4 English as a world language, and disadvantage
6.5 Concluding comments
    Suggestions for further reading

We have mentioned a number of times in this book that personal disadvantage can occur through intercultural interaction. It can be closely linked to people's use of language, but it can also involve other issues such as stereotyping and prejudice. In this chapter, we focus directly on such concerns. All of the intercultural competencies we have explored in Chapters 4 and 5 play an important role in this.

6.1 Impression management and disadvantage

In Chapter 5, we discussed the importance of face in the management of rapport, and noted that face sensitivity is associated with the positive attributes that people claim and want other participants to acknowledge. In this section, we consider people's claims to positive attributes from a different perspective – in terms of the impressions that they want to convey and the impressions that they hope others will perceive. This is always a subjective process, which is subject to considerable individual and contextual variation; nevertheless, cultural factors have the potential to impact significantly on the process and this can result not only in people misjudging each other but also in people being unfairly disadvantaged.

6.1.1 What is impression management?

Rosenfeld, Giacalone and Riordan (2002: 4) define impression management as the 'process whereby people seek to control or influence the impressions that others form'. It is often called self-presentation when it relates to the impressions that an individual wishes to convey of him/herself, and in fact one of the first books on this topic, which was written by the sociologist Erving Goffman in 1959, was entitled *The Presentation of Self in Everyday Life*.

Very frequently, impression management is an unconscious process. We may automatically manage impressions, such as politeness, respectfulness and thoughtfulness, because the behaviour associated with those attributes is so familiar to us. However, impression management may also be a very conscious process. Consider Experiential Example 6.1, for instance. This example concerns the same Chinese business visitors discussed in Experiential Example 5.1, and describes part of what happened on the last day of their visit. The group were arguing bitterly with their British hosts, for over four hours, about money and other contractual matters. Towards the end of this time, one of the Chinese delegation members stated very explicitly the specific attributes he felt they ought and ought not to be conveying. In other words, he was very conscious of the impression they were leaving on the British and he wanted them each to deliberately control this. Such conscious attention to impression management is particularly common in interactions that are strategically important to us, such as job interviews, performance appraisals, first dates and so on.

Experiential Example 6.1   Conscious concern about managing impressions

A group of Chinese businessmen, at the end of a visit to a British company with which they had been doing business, got embroiled in a protracted argument with their British hosts over money. One of the Chinese became concerned about the impression they were conveying, and said privately to the others: *One thing is that we should not let people say we are stingy; secondly, we should not give the impression of being too weak; thirdly, we should negotiate in a friendly manner.*

(Spencer-Oatey, 2007a: 645)

However, impression management is a very complex process (see Concept 6.1). As Leary (1995: 11) points out, we cannot control the impressions that others form of us by pushing a button or flicking a switch. Many things can go wrong, because a given behaviour can be interpreted in more than one way. For example, a consultant may want some potential new clients to perceive him/her as a well-informed and competent professional, yet the clients may in fact perceive him/her as pompous and arrogant. Many individual and contextual factors impact on the process, and so do cultural factors. In this chapter, we focus particularly on the ways in which cultural factors can affect both impression management and impression perception, and then consider this from an equal opportunities and from a discrimination point of view.

Concept 6.1   Goffman on impression management

Regardless of the particular objective which the individual has in mind and of his motive for having this objective, it will be in his interests to control the conduct of the others, especially their responsive treatment of him. [...] Sometimes the individual will act in a thoroughly calculating manner, expressing himself in a given way solely in order to give the kind of impression to others that is likely to evoke from them a specific response he is concerned to obtain. [...] Sometimes the traditions of an individual's role will lead him to give a well-designed impression of a particular kind and yet he may be neither consciously nor unconsciously disposed to create such an impression. The others, in their turn, may be suitably impressed by the individual's efforts to convey something, or may misunderstand the situation and come to conclusions that are warranted neither by the individual's intent nor by the facts.

(Goffman 1959: 15, 17, 19)

6.1.2   Managing and perceiving impressions in intercultural interaction

In all interaction, if people are to convey the impressions that they want others to perceive, and if others are to perceive the impressions that people intend, then the more they all have in common in terms of knowledge (linguistic, pragmalinguistic, sociopragmatic and world knowledge – see Chapter 4) and values, the greater the likelihood that they will be able to achieve this (although there will always be considerable individual and contextual variation). Conversely, the greater their differences, the more problematic it is likely to be. This is because the perceptual set, and the resulting perceptual selectivity that this knowledge and these values shape in the participants (and which are necessary for managing the complex multitude of stimuli in any inter-action), may lead to a mismatch between the impressions that people intend or desire to convey and the impressions that people actually perceive. In intercultural interaction, this can be particularly problematic. Let us consider some examples.

Experiential Example 6.2 is an extract from a role-played interaction between a white manager and a South Asian worker. Gumperz and Roberts (1980; cited by Roberts 1998) asked a group of white British managers/white-collar workers and a group of South Asian workers what impressions they each had of these two people, on the basis of this extract, and they found that there were marked differences in the two groups' evaluations. The white staff were critical of J's explanation, arguing that it was unconvincing and confusing. To them it sounded like a poor excuse, which could convey an impression of incompetence and/or unreliability. The South Asian participants, on the other hand, found J's explanation quite adequate. To them, it was the manager's behaviour that was inappropriate. They felt his use of 'why the devil' sounded critical and conflictive, and they perceived him as unpleasantly aggressive.

Experiential Example 6.2   Roberts (1998) on impression management in the workplace

A (white manager):   Jaswinder/<u>why</u> the <u>devil</u> didn't you tell me about the <u>pallets</u> before//

J (South Asian worker):   Well/I wanted to <u>tell you</u> but I couldn't leave the <u>line</u>/we are having a few <u>problems</u> / and Mr Smith told me/ not to move from the <u>line</u>// I..I think there was <u>time</u>/ to come and <u>report</u>/ but..but said there <u>wasn't</u>//

(Roberts 1998: 111)

Roberts explores possible reasons for these differing impressions. With respect to the worker, she notes that if J is to make a good impression on his manager, he needs to know what will count as a 'good' excuse in his manager's eyes. She suggests that personally *wanting* to report the problem is something the manager would have wanted to hear. However, J does not stress key words such as 'wanted' and 'I couldn't', and so to white listeners he sounds uninvolved in the matter. This could, of course, be an individually idiosyncratic style of speech, yet a number of other studies (e.g., Gumperz 1982) have found similar differences between white British and South Asian use of contrastive stress. So this suggests that a difference in people's pragmalinguistic conventions is a key factor which underlay the differing impressions of J that the two groups formed.

With regard to the white manager, Roberts explains that the white group saw his language as reflecting the relatively informal relationships of the workplace. 'The South Asian group, on the other hand, drew on workplace discourses which assumed more hierarchical relationships characterised by less informal and personal exchanges. They explained that joking, casual use of invective and similar informalities tended to be used only among equals who knew each other well. In more formal work situations, such behaviour would be regarded as unseemly displays of emotion' (Roberts 1998: 112).

In other words, the impressions that both the manager and the worker conveyed to others was different from what they intended, and cultural differences in interactional conventions and styles significantly influenced people's perceptions and judgements. Neither participant was aware of the impact of these cultural differences, and greater intercultural interaction competence on both sides could have created better interactional outcomes.

Roberts (1998) provides a second example which illustrates the impact of cultural factors on impression management and perception (Experiential Example 6.3). Molly's interactional style is more self-effacing (see Concept 5.7), more status-oriented (see Concept 5.8) and more restrained (see Concept 5.6) than Anne's, and Roberts explains that this results in the manager giving Molly a higher number of admonitions than she does Anne, even though Anne's performance is not really any better than Molly's. Presumably Nancy, the manager, perceives Molly as being less pro-active and less personally involved in her work and thus in need of more admonition. However, these impressions are influenced by Nancy's culturally-based expectations of the type of interactional style that an effective employee will or should display.

Experiential Example 6.3   Impression management in performance appraisal

Roberts presents two interactions that are role played reconstructions of authentic appraisal interviews at the Bank of America, filmed as part of the BBC film *Crosstalk at Work* (Twitchin and Roberts 1992). In Data Example 1, Nancy, the senior manager is appraising Anne – a white American. In Data Example 2, she is appraising Molly who is of Chinese background.

Data Example 1

1	A:	Hi, how are you, Nancy
2	N:	Good and you
3	A:	Good
4	N:	Are you ready for year end results here
5	A:	I think so. I think it's been a pretty good year. I've learnt a lot and er I think it's been good
6	N:	As you know, we are still a little short on transaction accounts. I know we talked about it last time in terms of being a little more pro-active

Data Example 2

1	N:	Good morning Molly
2	M:	Hi
3	N:	We received our year end results today and we did well on deposits, transaction accounts and overall in customer service, though we're weak in two areas – sundry losses which we've continued to talk about throughout the year and non-interest revenue. Do you want to tell me a little bit about sundry losses
4	M:	We did have someone from corporate security give us a meeting on loss prevention and that really helps
5	N:	Did anything get by you
6	M:	Couple of times – yeah couple of transactions. And then the customer just took off
7	N:	I'd like you to pay attention to that area because we're still going to have a really strict goal in that category

Roberts analyses the modes of self-presentation used by Anne and Molly:

'Anne, for example, in turn 5, treats Nancy's opening gambit as an opportunity to evaluate the year and herself positively. She asserts her right to speak and to make explicit her opinion of the year. Grammatically, she presents herself as an active agent: 'I've learnt a lot', 'I've used the resources' and so on, as if the act of putting these activities into words will form part of the evidence on which Nancy's appraisal of her will be made. [...]. Molly, by contrast, takes a different position on speaker rights, waiting for Nancy's direct question at the end of turn 3: 'Do you want to tell me a little about sundry losses'. She also avoids presenting herself as an active agent and answers Nancy's implied criticism with brief, factual narrative accounts of how the team has responded to the weak area of sundry losses (turn 4).'

Roberts then uses this example to draw attention to the sociopolitical dimension of discourse, pointing out that in multilingual societies such as Britain, it is the white majority group who define what is allowable or otherwise in a workplace interaction.

(Roberts 1998: 115–16)

Both of these examples demonstrate that there can be significant differences between the impressions that people intend to convey and the impressions that others perceive, and that differences in cultural knowledge and values can play a critical role in the emergence of such mismatches. So this raises a very important issue: when people are in less powerful positions, such as when they are employees or selection candidates, will they be disadvantaged because of the unintended impressions they give to their bosses or selection panel? This is clearly a distinct possibility and research (e.g., Roberts, Davies and Jupp 1992) has provided evidence to demonstrate that this occurs. Even though the disadvantage and/or discrimination may be unintended, this of course is no excuse. People can be denied legitimate access to, for example, education, healthcare, legal advice and representation, and employment, and that is why diversity training is of such importance nowadays in many countries.

The intercultural competencies that we explored in Chapters 4 and 5 denote some of the capabilities that are needed to handle such matters. There are other important intercultural competencies that concern knowledge and ideas and these are shown in Concept 6.2. Openness and valuing of differences are particularly important for the issues we are focusing on in this chapter.

Concept 6.2 Intercultural cognitive competencies	
Knowledge information gathering	Gathers information about the micro and macro interactional context using a wide range of suitable methods
New thinking – Openness	Open to new ideas, curious, and willing to challenge assumptions
New thinking – Synergistic creation	Finds creative solutions that can reconcile different opinions/ procedures
Goal management	Willing to accommodate to local ways and priorities
Valuing of difference	Looks beyond stereotypes and explores what contrasting people have to offer

6.2   Stereotypes and disadvantage

Another very important factor that can intervene in the process of impression perception is that of stereotyping. Stereotypes can blinker people's judgements, leading them to focus on certain pieces of 'evidence' and to overlook other, contradictory 'evidence'. Let us first consider an example.

6.2.1   Stereotypes and intercultural interaction

Birkner and Kern (2008) researched job interviews involving employers who were based in former West Germany and applicants who came from both former West and East Germany. They found that the West German employers expected applicants to be assertive in their handling of conflict management, and they negatively evaluated candidates if they failed to convey this impression (see Experiential Example 6.4). In this example, the candidate demonstrated at one point in the interview a clear ability to deal effectively with conflict. However, the interviewers overlooked this evidence, because they had already formed the – in fact, wrong – impression that she was weak in this respect, because of her earlier response to a direct question about arguing. In this earlier response, she wanted to convey her deference for her boss (status-oriented interactional style), but they misinterpreted this as lack of assertiveness.

Experiential Example 6.4   Birkner and Kern on inadvertent discrimination in job interviews

In our data we find an example of an East German applicant who is asked if she has ever had an argument with a superior.
I = Interviewer; A = Applicant

```
 1  I2:  and mit ihrem CHEF? ham=se auch mal, (0.5) so=n paar~
 2  A:   [empört] NE:IN:
 3  I2:  (0.5) disKURse gehabt, NEIN?
 4  A:   =nie.
 5  I2:  weil s=sich so gut mit dem verSTANden haben.
 6  A:   (0.5) nee das hat damit nischt zu   [TUN; (da hab ich?) reschPEKT.
 7  I2:                                      [nee,
 8  A:   (hi [hi)
 9  I2:      [sie haben resPEKT.
10  A:   ja; resPEKT;
```

```
 1   I2:   and with your BOSS? did you ever, have (0.5) well any~
 2   A:    {indignant} NO:;
 3   I2:   (0.5) ARgument, {lit. 'discourses'} NO?
 4   A:    =never.
 5   I2:   because you got ON with him so well.
 6   A:    (0.5) no that's got nothing to DO with [it; (I'm?) resPECTful.
 7   I2:                                          [no,
 8   A:    (hi [hi)
 9   I2:       [you are resPECTful.
10   A:    yes; resPECTful;
```

The applicant emphatically denies having had any conflicts with a superior, and gives 'respect' as the reason. The team of interviewers come back to this in their post-interview evaluation, and it seems to be an important factor in their judgement of her:

Interviewers' evaluation

I2:   conflicts are something she has problems with, because she also has (0.5) as we have seen in the course of the interviews, the Eastern mentality, that she keeps quiet about them, no question.

I1:   (...) she probably isn't able to cope with conflicts with her team colleagues. We have clear evidence that she can't easily handle conflict with management.

The interviewers' assessment of the applicant corresponds with our findings in the ethnographic interviews. Yet looking more closely at the job interview with the applicant concerned, we find a narrative later on where, discussing something else, she gives a detailed account of how she once confronted her boss who had been criticizing her performance behind her back. It is a perfect example of using initiative in dealing with conflict with a superior. This suggests that although Eastern applicants' communicative norms differ from Western ones in job interviews, their behaviour in real life may in fact be quite similar.

(Birkner and Kern 2008: 253–4)

This example illustrates the same type of 'unfair' formation of impressions and subsequent disadvantage that we discussed in the last section. However, the situation is even more complex than this, because stereotyping almost certainly played an important role. From the interviews that Birkner and Kern conducted with the interviewers, we learn that they had clear stereotypes of East and West Germans (Research Report 6.1). Their belief that East Germans are 'submissive and servile, and lack the ability to deal with conflict successfully' no doubt led them to perceive 'respectfulness for the boss' (cf. status-oriented style) as submissiveness, and caused them to overlook or ignore contradictory evidence that emerged later in another part of the interview. The interaction itself, and the impressions they formed, would in turn have reinforced their original stereotype, leading to ongoing disadvantage and discrimination of future candidates.

Research Report 6.1   Stereotypes of East and West Germans

In one ethnographic interview, [...], a personnel manager (who also took part in the job interviews) commented: 'If we count assertiveness and conflict management as elements of team work, it's true that they are a bit more reserved, the East Germans.' Later he assesses East Germans as 'very submissive, at times, what the boss says goes and you don't question it.' Asked for the causes he assumes 'because they never had to or it wasn't allowed.' This indicates that some interviewers perceive East Germans as submissive and servile and even assume that they lack the ability to deal with conflict successfully. West Germans, on the other hand, are considered more self-confident and better prepared to handle conflict.

(Birkner and Kern 2008: 253)

This example clearly underlines the harmful impact that stereotypes can have on intercultural interaction. It is very important, therefore, to consider them in greater detail.

6.2.2   What are stereotypes?

Despite the widespread use of the term 'stereotypes', there is no real consensus among social psychologists as to exactly what they are. As the definitions in Concept 6.3 indicate, there are differences of opinion on the following points: how accurate/inaccurate stereotypes are in their generalizations (e.g., do they have a kernel of truth?), whether they are bad (e.g., do they only emphasize negative features of groups or include positive ones?), and whether stereotypes need to be shared among a number of people rather than be held by just one person.

Concept 6.3   Definitions of stereotypes

Stereotypes are grossly oversimplified and overgeneralized abstractions about groups of people and are usually highly inaccurate although they may contain a grain of truth.

(Pennington 1986: 90)

A stereotype refers to those folk beliefs about the attributes characterizing a social category on which there is substantial agreement.

(Mackie 1973: 435; cited by Schneider 2004: 16)

Stereotyping has three characteristics: the categorization of persons, a consensus on attributed traits, and a discrepancy between attributed traits and actual traits.

(Secord and Backman 1964: 66; cited by Schneider 2004: 16)

[A stereotype is] a positive or negative set of beliefs held by an individual about the characteristics of a group of people. It varies in its accuracy, the extent to which it captures the degree to which the stereotyped group members possess these traits, and the extent to which the set of beliefs is shared by others.

(Jones 1997: 170; cited by Schneider 2004: 17)

Stereotypes are qualities perceived to be associated with particular groups or categories of people.

(Schneider 2004: 24)

Stereotypes can be conceived of as processes which have the function of simplifying judgement and which occur in situations characterized by little information, high complexity and pressure of time. [...] They are thus tools for the management of one's environment with more or less distorting effects.

(Schäfer 1994: 461; translated by Franklin)

According to Schneider (2004: 24, 562), stereotypes are simply generalizations about groups of people, and people use them on a regular basis. For example, in writing this book, we regularly ask ourselves 'what kind of people' will be reading it; similarly, when preparing a guest talk, most speakers ask the host organizer 'what types or groups of people' will be attending the lecture. Then, having identified the likely groups, people frequently infer certain features for the target audience, such as their expected amount of prior knowledge, topics that will be of interest/ relevance to them, and their ideological beliefs and/or assumptions. This kind of generalizing is thus an integral part of our everyday lives.

However, such generalizing does not always lead to 'accurate' assessments, and one of the reasons for this is the complexity of the relationship between category and features. Schneider (2004: 90) usefully distinguishes between three types of features:

1. *Essential features*: those that are absolutely essential for category membership and that usually simultaneously preclude membership from other categories; e.g., for 'senior citizens'/pensioners, it is essential for them to be over a certain age, and they cannot simultaneously be a 'senior citizen' and 'underage';

2. *Identifying features*: those that we use (but cannot always reliably depend on) to identify category members; e.g., for pensioners we may look at their hair colour, number of wrinkles, degree of stoop and so on;

3. *Ascribed features*: those that are associated with a given category but are not in any way integral to it and may be inaccurate; e.g. for 'senior citizens'/pensioners, we may think of them as having plenty of time on their hands, as physically not very strong, and as forgetful.

One way of judging the accuracy of stereotypes is to compare a group's stereotypes of themselves with the stereotypes held by non-group members. If there is convergence, then the stereotype could be regarded as accurate. However, even if a stereotype is empirically found to be accurate, we need to bear in mind several things. Firstly, people may differ in their evaluations (positive/negative) of a given stereotype. Secondly, stereotypes are subject to change, and so we must not assume that they are fixed and immutable (see Smith, Bond and Kağıtçıbaşı 2006: 227). Thirdly, as Schneider (2004: 337) points out, 'The major problem with stereotypes is not their putative accuracy, but how they are applied. [...] Even stereotypes that are generally accurate can be mis-applied to individuals.' (See the discussion in the next section.)

Stereotyping is often associated with prejudice and/or discrimin-ation, and as the definitions in Concept 6.4 indicate, the concepts are interrelated but not equivalent.

Concept 6.4   Prejudice and discrimination

Prejudice can be defined as the set of affective reactions we have toward people as a function of their category memberships.
(Schneider 2004: 27)

A stereotype is a group of beliefs about persons who are members of a par-ticular group, whereas prejudice can better be thought of as an attitude, usu-ally negative, towards members of a group.
(Smith and Bond 1998: 184–5)

Discrimination is the treatment of a person or a group of people unfairly or differently because of their membership of a particular social group.
(Chryssochoou 2004: 36)

Whereas prejudice represents the affective or emotional reaction to social groups, stereotypes are the cognitive manifestation of prejudice, and discrimination is the behavioral manifestation of prejudice. Using this model, a person's negative attitude toward a group [...] may be conceptualized as:

Negative stereotype: members of Group X are lazy, unreliable and slovenly
Prejudiced attitude: I don't like (people who belong to) Group X
Discrimination: I prefer to exclude them from the neighbourhood, avoid hiring them etc.

(Jones: 2002: 4)

The Parekh Report (Runnymede Trust 2000: 72–3), which deals with the future of multi-ethnic Britain and racial issues, emphasizes that the cause and effect relationship between prejudice, discrimination and exclusion and inequality is complex and multi-directional. Although the interrelationship is sometimes thought of in unidirectional terms (stereotyping leads to prejudice, which leads to discrimination, which leads to exclusion and inequality), in fact, discriminatory behaviour can create as well as be the consequence of prejudice. Similarly, exclusion and inequality can generate the very beliefs, attitudes and behaviours that then act to reinforce them.

6.2.3   Are stereotypes harmful?

Experiential Example 6.4 clearly demonstrates the harmful nature of the application of stereotypes in intercultural interaction. Many researchers have also taken such a view, arguing that stereotypes are by nature harmful because they lead to the ignoring of the individuality of individual members of other cultures and create expectations and self-fulfilling prophecies (Gudykunst 2004) to the detriment of the individual concerned. It is argued that they influence the way in which information is processed (cf. Hamilton Sherman and Ruvolo 1990) and remembered (cf. Hewstone and Giles 1986), and that such processes may well be based on little or no sound knowledge or experience of the individual or group concerned. At the worst, it can lead to prejudice. However, Smith and Bond (1998: 185–6) point out that 'this liberal distaste for stereotyping was held by many social scientists and reinforced by the cultural emphasis on personal uniqueness [...] characteristic of the individualist societies where most research into stereotypes is conducted', an observation which can be viewed as a more general warning about the problems which can be caused by the culture-centredness of much research (cf. Chapter 11).

One of the major problems with stereotypes is that they easily take on an essentialist character, with the result that group members are treated as having certain invariable and fixed properties, and as being essentially different from members of other groups. Yet most social groups have few or no essential features; they only have identifying and ascribed features that just have a probabilistic association, of varying degrees of strength, with a particular group (both in terms of how well the features predict the group, and how well the group predicts the features). Holliday, Hyde and Kullman (2004) explain the dangers of holding an essentialist notion of culture (Concept 6.5).

Concept 6.5 Stereotypes, essentialism and intercultural interaction

Holliday, Hyde and Kullman describe a series of interactions between an Australian lecturer and a black South African student studying in Australia, which are a reconstruction of a number of authentic occurrences. The lecturer had previously worked on a South African education project and felt he knew a lot about the country. He often told the student he understood something about 'black culture in South Africa', would be able to help her meet deadlines and seemed surprised if she did well. One day she overheard him talking to a colleague, saying 'Well, she does have some difficulty meeting deadlines; but of course that's something deep in black African culture, isn't it?' Yet the student knew she was having no more difficulty than any of the other students, and that in any case, this did not have anything to do with being black. Another student always missed deadlines; he was Welsh but no one suggested this was anything to do with being Welsh.

Holliday and his colleagues point out several ways in which the lecturer's behaviour is inappropriate:

- He interacts with her not so much as an individual as with an image of who she is.
- He treats her as being different from the other students.
- He rationalizes her shortcomings in terms of her culture, implying the inferiority of her cultural group.
- He over-emphasizes 'exotic' aspects of her culture, which could imply backwardness.
- He speaks slowly and carefully, making her feel patronized.
- He uses words and phrases that identify her as being different.

They acknowledge that the lecturer is trying to do his best for the student, but argue that his essentialist notion of her culture give rise to the above basic mistakes.

(Holliday, Hyde and Kullman 2004: 31–2)

However, some aspects of the lecturer's behaviour need not necessarily have been inappropriate – the student might have appreciated him speaking slowly and carefully if her English was weak; she might have wanted to be treated differently from the other students if she felt some of her beliefs and/or practices required it. So the key is not to ignore completely any differences between cultural groups that may exist at a generalized level, but, as Devine (1989) seems to suggest, rather to be highly attuned (see Chapters 4 and 5) when engaging with them in interaction.

In fact, some scholars (e.g., Hamilton 1979; Tversky and Kahnemann 1983) have proposed that cognitive processes, such as categorization and generalization, with which stereotyping has much in common, are inevitable in interaction. The psychologist, David Schneider, for example, argues as follows: 'stereotypes cannot easily be divorced from more 'normal' ways of thinking about people. As a cognitive process, stereotyping seems pretty much like business as usual. Stereotypes are simply generalizations about groups of people, and as such they are similar to generalizations about dogs, computers, [...] city buses, or Beethoven piano sonatas. We have them because they are useful. I use stereotypes about students when I prepare my lectures (and, for that matter, stereotypes about prospective readers of this book while I write it)' (2004: 562). In the intercultural field, some people argue that the application of the 'right kind' of stereotypes can be beneficial as a tool for managing the complexity of intercultural interaction. This counterintuitive and 'politically incorrect' view is one which the management scholar Adler (2001: 81), for example, advocates. She describes the characteristics of the helpful rather than harmful stereotype: it must be a *consciously held* description of the *group norm*, *descriptive* rather than evaluative, *accurate and soundly based on research* rather than hearsay and limited experience; it should only be used as the *first best guess* prior to direct information about the person or persons concerned; and it should be *modified* as a result of observation and experience.

Whatever view one chooses to identify with, researchers and practitioners involved in intercultural interaction need to come to grips with the concept of stereotyping and its ramifications. From a research point of view, description, categorization and generalization are key activities of many researchers. Indeed, some of the categories most frequently used by researchers into intercultural interaction, for example, Hofstede's value orientations, Hall's interactional orientations and, in Germany, Thomas's culture standards (see Chapter 2) can all be described, when applied to particular cultural groups, as amounting to 'stereotypes' – helpful or harmful depending on one's standpoint. In intercultural development interventions, experience shows that intercultural interactants possess both harmful and helpful stereotypes, apply them in their interaction and certainly use them when asked to reflect upon their intercultural interaction. Furthermore, teaching and learning materials make ample use of what may be described as helpful or harmful stereotypes, and so it is important to consider some fundamental questions associated with stereotyping when planning the development of intercultural competence:

- How useful, feasible or harmful is it to talk about the characteristics of a particular group, such as a national group or an organizational group?
- If it is useful, how can these characteristics best be identified?
- If it is harmful, how can people best be helped to interact with members of groups they are unfamiliar with?

We return to these questions in Chapter 9.

6.3   Prejudice, conscious discrimination and deliberate domination

In the examples we have considered so far, we may have implied that failure to provide people with equal opportunities is an inadvertent mistake rather than a deliberate strategy. However, as the Parekh Report (Runnymede Trust 2000) makes clear, lack of awareness is no excuse:

> Nor is unwittingness an excuse. If officials do not predict the discriminatory consequences of established policies and routine practices, they are failing in elementary duties of professionalism and care.
>
> (Runnymede Trust 2000: 70)

The report also points out that 'the unequal power relations between police officers and members of the public, teachers and pupils, health professionals and patients, employers and employees, and so on, are fertile ground for a wide range of prejudices and negative stereotypes, particularly at times of stress and conflict', and that 'some discrimination is entirely explicit and intentional' (Runnymede Trust 2000: 73, 70).

Eades (2007) provides a shocking example of this from another cultural context. It concerns the Pikenba Case, the background to which is as follows. In May 1994 three Aboriginal boys, aged 12, 13 and 14, were walking around a shopping mall near the centre of Brisbane. It was shortly after midnight, and six armed police officers approached them and told them to get into three separate vehicles. They were driven to an industrial wasteland area about 14 kilometres away, and then simply abandoned. They were not taken to a police station or charged with any offence; they were just taken to this remote spot, according to the police, so that they could 'reflect on their misdemeanours'. The boys complained to the Aboriginal Legal Service, and a subsequent investigation recommended that criminal charges be laid against the six police officers. The case came to court in 1995, and most of the four-day hearing consisted of evidence from the three boys. This comprised lengthy cross-examination by each of the two defence lawyers who were representing three of the police officers (Experiential Example 6.5). Eades explains how these lawyers took deliberate advantage of their understanding of Aboriginal communication conventions to destroy the credibility of the witnesses, and argues that the case highlights the importance of power relations in intercultural interaction.

Experiential Example 6.5   The Pikenba Case: deliberate domination in court

Perhaps the most pervasive linguistic strategy used by defence counsel was their exploitation of the Aboriginal tendency to freely agree to propositions put to them in Yes-No questions, regardless of their actual agreement, or even their understanding of the question. Termed 'gratuitous concurrence' (Liberman 1981), this conversational pattern is widely found in intercultural interactions involving Aboriginal people, and is considered a major problem for the way in which Aboriginal people participate in the criminal justice system (Eades 1992, 2002).

   A number of factors increase the likelihood of an Aboriginal witness in court using gratuitous concurrence, including interviewer hostility, for example shouting or haranguing. The following example occurred during the cross-examination of the oldest of the three boys, who was 15 at the time. It typifies much of the cross-examination by the first of the two defence counsel, who used shouting and repeated question tags (such as *didn't you*), in response to answers that he did not accept. As we see in this example, the witness's response to such harassment (in turn 4) often appears to be gratuitous concurrence.

Example

1   DC1:   And you <u>knew</u> (1.4) when you spoke to these six police in the Valley that you didn't have to go anywhere with them if you didn't want to, didn't you?
2   BARRY: (1.3) No.
3   DC1:   You <u>knew</u> that, Mr (1.2) Coley I'd suggest to you, PLEASE DO NOT LIE. YOU KNEW THAT YOU DIDN'T HAVE TO GO ANYWHERE if you didn't want to, didn't you? (2.2) DIDN'T YOU? (2.2) DIDN'T YOU, MR COLEY?
4   BARRY: (1.3) Yeh.
5   DC1:   WHY DID YOU JUST LIE TO ME? WHY DID YOU JUST SAY 'NO' MR COLEY?

(Eades 2007: 291–2)

Examples such as this raise challenging questions for us. Dealing with conscious discrimination and domination is a very complex issue that goes beyond the scope of this book. However, in Chapter 9 we return to many of the issues discussed in this chapter to consider how they can be addressed when aiming to develop ICIC.

6.4   English as a world language, and disadvantage

In this final section, we turn to another aspect of potential domination in intercultural interaction – the use of English. English is now a world language: it is spoken by large numbers of people in widely distributed territories, it has priority status in many countries, it functions as an international lingua franca, and it displays global ownership (see Crystal 1997; Graddol 1997; Smith 1993). Linguists such as Phillipson (1992) and Pennycook (1994) argue that this raises a number of concerns associated with linguistic imperialism; for example, they maintain that:

- The 'export' of English often goes hand in hand with cultural elements, such as consumerist values, religious beliefs, scientific approaches, bodies of research knowledge and popular culture, and thus can lead to cultural domination by the originating countries, such as the United States or the United Kingdom.
- English offers linguistic and economic power to those who are proficient in it, but conversely puts those who are less proficient in it at a major disadvantage.
- English can be a language killer, in that members of minority language groups may feel less need to learn and maintain their own language. These minority languages could thus die out unless specific steps are taken.

However, as Pölzl (2005) points out, these same concerns can be viewed from a different perspective:

- The spread of English and its cultural concomitants is more likely to lead to hybridization than the straightforward 'export' of culture.
- Social disadvantage is not 'the fault' of English *per se*, but rather results from social and institutional practices; the key is thus to identify the most effective ways of combating the inequality.
- If members of minority language groups are not provided with the opportunity to learn English, they will suffer from linguistic

isolation, and they will suffer from educational, social and economic marginalization.

A key issue underlying all of these arguments is the interrelationship between language and community identity. Pölzl (2005) identifies three main possibilities for the interrelationship, as shown in Concept 6.6, which she suggests represent salient stages on a continuum of language function and speakers' identification.

In intercultural interaction, all of these interrelationships between cultural identity and language choice may occur, and the situation is further complicated by the fact that language use (the language(s) chosen and levels of proficiency) is not only associated with community

---

Concept 6.6 Functional varieties of language and their impact on identity perceptions (Pölzl 2005)

Lingua culturae	Language and community identity are closely interconnected. Speakers closely identify with the language as a symbol of their native community and link it closely with their identity. English as a lingua culturae emerges in areas where speakers use it as a native language, such as native speakers of English in the UK, USA, Australia and New Zealand.
Lingua converta	A *lingua converta* is a language that has been established alongside an existing *lingua culturae* and is used in addition to the latter. Speakers have creatively adapted it to reflect their own community contexts and they include it as part of their expression of identity. In the case of English, this applies to countries in South Asia, South-East Asia and Africa where English is institutionalized as a second (official) language, mainly as the result of colonization.
Lingua franca	A language that is used predominantly for communication purposes. Speakers use it as a medium of communication only, and do not identify symbolically with it. They retain their allegiance to their primary language, and use the lingua franca simply to be intelligible to others. In terms of English, English is acquired as a foreign language in a growing number of countries for international purposes.

identity, but also impacts on individual and relational identity. For example, if I am just moderately proficient in English as a lingua franca, yet others speak very quickly to me and use complicated vocabulary, this can challenge my personal identity as a competent person. These are issues that we consider in greater detail in the next chapter.

The fears of linguistic imperialism and related issues discussed above are concerned more with the results of the pre-eminence of English than its effects on intercultural interaction in the communication situation itself. Those working in trans- and supra-national political institutions and NGOs may experience such concerns, and they are reflected in the 'mother tongue plus two foreign languages' policy of the European Commission (in which one of the two foreign languages is nevertheless tacitly assumed to be likely to be English). People may sometimes express their fears, not least to document their cultural neutrality. However, in international business and management, and in other areas in which overt respect for political sensibilities is perhaps less necessary or at least less common, people by and large experience the spread of English as a welcome simplification and very often a *sine qua non* of intercultural interaction.

6.5   Concluding comments

In this chapter, we have discussed the impressions that people may aim to convey of themselves, and the impressions that others may perceive. We have argued that mismatches can have serious implications for equality of opportunity, and we have demonstrated how cultural factors can play a crucial role in this process. Sometimes discrimination can be inadvertent, but it can also be deliberate.

Impression management is closely associated with the notion of identity because it involves the self attributes that people want to convey to others. In the next chapter we continue with the theme of identity, focusing on the challenges to identity that people may face when they experience cultural change.

Suggestions for further reading

Rosenfeld, P., Giacalone, R. A. and Riordan, C. A. (1994) Impression management and diversity: Issues for organizational behaviour. Special Issue of *American Behavioral Scientist*, 37(5). This special issue comprises nine articles that all address the interconnection between impression management and diversity.

Alim, H. S. (2005) Hearing what's not said and missing what is: Black language in white public space. In S. Kiesling and C. Bratt Paulston (eds) *Intercultural Discourse and Communication: The Essential Readings*, pp. 180–97.

Oxford: Blackwell. This chapter analyses the 'battlin' linguistic practices of Black American Hip Hop culture. It reports that while Black youth attach very great value to the verbal inventiveness and competition involved in battling, white teachers misinterpret it as 'violence' and 'not appropriate' on school grounds.

Gumperz, J. and Roberts, C. (1991) Understanding in intercultural encounters. In J. Blommaert and J. Verschueren (eds) *The Pragmatics of International and Intercultural Communication*, pp. 51–90. Amsterdam: John Benjamins. This chapter gives many examples of encounters between white and Asian British people in Advice Centres in Britain, and analyses the impact of cultural factors.

Roberts, C., Davies, E. and Jupp, T. (1992) *Language and Discrimination*. London: Longman. This book provides a detailed analysis of communication in multi-ethnic workplaces, and the discrimination that may occur.

Gudykunst, W. B. (2004) *Bridging Differences: Effective Intergroup Communication*. Thousand Oaks, CA: Sage. This book contains numerous and stimulating thoughts on stereotypes and prejudice.

Chryssochoou, X. (2004) *Cultural Diversity: Its Social Psychology*. Oxford: Blackwell. This book provides a social psychological perspective on stereotypes, prejudice and perceptions of others, and includes numerous helpful definitions of concepts and brief research reports.

7
Adapting to Unfamiliar Cultures

> If you're not willing to be changed by a place, there's no point going.
>
> Mifflin 1996

Chapter outline

During the last three chapters we have explored the intercultural competencies needed for effective and appropriate intercultural interaction, focusing particularly on the process of interaction. In this chapter we turn to the individual and consider the impact that intercultural interaction can have on the psychological welfare and growth of those who experience such interaction, especially in unfamiliar cultural settings. In Chapters 10 and 11, we examine ways of researching this adaptation process and the extent to which people feel they have adapted well.

7.1 Culture shock and stress

7.1.1 Understanding culture shock and stress

Culture shock is a common experience for people who spend an extended period of time in a different cultural environment. The term refers to the psychological (and physical) consequences of changes in circumstances, when people experience feelings such as the following:

- *Sense of loss and feelings of deprivation*, in relation to friends, status, profession and possessions.
- *Feelings of helplessness*, not being able to cope with the new environment.
- *Irritation, anger* about 'foreign' practices.
- *Feelings of isolation*, feeling rejected by (unable to get close to) members of the new culture, or own rejection of them.
- *Confusion* in role, values and self-identity.

(See Experiential Example 7.1.) Less severe forms of such discomfort can also be experienced by those interacting with members of other cultures in their home culture, working in multicultural virtual teams or making a short trip abroad to visit a subsidiary of the home organization.

Experiential Example 7.1   Culture shock in Britain

It was in the seventh or eighth month that I clearly was having symptoms of culture shock: I was confused, annoyed, I asked questions like: 'Why are the banks not better?' I was looking at identifying all the inefficiencies of the British system. I hated the British business culture which I saw as slow, bureaucratic, cumbersome, lacking customer service, lacking initiatives. Fortunately, I had a very good mentor and I could go on Friday afternoons and moan and talk to him about my experiences. I was able to make a much better adjustment, and after about 12 months I felt integrated and also reconciled.

(Female US Manager, cited by Marx 2001: 9)

The result of culture shock can be anxiety, depression, frustration, anger and/or self-pity, and there can also be physiological and behavioural consequences which vary from person to person. Some people eat more and some eat less; some people sleep a lot and some have difficulty sleeping; many people get frequent minor illnesses, and some lose their ability to work effectively. Some people may withdraw, and, for example, spend excessive amounts of time reading, or they may interact only with fellow nationals and avoid contact with host nationals.

In fact, all of these symptoms stem from stress, and Berry (2006: 43) argues that 'acculturative stress' is a more suitable term. Any kind of significant change in our lives, whether positive or negative, and whether involving cultural change or not, can be stressful. However, cultural change, such as moving overseas, typically involves a particularly large number of changes, such as changes in living conditions, food, social activities, recreational activities, working hours or conditions, work responsibilities, family circumstances (e.g., there may be marital separation, or new schools for children), and so on. It is this unusually large number of changes that can be particularly stressful, and has given rise to the notion of culture shock.

Oberg (1960), in a classic paper on culture shock, argued that people's emotional reactions to cultural change follow a U-curve: initial positive reactions, followed by negative reactions, and then recovery and adjustment to positive health (see Concept 7.1). However, longitudinal studies have offered little support for precisely this pattern. For example, Ward and colleagues (2001) report a study of overseas students which displays the complete opposite: the degree of depression experienced by students at month 1 and month 12 was significantly higher than at month 6. So these authors, on the basis of a number of studies, argue that 'psychological adjustment difficulties appear to be greatest in the early stages of transition [...], drop in the first 4 to 6 months, and are then somewhat variable over time' (Ward, Bochner and Furnham 2001: 81). Anecdotal accounts also tend to question the U-curve pattern, although they highlight the stress that individuals may experience (e.g., see Experiential Example 7.2).

Concept 7.1   Oberg's stages of emotional reaction to cultural change

1. The 'honeymoon', with emphasis on the initial reactions of euphoria, enchantment, fascination, and enthusiasm;
2. The crisis, characterized by feelings of inadequacy, frustration, anxiety and anger;
3. The recovery, including crisis resolution and culture learning; and finally,
4. Adjustment, reflecting enjoyment of and functional competence in the new environment.

(Oberg 1960; cited by Ward, Bochner and Furnham 2001: 80)

Experiential Example 7.2   Culture shock over time

I had a very negative phase after the first year. I cannot see clearly defined stages that run in a linear fashion as described in the original culture shock model. It is more like a lot of ups and downs and maybe something like a mini repetition of the culture shock cycle throughout one's stay abroad. The way I coped with my own emotions was to talk to someone close about it.

(German manager working in Africa; cited by Marx 2001: 11)

Superficially it might seem as though stress is a negative phenomenon, yet an appropriate amount of stress can actually be beneficial. Kim (2001: 60) reports a number of studies which found that people with a greater frequency of stress-related symptoms were more effective in their adaptation in the longer term. So both Kim (2001) and Berry (2006) argue that stress can positively promote adaptation and can help people grow towards richer and more self-fulfilling personhoods (Concept 7.2).

Concept 7.2   Kim on the stress-adaptation-growth dynamic

Stress, adaptation, and growth [...] highlight the core of strangers' cross-cultural experiences in a new environment. Together, they constitute a three-pronged *stress-adaptation-growth dynamic* of psychic movement in the forward and upward direction of increased chances of success in meeting the demands of the host environment. None of the three occurs without the others, and each occurs because of the others. Stress, in this regard, is intrinsic to complex open systems such as humans and essential in their transformation process – one that allows for self-organization and self-renewal.

The stress-adaptation-growth dynamic plays out not in a smooth, linear progression, but in a cyclic and continual 'draw-back-to-leap' representation of the present articulation of the interrelationships among stress, adaptation, and growth. Strangers respond to each stressful experience by 'drawing back,' which in turn activates adaptive energy to help them reorganize themselves and 'leap forward.' As growth of some units always occurs at the expense of others [...], the adaptive journey follows a pattern that juxtaposes novelty and confirmation, attachment and detachment, construction and destruction. The process is continuous as long as there are new environmental challenges.

(Kim 2001: 56–7)

Nevertheless, too much stress can be counter-productive, so any kind of stress needs to be managed appropriately for growth to occur. What competencies and what types of strategy are most effective for promoting this? The next section turns to this issue, and we return to it in Chapter 9.

7.1.2   Managing culture shock and stress

As we noted in Chapter 3, most frameworks that conceptualize ICIC identify a number of personal qualities that are helpful for managing culture shock and stress. Matsumoto and his colleagues (e.g., Matsumoto, Yoo and LeRoux 2007) have researched this empirically and propose, on the basis of their studies, that there are four key ingredients for the effective management of cultural stress and the promotion of personal growth. These are: emotion regulation, openness, flexibility and critical thinking. They argue that emotion regulation functions as a gatekeeper, because people have difficulty engaging in critical thinking and assimilating new cognitive schemas to aid adjustment unless they have first been able to control their emotions. The WorldWork framework (see Concept 3.7), in common with the Cross Cultural Adaptability Inventory, includes emotional strength as one of its foci. The WorldWork framework identifies three different elements: resilience, coping and spirit of adventure (see Concept 7.3). Resilience seems to correspond closely to Matsumoto and colleagues' concept of emotion regulation. In the related competency of personal autonomy the WorldWork framework identifies inner purpose as a quality which contributes to the management of culture shock and stress.

A number of researchers have explored the range of strategies that people use to cope with stress and thus put the quality of resilience into practice. Carver and his colleagues (1989) have identified 15 such strategies (Concept 7.4) and these have been used in a few cross-cultural studies.

Concept 7.3   Intercultural competencies associated with emotional strength

Resilience	Ability to cope well with stress, uncertainty and anxiety and to bounce back after making mistakes.
Coping	Has well-developed methods for dealing with stress, builds local support networks and uses humour to relieve tensions.
Spirit of adventure	Searches out and enjoys new experiences, even if they are unpredictable and outside the normal comfort zone.
Inner purpose	Possesses an inner strength and well-defined personal values, self-reliance and determination that provides a clear sense of purpose and direction.

(based on WorldWork, n.d.)

Concept 7.4   Carver, Scheier and Weintraub's list of coping strategies

Coping strategy	Example
Positive reinterpretation and growth	*I look for something good in what is happening*
Mental disengagement	*I turn to work or other substitute activities to take my mind off things*
Focus on and venting of emotions	*I let my feelings out*
Use of instrumental social support	*I ask people who have had similar experiences what they did*
Active coping	*I concentrate my efforts on doing something about it*
Denial	*I act as though it hasn't even happened*
Religious coping	*I seek God's help*
Humour	*I kid around about it*
Behavioural disengagement	*I give up the attempt to get what I want*
Restraint	*I make sure not to make matters worse by acting too soon*
Use of emotional social support	*I get sympathy and understanding from someone*
Substance use	*I use alcohol or drugs to make myself feel better*
Acceptance	*I accept that this has happened and that it can't be changed*
Suppression of competing activities	*I focus on dealing with this problem, and if necessary let other things slide a little*
Planning	*I make a plan of action*

(Extracts from the COPE Scale: http://www.psy.miami.edu/faculty/ccarver/sclCOPEf.html (accessed 23 November 2008)

Typically, self-ratings of these items are correlated with self-ratings of measures of psychological well-being. These have yielded mixed findings as to which strategies are associated with psychological well-being, and Cross (1995) has speculated that a possible reason for this could be cross-cultural differences in the effectiveness of different coping strategies.

Experiential Examples 7.1 and 7.2 both point to the value of social support for handling stress, and Ward, Bochner and Furnham (2001) report some empirical evidence which substantiates this. This raises an important question: who can provide the most effective social support – people from the 'host' culture, people from one's own culture, or other 'foreigners' or 'outsiders'?

The psychologist Stephen Bochner explored this issue by studying the friendship patterns of overseas students (e.g., Bochner, McLeod and Lin 1977). He found that people tend to belong to three distinct social networks, and that each of these serves important but different psychological functions. He found that overseas students prefer local students for help with language and academic difficulties, but prefer co-nationals for emotional support (Concept 7.5). Spencer-Oatey and Xiong (2006) report similar findings.

Despite the importance of social support from one's own cultural group, a number of researchers (e.g., Ward and Kennedy 1993) have found that in the longer term a greater amount of interaction with host nationals is associated with fewer social difficulties, improved communicative competence and facilitates general adaptation to life overseas. Of course, interaction with the host cultural group is a two-way process that requires both parties to be both willing and interested in interacting. Some social settings make that more difficult than others, and this is an issue that we return to in Section 7.3.

Ward and Kennedy (2001) point out, though, that there has been surprisingly little research into the coping strategies that people actually use to deal with the stressful changes associated with cross-cultural transition, and how effective they are. This is clearly a topic that would benefit from further research.

Concept 7.5 Functional model of the friendship patterns of overseas students		
Network	**Membership**	**Typical function**
Primary monocultural	Co-nationals	Provide close friendship (compatibility of cultural and ethnic values)
Secondary bicultural	Significant host nationals, such as academics, fellow students, advisors and officials	Help the student succeed at university and adjust to the new culture
Tertiary multicultural	Other friends & acquaintances	Provide companionship for recreational and non-task-oriented activities
(Bochner, McLeod and Lin 1977)		

7.2   Personal growth

A key feature of much theory and research into cultural adaptation and change is the notion of development and growth. This section explores theorizing and research into this ongoing process.

7.2.1   Sensitivity to difference and personal growth

Bennett (1986: 180) argues that if we are to understand the notion of growth, and to help people (through mentoring, coaching or more conventional development interventions) to make progress on their personal journeys to 'becoming intercultural' (Kim 2001: 194–5), then we need to map the staging points in this process. He proposes a six-stage model known as the Developmental Model of Intercultural Sensitivity (DMIS) (Bennett 1986) (Concept 7.6). He labels the first three stages as ethnocentric, and the last three stages as ethnorelative.

Concept 7.6 Bennett's developmental model of intercultural sensitivity		
Stage	**Summary description**	**Illustrative viewpoints**
1. Denial of difference	The inability to <u>construe</u> cultural difference, indicated by benign stereotyping (well-meant but ignorant or naïve observations) and superficial statements of tolerance. May sometimes be accompanied by attribution of deficiency of intelligence or personality.	*All big cities are the same – lots of buildings, too many cars, McDonalds.* *I never experience culture shock.* *With my experience, I can be successful in any culture without any special effort.*
2. Defence against difference	Recognition of cultural difference coupled with negative evaluation of most variations from native culture – the greater the difference, the more negative the evaluation. Characterized by dualistic us/them thinking and frequently accompanied by overt negative stereotyping.	*I wish these people would just talk the way I do.* *When you go to other cultures, it makes you realize how much better the US is.* *What a sexist society!* *Boy, could we teach these people a lot of stuff!*

3. Minimization of difference	Recognition and acceptance of superficial cultural differences such as eating customs, etc., while holding that all human beings are essentially the same. Emphasis on the similarity of people and commonality of basic values.	*The key to getting along in any culture is just to be yourself – authentic and honest!* *Customs differ, of course, but when you really get to know them they're pretty much like us.*
4. Acceptance of difference	Recognition and appreciation of cultural differences in behaviour and values. Acceptance of cultural differences as viable alternative solutions to the organization of human existence. Cultural relativity.	*The more difference the better – more difference equals more creative ideas!* *Sometimes it's confusing, knowing that values are different in various cultures and wanting to be respectful, but still wanting to maintain my own core values.*
5. Adaptation to difference	The development of communication skills that enable intercultural communication. Effective use of empathy, or frame of reference shifting, to understand and be understood across cultural boundaries.	*To solve this dispute, I need to change my behaviour to account for the difference in status between me and my counterpart from the other culture.* *I can maintain my values and also behave in culturally appropriate ways.*
6. Integration of difference	The internalization of bicultural or multicultural frames of reference. Maintaining a definition of identity that is 'marginal' to any particular culture. Seeing one's self as 'in process'.	*I feel most comfortable when I'm bridging differences between the cultures I know.* *Whatever the situation, I can usually look at it from a variety of cultural points of view.*

(Based on Bennett, n.d.)

Bennett (in collaboration with Hammer) has developed an 'Intercultural Development Inventory' which he claims is a reliable and valid measure of five of these stages (see Section 11.2.3 for more details), and he suggests training procedures for challenging people at any of these stages to grow in their sensitivity.

However, there are a number of controversial issues associated with Bennett's model; for example, whether people necessarily have to move sequentially through each of the stages, and whether people may (appear to) be at different stages with respect to different cultural groups and/or different issues. Sparrow (2000) argues that identity development should be viewed as more interactive and highly dependent on context. Another issue is whether there is/should be a limit to ethnorelativity when a cultural group engages in behavioural practices that most or many others regard as unethical (e.g., enforced female circumcision, bribery in business, arranged marriages), but are a norm or at least usual or common within the group. Problems associated with Bennett's assessment tool are discussed in Chapter 11.

7.2.2   Identity and personal growth

Another way of conceptualizing personal growth is in terms of identity. This is a fruitful perspective that can yield valuable insights into the process of growth, especially when combined with analytic concepts from humanistic geography and cultural studies.

As Simon (2004) points out, identity is both cognitive and social in nature, both stable and dynamic (Concept 7.7). It has numerous facets, and comprises people's self-beliefs in terms of personal (individual) characteristics, interpersonal relationships and group (collective) affiliations.

Concept 7.7   Conceptualizations of identity

Identity results from interaction in the social world and in turn guides interaction in the social world.

(Simon 2004: 2)

The self-concept is a multi-faceted, dynamic construal that contains beliefs about one's attributes as well as episodic and semantic memories about the self. It operates as a schema, controlling the processing of self-relevant information.

(Based on Campbell, Assanand and Di Paula 2000: 67)

Identity can *only* be understood as process, as 'being' or 'becoming'. One's identity – one's identities, indeed, for who we are is always singular *and* plural – is never a final or settled matter.

(Jenkins 2004: 5)

When people move into culturally unfamiliar contexts, such as when they go abroad to live or study, or when they take up a job in a very different type of organization, they often experience some challenges to their senses of identity – their individual, interpersonal and community identities. For example, they may find that their perception of themselves as 'competent persons' is brought into question, they may be unsure how to fulfil their role, and/or they may feel unsure which group they 'really' belong to. Experiential Examples 7.3, 7.4 and 7.5 provide some authentic illustrations of such experiences.

Experiential Example 7.3   A competent speaker?

[A British student on a placement in Spain] [...] every time I asked her a question, she'd assume I hadn't understood anything. She'd therefore sigh heavily [...] and repeat EVERYTHING she'd just said. [...] she speaks deliberately slowly and loudly *at* me (not *to* me), even though I'm now at such a stage with my Spanish where I can easily understand her talking at normal volume and speed. Annoying bitch! [...] it occurred to me that I hate them [my landlady and her mother] [...] for one reason above all others: they make me feel that I know no Spanish. This is highly annoying because I know I can speak Spanish. With every other Spaniard I speak with now I have normal conversations, sometimes quite complicated ones.

(Crawshaw and Callen 2001: 117)

Experiential Example 7.4   New ways of interacting with teachers

[A Chinese student studying in Britain] Although we were scornful of the Greek students' somewhat showy performance [in class], in fact, in the back of our minds we were really envious of their courage. We felt upset about ourselves; after all, they have gained from the interactions. From the bottom of our hearts, we Chinese want to interact with the teacher and are willing to talk to them, but we are just constrained by old mindsets and cannot pluck up the courage.

(Xiong 2005: 157)

Experiential Example 7.5   Who am I?

[A bilingual South Asian living in the UK] R. said to me, 'Well, Rabia, are you a British citizen? [...]. And I sat there and I honestly could not say. I could not answer that question by confidently saying, 'Yes, I'm a British citizen' because what I did say to her, I said, 'Well, who am I really?' That's true like

> what I've told you, I've lived the two lives. I have got a British passport and
> all that stuff, but let's turn it the other way. If I was walking down a road,
> who would R see me as? And then I asked her that and she said, 'British,
> because you speak English really well.' I said, 'Yeah, but that's because you
> know me.'
>
> (Mills 2004: 171)

People need to 'make sense' of experiences such as these; in other
words, the stress that they experience pushes them to account to themselves why the situation has occurred. This sense-making usually takes
the form of a narrative, and a rich analytic framework for exploring
people's identity narratives is offered by the metaphors of 'place', 'space',
'borderlands' and 'third spaces' (Bhabha 1990). These theoretical constructs facilitate multiple perspectives on the complex issues of identity
challenge, development and change.

Thinking first of 'place', Fougère (2008: 196) explains that 'place
accounts for a fixity and a familiarity', which provides us with a sense
of belonging. We can be either outside a 'place' or inside it, and this can
affect the extent to which we identify with it and feel we belong to it.
According to Relph (1976; cited by Fougère 2008), we can be inside or
outside a place in various ways (Concept 7.8).

Concept 7.8   Relph on insideness/outsideness of place

Insideness		Outsideness	
Behavioural insideness	Interest in the physical characteristics of a place	Incidental outsideness	Places are merely backgrounds for other activities
Empathetic insideness	'Emotional participation' in a place	Objective outsideness	Places are treated as concepts and locations
Existential insideness	Complete and unselfconscious commitment to a place	Existential outsideness	Profound alienation from a place
Vicarious insideness	Experience of places through novels and other media		

(Derived from Relph 1976: 50–5, cited by Fougère 2008: 192)

In intercultural contexts, people can experience a range of feelings and reactions that can be conceptualized in these terms. For example, people may be curious about their new physical surroundings and want to explore them (behavioural insideness); they may develop a sentimental attachment to a place (empathetic insideness); they may regard their current placement as an inconvenient but necessary stepping-stone for getting somewhere else (incidental outsideness); or they may feel deep discomfort and antagonism towards it (existential outsideness). Very frequently, people feel confusion as to where they belong; they do not know whether they belong to this place or to that place, as Experiential Example 7.5 illustrates. In other words, they are in the 'borderlands'.

The concept of place is complemented by the concept of 'space'. According to Fougère (2008: 196), 'space is something one can explore, seemingly for ever, and thus represents a possible emancipation from the pressure of one's place, in a way at once exciting, because of the promises of new experiences it offers, and worrying, because of its unknown character.' People's identities are continually developing and changing, and 'space' provides them with the opportunity to do so. People's self-narratives emerge as they move from an original place into a space, and then use that space to lead themselves to a new place. In exploring spaces, people may be grappling with a range of challenges; for example, they may be striving to bring coherence to their sense of identity, and addressing questions such as *'How can I be both a Jew and a Christian? Or How can I be both a competent professional and a dedicated mother or father?* When people perceive they have multiple identities that are seemingly incompatible, this can be very unsettling. Bilingual and bicultural individuals, or people who have lived for extended periods of time in different cultural contexts, frequently report such internal conflicts, and they continue with this pain until they are able to develop a coherent conception of themselves. As Experiential Example 7.6 illustrates, people's initial reaction is often to feel that they have to choose either one or the other identity; in this case, the young man felt that he had to be either English or French but could not be both. He needed to be able to work through these feelings of conflict, and find ways of developing a sense that he could be both English and French.

Experiential Example 7.6   The pain of biculturalism

[French young man returning home after 10 years of schooling in England]
Realizing that I was neither English nor French, I came to the conclusion that I had to choose one country and one culture. As I was living in France,

I decided to reject my English background and consciously strove to become French. [...] For a long time I felt that it was impossible to be bicultural – that it was too painful – and I therefore strove hard to adopt one culture and reject the other. Now that this is done, and with the years gone by, I realize that had the circumstances been different and had I been helped more by my family and friends when I first came back to France, life would have been easier and I could perhaps have retained both cultures.

(Grosjean 1982: 165)

Similar confusion can be felt by business people involved in cross-border mergers and acquisitions, and professionals working in supra-national organizations like the European Parliament. They may find that core elements of their identities (e.g., member of Company X, representative of Party Y) are ignored or questioned by their new work/role, and that they are expected to generate new social identities which may seem to conflict with their familiar ones (e.g., member of Company Z rather than Company X). This can be very unsettling and clearly affects interaction and cooperation. As Experiential Example 7.6 indicates, appropriate support (see Section 7.2.2 above) may be able to ease this process of achieving a coherent sense of identity, and we take up this issue again in Chapter 9 on intercultural development.

For some people, residence abroad and the exploration of the 'space' that they experience, leads not to a discovery of a new place, but to a clearer understanding of their original place. For example, Fougère (2008: 191–2) reports that one of his interviewees, a French young graduate who went to work in a company in Finland, gained a new understanding of his nationality, saying 'I think that if one doesn't go abroad, one doesn't realize what it is to be French, that is, well, what is it that says that I am really French [...] there's a whole lot of things, which belong to daily life and are commonplace, and which, when one goes abroad, one realizes that they're typically French.' Similarly, one of Marx's (2001: 17) business manager interviewees gained a new understanding of his personal qualities: 'My most positive surprise was to realize that I was a born survivor and that I could deal with problems. It was very good for my self-image and I learned that I had a lot of staying power.'

For many people, their exploration of space results in developmental changes to their senses of identity, not just a clearer awareness of their existing identity. For example, people may acquire new traits and qualities, they may develop new conceptions as to how given social roles should be fulfilled, and they may acquire new affiliations to certain social groups. It is not a matter of replacing certain identity characteristics with others; rather, it is a question of expansion and development. Bhabha (1990) uses the term 'hybridity' in relation to this, and labels the spaces in which hybrid identities can develop as 'third spaces'. These are 'heterogeneous relational spaces' (Soja 1989, cited by Fougère 2008) or 'heterotopias' that are 'capable of juxtaposing in a single real place several spaces, several sites that are in themselves incompatible' (Foucault 1986). Others (e.g. Kim 2001) refer to this process as 'becoming intercultural' or developing an 'intercultural personhood'. A key practical application question is how third spaces or heterotopias can be facilitated, and how hybridity or intercultural personhood can be nurtured.

Concept 7.9   Becoming intercultural

For me the importance of hybridity is not to be able to trace two original moments from which the third emerges, rather hybridity to me is the 'Third Space', which enables other positions to emerge.
(Bhabha 1990: 211)

Becoming intercultural [...] is a continuous process of psychic transformation in which the person 'brings all parts within himself together into a complete and harmonious whole that is organically in order' (Kao 1975: 33).
(Kim 2001: 194)

The process of becoming intercultural is not one of having to replace one culture with another. It is, instead, a 'working through' of all cultural experiences, so as to create new constructs – that is, constructs that did not exist previously.
(Kim 2001: 196)

7.3   Adaptation and the social context

The discussion in the last section illustrates an important challenge that people face in adapting to unfamiliar cultures: how to manage (cognitively and affectively) the interrelationship between the 'old' and the 'new' culture. Berry (e.g., Berry and Sam 1997) suggests that people face two fundamental questions in relation to this: (1) how much value they attach to maintenance of their heritage cultural identity and characteristics, and (2) how much value they attach to building/maintaining relationships with the larger society. He has proposed a very well known acculturation framework which maps people's different combinations of preferences over these two issues (Figure 7.1).

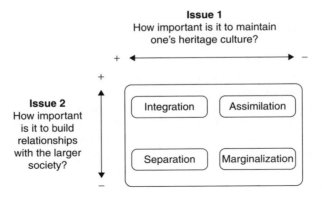

Figure 7.1   Berry's acculturation orientations (based on Berry and Sam 1997: 296).

However, as Berry (2006) rightly points out, people cannot necessarily pursue independently their preferred acculturation orientations; they are also constrained or facilitated by the preferences of others. For example, people can only pursue integration or separation if other members of their cultural group similarly want to maintain their heritage culture. Perhaps even more importantly, the attitudes and social policies of the dominant group may restrict people's opportunities for integration. He explains this as follows:

> [...] integration [...] can only be freely chosen and successfully pursed by non-dominant groups when the dominant society is open and inclusive in its orientation towards cultural diversity [...]. Thus a mutual accommodation is required for integration to be attained, involving the acceptance by both dominant and non-dominant groups of the right of all groups to live as culturally different peoples within the same society. This strategy requires non-dominant groups to adopt the basic values of the larger society, while at the same time the dominant group must be prepared to adapt national institutions (e.g., education, health, labor) to meet better the needs of all groups now living together in the plural society. This latter arrangement [...] [is] called multiculturalism.
>
> (Berry 2006: 35–6)

Unfortunately, however, the policy of multiculturalism does not necessarily promote integration, as societies across the developed world have experienced and as a number of opinion leaders around the world have recently argued. For example, Sir Trevor Phillips, Chair of the Commission for Racial Equality in the United Kingdom, and George Alagiah, a prominent British journalist who was born in Sri Lanka, both argue that multiculturalism has led to segregated communities and economic disadvantage for many (Quote 7.1). In addition, 'local' people often dislike the policy, feeling that it is 'unfair' (e.g., a belief that local authorities give priority to immigrants in allocating social housing, etc.) and that it is undermining their traditional customs and ways of life. This fuels prejudice which exacerbates the situation. The British experience is only one example of how the processes of acculturation raise broader social and political questions, and how these questions provoke often heated discussion in those countries of the world that are facing increasing cultural heterogenization.

Quote 7.1   Multiculturalism: integration or segregation?

The philosophy of multiculturalism begins by defining people as different and then treating them differently. This lazy ambition, where we have a rich diversity of peoples who make little or no effort to reach out to each other, is insufficient [...] Some communities have found it difficult to break out of their isolated clusters, leaving them culturally and sometimes even physically ring-fenced within cities. In these segregated ghettos minority communities can feel intimidated and under siege, and even neighbouring majority communities can feel excluded, so the two simply never meet or learn to appreciate each other.

(Phillips 2004)

Throughout the seventies and eighties [in Britain] local authorities up and down the country followed suit – setting up race relations units, drawing up equal opportunity policies and, crucially, funnelling tax-payers' money towards myriad groups based on ethnicity. This flow of cash created a perverse incentive for communities to show just how different they were. Instead of encouraging [...] 'mutual tolerance' [...], multiculturalism began to encourage something entirely different – ethnic exclusivity. [...] Multiculturalism, with its emphasis on diversity and cultural retention, has been a poor medium through which to tackle economic disadvantage. Segregation alone is bad enough, but when it is coupled with poverty its effect can be truly poisonous [...]. For those people caught between the twin evils of racism and penury, marginalized socially and geographically, multiculturalism is failing to deliver what it promised all those years ago.

(Alagiah 2006: 191, 211)

What, then, can be done about this? Phillips (2004) recommends two types of strategies:

- public policy initiatives that will bring communities closer together physically (e.g., ensuring supermarkets, schools and other services are built to be shared between communities and not for one at the expense of the other);
- cultural interaction initiatives that will help people from different communities to understand each other.

Both of these work on the assumption that contact is the key to promoting integration. Contact is certainly a prerequisite, but it is insufficient in itself (Concept 7.10). Research indicates that the conditions of contact need to be managed, and that people need to be helped to reap the benefits of the contact. So we turn to these practical concerns in Part 2 of this book and explore the various ways in which this can be achieved.

Concept 7.10   Bochner on the contact hypothesis

[...] the 'contact hypothesis' [...] is based on the belief that inter-ethnic conflict is fuelled by ignorance of each other's cultures. It is assumed that once culturally diverse individuals come into contact with each other, through their interactions each will get to know the other's point of view, leading to better mutual understanding, greater tolerance and better cross-cultural acceptance. However, the evidence regarding the contact hypothesis [...] is mixed. That is because cross-cultural contact promotes better inter-group relations only under quite specific conditions. These include equal status of the participants; no history of inter-group conflict; both parties gaining a benefit from the interaction; and that the meetings are a pleasant experience for everyone taking part. If these conditions are not met, then the contact can intensify existing hostility and increase ethnocentrism.

(Bochner 2006: 188)

Berry's model has been applied in adapted form to another area of intensive intercultural interaction, namely to organizations that come into being when one company merges with or acquires another, a situation which is further complicated when these mergers and acquisitions (M & As) take place across national borders. Nahavandi and Malekzadeh (1988) describe four possible results of M & As at the cultural level: deculturation (the old culture is discarded or a new one is adopted); assimilation (members of an organization adopt the culture of the other); separation (original cultures are retained); integration (some cultural change takes place in both organizations).

Acculturative stress results when there is no agreement as to how to proceed after the M & A has taken place or when the desire on one side to retain a culture is challenged by a strong desire on the other for integration. This can result in resistance to acculturation and conflict between the merging organizations. One of the key tasks for those developing intercultural interaction competence is to enable individuals and organizations to address these problems, for example, in the form of bi- or multicultural team building.

Cultural due diligence – an audit of the cultural conditions prevailing in the two companies before merger – to accompany the usual financial, legal and commercial due diligence processes is a desirable, but rare way of preparing organizations for the cultural challenges ahead and is a strongly research-oriented area in which interculturalists can expand their portfolio of knowledge-intensive services.

7.4   Concluding comments

In this chapter we have focused on the affective and cognitive adjustments that people need to make when they cross cultures for extended periods of time. We have argued that people need to manage stress, deal with threats to their identities, develop new understandings of themselves, and handle social contexts that may be more or less welcoming. Yet all this should not, and cannot, be a one-sided process. Integration requires mutual involvement – newcomers and hosts both need to take responsibility for facilitating the process. In Part 2 of the book, we explore some of the practical steps that can be taken to promote adaptation and the development of ICIC.

Suggestions for further reading

Ward, C., Bochner, S. and Furnham, A. (2001) *The Psychology of Culture Shock*, 2nd edn. Hove: Routledge. This book provides a clear and detailed discussion of issues associated with crossing cultures. It contains numerous references to interesting studies.

Kim, Y. Y. (2001) *Becoming Intercultural*. London: Sage. This book presents an integrative theory of cross-cultural adaptation that places particular importance on communication. A summary of the theory is available in:

Kim, Y. Y. (2005) Adapting to a new culture: An integrative communication theory. In W. B. Gudykunst (ed.) *Theorizing about Intercultural Communication*, pp. 375–400. London: Sage.

Hoffman, E. (1989) *Lost in Translation*. London: Vintage. This autobiography movingly describes the experiences that the author went through when she was exiled from Poland as a child and needed to build a new life in America.

Alagiah, G. (2006) *A Home from Home: From Immigrant Boy to English Man*. London: Little, Brown. This autobiography not only describes the author's experiences of adjusting to life in Britain but also reports and discusses people's experiences of multiculturalism.

Part 2

Promoting Competence in Intercultural Interaction

8
Assessing Competence in Intercultural Interaction

The ultimate **measure** of a man is not where he stands in moments of comfort and convenience, but where he stands at times of challenge and controversy.

Martin Luther King

Chapter outline

In Part 1 of the book we explored the various ways in which intercultural interaction can be conceptualized, including the interrelationship between culture, interaction processes and interaction competencies. In Part 2 of the book we turn to a related issue: how competence in intercultural interaction can be promoted. In this chapter we explore how such competence can be measured and in the next chapter we consider how it can be developed.

The use of tests and instruments is widespread in applied linguistics and foreign language education. They may have two purposes. On the one hand, they may be used to investigate the mastery of language from a proficiency point of view. On the other, they may be applied in teaching and learning contexts to support the development of the mastery of a language. Similarly, there are instruments which can be used to help both assess and develop ICIC. Some focus on the assessment of people's value orientations (cf. Section 2.2.1); others focus on the assessment of people's ICIC. This chapter overviews a range of both of these types, and suggests guidance criteria for selecting among them. Chapter 9 discusses how they can be used for developmental purposes. In Part 3, Researching Intercultural Interaction, we consider instruments that can be used in research. Chapter 10 presents studies in which assessment of ICIC is a key element of the research and Chapter 11 deals with instruments that can be used for research purposes. Part 4 of this book, Resources, contains a comprehensive list of instruments, including those discussed in this chapter.

8.1   Assessment instruments

We use the term 'assessment instrument' to mean a device, frequently a pencil-and-paper or online questionnaire, which identifies and measures features of an individual's value preferences or of his/her ICIC. (Instruments also exist to assess features at the organizational level and they are very briefly considered at the end of this chapter.) The instruments are very largely *self*-assessment in character, that is they ask the respondent to make an assessment and indicate this assessment by choosing a position on a rating scale.

Assessment instruments thus involve the respondent in the production and collection of the relevant data but they generally do not require the teachers, trainers, consultants or researchers using them to apply their expert knowledge in making the assessment, for example, by comparing samples of intercultural interaction with implicit or explicit behavioural indicators, as is familiar, for example, from oral testing of foreign language proficiency. An exception is the INCA suite of instruments, also discussed below. Some instruments use the assessment of non-expert others, for instance, colleagues (as, for example, in Global View which is also discussed briefly below). However, all instruments clearly demand the greater or lesser involvement of the investigator in conducting the assessment, scoring and interpreting of the results and, when the instrument is used for developmental purposes, passing them on to the respondent as part of a learning process.

In the intercultural field, 'instrument' is a term which is preferable to 'test', given a test's requirements of demonstrable validity and reliability (see below), and also to 'inventory', which for many readers may be unfamiliar in this context, although it is frequently found in the designation of instruments.

Assessment instruments are to be distinguished from other methods of assessment such as written examinations, interviews, case studies, the analysis of narrative diaries, portfolios and observation by trained assessors, which are more usual in the school and university context when it is a matter of judging the learning progress achieved by a pupil or student and/or of certifying levels of competence. In this chapter we focus on assessment instruments, since this method of assessment is likely to be the least familiar to readers coming to intercultural interaction from applied linguistics and language education. However, in Sections 8.5 and 8.6 we also devote some attention to other methods of assessing ICIC which may be more suitable for measuring learning progress and for certification purposes.

8.1.1   Purposes of assessment instruments

The instruments discussed here aim to present a picture of an individual's personal value orientations or their ICIC.

The development of instruments to assess value orientations and ICIC originated in the concerns that US scholars and intercultural developers felt in the 1960s and 1970s. They wanted to *explain* the failure and *predict* the success of individuals working abroad – such as members of the US diplomatic service and Peace Corps volunteers – and thus to *select* people to work more effectively in unfamiliar cultures and to *develop* their abilities in this respect. The internationalization of business has led to the further development of such instruments to satisfy these purposes.

The assessment instruments in current use still have such purposes, although they are now primarily used for broadly pedagogical and development purposes. Self-assessment tools are in themselves a teaching and learning procedure which stimulates greater self-awareness and reflection in an individual and may thus usefully form a phase in a guided development process. This phase will often be at the beginning or in the course of a learning process and signals to the learner and developer alike where strengths and growth potential may lie. This chapter focuses on this diagnostic use of assessment instruments; how they may be used for development purposes will be dealt with more fully in the next chapter.

An assessment instrument of the kind described so far is probably inappropriate as the sole means of assessing growth in competence as a result of a development or learning process in educational contexts such as school or university and as a way of certifying a competence level for a qualification. (As we show in Chapters 9 and 10, they may be used at the end of a learning process by researchers interested in examining the effectiveness of a particular development intervention.) Few, if any, are statistically robust enough to justify the exclusion of the teacher's assessment and, especially in formal educational contexts, forms of assessment which have a close link to the preceding teaching and learning activities are rightly conventional, having as they do a greater face validity (see below) and thus acceptance by learners and teachers alike. Suitable 'instruments' for this purpose, which are rather different in nature to those described so far, are discussed below in Section 8.5.

Statistical and other forms of analysis show that a number of instruments possess the validity and reliability (see below) that allow them to be used with confidence for research purposes, for example, explaining the failure and success of expatriate assignments. A number of instruments have been developed purely or mainly with research purposes in mind and some of these are discussed in Chapter 11.

8.1.2   Criteria to guide the selection of assessment instruments

Clearly, chief among the criteria for selecting an assessment instrument is the extent to which it fulfils the purpose the user has in mind. It is also important that the instrument is reliable and valid in various ways so that the user can be sure that conclusions drawn from the data generated by the instrument are soundly based. This is particularly the case when it is used for research purposes.

The stability of the instrument over time (test-retest reliability) in producing similar results with the same respondent, and the internal consistency of the instrument (split-half reliability) can be examined statistically and an assessment of the instrument's reliability made. It is important for the user to know that the results obtained when applying the instrument are not purely a matter of chance and that the test repeated with the same respondent and in the same conditions will produce adequately similar results.

Users also need to be sure that the instrument measures what it is intended to. Judgements can be made as to what an instrument measures and whether it actually measures what it claims to measure (construct validity). Construct validity is, however, hard to demonstrate because it is necessary (although often difficult) to test the construct more directly than through the instrument itself. Indirect demonstrations of construct validity may include showing that the instrument has a solid conceptual pedigree and that unsound or irrelevant research insights or items in the instrument have been omitted. Depending on the research question, the correlation between the assessment made by the instrument itself and external criteria such as the degree of success in the selected field (predictive validity) may be important.

For development purposes, reliability and validity of the kind discussed above are generally considered to be less crucial than in research. For example, the results of an assessment for development purposes are often discussed with the respondent who thus has a chance to react to, and correct for the developer, what may seem to be a wayward assessment. However, in this situation a different type of validity is important. It is necessary that the questions contained in the instrument are regarded by the respondent as relevant to the dimensions being assessed (face validity). Some items may detract from this face validity. For example, agreement with the perhaps naïve-seeming item taken from the Intercultural Sensitivity Inventory (ICIS) discussed below, 'I decorate my home or office with artefacts from other countries' may indeed be interpreted as indicating a certain openness to culture whereas a negative answer may well be seen as saying more about preferred styles in home decoration than cultural open-mindedness. If an instrument does not have face validity, there is a danger that the respondent will not complete the questionnaire or will not accept the assessment that results. The latter is problematic as assessment instruments are used as a development tool to form the starting point for a process of reflection, introspection and learning. However, if an instrument is being used for the purpose of personnel selection rather than development, face validity should be lower because transparent questions may lead to respondents choosing answers to suit the questioner's intentions.

The topic that the instrument focuses on is a further criterion to be taken into account when choosing an appropriate instrument. The range of topics covered is very broad; here we shall restrict our discussion to those which assess value orientations on the one hand, and some of the myriad aspects of ICIC on the other.

A final criterion to be considered is cost. Some instruments can be obtained at no greater cost to the user than the printed medium in which they are published. An example of such an instrument is the Cross-Cultural Adaptability Inventory discussed below. Other instruments, such as the International Profiler, also presented below, may require the involvement of third parties in the administering, scoring and feedback process and are therefore more expensive. Such factors also influence availability: some instruments are clearly readily available while others can be used only by trained consultants who have acquired certification after taking part in a sometimes costly training course.

The variety and number of instruments available is unsurprisingly very great. Paige (2004: 85–128) lists 30 instruments for personal assessment and development alone. The SIETAR Europa documentation centre (http://www.sietar-europa.org/SIETARproject/index.html) listed more than 50 at the time of going to press. Section 12.5 of the resources chapter of this book contains a list totalling 77 instruments, including references and details of providers. Readers wanting more comprehensive and systematic guidance in choosing a particular instrument are advised to consult Paige's review.

8.2   Assessing value orientations

A number of instruments assess the respondents' value preferences in relation to the dimensions/orientations that can vary across cultures (see Chapter 2). The use of this kind of instrument in research contexts is described in Section 11.1.2. Here we deal with the development context.

Instruments with this purpose are often proprietary instruments developed by training organizations and are therefore not easily available for scrutiny by outsiders not paying for a training programme or other intervention. They are often designed to dovetail into the training content, in the area of awareness raising and cultural knowledge which rely on the work of Hofstede, Trompenaars and Hall. Such work tends to form the conceptual framework for much culture-general development and indeed – for better or worse – for some culture-specific development. This is elaborated on in the next chapter.

Such instruments may be useful in raising awareness of the culturally-based values and preferences an individual may have, of the existence of differences between individuals and cultural groups, and of the dimensions underlying such differences. They may thus contribute to the development of (a) self-awareness and (b) specific cultural knowledge (knowledge both of one's own culture and of a target culture or cultures), which are two of the key dimensions of ICIC discussed in Chapter 3. They may also predict a cultural fit, or lack of it, for interaction with specific cultures. However, they do not as such make a statement about a respondent's ICIC. Moreover, although they may sensitize the respondent to issues that may occur in interaction with members of a new culture, they offer no solutions and, by possibly suggesting cultural fit, they may predict a comfort in interaction which the respondent may not experience. This also begs the question of whether cultural fit is actually desirable in intercultural interaction or whether cultural unfit may in fact be more suitable for generating the synergies, creativity and potential intercultural interaction is believed to offer.

A further criticism of the use of such instruments for development purposes is that they do not equip respondents with any insights about possible areas for personal growth.

An example of an instrument which attempts to assess respondents' value orientations is the Value Orientations Survey (Instrument 8.1). It forms a part of the Value Orientations Method and is based on the work of Kluckhohn and Strodtbeck (1961/1973) (see Section 2.2.2). The instrument itself is reproduced as an appendix in Russo (2000a), which also contains a detailed description of how to analyse the data collected, a sample analysis and guidelines on administering and modifying the survey.

There are published reports of the survey being used for development purposes in areas as diverse as the language classroom (Ortuno 1991, 2000), mental health care (Spiegel and Papajohn 2000) and conflict resolution (Gallagher 2000). There is little information about its reliability and validity and it seems that the Values Orientations Survey has only rarely been used for research purposes (e.g., Yau 1994).

Instrument 8.1   The Value Orientations Survey (VOS)

The Value Orientations Survey is based on a theoretical framework, which in turn rests on three assumptions:

1. There is a limited number of problems in life for which all people must find solutions.
2. The solutions that exist are neither limitless nor random but vary according to value orientation.
3. The possible value orientations exist in all people and cultures but are preferred to different degrees.

The order of preference for the possible solutions profiles the value orientations of the individual and the individual's group.

The value orientations examined in the survey are described in detail, for example, in Russo (2000b: 8–13) and paraphrased here:

Person-Nature Value Orientation

Mastery Over   Human beings can and should exercise total control over the forces of nature within and around them.

Harmony With   Human beings can and should seek a balance of control with the forces of nature.

Subject To   Human beings have little or no control over these forces.

Time Value Orientation

Past   The focus is on the past, and on preserving or restoring traditional teachings and beliefs.

Present   The focus is on the present, and on accommodating changes in beliefs and traditions.

Future   The temporal focus is on the future, on seeking out change and new ways to replace the old.

Activity Value Orientation

Doing   Meaning is found in activities which lead to concrete rewards valued by the individual and the group.

Being   Meaning is found in activities which lead to intangible rewards that satisfy the need of the individual or group for the spontaneous expression of impulse and desire.

The Being-in-Becoming dimension (see Concept 2.7) is not included in the VOS.

Human Relations Value Orientation

Collaterality   Emphasis is placed on consensus, reciprocity and participation in decisions that affect the group.

Lineality   Emphasis is placed on hierarchical principles and deferring to higher authority in the group.

Individualism   Emphasis is placed on independent action and independent decision-making.

The original survey contained these four dimensions and did not include the dimension referred to as 'Belief about basic human nature' (see Section 2.2.2). Later surveys, developed by other social scientists, include this fifth orientation.

The items in the survey, which the developers recommend is administered orally (Russo 2000b: 15), consist of a brief description of a situation followed by a description of a number of possible ways to react to it from which respondents have to choose the 'best' or 'most true' answer. Some of the situations have been made famous to management audiences by the work of Trompenaars and Hampden-Turner (1997). Here is an example called Ways of Living, which examines the activity orientation of the respondent:

There were two people talking about how they liked to live. They had different ideas.

1) One said, 'What I care about most is accomplishing things – getting things done just as well or better than other people do them. I like to see results and think they are worth working for.

2) The other said, 'What I care most about is to be left alone to think and act in the ways that best suit the way I really am. If I don't always get much done but can enjoy life as I go along, that is the best way.'

Which of these two people do you think has the better way of thinking?
Which of these two people are you really most like?
Which kind of these two people do you think most other people in _____(your family, group, or community) would think has the better idea?

(Russo 2000a: 208)

Another example, called Ceremonial Innovation, examines the respondent's orientation to time:

Some people in a community like your own saw that the religious ceremonies were changing from what they used to be.

1) Some people were really pleased because of the changes in religious ceremonies. They felt that new ways are usually better than old ones, and they like to keep everything – even ceremonies – moving ahead.

2) Some people were unhappy because of the change. They felt that religious ceremonies should be kept exactly – in every way – as they had been in the past.

3) Some people felt that the old ways for religious ceremonies were best but you just can't hang on to them. It makes life easier just to accept some changes as they come along.

Which of these three felt most nearly what you believe is right?
Which of the other two do you think is most right?
Which of the three ways do you think most other people in _____ (your family, group, community) would say is most right?
Which of the three ways do you think most _____ (people in another group, community or cultural group) would say is most right?

(Russo 2000a: 207)

The development aim is initiated as with all instruments by the mere answering of the questions but can be continued in workshops which follow the interviews. Similarities and differences in individual and group orientations can be discussed and understanding of and for difference created.

Some instruments may also take account of the interactional orientations and styles described by Parsons and Shils (1951), again popularized by Trompenaars and Hampden-Turner (1997) and by Hall (1976, 1983), again also in part adopted by Trompenaars and Hampden-Turner (1997).

Examples of more recent proprietary instruments of this kind are: the Intercultural Awareness Profiler available to clients of Trompenaars-Hampden-Turner Consulting; the Cultural Orientations Indicator, which is part of the Cultural Navigator available to clients of TMC; the Worldprism Profiler available from TMA; and the Intercultural Personality Test available from ICUnet AG, details of all of which can be found in Chapter 12.

To what extent they are valid and/or reliable instruments is generally unknown because studies do not exist or the results of them are not readily available. They have rarely been the subject of investigation in cooperation with independent researchers. Indeed, a forerunner of the Intercultural Awareness Profiler instrument was at the centre of a bitter dispute between Hofstede and Trompenaars. In an article entitled 'Riding the Waves of Commerce', a provocative allusion to Trompenaars' best-selling book, Hofstede (1996) raises concerns about Trompenaars' conclusions and his methodology. After correlation and factor analysis of the data, Hofstede claims that the instrument Trompenaars used lacked content validity.

8.3 Assessing intercultural interaction competence

As a result of the multi-faceted nature of ICIC, which we discussed in Chapter 3, there is a correspondingly large variety of instruments which can claim to assess some element of ICIC. Paige's taxonomy (2004: 94) lists some of them: intercultural development; cultural identity; learning styles; global awareness and worldmindedness; cultural adjustment, culture shock and cultural adaptation; intercultural and multicultural competence; prejudice and racism.

This variety also reflects the increasing internationalization of society, driven not only by increasing flows of economic and refugee migrants but also by the massive increase in cross-border business activity and a concomitant increase in its complexity. It is this latter development which has led to the development of more instruments which attempt to provide data mainly for development purposes but also for research into the complexity of intercultural interaction.

This kind of assessment captures a person's views of selected affective, behavioural and cognitive components of his/her ICIC. The use of this 'picture' to give feedback skilfully and sensitively to a trainee can contribute to the development of ICIC. The creation of self-awareness (in itself a crucial component of ICIC), making clear where strengths and deficits may lie, and pointing out developmental strategies and techniques, are the key objectives of instruments assessing ICIC. Such instruments can initiate a process of introspection and/or lead to group learning activities or to the implementation of a personal development plan to support learning and development. We present two such instruments here. A further instrument which can be used both for developmental and research purposes is described in Section 11.2.2.

The Cross-Cultural Adaptability Inventory

Mainly suitable for tackling the issues of cultural adaptation and culture shock, the 50-item, self-assessment Cross-Cultural Adaptability Inventory (CCAI) (Instrument 8.2) was developed by Colleen Kelley and Judith E. Meyers, who describe it as 'a training instrument designed to give feedback to an individual about his or her potential for cross-cultural effectiveness' (Kelley and Myers 1993: 1).

Instrument 8.2   The Cross-Cultural Adaptability Inventory

The CCAI is based on a set of what the developers describe as skills or skill sets derived from a survey of the research literature in psychology, communication and international management, much of it already reviewed in Chapter 3, and which have been shown to be critical for adapting to other cultures. The four skill sets are:

emotional resilience with items in the inventory focusing on coping with stress and ambiguity, bouncing back from imperfections and mistakes, trying new things and experiences; and interacting with people in new or unfamiliar situations;

flexibility/openness with items focusing on a liking for and interest in people and ideas different from oneself, tolerance and nonjudgementalness and flexibility;

perceptual acuity with items focusing on attention to verbal and non-verbal communication cues and skills and their accurate interpretation across cultures;

personal autonomy with items focusing on values, belief and personal identity in the context of unfamiliar cultures and divergent values.

The inventory is a self-report instrument that requires people to respond to statements about cross-cultural adaptability along a six-point Likert scale, ranging from 'Definitely true about me right now' to 'Definitely not true about me right now'.

As examples of the kind of items included in the CCAI, we present the first ten items of the instrument:

I have ways to deal with the stresses of new situations.
I believe I could live a fulfilling life in another culture.

I try to understand people's thought's and feelings when I talk to them.
I feel confident in my ability to cope with life, no matter where I am.
I can enjoy relating to all kinds of people.
I believe that I can accomplish what I set out to do, even in unfamiliar settings.
I can laugh at myself when I make a cultural faux pas (mistake).
I like being with all kinds of people.
I have a realistic perception of how others see me.
When I am working with people of a different cultural background, it is important
to me to receive their approval.

It is available both online and in a self-scoring format. In the latter, a circle graph portrays the person's scores in the four skill sets and compares them with each other. The developers explain that 'it is most effective when used as part of a training event – both as a means of developing self-understanding [...] and as a take-off point for further awareness and skill training' (Kelley and Meyers 1993: 1), this latter use being a variety of needs analysis.

The CCAI is available with a handbook that gives background information on the development of the tool, the insights and theories on which it is based and the statistical data supporting it. Training tools are available that provide a full-day training design, as well as follow-up materials in the form of an action-planning guide and a participant workbook. A 360° feedback version is also available.

A weakness of the CCAI reported by some intercultural trainers concerns the somewhat transparent nature of the statements which have to be responded to. Statements such as 'I believe that all cultures have something worthwhile to offer' and 'I try to understand people's thoughts and feelings when I talk to them' could well prompt answers which are more socially desirable than honest and therefore unlikely to make a meaningful contribution to the profile created.

The fact that the Inventory is not available in other languages may also be a disadvantage: an informal test of the comprehension of the statements among German first-semester students of English studies who had learned English at school for between six and nine years, revealed considerable difficulties in understanding.

Ward, Berno and Main (2002), in their presentation of two studies of the CCAI, showed that the four dimensions of the CCAI relate to psychological and sociocultural dimensions of sojourner adjustment. Their findings 'suggest that the instrument can be used effectively as a training tool to prepare sojourners for cross-cultural transitions. Specifically, it can be employed to provide realistic feedback on an individual's strengths and weaknesses, to identify training needs in these areas, and to predict potential for successful adaptation' (Ward, Berno and Main 2002: 421).

In contrast, Davis and Finney (2006: 328), who conducted a factor-analytic study of the CCAI, conclude with the damning judgement that the CCAI should 'not be used to assess the cross-cultural adaptability of any population until it has been studied more extensively. Further work at both the construct and item level seems necessary. Subsequent refinement and/or development of this instrument needs to be clearly tied to theory and supported by empirical evidence.' Clearly, such a conclusion does not necessarily place the usability of CCAI as a *development instrument* in doubt but underlines the need for the psychometric properties of all such instruments to have been thoroughly investigated if they are to be used for research purposes.

The International Profiler (TIP) and Global View 360

Using the framework of ten international competencies, broken down into 22 dimensions, outlined at the end of Chapter 3, WorldWork Ltd have developed two instruments to assess aspects of ICIC: the International Profiler (TIP) and Global View 360 (Instrument 8.3).

Instrument 8.3 The International Profiler (TIP) and Global View 360

The International Profiler (TIP) consists of an online, normed psychometric questionnaire, together with a Feedback Book, a Coaching Manual and other development materials, based on a set of competencies identified as enabling their possessors 'to become rapidly effective in unfamiliar cultural settings' as the WorldWork Ltd Website[1] puts it. It is available in English, French, German and Italian, a considerable advantage for its target audience in international business.

The purpose of the International Profiler is, according to the developers' website, 'to help managers and professionals understand where they typically put the emphasis when working internationally. It helps to raise their awareness of potential areas in which they may require future development, and suggests actions they can take to fill the gaps.' The developers emphasize that the International Profiler is not a selection tool and indeed not 'a hard-edged assessment tool', but is developmental in character and forms 'the basis for a structured exploration of an individual's international competency requirements'[2].

The set of ten competencies, which is broken down further into a total of 22 dimensions (see Concept 3.7), was derived from an examination of a wide range of relevant research literature covering insights from psychology, applied linguistics and management science amongst others, much of it discussed in Chapter 3. The competencies and their dimensions include factors which change and can be developed only slowly and with difficulty, such as values and motivational traits, as well as those which are easier to develop, such as knowledge and skills. The competencies with the related dimensions in brackets are as follows:

Openness (New thinking – Welcoming strangers – Acceptance)
Flexibility (Flexible behaviour – Flexible judgement – Learning languages)
Personal autonomy (Inner purpose – Focus on goals)
Emotional strength (Resilience – Coping – Spirit of adventure)
Perceptiveness (Attuned – Reflected awareness)
Listening orientation (Active listening)
Transparency (Clarity of communication – Exposing intentions)
Cultural knowledge (Information gathering – Valuing differences)
Influencing (Rapport – Range of styles – Sensitivity to context)
Synergy (Creating new alternatives)

Whereas some of these terms are self-explanatory, others are less so and readers are advised to consult Section 3.4.2, and the very informative WorldWork Ltd website for clarification. (See also Chapters 4–7 which expand on many of these competencies.)

The questionnaire, which is generally filled in online, has 80 items, each consisting of a stem and three ways of completing the statement. The respondents are required to select the completion which best describes them, their behaviour or their attitudes, and then to select the second-best completion in the same way. The respondents are asked to score their first choice with a 5 or a 4 depending on how accurate a description they think it is, and in the same way they have to score their second choice with a 3 or 2. The third completion, which though unchosen by the respondent is also a statement about the accuracy of the description, is left un-scored. There are approximately ten statements which refer to each of the 22 dimensions.

An example of an item which is used in presentations of the tool is as follows:

	MOST	NEXT
When travelling abroad I		
a. think about the impression I make on local people	☐5 ☐4	☐3 ☐2
b. adapt to the local way of doing things	☐5 ☐4	☐3 ☐2
c. actively find out about the country and its people	☐5 ☐4	☐3 ☐2

The feedback on the results of the questionnaire responses is given by a trained and licensed developer or consultant, on the basis of two graphics depicting the profile of the respondent. The graphics are generated by the provider and are sent by email to the person giving the feedback, who then discusses them with the respondent so that they can contribute to that person's personal development. An interpretive report of 25 to 30 pages explaining the profile in detail and outlining the advantages and disadvantages of the highest and lowest scores among the 22 dimensions can also be generated at extra cost.

One of the graphics shows the respondent's ranged scores, i.e. the extent on a scale of 1 to 100 to which s/he places more or less emphasis on a particular competence when working internationally, and the other graphic (see below) shows normed scores, i.e. how the respondent's scores compare with those of all the other respondents recorded in the database or with selected sub-groups. Thus the score of 9 indicated in the right-hand column of the normed profile below indicates that 91 percent of the other respondents scored higher on the New Thinking dimension of the Openness competence (Figure 8.1).

As of November 2008 the norm base contains information from more than 4000 International Profiler questionnaires.

The primary strength of TIP lies in the fact that it does not deliver an overall assessment, with all the negative connotations of a single verdict, but a differentiated profile of a person with respect to the emphasis and attention paid to each of the 22 dimensions in the competency set.

A second strength is the high face validity of the instrument. In the eyes of the respondents, the items and the competencies profiled clearly relate to management in international settings as they experience it. Indeed, respondents often comment on the general rather than international management character of many of the competencies. This characteristic of TIP lends it a high degree of credibility in the eyes of respondents who otherwise may be sceptical of the value of an intercultural assessment.

A weakness may be its lack of validation. WorldWork Ltd writes on its website that it 'is currently seeking opportunities to carry out full reliability and validity tests, and will be pleased to work with any organisation willing to provide the necessary facilities to enable this to take place'. Such investigations were in progress at the time of writing.

It remains to be seen whether TIP sets a trend for instruments which offer multi-faceted assessments of more than the usual four or six components of competence or effectiveness. Instruments which offer a wider range of categories than, for example, the single stage of intercultural development yielded by the Intercultural Development Inventory (IDI) (see Section 11.2.2) are a response to changing development settings. How TIP can be used in a developmental setting will be described in the next chapter.

Based on the same framework of competencies, Global View, according to the WorldWork Ltd website, is 'a panoramic version of the International Profiler. It can be used by individuals wishing to obtain feedback from international colleagues, clients, friends etc. who have been able to work with them, or directly observe them working across international boundaries'. In this way it can help 'an individual to understand the impact that he or she makes on people from different cultures, as a basis for personal growth and development'.

The International Profiler

Normed Profile

Mimi Lee

Emphasis	LOW	LOW-MID	MID-RANGE	HIGH-MID	HIGH

Openness

Scale: 5 10 15 20 25 30 35 40 45 50 55 60 65 70 75 80 85 90 95 99 | Score

Dimension	Score
New Thinking	9
Welcoming Strangers	25
Acceptance	7

Flexibility

Dimension	Score
Flexible Behaviour	95
Flexible Judgement	16
Learning Languages	66

Personal Autonomy

Dimension	Score
Inner Purpose	97
Focus on Goals	99

Emotional Strength

Dimension	Score
Resilience	83
Coping	67
Spirit of Adventure	52

Perceptiveness

Dimension	Score
Attuned	87
Reflected Awareness	36

Listening Orientation

Dimension	Score
Active Listening	41

Transparency

Dimension	Score
Clarity of Communication	30
Exposing Intentions	46

Cultural Knowledge

Dimension	Score
Information Gathering	55
Valuing Differences	74

Influencing

Dimension	Score
Rapport	32
Range of Styles	66
Sensitivity to Context	43

Synergy

Dimension	Score
Creating New Alternatives	66

Emphasis	LOW	LOW-MID	MID-RANGE	HIGH-MID	HIGH

© WorldWork Limited 2002

Figure 8.1 The page from an International Profiler report which shows the participant's normed scores across 22 dimensions.

In contrast to conventional 360 degree instruments, the user can choose how s/he groups the observers, so that, for example s/he may ask for feedback from foreign colleagues s/he is working with. The website explains that the 'feedback from these different nationalities can be grouped together, so that the user will then receive feedback which separately identifies the views of people from different countries or regions'. Global View thus meets the need seen by Hammer (1989: 254) for 'competence judgments from significant others' to be included in ICIC assessment procedures.

8.4 Assessing both value orientations and intercultural interaction competence

Some instruments claim to assess both value orientations and elements of ICIC. We present one example here.

Instrument 8.4 Intercultural Sensitivity Inventory (ICIS)

The Intercultural Sensitivity Inventory (ICSI) ICSI is a self-scoring, 46-item, self-report instrument in which respondents react to a set of items on a Likert-type seven-point scale. The instrument assesses the constructs of **individualism, collectivism, flexibility** and **open-mindedness**. The instrument can be used to raise respondents' awareness of certain cultural value orientations and of their flexibility and open-mindedness when it comes to encounters with unfamiliar cultures.

Items are divided into three sections. In the first section, respondents are required to respond to items by imagining that they are living and working in the United States. In the second section they are required to respond to the same set of items by imagining they are living in Japan. Whereas the items in the first two sections measure individualism and collectivism, those of the third section refer to flexibility and open-mindedness. The developers of the ICIS write that 'All of the items were written to capture behaviours rather than attitudes or traits. This was done to avoid obtaining responses that would be limited to a cognitive level' (Bhawuk and Brislin 1992: 420).

Examples of items assessing individualism are: 'I prefer to be direct and forthright when dealing with people' and 'To increase sales, I would announce that the individual salesperson with the highest sales would be given the "Distinguished Salesperson" award'. Examples of items assessing collectivism are 'I am very modest when talking about my own achievements' and 'If I want a person to perform a certain task I try to show how the task will benefit others in the person's group'. Examples from the third section are 'Given acceptable hygienic conditions, I would not mind if my children ate local food at school, when I am living in another country' and 'I do not like to meet foreigners'.

Bhawuk and Brislin (1992) report on a study of two groups which gives statistical evidence of the soundness of the assessments undertaken with the instrument.

8.5   Assessing intercultural interaction competence in the school and university education context

The school-level national curricula for modern foreign languages in a number of countries (e.g., England, Germany) identify intercultural competence as a key objective; however, there are often no specific attainment targets for this element of the curriculum, and no clear guidelines as to how it should be assessed (Cf. Section 9.3.1). Byram (1997) makes a number of suggestions as to modes of assessment – test, test simulation, continuous assessment, coursework and portfolio and supplies some concrete examples, but these do not seem to have found their way to any great extent into the assessment of intercultural interaction competence in the school context. The LACE study,[3] which examined the development of intercultural competence in compulsory foreign language education in 12 nations in Europe and which was conducted in 2007 for the European Commission, found that whereas the curricula investigated generally prescribed relatively vaguely formulated objectives to be attained by language learners in the area of intercultural competence, levels of attainment and assessment methods were not described in any useable detail or clarity. The teachers surveyed in the same study reported that both the development and assessment of intercultural competence tended to be neglected not least because of a lack of guidance in their professional education and in the curricula they had to follow. (Intercultural competence development in the school context is dealt with in greater detail in Section 9.4 of the next chapter.)

At university level, courses in intercultural interaction/communication are becoming increasingly more widespread, and include undergraduate level 'global citizenship' skills training courses as well as more specialized master's degree courses in intercultural communication/studies. In addition, study abroad opportunities are often assessed from an ICIC point of view. Assessment of ICIC is therefore an important issue within the education sector, and includes both formative and summative assessment.

Portfolios are increasingly being used for assessment purposes in a range of contexts, including in universities. When a portfolio is used for assessment purposes, a collection of a learner's work and experience document his/her learning progress and achievement, and this collection of evidence is evaluated. Here we briefly consider the use of a *portfolio* in the assessment of ICIC.

Concept 8.1   Portfolio assessment

a purposeful collection of a learner's work assembled over time that documents one's efforts, progress, and achievements.
(MacIsaac and Jackson 1994: 64)

[...] portfolio assessment recognises that learning is not always easily quantifiable, and calls on students to demonstrate their learning by selecting and presenting examples of their best work.
(Jacobson, Sleicher and Burke 1999: 467)

The main advantage of portfolio assessment is that it allows an individual student's growth to be demonstrated. It is a personalised approach and takes a longitudinal view of the learning process.
(Ingulsrud et al. 2002: 479)

The use of a portfolio to document competence allows a combination of atomised and holistic assessment. It also provides the means of maintaining a close relationship between testing and teaching since some documentation would be chosen from the teaching and learning process.
(Byram 1997: 107)

Learning through a cross-cultural experience involves a multitude of factors. To account for as many factors as possible, an authentic assessment tool like the portfolio is an appropriate approach. [...] An impressionistic evaluation of portfolio contents, together with a quantifiable analysis of a central text, provides a balanced assessment for course evaluation.
(Ingulsrud et al. 2002: 489)

Portfolios are not easy to assess reliably in order to establish degrees of ICIC. Jacobson, Sleicher and Burke (1999), for example, describe portfolio procedures for introducing, developing and evaluating intercultural communication skills among university students learning English as a foreign language. Although they regard it as 'a positive experience for most students and a productive use of class time', they report on the considerable problems they encountered. These include: making the concept and the purpose of the portfolio clear to the students; students' difficulties in describing the cultural knowledge they have acquired and in reflecting on their interactional skills; the time-consuming nature of the portfolio creation; the lack of structure to the task; and evaluating the 'qualitative, holistic nature' of portfolios. When Jacobson, Sleicher and Burke (1999: 491) write, 'We have not even approached the problem of attempting to grade portfolios or incorporating them into a grade for an individual's overall class performance', it becomes clear that the portfolio approach was problematic for them as a means of assessment, even though it may have offered some students valuable learning opportunities.

Ingulsrud and colleagues (2002), on the other hand, propose a method for assessing portfolios that they claim has worked well. Using a critical text analysis approach, they illustrate how a piece of written work can be examined for 'recognition' and 'reflection'. They explain it as follows:

> We developed a method of critically examining the reports. This involved going through the text and locating instances where students noticed or 'recognized' spaces, items, events, or behaviors that to them were significant. [...] Based then on their recognition, we checked to see whether there was any 'reflection' on the 'recognition'. Reflection involves relating what they observed to something in their own culture, life, or plans for the future.
>
> (Ingulsrud et al. 2002: 480)

The authors describe how they worked out a quantitative measure of the amount of recognition and of reflection displayed in a student report, and they suggest a formula for calculating overall cross-cultural awareness. They used two raters to do this, and found interrater reliability to be satisfactory. Ingulsrud and colleagues conclude:

> The approach we have developed to assess cross-cultural experience has found acceptance in our institution because it accommodates the personal and multifaceted nature of the experience on the one hand, and on the other, the need for a rigorous measure of what has been attained.
>
> (2002: 489)

8.6   Assessing intercultural interaction competence for certification purposes

The combination of atomized and holistic assessment put forward by Byram (see Concept 3.5) is particularly appropriate when it comes to the bench-marking of ICIC for certification purposes:

> A portfolio would [...] allow levels to be set for each component and for holistic performance, with criteria specifying levels of attainment

appropriately for each competence and savoir. A portfolio also allows a combination of criterion-referenced documentation with objective, norm-referenced tests if this is thought desirable, for example where the portfolio is to be used as a passport to further education opportunities.

(Byram 1997: 107)

It is this conceptualization of the portfolio which provides the methodological framework for the INCA approach to benchmarking assessment. On the basis of a grid of ICIC competencies (see Concept 3.6), the INCA project has developed a Portfolio and a suite of tools for assessment purposes.

In contrast to most intercultural instruments, which are usually in the form of self-assessment, the INCA approach includes assessment by observers. There are two reasons for including assessment by observers. Firstly, it is assumed that being well-motivated and possessing a sound knowledge of intercultural competence, which may influence the way in which people assess themselves (so goes the argument), do not necessarily translate into effective behaviour. Secondly, self-assessment tools may prompt socially acceptable answers rather than a more objective assessment. Connections between the project and the Council of Europe's European Language Portfolio and its assessment model also meant that behavioural assessment needed to be included.

What emerged was a combination of two different assessment procedures. On the one hand, written exercises involving scenarios have been developed which are aimed at profiling affective and cognitive aspects of intercultural competence and which can be completed online or offline The nature of the written exercise items is described thus: 'Candidates are presented with critical incidents, along with a series of open-ended questions, such as: "What advice would you give the teams involved for improving their communication?"' (Prechtl and Lund 2007: 483)

On the other hand, group exercises (role plays) have been developed which are aimed at assessing behavioural aspects of intercultural competence and which are described thus: 'the assessees work together in a team with counterparts from another culture. They are observed by trained assessors, who score their behaviour against the INCA grid' (Prechtl and Lund 2007: 483) (see Instrument 8.5). (For more details, see Prechtl and Lund 2007, and http://www. incaproject.org/)

Instrument 8.5   Extract from a completed INCA assessment sheet

Element of intercultural competence: respect for otherness (See Concept 3.6, this volume)

Positive indicators	Score	Negative indicators	Score
Shows respect for values and norms of both interlocutors	+	Describes one person's behaviour in negative terms	
Describes behaviour of both persons in positive / neutral terms	+	Insults the interlocutor	–
Avoids prejudiced statements	+	Makes prejudiced statements	
Takes both parties' views into account	+		
Total score 3+			

The number of pluses (+) or minuses (–) achieved in the total score corresponds to a three-level (basic, intermediate and full) grid of competencies.

(adapted from Prechtl and Lund (2007: 484))

In many respects, the variety of assessment tools in the INCA suite is its unique-selling proposition, yet at the same time it is its most vulnerable aspect. Although behavioural testing may increase the face-validity of the instrument, it raises serious questions about its reliability. Will the procedure produce the same assessment of the assessee when the behaviour is assessed by different assessors and, more critically, when it is repeated with different counterparts from different cultures? Much must depend on the knowledge, skill and experience of the assessors and on their training in the use of the assessment grid.

Questions of validity pose themselves as well: to what extent can a culture-general intercultural competence be assessed on the basis of what would appear to be interaction with members of a restricted selection of probably Europe-biased cultures?

Generally, developers of self-assessment tools are rightly reluctant to recommend the use of their tools for selection and career advancement purposes, especially if they have not been satisfactorily validated. Such reluctance would also seem to be appropriate here until validation has taken place.

The results of the INCA assessment are among the items that can be included in a collection known as the Dossier, a file of evidence to support the individual's own record of his/her learning and competence, which forms a part of the INCA Portfolio.

The other parts of this Portfolio are a Biography section and a Passport section, 'which allow the individual to keep a record of significant intercultural experiences' (Prechtl and Lund 2007: 482) and to 'evaluate his/her experiences, learning and progress' (Prechtl and Lund 2007: 482). Using the INCA grid of six components and three levels (see Concept 8.2), the individual plots his/her 'level' against each competence. 'The INCA Portfolio thus offers the individual a comprehensive means of recording his/her developing intercultural competence' (Prechtl and Lund 2007: 482).

8.7 Assessing and developing value orientations and intercultural interaction competence at the organizational level

This kind of assessment involves taking, not a portrait photograph of an individual, but a group shot which gives an account of circumstances in a particular group or organization. Assessment instruments are increasingly being used for this purpose, and this is understandable, partly in view of the pressure from the continuing internationalization of economic activity: not only individuals but also organizations and their management are challenged in culturally mixed environments, for example in international and supra-national organizations. These contexts may not only question the cultural orientations, values and norms of the individual and require ICIC of him or her, but may also demand an intercultural competence of the organization that the person is a part of, something which clearly raises management questions at the strategic and operational level (in other words, beyond the individual level we are accustomed to in assessment contexts).

This pressure is compounded by the issue of disadvantage. As discussed in Chapter 6, intercultural interaction situations may lead to people being disadvantaged. Acknowledging this kind of disadvantage, drivers of political and social change in Western societies at large are increasingly aiming at more active support for cultural groups in all areas, not only in the more conventional and familiar fields of national or ethnic culture, sometimes referred to in the literature as 'global diversity'. As a result, collective actors are being compelled to examine the extent to which the competence of the organization in question meets the challenges posed at the organizational rather than the individual level in supporting 'domestic diversity', for example, in the areas of gender, physical ability, age and sexual orientation.

Anti-discrimination legislation means that in Europe, too, organizations will increasingly need to demonstrate compliance with legal requirements that outlaw discrimination on the basis of global and domestic diversity and that imply the fostering of such cultural diversity. One possible such indication may be the demonstration of organizational competence and measures for developing diversity management, and intercultural instruments can be employed at the organizational level for this purpose. Examples of such instruments are the Culture for Diversity Inventory (Cooke and Lafferty 1995), Assessing Diversity Climate (Kossek and Zonia 1993) and the University Equal Opportunity Climate Survey (Landis, Dansby and Tallarigo 1996).

The IDI instrument (see Instrument 11.2. and Section 11.2.3) and other related publications (e.g., Hammer, Bennett and Wiseman 2003: 441) state that the IDI can be used to establish group profiles of intercultural competence. In a review of the Bennett (1993) Developmental Model of Intercultural Sensitivity, Bennett and Bennett (2004) focus not as in previous publications on the pedagogical implications of the various stages of the model, but on its organizational implications in a global and domestic diversity context. As a result, it can be inferred that an instrument based on the model, if not the IDI instrument itself, could be used to determine organizational intercultural competence. Indeed, Paige (2004: 88) briefly describes one such use of the IDI in a large metropolitan school district aiming at improving intercultural sensitivity. Similarly, one of us (Franklin), and others have used the International Profiler (see above) to generate group profiles within a rapidly internationalizing company.

However, one question needs to be addressed by research: does the aggregate of the intercultural competence of the members of a group amount to a profile of organizational intercultural competence? In other words, do collective actors such as companies and not-for-profit organizations reflect the competence of the sum of the individual actors residing in it or are organizations capable of actions which display a different (either smaller or greater) competence? Given the significance attached to voluntary corporate codes of conduct or to strategies guiding, for instance, corporate and social responsibility, and indeed in view of legislation on corporate governance, the answer may well be no. It would appear necessary to develop and/or apply other, more management-oriented models and measures of organizational intercultural competence to determine the legitimacy of applying assessment instruments designed for individual use in this way.

8.8 Concluding comments

In this chapter we have discussed the nature and purpose of instruments which assess two features of intercultural interaction: people's value orientations and their competence at handling the interaction. Both of these types of instrument attempt to examine and measure extremely complex phenomena, so it is only rarely that they have been shown to have the degree of validity and reliability which, for example, applied linguists require of language tests used in research contexts. However, for the purpose of developing intercultural interaction competence in professional contexts, when instruments are used as a pedagogical tool rather than a yardstick, there is less need for the assessment instruments to satisfy demanding quality criteria and the next chapter will discuss, amongst other topics, what role such instruments have in the development process.

In the education and certification context, where instruments in the broadest sense are urgently needed to certify the progress of learners and their qualification as intercultural interactants, the self-report nature of most instruments described in this chapter make them unsuitable for this purpose. More work needs to be done to develop instruments and procedures which actively involve teachers and assessors (despite the difficulties relating to validity and reliability mentioned in Section 8.6), so that especially language teachers in schools, as well as university-level educators, are better able to assess the ICIC of their students.

For this to be possible, observable and assessable indicators of ICIC need to be defined for particular target groups and some work is already being done in this area. Building on the INCA project, CILT, The National Centre for Languages in the United Kingdom completed in July 2008 the development of National Occupational Standards (NOS) in Intercultural Working for the UK.[4] But further such work on standards and on attainment objectives (including a hierarchy of levels) which are achievable as a result of teaching and learning at school is required. Going beyond the work of the Common European Framework of Reference for Languages, this could usefully occur at the European level and is one of the key recommendations of the LACE study mentioned in Section 8.5 and described in detail in Section 9.4. The question of the objectives of ICIC development is dealt with in the next chapter.

The need for standards and attainment objectives in turn demands conceptualizations of ICIC which are clearer and in particular easier to handle than those which currently exist, in order to make a successful move from the theory of intercultural competence to the practice of developing and assessing it. Here considerable research and development work remains to be done.

Notes

1. http://www.worldwork.biz (accessed 21 Nov. 2008).
2. http://www.worldwork.biz/legacy/www/docs2/tip.phtml (accessed 21 Nov. 2008).
3. http://ec.europa.eu/education/policies/lang/doc/lace_en.pdf
4. http://www.cilt.org.uk/standards/intercultural.htm

Further reading

Byram, M. (1997) *Teaching and Assessing Intercultural Communicative Competence.* Clevedon: Multilingual Matters. Useful chapters on the assessment of ICIC in the school education context.

Paige, R. M. (2004) Instrumentation in intercultural training. In D. Landis, J. M. Bennett, and M. J. Bennett (eds), *Handbook of Intercultural Training*, vol. 3. Thousand Oaks, CA: Sage: 85–128. A very comprehensive overview of the state of the art in the United States.

Prechtl, E. and A. Davidson-Lund (2007) Intercultural competence and assessment: perspectives from the INCA project. In H. Kotthoff and H. Spencer-Oatey (eds), *Handbooks of Applied Linguistics.* Volume 7: *Handbook of Intercultural Communication.* Berlin and New York: Mouton de Gruyter, pp. 465–90. A useful article about an assessment approach for certification purposes developed in Europe.

9
Developing Competence in Intercultural Interaction

> Education and training in intercultural communication is an approach to changing our 'natural' behaviour. [...] This attempt at change must be approached with the greatest possible care.
>
> Bennett 1993: 21

Chapter outline

We mentioned several times in Chapter 8 that one important purpose of intercultural assessment is to promote reflection and to aid the development of ICIC. This chapter focuses specifically on the development process, and deals with two main contexts: professional contexts and school education contexts.

9.1 The term 'development' and its conceptualization

We deliberately use the term 'developing' in this chapter, and not 'training', 'teaching' or 'promotion', because it allows us to use it with both its intransitive and transitive meanings. It is true that the various sub-competencies, which we showed in the previous chapters make up intercultural interaction competence (ICIC), can *be developed* to varying extents as a result of a pedagogical activity – for example, training, coaching or teaching of various kinds. But it is also the case that they can *develop* by themselves as a result of an interplay among personality, upbringing, socialization (including school education) and, at a later stage, life experience. This dual use of 'development' thus covers a distinction similar to that contained in the contrasting concepts of *foreign language teaching* vs. *foreign language acquisition* or *instructed acquisition* vs. *natural acquisition*.

We think this distinction is also advisable because the components of ICIC vary in their susceptibility to *being developed*. Different types of activity, settings and time-scales may be necessary to develop them.

Let us take two component competencies as examples. We have suggested that *openness* and *active listening* are both constituents of ICIC. It is possible in the short to medium term to acquire or improve through training and practice a repertoire of behaviours or skills which go to make up *active listening* and therefore to teach or train somebody in them. On the other hand, *openness* to new ideas, unaccustomed behaviours and unfamiliar people is linked to *personality* which is probably impossible to develop in the *short* term. It is a competence which can probably *develop* but one which may also *be developed* in the *medium to long* term. For this to happen it needs to be given space and time to flourish so that growth can occur. It may change slowly as a result of experience, such as that provided quite simply and unintentionally through living; it may also change as a result of experience provided intentionally through educational activities at school, such as trips abroad or exchanges (see Section 9.4 below). In this case, 'teach' and 'train' in our view would also be inappropriate terms.

The significance of these processes of *developing* and *being developed*, which require different time-scales, and traditionally involve different activities and settings, has led us to divide this chapter into two distinct contexts. The first context is that of adult *professional development*, in which intercultural development interventions are generally short term. The second context we deal with is the primary and secondary *school education* context, which is long term in nature.

University education occupies a position which is not always clear to the outside observer. It may pursue a mixture of the objectives of both the professional development context and the school education context. Some university courses include modules aimed at developing ICIC as a general educational objective and some have a decidedly vocational intention. For this reason and because of the lack of research insights on the situation at universities, we do not consider the university context here.

9.2 Aims and outcomes of ICIC development

All development activities both in school education and in professional development contexts are aimed at bringing about change in people. They are intended to enable participants to know something or do something or feel something they did not before the development intervention took place or something they knew or did or felt less completely beforehand. In this case, the *general aim* of ICIC development is to bring about change in the various components of an individual's ICIC, either by establishing them or by enhancing them. More generally, and to use our conceptualization of ICIC as described in Chapter 3, these intended changes are aimed at enabling the participant to achieve intercultural interaction that is (more) effective and (more) appropriate.

As explained at the end of Chapter 3, the components of ICIC are often grouped into three broad categories: affective, behavioural and cognitive. Similarly, the *outcomes* of ICIC development are frequently grouped into *knowledge, skills* and *attitudes*, which can be related to the cognitive, behavioural and affective components of ICIC:

- *Knowledge* as an outcome will enable the participant to *understand* aspects of intercultural interaction and may often be acquired in the short term. This knowledge may consist, for example, of knowledge about the values and norms of particular cultures with which people may come into contact, contrastive knowledge about cultures generally and knowledge about the process of intercultural interaction. This knowledge may be needed to use some of the skills and to support the modification or adoption of attitudes, perspectives and values necessary for successful intercultural interaction. This outcome is clearly cognitive in nature.
- *Skills* as an outcome will enable the participant to *do something* in the intercultural context effectively and appropriately and may be acquired in the short to medium term. These include, for example, the skills of active listening, linguistic accommodation and other behaviours associated with the competencies of communicating messages (see Concept 4.1), managing rapport (see Concept 5.1), handling knowledge and ideas (see Concept 6.2) and displaying emotional strength (see Concept 7.3). This outcome is largely behavioural in nature but is promoted by the understanding that comes from acquired knowledge and by supportive attitudes. The task of skills development is to facilitate the transformation of cognitive and affective factors so that they support newly learned behaviours.

- *Attitudes* as an outcome will enable the participant to see members of different cultures, and experience interaction with them, with different attitudes, from different perspectives and with different values, and may be acquired in the more medium to long term (Spencer and Spencer 1993) and sometimes with difficulty. These consist, for example, of affective factors included among rapport management competencies (emotion regulation), among cognitive competencies (new thinking, openness, valuing of differences) and among competencies associated with emotional strength (inner purpose, spirit of adventure). This outcome is affective and also cognitive in nature.

An awareness of these distinctive kinds of outcomes is key for three reasons. Firstly, they repeatedly occur in publications dealing with intercultural development in both of the contexts we deal with here. Secondly, this awareness gives developers simple criteria for assessing the needs of participants in interventions, selecting from the mass of methods and materials, and designing new development activities. Thirdly, awareness of these outcomes can act as a mechanism to correct a tendency in much ICIC development to emphasize the passing on of knowledge at the expense of developing attitudes and in particular skills.

9.3   Developing ICIC in professional context

Development interventions in the professional development context differ from those in the educational context in the following ways:

- the target group is generally composed of mature adults rather than children and maturing adults;
- the duration of the development intervention is generally much shorter;
- the aim is job-related rather than generally educational;
- the beneficiaries of the development intervention are the individual participant and his / her *organization* (or other users of his / her professional qualifications) rather than the individual and *society*.

Apart from these general characteristics, which practically always apply, the professional development context is extremely heterogeneous in nature, as the table of examples of authentic development scenarios below shows:

Sample 9.1   Authentic development scenarios in professional development contexts

Target group	Aim	Duration
C1* university researchers	To improve virtual and face-to-face cooperation with C2* colleagues in a joint research project	0.5 days
Prospective C1 expatriate manager, spouse and children	To prepare for 3-year assignment in C2 and to ease adjustment to C2	2 days consecutively
C1 management staff	To enhance post-acquisition integration after takeover by company from C2 and merger with company in C3	5 days over 9 months
Academics from various C1 universities teaching foreign students from various cultures	To improve teaching and learning in intercultural groups	1 day
Engineers from C1 parent company and C2 subsidiary	To facilitate the establishment of working relationships, communication and cooperation in a newly created virtual team	1.5 days consecutively
180 investment bankers from 20 cultures working for an international company with a strong C1 influence	To make participants aware of challenges *and* potentials of an international company	45 minutes

*C1 = 'home' or first national or ethnic culture, C2 = 'host' or contact culture

9.3.1   Preparing development interventions

Writing of the general aims of 'cross-cultural training programmes' (which fall into the category of 'professional development contexts'), Brislin and Yoshida (1994: 4) name four. They should:

1. help people 'in overcoming obstacles that could interfere with their enjoyment of their cross-cultural experiences' and thus help them 'find satisfaction in their work and in their everyday lives';

2. 'develop positive and respectful relationships with others in the culture';
3. 'help people overcome tasks associated with their work'; and
4. assist people with the inevitable stress that they will experience'.

This list of aims would coincide with the problem-solving intentions motivating much ICIC development in professional development contexts. But it neglects the further aim which professional development specialists are currently more and more seeking to achieve, namely the *leveraging* of cultural diversity to realize its potential in creativity, problem-solving and so on. The greater interest in diversity management (see Section 8.7) in organizations of the Western world is doubtless to a certain extent motivated by the need to comply with anti-discrimination legislation in the United States and at European Union and member state level. But there is also a genuine interest in tapping the assumed potentials of diversity.

The challenge to intercultural developers in *dealing with the problems* posed by diversity and in *using its potentials* is to translate an often rather vaguely recognized development *need* and weakly formulated development *aims* into rather more concrete development *outcomes*. This challenge can be met through *needs analysis*. Applied linguists may well be familiar with the notion of needs analysis from the area of languages for specific purposes. The intentions, and the concepts and procedures used to realize those intentions, are similar.

Necessities

Just as it is not possible or necessary to aim at a total proficiency in a foreign language to master a specific communication situation in that language, so too is it not practicable or even necessary to develop ICIC in all its facets as described in the previous chapters for every identified need for intercultural development. The demands of any particular target situation for which the participants are being prepared correspond to a subset of all the components of ICIC and will vary from target situation to target situation. This subset renders a list of needs known as target-situation *necessities*. For example, the extensive research literature on culture shock would suggest that a manager being prepared to work with colleagues from other cultures in his / her home culture rather than abroad is likely to require stress management skills to a lesser extent and less factual knowledge about everyday life in the other culture than a prospective expatriate. This list of *necessities* forms an ideal range of competencies which the participants should possess at the end of the intervention. One of the intentions of the needs analysis is thus to gain a picture of the target situation for which the participant is being prepared in order to determine the *necessities* for handling it.

Lacks

Every participant is of course not completely devoid of intercultural competence but brings an individual set of knowledge, attitudes and skills to the development intervention. This is a subset of the *necessities* identified for a particular situation. By subtracting the participant's individual set of knowledge, attitudes and skills from the *necessities,* the developer arrives at a set of needs known as *lacks.* This set of needs is what can be called the *development gap* and allows the developer to formulate *outcomes* for the intervention which will fill this gap. A second intention of the needs analysis is thus to gain a picture of the participant's relevant knowledge, attitudes and skills so that *lacks* can be ascertained.

The information required for this analysis can be gathered in a number of ways: the most usual are interviews with the HR department which has commissioned the development intervention and regrettably these are sometimes the only source of information. Insights into general organizational needs (e.g., successful post-merger integration, setting up international teams) and information and assumptions about the individual needs of those thought to require development are likely to be the outcomes of these interviews. Interviews with the participants themselves are rarer, desirable though they would be; more common are questionnaire surveys, increasingly in online form. An example of the text of one such pencil-and-paper needs analysis questionnaire is reproduced in Sample 9.2.

Sample 9.2   A needs analysis questionnaire

Dear Participant

Successful British-French
Management Communication and Cooperation
between French Parent Company X and British Subsidiary Company Y
A workshop to be conducted by N.N.

We are looking forward to meeting you at the Anglo-French cross-cultural workshop. As we would like to tailor it to your experience, needs and expectations, we would appreciate it very much if you could take the time to fill in the attached questionnaire and send it back by e-mail by [...] to [...].

Yours sincerely

N.N.

1. Surname: First name:

2. May we contact you? If so,
   Email: Telephone:

3. What is your mother tongue?

4. What national or ethnic culture(s) do you regard yourself as a member of?

5. What foreign languages do you speak and how well? (basic (–), good (+), very good (++) native-like (+++))

6. What is your educational background?

7. Please describe your work. Mention what parts of your work involve contacts with other cultures.

8. Have you ever taken part in any kind of intercultural training? If so, please describe briefly.

9. Have you ever lived or worked abroad for a period of more than three months? How long? Where? Doing what kind of work?

10. What kind of contact do you already have with your British / French colleagues?

Nature of contact	Frequency	Challenges
Telephone		
Video conferences		
Virtual communication e.g. email, shared database		
Face to face meetings in my country		
Business trips abroad		

11. When you consider your experience with past and present British (if you are French) or French (if you are British) colleagues, in what areas of communication and behaviour at work have you observed different perceptions, points of view and ways of doing things?

12. In what areas of work have you observed problems, if any, in the communication and cooperation between the British and French?

13. What do you believe would be helpful for your future cooperation with your French / British colleagues?

14. What topics would you like the workshop to cover?

15. What are your aims for this workshop?

16. Please complete this sentence: This workshop will be a success for me if [...].

17. Any other comments?

Thank you for answering these questions. Your answers, which will only be used in preparing the workshop, will be treated in strict confidence and will not be made available to third parties without your permission.

Organizational and budget constraints will mean that a needs analysis will often not go beyond what is illustrated above. The information generated by such interviews and questionnaires, while essential and useful for the intervention designer, is hardly comprehensive. A way of obtaining more comprehensive data is to conduct individual and/or organizational assessments of cultural orientations and ICIC. The assessment of intercultural interaction competence at the organizational level is dealt with in Section 8.7 and selected instruments and frameworks used at the individual level to assess ICIC are presented in Sections 8.3, 8.4 and 8.6.

We now describe briefly how ICIC assessment can be embedded in a development intervention both as a kind of needs analysis and as a development action.

Before the face-to-face intervention takes place, participants complete an ICIC assessment instrument, such as one of those described in Chapter 8. On the basis of the results, the intervention designer determines outcomes in terms of knowledge, attitudes and skills. Constraints of time for the intervention will mean that the developer usually has to select the more prevalent lacks in the group. The outcomes of the intervention he/she selects will not fill the development gap in its entirety for every individual.

However, an assessment instrument can be used both for needs analysis and as a development tool at the individual level. The participant completes the assessment and takes part in a feedback session with the person trained and experienced in the use of the instrument. In the course of the one-to-one feedback session, which can last from between one and three hours, the developer explains the assessed sub-competencies to the participant and discusses those identified as being present or absent in the participant to a lesser or greater degree. Crucially, the developer assesses with the participant their relevance to the necessities of the target situation.

Instruments may provide developers with material to support this feedback process. For example, The International Profiler (see Section 8.3) provides its licensed consultants with a feedback book, which contains detailed definitions of competencies, interpretations of high and low scores and case studies; a coaching handbook, which contains descriptions of the rationale behind the possible development of a particular competence and suggested action steps for achieving that development; and a set of competency cards for use in the feedback session, which define each competency and illustrate it with a striking photograph. A comprehensive interpretive report on each candidate can also be generated by the database which compares the completed questionnaire with responses given by all previous respondents.

Towards the end of the feedback session, the participant identifies areas of need for individual development in consultation with the developer and various development steps are agreed. In the case of the International Profiler, for example, the participant may be given a blank action plan to be filled in after reflection by the participant. The action plan contains space for the participant to identify development objectives, the benefits likely to arise from their achievement and steps to help achieve them. When the participant has devised his/her own action plan, it is returned to the licensed consultant, who makes further development suggestions and in turn sends it back to the participant.

The very individualized, needs analysis-oriented aspect of this procedure can be seen in the fact that the action plan can also be made available to other developers involved in subsequent elements of the development intervention, for example, the facilitator of a further culture-specific (see Section 9.3.2 below) session, who can then devote attention to a particular identified need and the corresponding outcome.

An extract from an International Profiler action plan filled in by the participant and the consultant is reproduced below. The consultant filled the third column headed S.M.A.R.T. actions, the participant the rest.

Sample 9.3   An extract from a personal development plan based on an intercultural assessment

WorldWork International Development Plan

To fulfil the international requirements of my role, I need to:

1. observe non-verbal and between-the-line communication among my new international colleagues

2. observe informal structures of hierarchy and power

3. [...]

To help me meet these requirements I need to

> ➤ identify my key areas for development

> ➤ clearly understand the benefits of shifting my focus of energy

> ➤ commit to realistic actions which will close the gap I have identified.

Development areas	Benefits for me	S.M.A.R.T.* Actions
1. Low attuned: observation of body language and implicit messages among my new international colleagues	– understanding my new colleagues; – being understood as a result of adapting my communication styles; – developing personal relationships	1) Become aware of how body language may vary across cultures by reading, for example, E.T Hall's 'The Silent Language' and find examples of posture, gesture, etc amongst your *international* colleagues which are less common in your own culture. 2) Ask your trainer in the Intercultural Awareness Session whether he/she agrees with what Greg Nees writes about *German* body language on pp. 90–4 of his book 'Germany. Unravelling an Enigma'. 3) Try reading pp. 163–92 of Sylvia Schroll-Machl's book 'Doing Business with Germans' on communication style and esp. pp. 179–80 on 'reading between German lines'.
2. Low sensitivity for context: observation of informal power structures	– understanding my new environment; – discovering new possible channels of influence	Train 'your political nose' by observing over time what was critical in helping or preventing the implementation of ideas in your organisation: the quality of the idea, the resources made available, the sponsor(s) of the idea or the key decision-makers along the way. Who has influence? How is this influence gained? How do these factors differ from your home culture?
3. [...]		

*Make them Specific, Measurable, Achievable, Realistic, Time-scaled

Another possibility is for the results of the assessment to be made available to the participants during a group face-to-face intervention, which gives them the opportunity to satisfy individual needs through targeted learning and questions put to the facilitator.

Having analysed the needs of the participants, using a questionnaire and/or an assessment instrument (which the developer can also use for development purposes at the individual level) and specified the desired outcomes of the intervention, the developer is ready to conduct the development intervention.

9.3.2   Conducting development interventions: content

In this section we briefly describe what the content of development interventions may be and some of the problems connected with choices of content.

Developing knowledge and awareness

Cultural knowledge, both of other cultures and also one's own culture(s), is a key component of ICIC. But this is not the only reason why it occupies such a central place in the outcomes of intercultural development in the context of professional development. In contrast to skills and attitudes, it is relatively simple for a developer to pass on knowledge and for participants to acquire it.

The knowledge passed on can vary from simple information about everyday life and the nature of professional activity to concepts of culture, cultural models and insights into the culturally based values, attitudes and behavioural norms of a particular culture and its institutions. This broad body of knowledge is part of the repertoire of the intercultural developer and makes clear the developer's need for a sound multidisciplinary background (see Section 9.5 below).

In what are known as *culture-general* interventions, that is those preparing participants for dealing with all types of cultures, the knowledge passed on by most intercultural developers is very frequently that generated by Hall, Hofstede and Trompenaars. Berardo and Simons (2004), in a study conducted in collaboration with SIETAR Europa (see Associations section of Chapter 12), asked 261 intercultural trainers working in the professional development context, to record the particular sources – and incidentally the significant influence – of the knowledge they pass on in their interventions. Asked to name their first and second preferences among 'cultural models', the interculturalists surveyed overwhelmingly indicated Hofstede and Trompenaars (occasionally in combination with co-author Hampden-Turner) with 89 of 170 mentions.

Despite (or perhaps precisely because of) the widespread influence of Hofstede and Trompenaars, developers and participants increasingly criticize the usefulness and quality of the knowledge they offer. What may be regarded as monolithic concepts of culture as something related chiefly to national or ethnic group membership does not chime with professionals' increasing experience of a professional environment in constant flux and with their confrontation with other salient bearers of culture, such as gender, age, religion and not least the organization. As we pointed out in Chapter 7, the complexity of the international assignments of many professionals underlines the need for the culture concepts used in development in the professional context to include at least organizational culture as a significant complicating factor in the intercultural interaction. The *culture-comparative* approach of these predominant models also means that the studies are not of course *culture-interactional* (see Chapter 1 for an explanation of these terms) and as such do not offer developers and participants many insights about interaction and how to handle it. As Franklin writes, such studies deliver insights which are:

> relatively far removed from the daily communication situations and interactions of (international) cooperation and thus offer little help to international managers in the area of communication itself – in assisting managers actually to interact across cultures. Hofstede devotes only just over one page of 466 to the principles of intercultural communication and cooperation (2001: 423–5) and less than a page to language and discourse (2001: 425). Trompenaars and Hampden-Turner (1997: 74–6) deal with the topic in something under three brief pages.
>
> (2007: 264–5)

Both developers and participants themselves sometimes also question the age of the studies (e.g., Hofstede's *Culture's Consequences* first appeared in 1980 and Trompenaars *Riding the Waves of Culture* in 1993) and their corporate origins (IBM and Royal Dutch-Shell respectively). Hofstede's counter-argument that the IBM source of his data adds validity to the study as the data is derived from a matched sample frequently fails to convince. Nevertheless, such knowledge has found many users in the development community – it offers some empirical security in a field notoriously susceptible to the perverting effects of anecdote and stereotype, and to the inherent *culture-centredness* (see Section 11.1.2) of the developer.

When it comes to *culture-specific* development interventions, that is those preparing participants for dealing with a particular culture, criticism of the quality of the knowledge passed on is also often justified. Developers are not always country-experts with comprehensive, up-to-date knowledge, and information and facts about specific national and ethnic cultures in books and websites for non-specialists are often outdated or over-generalized. This may become obvious, for example, when C1 natives (or long-term C2 residents in a C1 culture) read material about the C1 designed for others. Such sources are frequently the result of work by practitioners with perhaps limited experience of the culture they are describing and with little knowledge of the research literature and methods of investigation.

A further frequent problem with written material is the usually implicit presence of a *reference culture* in the text. To read, as is possible in country-briefings on Germany for example, that 'fridges tend to be rather small in Germany' may be helpful for the US reader for whom the information was written and with whose fridge its German counterpart was implicitly compared; yet it may tell non-US readers nothing useful about German fridges, for whom they are of a 'normal' size, but probably quite a lot about the capacity of the average US fridge. 'Cultural information' originating, for example, in the English language both in books and on the internet is often not very useful to members of other cultures because of the reference culture (usually the USA or UK) guiding both choice of information and its interpretation. Here again we see an example of *culture-centredness*, a topic we deal with in Section 11.1.2.

In its extreme form, the quality deficit in knowledge-oriented materials and development may lead to criticism from participants that the material or intervention is merely perpetuating stereotypes, an activity which is regarded as harmful (see Section 6.2.3). In Chapter 2, we pointed out that the cognitive representation of categories (such as cultural groups) naturally entails a certain amount of reductionism. This complexity reduction is all the more evident when knowledge is justifiably simplified for pedagogical reasons. Materials producers and developers alike run the risk of producing descriptions of cultures for participants which to liberal observers, especially those from individualist cultures with a high regard for human uniqueness (Cf. Smith and Bond, 1998: 186 and Section 6.2.3) may appear to reproduce stereotypes. Because stereotypes ignore the quality of uniqueness in human beings, such materials are therefore *per se* especially likely to be unacceptable in individualist cultures.

Evidence-based descriptions of culture on which pedagogical material is based will ensure that authors and developers will be able to defend themselves against such criticism and at the same time meet the understandable need of participants for manageable descriptions of cultures. They will also meet the need of developers to tackle the stereotypes of cultures that participants bring to their intercultural interactions and the development intervention itself. The development field is in urgent need of such evidence-based emic and etic descriptions so that its reliance on unsatisfactory sources can be reduced.

Whereas the acquisition of knowledge about *cultures* is clearly a very frequently targeted outcome of ICIC development, we believe on the basis of experiential and anecdotal evidence that knowledge about the *process* of intercultural interaction is more rarely the focus of ICIC development interventions. Some evidence for this assertion is given by Berardo and Simons (2004), who surveyed which models were used in development interventions. They found that applied linguists and psychologists who could be said to have generated knowledge about the *process* of intercultural interaction were mentioned only 16 times out of a total of 170 mentions.

This lack of attention to the *process* of intercultural interaction is clearly a challenge to those researchers working in this field to produce useful and usable research insights and to help to transfer this to the practice of intercultural development. This transfer is a process which must not stop at the gathering of authentic data but one which also demands more extensive cooperation with practitioners, both those involved in intercultural interaction itself and those involved in developing ICIC, and also a greater understanding of and sympathy for their respective needs.

Developing skills and behaviours

As we pointed out at the beginning of this chapter, developing skills and behaviours to handle effectively the processes of intercultural interaction takes longer than merely passing on and acquiring knowledge. At the same time, however, skills and behaviour are more central to the needs of professionals. Certainly, as Ting-Toomey (1999) points out, knowledge forms the foundation for the state of mindfulness (see Section 3.2.3) and is as such the first step to the skills needed to manage intercultural interaction. But in the professional development context, with its understandable emphasis on solving problems rather than merely understanding them, professionals may see cultural knowledge as a 'nice to have' but what they really require are skills and behaviours which lead to competence in the target situation.

Some skills and behaviours are relatively easier to develop and include common behavioural conventions and social rituals. A more difficult aspect of this kind of development is the necessary but hard-to-define distinction between flexible normative conventions and inflexible prescriptive/proscriptive conventions (see the discussion of behavioural expectations in Section 5.4). It is also hard but necessary to distinguish between individual and shared perceptions of what is normative and what is prescriptive/proscriptive for a particular group. This difficulty can be illustrated by asking a C1 group of professionals to agree on a description of such conventions; for example, for running a meeting or conducting a sales pitch in their C1, which could be useful to colleagues from a C2. Experience shows that they often find it difficult to achieve consensus. However, the urgent need felt by professionals dealing with another culture for this kind of skill and behaviour is captured in needs analyses. It is also reflected in the existence of the 'dos and don'ts'/business etiquette genre of cultural information. The difficulty encountered in this behavioural area of ICIC development underlines the insight that ICIC depends not only on knowledge and skills but to a large extent on a sensitivity that is itself dependent on attitudes, affective qualities and values which can only be developed in the medium to long term.

Perhaps more important – and especially so in view of our criticism of the appropriateness criterion for ICIC (see Section 3.2.1) – is the development of the competencies associated with message communication and rapport management (see Concepts 4.1 and 5.1). These are vital in intercultural interaction situations. Here, the very frequent absence of native speakers of the language in use means that the transfer of message meaning in particular may well be impeded by a lower level of language proficiency. Native speakers of the language in use may also fail to accommodate their language and may be weak in active listening and thus poor at negotiating meaning and creating understanding.

Such skills are crucial but strangely neglected in intercultural development interventions. Neither older intercultural development publications such as Paige (1993), Brislin and Yoshida (1994), Kohls with Brussow (1995), Cushner and Brislin (1996) and Singelis (1998), nor more recent handbooks such as Landis, Bennett and Bennett (2004) or Gardenswartz and colleagues (2003) deal with them. In their review of the intercultural training profession, Berardo and Simons (2004) also offer no evidence that this is a skill which is being developed in interventions.

Exceptions here are, for example, to be found in Ewington and Trickey (2003), Comfort and Franklin (2008), and Spencer-Oatey and Stadler (2009). Ewington and Trickey elaborate on and exemplify 'transparency strategies' (2003: 48). Comfort and Franklin discuss what they call 'clarity skills' (2008: 93–4) and 'active listening skills' (2008: 94–5) and list examples of how they might be realized in English (2008: 99). Spencer-Oatey, Ng and Dong (2008) give authentic examples of a range of message communication and rapport management competencies, using data from the eChina-UK Programme. There is a pressing need in the practice of intercultural development for more work to be done in this area by applied linguists working on linguae francae of intercultural interaction.

The acquisition of other skills and behaviours which go beyond behavioural conventions, social protocols and rituals on the one hand, and message and rapport competencies on the other, may be considerably more difficult. It may indeed necessitate a thoroughgoing adjustment in behaviour rather than involve a relatively simple learnable skill. As we pointed out in Section 7.2.2, this adjustment may go against a participant's values. Consider the authentic case of the German manager of a balsa-wood plantation in Ecuador. His large power-distance (see Concept 2.4) workforce expected detailed instructions in the workplace, whereas his own small power-distance values made him expect initiative and participation from his staff. The adjustment in behaviour expected of him so that it was appropriate and effective in the Ecuadorian context demanded behaviours which conflicted with important beliefs he held about the nature of human beings and how to manage them. The behaviour he wanted of his staff demanded an equally far-reaching adjustment in their values. In the absence of tried and tested ways of nurturing and managing the hybrid identities and intercultural personhood we discussed in Chapter 7, a cognitive appeal to the pragmatic value of a change in the behaviour of a professional may or may not be effective but is often the only thing the developer can do. Such a change may not necessarily lead to a sacrificing of important, individually held values.

Another key skill in the range of sub-competencies making up ICIC which is difficult to acquire, but for different reasons, is skill in a second language. This is a skill that is clearly especially important for those who are not native speakers of a widely used lingua franca. In the professional development context, foreign language training will indeed sometimes be the only form of ICIC development routinely offered to staff with international contacts and as part of preparation for expatriate assignments.

Foreign language teaching and learning materials aimed at the professional have long since incorporated a cultural aspect to the communication situations for which they aim to develop the necessary language skills. But this cultural aspect in the case, for example, of business English as a foreign language tends to limit itself to knowledge about culturally-based variation in the nature of communication situations rather than skill in handling them. Another area in which language teaching and learning materials for business English as a foreign language may take account of the cultural factor is in a preoccupation with indirectness of disagreement and requests in professional contexts. However, this is aimed at promoting a near-native appropriateness in these areas in interaction with native speakers of British English and other varieties of English and is less important for dealing with situations in which English is used as a lingua franca, where Byram's model of the 'intercultural speaker' (see Section 3.4.2) is a more appropriate target. The intercultural speaker's message communication competencies for handling the intercultural interaction situation may be touched upon when the language of presentations and negotiations is dealt with and rapport management competencies may be touched on when it comes to teaching the language of small talk and social conversation.

Developing attitudes

Enabling the participant to *adopt or change attitudes, perspectives and values* is a much more difficult undertaking in the short timeframes usually available in the professional development context than is passing on knowledge or developing skills (Cf. Spencer and Spencer 1993: 11). Attitudes, perspectives and values, such as seeing intercultural interaction not only as a potential problem but also as an opportunity, or recognizing that cultural diversity requires flexibility in behaviour, may change as a result of exposing people to new situations and giving them new experiences. This generally takes place over a longer period of time.

However, human resource development specialists and intercultural developers believe that such changes may at least be *initiated* even in short development interventions. Fowler and Blohm, in their description of the development of attitudes write: 'If the outcome of the training is that trainees will modify their attitudes, methods need to touch trainees' belief systems, often intensely' (2004: 46). This intensive touching of belief systems can result in particular from participation in intercultural exercises, simulations, role plays and games described briefly in Section 9.3.3 below and listed in the Resources for Developing Intercultural Interaction Competence section of

Chapter 12. Intercultural development methods such as the contrast-culture method, cross-cultural dialogues and the culture assimilator, also described in Section 9.3.3 below, may have this effect as well.

A gentler encounter with trainees' belief systems can be achieved by requiring participants to complete a values orientation assessment instrument (see Section 8.2). This can familiarize them with their own culturally-based values, just as a competence assessment (see Section 8.3.2) can bring out personal attitudes, values and competencies related to the mastery of the intercultural interface. (How the latter can be embedded in a development intervention is described in Section 9.3.1 above.)

Assessment can produce information about attitudes or values held by the participant. It can thus form the point of departure for changing the attitudes held if the participant recognizes that the attitudes or values highlighted are not conducive to effective intercultural interaction generally or are not usual in the participant's C2. A values orientation assessment can point out similarities and differences between the participant's values and those of the C2 and thus help the participant become aware of, and to some extent prepare for, possible areas of difficulty. In this way it can be used to suggest the possible culture-fit or culture-unfit that a participant might experience in a particular C2.

9.3.3 Conducting development interventions: methods

In this section we give an overview of the main methods intercultural developers may use in delivering the outcomes they have chosen for the intervention. Descriptions of teaching methods are notoriously dry and also difficult to follow and it is not surprising that trainer-training involves witnessing the methods in practice and trying them out. Nevertheless, what follows gives an impression of the repertoire of methods available and a detailed description of those which are rarely used outside the field of intercultural development.

In a seminal article in the first *Handbook of Intercultural Training* (Landis and Brislin (eds), 1983), Gudykunst and Hammer published a much imitated, but often unattributed 'classification scheme for training techniques' (1983: 126). They used two sets of contrasting concepts. The first set concerned the distinction between *culture-specific* and *culture-general* development already mentioned in Section 9.3.2 above. The second set concerned the methods employed in interventions – on the one hand, the 'university model', or *didactic/expository* set of methods and on the other, the *experiential/discovery* set of methods. Gudykunst and Hammer placed these two sets of concepts on intersecting axes, thus forming taxonomic quadrants. Gudykunst, Guzley and Hammer (1996) elaborate on the original classification and the diagram shown in Sample 9.4 can be constructed. Some of the methods listed are described in detail below.

Sample 9.4   Gudykunst and Hammer's classification scheme for training techniques

	Experiential / discovery			
	I. Experiential – culture-general		**II. Experiential – culture-specific**	
	Human relations training	Intercultural communication workshop	Bi-cultural human relations training	Bi-cultural communication workshop
	Culture-general simulations (incl. culture contrast)	Self-confrontation	Culture-specific simulations	Culture-specific role-plays
	Self-assessments			
Culture-general	Academic courses in intercultural communication, cultural anthropology and cross-cultural psychology	Kraemer's cultural self-awareness	Foreign language training	Area orientation briefings
	Written material	Lecture / discussion techniques	Culture-specific assimilators	Written material, e.g. CultureGrams Interacts
	Videotapes	Culture-general assimilators		
	III. Didactic – culture-general		**IV. Didactic – culture-specific**	
	Didactic / expository			**Culture-specifc**

(Based on Gudykunst and Hammer 1983: 126–40, and Gudykunst, Guzley and Hammer 1996: 66–72)

The diagram is important for three reasons. Firstly, it makes clear the multidisciplinary roots of intercultural development: psychology, sociology, communication studies, anthropology, area studies and foreign language education are all represented. Secondly, applied linguistics is notable through its absence. Thirdly, current best practice uses all these methods or elements of them to a greater or lesser extent, even if they are known by different names.

A later elaboration of this taxonomy by Bolten (2001: 9–10) is mostly terminological in nature but adds one substantially different method, namely discourse analysis-based training, such as that described by Liedke, Redder and Scheiter (1999) and Ten Thije (2001).

Another method or approach developed in Europe which is not included and which uses insights from linguistics is the Linguistic Awareness of Culture (LAC) programme (Müller-Jacquier 2000), which draws on Knapp and Knapp-Potthoff (1990) and other sources. One objective of LAC is to promote what Müller-Jacquier describes as 'meta-communicative skills'. This latter competency is – as Kühlmann and Stahl's (1998) research reported on in Section 3.4.1 indicates – a constituent of ICIC and relates to message communication competencies (see Concept 4.1 and Section 9.3.2 above for a discussion of their development). These are skills which, as we noted above, are frequently neglected in current development practice. These European approaches are reported on in English by Rost-Roth (2007: 499).

Fowler and Blohm (2004) develop a new taxonomy of methods and present an extremely valuable, exhaustive list of practically all methods and techniques that includes all those currently used. They use a largely different and more elaborate set of criteria to produce an effective tool for selecting methods for various development scenarios. They describe the methods, their strengths and weaknesses, adaptability, application, availability and so on.

Particularly useful is the characterization of various methods as 'cognitive', 'active' (although interactive may be a more appropriate term), 'intercultural' or 'other'; so too is the attempt to describe the methods' expected outcomes according to whether they tend to support the development of knowledge, skills or attitudes. (See Sample 9.5.) This allows developers to choose methods suitable for the outcomes they want to achieve. The table which follows reproduces these aspects of the 30-page description and also gives alternative names of methods to be found in the literature. We return to these methods in our discussion of research into methods used in school education to develop ICIC.

Sample 9.5   A classification of development methods and their expected outcomes

Nature of method	Method	Development outcome
Cognitive	Lecture, briefing	Knowledge
	Written material	Knowledge
	Computer-based training	Knowledge, skills
	Self-assessment	Knowledge
	Case studies	Knowledge, skills
Active	Simulations and games	Knowledge, skills, attitudes
	Role play	Skills, attitudes
	Exercises	Knowledge, skills
Intercultural	Contrast culture, contrast American	Attitudes
	Critical incidents	Knowledge, skills, attitudes
	Culture assimilator, intercultural sensitizer	Knowledge, skills, attitudes
	Culture analysis	Knowledge, skills
	Kraemer's cultural self-awareness, cross-cultural dialogues	Knowledge, attitudes
	Area studies	Knowledge
	Immersion	Knowledge, skills, attitudes
Other	Visual imagery	Knowledge, attitudes
	Art and culture	Knowledge, skills, attitudes

(adapted from Fowler and Blohm 2004)

Many of the methods described by Fowler and Blohm as 'cognitive', 'active' and 'other' are familiar from other areas of teaching and development, and for this reason we restrict our discussion to those methods and techniques that belong more specifically to the intercultural development field.

Language education specialists will recognize in the list above the use of role play and simulations in promoting interaction among participants. The intercultural development field has produced a number of well-known and frequently used simulations and games such as BaFá BaFá (Shirts, 1974, 1995), RaFá RaFá (Shirts 1976), Ecotonos (Nipporica Associates 1993), Barnga (Thiagaran and Steinwachs 1990), The Trade Mission and Follow-The-Sun Global Technology Team (both in Hofstede, Pedersen and Hofstede 2002). They use roles and tasks to stimulate behaviour and interaction from participants who are required to take on values, attitudes and norms different from their own. They generate feelings of discomfort, frustration and anger in an attempt to replicate the feelings which may occur in genuine intercultural encounters and cause participants to reflect on the nature of culture and on their own attitudes to otherness.

Selected 'intercultural' methods for delivering outcomes

Six of the methods are described above as 'intercultural' methods, meaning that they have either their origin or a particular usefulness in the intercultural development area. In what follows we describe four methods which have found their way into the standard repertoire of ICIC development in the professional development context either in their original or in an adapted form. All of those described here involve a *critical incident* in an intercultural interaction.

Critical incidents

Critical incidents have become so widely used in the intercultural field that any ICIC development intervention is unthinkable without their appearance in one form or another.

Concept 9.1   Critical incident

The term 'critical incident' in the intercultural context is used with two slightly different meanings.

Firstly, it denotes an intercultural interaction or repeated experience which one or all parties to the communication experienced as ineffective and/or inappropriate and/or unsatisfying. This is the meaning it has when an interactant recounts such an occasion or when it is used in the research context. For example, critical incidents can be gathered as self-report data (see Section 11.2.2). Thomas (1988, 1996a) also embeds the collection of critical incidents in a technique for researching culture standards (see Section 2.3).

Secondly, the term 'critical incident' in the intercultural *development* context denotes a description of such an interaction so that it can fulfil a pedagogical purpose. The short prose text merely describes what happened and often the unspoken feelings and thoughts of one or all parties to the incident. Critical incidents of this kind were first used in the intercultural field in the 1960s by Triandis (see description of the culture assimilator below) for development purposes and by others in selecting US Peace Corps volunteers.

Wight (1995: 135–6) distinguishes between Critical Incident Exercises (CIE) and the use of critical incidents in culture assimilators (see below) and locates CIE in the experiential/discovery learning tradition (see Sample 9.4 above) in ICIC development.

Sample 9.6   Critical Incident

A group of German academics were meeting for a Friday afternoon seminar. A paper was presented and then there was a heated discussion. A US guest professor was disturbed by the atmosphere and had the impression that the professors didn't like each other at all. She was surprised that after the discussion had ended they left the room in a good mood wishing each other a good weekend.

(Gibson 2000: 45)

In the discussion of such an incident, the absence of interpretations to choose from (unlike in culture assimilators) forces participants to generate their own probable reactions and ways of handling the situation. They discuss with the developer the likely effectiveness and appropriateness of the suggestions. The developer may also ask the participants how they would feel in the situation and also get them to take the perspective of the various parties. In particular, the developer elicits from the participants possible explanations for the incident which are to be found in differences between culturally motivated values and norms. If none are forthcoming, the developer provides such insights him/herself, thus helping participants to achieve more accurate attributions of culturally-based behaviour in other contexts.

Gibson (2002) contains a wide variety of short and generally convincing critical incidents and Hofstede, Pedersen and Hofstede (2002) present critical incidents relating to the Hofstedian dimensions in a novel form.

Culture assimilator/intercultural sensitizer

Originated in the early 1960s and reported on by Fiedler, Mitchell and Triandis (1971), the culture assimilator uses critical incidents in a way which allows them to be applied not only in the classroom but also for self-study. The description of the critical incident is followed by a question designed to get the participants to reflect on the critical incident and assess what happened. Then he/she compares his/her assessments with four or five explanations of the critical incident, which sometimes offer behavioural choices for the parties to the critical incident. (One explanation may account for the incident from the C1 viewpoint, another from the C2 viewpoint.) As indicated in Sample 9.7, these explanations are followed by discussions of the explanations, which also indicate which of the explanations is the preferred answer in the given circumstances. (Space prevents us from reproducing this part of the culture assimilator here.)

Sample 9.7   Culture assimilator/intercultural sensitizer

Office hours

Karl had recently joined the faculty at a prestigious university in the United States. [...] He was excited about this upcoming opportunity, as it would enable him to work closely with colleagues and students in his area of interest. [...] A month into his teaching, Karl's enthusiasm began to wane. He had prepared quite detailed lectures and had chosen what he thought were adequate textbooks to supplement his course. He had become quite bothered, however, by two unanticipated occurrences. First, despite his enthusiasm for his material, his students never asked questions or engaged in dialogue in class. Rather, they seemed quite content simply to record everything in their notebooks in a passive manner. But what really was confusing was that many of the students seemed to show up during his office hours, wanting to discuss rather basic material he had already presented in class. Karl wondered why these students were wasting his time with such trivialities. Office hours should be used for serious issues. Why did the students not ask these questions in class?

If Karl came to you with this question, what would you suggest?

1. The students considered interrupting the professor during class to be impolite and discourteous.
2. The students were afraid of asking 'stupid' questions in front of their peers.
3. The students felt they must review their class notes before speaking alone with the professor, so they could speak intelligently.
4. The students felt that it was important for their final grades for the professor to know them individually.

(Cushner and Brislin 1996: 215–16)

Cushner and Brislin discuss these alternative explanations a few pages later.

Albert (1995) lists sources of culture-specific culture assimilators. Thomas and his various collaborators have published a long series of research-based culture-specific assimilators in German. Triandis (1995) describes briefly and Albert (1983) more thoroughly how to construct culture-specific culture assimilators, a topic which is the subject of a research project listed in Section 10.5.

Cross-cultural dialogues

Acknowledging his debt to Kraemer's work in the 1970s (reported on in Kraemer 1999), the originator of this method, describes a cross-cultural dialogue as:

> a brief conversation between two people from different cultures, during the course of which the speakers make statements which reveal or betray very different values, attitudes, or views of the world – in short cultural differences. [...] one of the speakers projects a value or assumption about the other person's culture that is not accurate, and, as a result, the communication between these two people either breaks down entirely or is extremely confusing or frustrating.
>
> (Storti 1999: 203)

Cross-cultural dialogues (or more accurately and in accordance with the terminology used in this book, *intercultural* dialogues), are thus a critical incident in dialogue form. When properly written (Storti 1999: 208–9) and facilitated (Storti 1999: 204–6), they can be used to pass on knowledge about cultures and also to help to develop attitudes of openness and flexibility.

Contrast culture/contrast American

A critical incident may well also be at the heart of the contrast-culture method. Based on research and development carried out in the early 1960s (see Stewart 1995, for a retrospective report), the contrast culture (or contrast American) method involves a participant (conventionally named Mr/Ms Smith) interacting in a role play situation with a trained actor who plays the role of a foreigner (conventionally named Mr Khan) in front of a group of participants, followed by a debriefing of the participants – sometimes in connection with a video recording of the interaction – which highlights values and norms of the cultures involved. Stewart describes some of the benefits of the method thus:

> The critical dynamic of the contrast-culture method of training is the simulation in which trainees are confronted with their own cultural assumptions and strategies during interactions. The experience probes reference-culture values and cultivates understanding of cultural interaction with members of other cultures. Trainees gain subjective insight into how their own culture is perceived by others and how its assumptions and strategies contribute to or detract from cross-cultural interaction.
>
> (1995: 56)

Kimmel (1995) describes the facilitation of the contrast-culture method; Fowler and Blohm (2004) describe the strengths and weaknesses of the method; Bhawuk and Brislin praise the method for developing cultural self-awareness and because 'it emphasizes affective goals through experiential processes' (2000: 170).

Perhaps the true significance of the method lies in the fact that it is relatively common practice, especially for culture-specific interventions, to use a member of a C2 to take part in an observed, and then debriefed, role play. It is a procedure which often offers participants a memorable learning experience but which could be improved by using the careful facilitation process of the original culture-contrast method.

9.3.4 Evaluating development interventions

In the professional development context it is usual for a development intervention to be evaluated by the participants at, or very shortly after, its conclusion. This may be done in the form of a pencil-and-paper or online questionnaire and will provide an impression of the expertise of the developer and of the extent to which the participants feel that their needs have been met.

A much more valuable evaluation, but one which in practice seldom takes place, happens some months after the end of the intervention. After time has elapsed, the participants are better able to make a judgement about the extent to which a development in their own knowledge, attitudes and skills has occurred as a result of the intervention and whether this development has made them better able to deal with the professional challenges they have since encountered.

The effectiveness of development interventions has often been the subject of research and we return to this in Chapter 10.

9.4 Developing ICIC in the school education context

Given the broad range of sub-competencies making up ICIC, some of a very general and transversal nature, it is not surprising that school education in the Western world in particular has increasingly claimed ICIC as an educational objective. It tends to see the general purpose of developing ICIC as a contribution at the individual level to societal well-being; for example by facilitating a policy of multiculturalism, by improving the integration of ethnic minorities and thus by supporting social cohesion. Less emphasis is given to the benefits of improved communication and cooperation between economic actors at the collective and individual level. Indeed, this purpose may well be denigrated by some in the world of education as purely utilitarian and debasing the inherently ethical intentions of successful intercultural communication.

Whatever the purpose of developing ICIC may be, and however those different purposes may be regarded from an ideological point of view, it is clearly advantageous that ICIC development also takes place in schools and universities for reasons of effectiveness: as already observed, many of the sub-competencies of ICIC demand longer-term development and nourishing, and schools and universities can provide a suitable time frame. Educational institutions have students in their classes and courses over periods longer than the mere two days often available in the professional context and – perhaps even more importantly – at an age when it is possible to facilitate the development of the values, attitudes and other qualities linked to personality which go to make up ICIC. As well as making ICIC the overt aim of activity in the classroom, they can also provide continuity and a context for more or less guided out-of-classroom experiences, such as school trips, exchanges, study periods and internships abroad and exposure to other intercultural situations in which students can acquire and develop a broader range of competencies than in the professional context.

9.4.1   Aims in school curricula

In contrast to the professional development context, ICIC generally does not occupy a place of its own in the curriculum but is integrated into the teaching of other subjects. Foreign language education is often seen as the appropriate place for ICIC development to be located and indeed most foreign language curricula declare it to be a general aim, which is expressed with varying degrees of precision and given varying degrees of importance in the curriculum as a whole (Research Report 1).

The investigation entitled 'Languages and Cultures in Europe (LACE): The intercultural competencies developed in compulsory foreign language education in the European Union', commissioned by the Directorate-General for Education and Culture of the European Commission, published in 2007 and referred to hereafter as the LACE study, analysed foreign language curricula at primary and lower secondary level in 12 European countries to discover, amongst other things, what objectives in the area of intercultural competencies they prescribe and the degree of focus given to them (see Research Report 9.1 for a brief summary). The LACE study used three analytical frameworks, those elaborated on in Byram (1997), Chen and Starosta (2005) and in the Common European Framework for Languages.

Research Report 9.1   General aims of selected lower secondary foreign language curricula in Europe and the significance they give to the role of ICIC development (adapted from the LACE study 2007)

Country	
England and Wales (Level: ISCED 2)	There are five strands per year: words, sentences, texts (reading and writing), listening and speaking, and cultural knowledge and contact. Objectives are identified for each strand – 8 each year for words and sentences, 7 each year for texts, 6 for listening and speaking, and 5 for cultural knowledge and contact. However, the assessment targets are only for listening, speaking, reading and writing. There are no assessment targets for cultural knowledge and contact. *Source*: Modern Foreign Languages, Keystage 3. (National Curriculum entitlements) 1999. Revised 2004. MFL (Modern Foreign Languages) Framework (2003)
Poland (Level: ISCED 2)	The objectives include acquisition of the foreign language at the level that ensures quite fluent language communication along with developing the knowledge of the target language culture and aspects of its everyday life. Objectives set out to be fulfilled by the school include: • developing self-esteem and belief in the learners' own linguistic abilities; • preparing the learner gradually for independence and autonomy in learning the foreign language; • developing in the learners an attitude of interest in and openness and tolerance towards other cultures. Generalized content areas related to intercultural competence include: • developing vocabulary with reference to everyday life, with particular account taken of the cultural background of the home country and the target language culture on the basis of authentic materials; • expanding the civilization and culture component, with particular focus on lifestyle and behaviour in the target language country. *Source*: Podstawa programowa języka obcego w gimnazjum (2003) (Core curriculum for foreign language in the gymnasium)

| Germany (Level: ISCED 2) | In its first pages, the document describes the development of intercultural competencies as a super-ordinate task of school education to which the foreign language classroom has a special contribution to make. This contribution is seen in the development of pupils' ability to communicate, thus making them open, tolerant and mature citizens in an integrating Europe, the document goes on.

The ability to compare their own attitudes, values and social conditions with those of other cultures in a tolerant and critical fashion and the willingness to display interest in and understanding of other ways of thinking and living and the values and norms of other cultures lead to an increase in experience and a strengthening of the identity of the learners, the document states.

It continues by saying that language education is regarded as making a prime contribution to the ability to take on more than one perspective through the acquisition of sociocultural knowledge of selected topics with respect to the target culture and the development of the capacity for intercultural communication.

At a later point in the document intercultural competence is described as one of three competence areas of the first foreign language. The other two are functional communicative competencies and methodological competencies.

Intercultural competence is at this point defined as consisting of sociocultural knowledge, an understanding of cultural difference and the ability to deal with it, and the practical mastery of intercultural encounters.

Source: Beschlüsse der Kultusministerkonferenz – Bildungsstandards für die erste Fremdsprache (Englisch/ Französisch) für den Mittleren Schulabschluss Beschluss vom 4.12.2003 (Decisions of the Standing Conference of the Ministers of Education and Cultural Affairs of the Länder – Standards in the First Foreign Language (English/French) for the General Education School Leaving Certificate). |
| Finland (Level: ISCED 2) | The curriculum states that the pupils will:

• 'Get to know the target language culture and come to understand it against their own cultural background.
• Learn to communicate and act in normal day-today situations in a manner acceptable in the subject culture.
• Learn to be aware of the culturally bound nature of values'

Source: Peruskoulun opetussuunnitelman perusteet 2004 (National Core Curriculum for Basic Education) |

(Extracts from country reports, contributed by Helen Spencer-Oatey, Andrzej Kurtyka, Peter Franklin and David Marsh respectively, which were used as source data in the LACE (2007) study)

Regardless of the framework used, the study came to the conclusion that, apart from there being important differences between countries and the primary and lower secondary level, the national curricula analysed 'pay most attention to the development of linguistic competencies and communication skills. (Inter)cultural competencies (if included in the curriculum) get considerably less consideration' and that 'intercultural competence as an objective focuses to a large extent on knowledge and attitudes' (LACE study 2007: 22).

Using the Byram framework of four types of competence (linguistic competence, sociolinguistic competence, discourse competence and intercultural competence), the LACE study researchers found that linguistic competence accounted for 50 per cent of the focus of the curricula across the 12 countries investigated, whereas intercultural competence received the least focus with only 15 per cent.

9.4.2   Aims and outcomes in the school classroom

What aims curricula contain, what actually happens in the classroom and what outcomes result in the form of knowledge, attitudes and skills acquired by pupils are three very different matters in any context. However, we can assume a greater disparity between aims and outcomes in the educational context than in the professional development context for three reasons.

- Firstly, the general nature of the needs which the classroom attempts to meet means that aims are fuzzily formulated leading to wide scope for different operationalizations of the described aims.
- Secondly, teachers in many cultures have the freedom to give not only their own interpretation but also their own weighting to the aims contained in the curriculum in terms of teaching time. For example, the LACE study (2007: 50) reports that '53.1% of respondents to the online survey report spending some 80% of classroom time on language learning, and 20% classroom time on developing intercultural competence, whereas as many as 32.9% spend 60% of classroom time on language learning and 40% on developing intercultural competence.'
- And thirdly and most significantly, because ICIC development is not a school subject in its own right, it is competing for attention with the main subject of the lesson, generally foreign language education. Castro and Sercu (2005: 20–2) show in their research that, unsurprisingly, language teachers prioritize language learning objectives over what they term culture learning objectives and general skills objectives.

For these reasons, research has concentrated on the teachers themselves as the mediator between curriculum and pupils to gain a picture of the aims and outcomes of ICIC development. To find out more precisely how teachers may interpret the ICIC aims in foreign language curricula, both Castro and Sercu (2005) and the LACE study (2007) questioned language teachers about their conceptualizations of the aims of ICIC development using the same set of aims for teachers to prioritize. Although the two surveys come to different rankings (see Research Report 9.2), generally developments in attitudes are more

Research Report 9.2　Teachers' conceptualizations of the aims of ICIC development

Competence area	Aim	Ranked by teachers	
		in Castro & Sercu (2005)	in LACE Study (2007)
Attitudes	Develop attitudes of openness and tolerance towards other people and cultures	1	1
Knowledge	Provide information about daily life and routines	2	5
Skills	Promote reflection on cultural differences	3	4
Knowledge	Provide information about shared values and beliefs	4	8
Knowledge	Provide experiences with a rich variety of cultural expressions (literature, music, theatre, film, ...)	5	7
Skills	Promote the ability to handle intercultural contact situations	6	2
Knowledge	Provide information about the history, geography and political conditions of the foreign culture(s)	7	9
Skills	Promote the ability to empathize with people living in other cultures	8	3
Skills	Promote increased understanding of students' own culture	9	6

clearly prioritized as aims, ahead of the skills area, which in turn comes ahead of knowledge in order of importance. This finding contrasts with the LACE study analysis of curricula (rather than of teachers' conceptualizations), which found priority being given to a large extent to knowledge and attitudes rather than skills.

9.4.3 Methods recommended in school curricula

The LACE study (2007) also investigated what didactic and methodological approaches to the development of intercultural competence are recommended by the curricula and found that the information regarding didactic and methodological approaches contained in the curricula is often very limited. Where recommendations are made, they concern most often the use of authentic materials in the target language such as TV programmes, newspapers, magazines, books; 'content and language integrated learning'; information about the other/another culture such as texts about the target country; oral teacher input; and online information. What is striking is that no mention is made in the curricula themselves of approaches or methods which are narrowly intercultural in nature (as described in Section 9.2.3 above), although the survey deliberately included these methods and techniques in the list teachers chose their answers from.

9.4.4 Methods used in the school classroom

The LACE study (2007) also questioned language teachers in an online survey and in telephone interviews about the methods, techniques and procedures they used when developing ICIC in the foreign language classroom. The list of methods they were given in part again deliberately duplicated the list used in Section 9.2.3 above, the intention being to discover to what extent methods firmly established in the professional development field have found their way into use in the schools. A summary of the results for all the countries surveyed is contained in Research Report 9.3, the number of stars indicating the frequency of a method being mentioned as used. The most striking findings are the dominance of traditional chalk-and-talk methods, the place firmly occupied by communicative methods of language learning and teaching (role play and task-based activities) and the low frequency of use of narrowly intercultural methods as described in Section 9.2.3 above and indicated in the table in italics.

If chalk and talk seem to dominate, what exactly is the talk about? Bandura and Sercu (2005) give us some idea in a ranked list of the activities teachers use in the language classroom and the nature of the

Research Report 9.3   Frequency of mention of methods used adapted from the LACE Study (2007)

Methods	Frequency	Methods	Frequency
Oral teacher input	****	*Cross-cultural dialogues*	**
Written information	***	*Immersion, school visits abroad and exchanges*	**
Online information	***	Tandem learning	*
Role plays	***	Self-assessment	*
Task-based activities	***	Case studies	*
Literature and the arts	***	*Critical incidents*	*
Content and language integrated learning	**	*Contrast culture training*	*
Information using other than online or written media	**	*Culture assimilator or intercultural sensitizer*	*
Internet-based collaborative learning	**	*Area studies*	*
Simulations and games	**		

Italics indicates 'intercultural methods' discussed on pp. 220–4.

ICIC outcome generated. The LACE study used the same descriptions of activities as in Research Report 9.4 and found those in italics in the table to be used frequently or from time to time by a majority of teachers in both primary and lower secondary foreign language education.

Both Bandura and Sercu (2005) and the LACE study (2007) asked teachers how frequently they dealt with certain topics in their ICIC development activities; the results are summarized in Research Report 9.5.

The striking finding is the very low priority given to values and beliefs, which in the professional development context would certainly achieve a higher frequency. Though this may be connected with the lower level of cognitive maturity of children compared with adults, it seems to be a curiously low ranking considering how essential a knowledge of values and beliefs of both C1 and C2 is to an understanding of culturally based difference.

There are a number of publications both in English (e.g., Tomalin and Stempleski 1993; Byram and Fleming 1998; Byram, Nichols and Stevens 2001) and presumably other languages, which provide language

Research Report 9.4   ICIC activities in the language classroom adapted from Bandura and Sercu (2005: 77–78)

Ranked activity	Score on a range 1 (never) to 3 (often)	Outcome
1. I tell my pupils what I heard (or read) about the foreign country or culture	2.67	Knowledge
2. I tell my pupils why I find something fascinating or strange about the foreign culture(s)	2.60	Knowledge, attitudes
3. *I ask my pupils to compare an aspect of their own culture with that aspect in the foreign culture*	2.50	Skills
4. *I talk with my pupils about stereotypes regarding particular cultures and countries or regarding the inhabitants of particular countries*	2.40	Knowledge, attitudes
5. I talk to my pupils about my own experiences in the foreign country	2.34	Knowledge, attitudes
6. I comment on the way in which the foreign culture is represented in the foreign language materials I am using in a particular class	2.29	Knowledge
7. I ask my pupils about their experiences in the foreign country	2.28	Knowledge, attitudes
8. I ask my pupils to describe an aspect of their own culture in the foreign language	2.22	Knowledge, skills
9. *I use videos, CD-ROMs or the Internet to illustrate an aspect of the foreign culture*	2.09	Knowledge
10. *I ask my pupils to think about the image which the media promote of the foreign country*	2.09	Knowledge, skills
11. I ask my pupils to think about what it would be like to live in the foreign culture	2.08	Knowledge attitudes, skills
12. *I decorate my classroom with posters illustrating particular aspects of the foreign culture*	2.05	Knowledge, attitudes
13. I bring objects originating from the foreign culture to my classroom	2.01	Knowledge, attitudes

14. I ask my pupils to independently explore an aspect of the foreign culture	2.00	Skills
15. *I ask my pupils to participate in role-play situations in which people from different cultures meet*	1.88	Attitudes, skills
16. I touch upon an aspect of the foreign culture regarding which I feel negatively disposed	1.83	Attitudes
17. I invite a person originating from the foreign country to my classroom	1.46	Knowledge, attitudes

Italics indicates those activities which the LACE study (2007) found to be used frequently or from time to time by teachers in both primary and lower secondary foreign language education.

Research Report 9.5   Subjects dealt with in ICIC development activities in the language education classroom

Bandura and Sercu (2005)			LACE Study (2007)			
				'I deal with this subject [...]		
Subject	Rank	score	Subject	[...] often'	[...] now and then'	[...] never'
Daily life and routines,	1	2.66	Daily life and routines	77%	23%	0%
living conditions,			Living conditions	42%	49%	8%
food and drink			Food and drink	73%	26%	1%
Traditions, folklore, tourist attractions	2	2.38	Traditions, folklore, tourist attractions	60%	40%	0%
Youth culture	3	2.24	Youth culture	51%	42%	7%

Education, professional life	4	2.17	Education	49%	48%	2%
			Professional life	7%	61%	32%
History, geography, political system	5	2.10	History	16%	71%	12%
			Geography	28%	67%	5%
			Political system	4%	44%	52%
Literature	6	2.06	Literature	21%	60%	19%
Values and beliefs	7	2.05	Values and beliefs	26%	60%	14%
Other cultural expressions (music, drama, art, [...])	8	2.05	Other cultural expressions (music, drama, art, [...])	34%	62%	4%
Different ethnic and social groups	9	1.89	Different ethnic and social groups	15%	62%	23%
International relations (political, economic, cultural) with students' own country and other countries	10	1.77	International relations (political, economic, cultural) with students' own country and other countries	4%	54%	41%

teachers with materials for the development of ICIC. However, the LACE study reveals that, after the lack of time, the lack of suitable resources is regarded by language teachers as the main problem in the development of ICIC in educational contexts. A large majority of respondents reported that they believed there should be more specific guidance for teachers concerning intercultural competence development in their classrooms. These two shortcomings are also revealed in Research Report 9.6, as are other forms of support language teachers feel are desirable.

Research Report 9.6 Support desired by language teachers in the development of intercultural competence (adapted from the LACE study, 2007)	
Examples of activities to do in the classroom	79.7%
Exchange programmes for teachers	70.1%
Workshops	63.5%
Examples of exercises	50.3%
More staff development (in-service training)	49.2%
Seminars	48.2%
Online forum to exchange ideas	47.7%

9.5   The qualification profile of the developer

Given the broad range of knowledge, attitudes and skills which make up ICIC and the varied methods needed to support their development, the developer must naturally have a role which goes beyond that of a chalk-and-talk developer. Although the latter might be suitable for passing on knowledge, it is likely to be less suitable for developing skills and attitudes. The 'facilitator of learning' role, familiar to applied linguists from classical communicative approaches to foreign language teaching (cf. Littlewood 1981: 92) is one which is an appropriate description of the developer's multi-faceted role. King (1993) once memorably described these two contrasting roles as the 'sage on the stage' as opposed to the 'guide on the side'.

The qualifications necessary for fulfilling this complex role are equally multi-faceted but vary considerably between the school context and the professional development context.

For the school context, Sercu (2005a, 2005b) has compared knowledge, skill and attitude profiles of language teachers, which she envisages as necessary for effective intercultural competence development in the language classroom, with empirical data on the profiles of teachers actually doing so. The results are summarized in Research Report 9.7.

Sercu concludes that the profile of foreign language teachers currently:

> does not meet all expectations of the 'foreign language and intercultural competence teacher' regarding knowledge, skills and attitudes. [...] The majority of teachers in all the countries participating in this research, however, either have what could be labelled 'a foreign language teacher profile', focusing primarily and almost exclusively on

Research Report 9.7 Ideal and actual knowledge and skills profiles of language teachers developing intercultural competence

Envisaged profile (Sercu 2005: 5–6)	Actual profile (Sercu 2005: 155–7)
Knowledge	
Sufficient familiarity with culture, frequent and varied contacts with culture	Frequent media contacts, travel to country concerned, extensive contacts with foreign culture at home
Familiarity with own culture	Teachers regard it as unimportant for pupils to acquire understanding of own culture
Possession of culture-general knowledge allowing comparisons and contrasts	Unclear
Knowledge about pupils' stereotypes	May have knowledge about pupils' stereotypes but do not take it into account when teaching
Skills	
Possession of appropriate teaching techniques	Possession of techniques to enlarge learners' knowledge of cultures
Ability to help pupils relate to own culture to foreign culture	Probably not
Ability to compare cultures	Yes
Ability to empathise with foreign cultures' perspectives	Probably not
Ability to select and adjust teaching materials	Can comment critically on cultural content but probably less able to select and adjust material for developing intercultural competence
Ability to use out-of-classroom experiential approaches such as school trips and exchanges	Little preparation and follow-up of such experiences
Attitudes	
Favourably disposed towards integrating intercultural competence development in foreign language teaching	Many are favourably disposed
Willing to work towards that goal	Many are willing to work towards that goal

| Definition of foreign language education should include intercultural competence development | Generally not the case |
| Should take account of pupils' perceptions and attitudes when designing learning process | Generally not the case |

the acquisition of communicative competence in the foreign language, or a 'foreign language and culture teaching profile', focusing primarily on the acquisition of communicative competence in the foreign language, but also teaching culture so as to enhance pupils' familiarity with the foreign culture as well as their motivation to learn the foreign language.

(2005: 158)

Intercultural interaction competence is extremely complex. In contrast, the conceptualization prevalent in much of foreign language education – referred to by Risager (1998) as the 'foreign cultural approach' – is rather restricted in scope. As a result, we would go further than Sercu (2005) above and suggest intercultural competence development in the language education in schools is an activity which probably develops few of the wide range of knowledge, attitudes and skills that the broader conceptualization includes. Its effectiveness thus probably leaves much to be desired. Without considerable changes in the education and training of foreign language teachers – an implicit conclusion of the LACE study as well – intercultural competence development in schools probably needs to be shared at present as a cross-curricular task with other subjects.

The professional development context is less thoroughly researched but what little is known about the qualifications of developers presents a rather different picture reflecting the multi-disciplinary nature of the area. Berardo and Simons (2004) in their survey of the intercultural profession also investigated the qualifications and experiences of intercultural developers. They found a broad range of subjects of study as a qualification held by developers although at bachelor's level as many as 43 per cent were graduates of linguistics, language and literature (2004: 12), with 36 per cent holding a degree in psychology, anthropology, history, sociology or political science. At master's level, linguistics, language and literature still dominate with 32 per cent; more closely followed by intercultural or international studies with 28 per cent; business, economics and marketing

(27 per cent); and psychology, anthropology, history, sociology or political science (26 per cent). Twenty-six per cent of those surveyed hold a doctoral degree, nearly half of them in psychology, anthropology, history, sociology or political science. Only 27 per cent of those questioned had a doctoral degree in linguistics, language and literature.

Berardo and Simons (2004: 80) also investigated the degree of preparation in training, coaching or consulting that developers active in the professional development field had:

> 48% report having attended a professional program or workshop in teaching, coaching or consulting while 75% have a certificate or diploma in one of these three categories. A large percentage of interculturalists also have either attended a professional program or workshop (64%) or have received a certificate or diploma (48%) in Intercultural or International studies.

In view of the relative lack of university degree courses preparing its graduates specifically for a career in intercultural communication and its development, other aspects of the qualification profile of developers are perhaps especially significant for those interested in becoming practitioners. The results of this research, also undertaken by Berardo and Simons (2004), are summarized in Research Report 9.8.

Research Report 9.8   Experiences beneficial and useful to intercultural developers in the professional development context (adapted from Berardo and Simons 2004)

	Beneficial / useful to respondents		Considered by respondents to be beneficial to those becoming professionals	
	Percentage of respondents ranking this aspect on a scale of importance from 1–7			
	1	2	1	2
Experience living abroad	68%	18%	39%	25%
International business experience	34%	19%	20%	13%
Cross-cultural relationships	33%	38%	8%	13%

Formal studies in the intercultural field	24%	24%	17%	21%
Formal training in OD coaching training facilitation	19%	24%	7%	15%
Having a diverse cultural heritage	17%	13%	7%	9%
Travel and tourism	12%	15%	3%	4%

9.6 Concluding comments

These findings highlight the significance of a discussion in progress in Europe at least about entry to the intercultural development profession and the qualifications of professionals in it or wanting to enter it. It is an occupation very attractive to many internationally minded and experienced graduates of a wide range of disciplines, who either try their hand as freelancers or start as interns for intercultural training providers. The entry barriers are extremely low. Anybody who can convince a client that they have the ability to conduct a development intervention can do so, and any graduate who appears qualified by virtue of a relevant university degree and other experience can become an often underpaid intern at a training company.

This is leading to an over-supply of potential developers, which in turn is seen as a threat in two ways by some of those established in the profession. Firstly, it bears the risk of diminished quality of delivery as more and more inexperienced developers acquire professional knowledge and skills by trial and error, which may have the back-wash effect of casting doubt on the effectiveness of ICIC development intervention. Secondly, even in a period of increasing demand from the market for development interventions, there is a fear of downward pressure on fees, which is becoming a reality for those offering standard services without special value added or the appeal of an established name.

One necessary consequence, but one which is realizable only in the medium term, would be the establishment of post-graduate professional qualification programmes which, on the basis of accreditation, could bring greater quality and transparency in both the professional and educational development contexts. For this to happen at university level, a rare cooperation of the disciplines would be required to ensure that the inherent multidisciplinary nature of the field is reflected in the qualification itself.

Further reading

Fowler, S. M. and Blohm, J. M. (2004) An analysis of methods for intercultural training. In D. Landis, J. M. Bennett and M. J. Bennett (eds), *Handbook of Intercultural Training*. London and Thousands Oaks, CA: Sage, pp. 37–84. An invaluable, state-of-the-art overview of the techniques of intercultural development as practised in the United States and many parts of Europe.

Fowler, S. M. and Mumford, M. G. (eds) (1995) *Intercultural Sourcebook: Cross-Cultural Training Methods*, Volume 1. Yarmouth: Intercultural Press; Fowler, S. M. and Mumford, M. G. (eds) (1999) *Intercultural Sourcebook: Cross-Cultural Training Methods*, Volume 2. Yarmouth: Intercultural Press. These two books give detailed and critical accounts of the methods of intercultural development, often written by the originators of the methods themselves.

Landis, D., Bennett, J. M. and Bennett, M. J. (eds) (2004) *Handbook of Intercultural Training*. London and Thousands Oaks, CA: Sage. Now in its third edition, this is a comprehensive overview of intercultural development by leading US and a number of European experts, mainly psychologists. The collection of specially written chapters includes a fascinating history of intercultural training as well as accounts of development contexts not dealt with in this chapter.

Sercu, L. et al. (2005) *Foreign Language Teachers & Intercultural Communication: An International Investigation*, pp. 1–18. Clevedon: Multilingual Matters. Very enlightening survey of the state of intercultural competence development in language education in Europe.

Part 3

Researching Intercultural Interaction

10
Research Topics in Intercultural Interaction

A sense of curiosity is nature's original school of education.

Smiley Blanton

Chapter outline

10.1   Researching intercultural interaction competence
10.2   Researching understanding and rapport in intercultural interaction
10.3   Researching disadvantage and domination in intercultural interaction
10.4   Researching adaptation to unfamiliar cultures
10.5   Researching intercultural interaction competence development
10.6   Concluding comments

This chapter and the next focus on research into intercultural interaction. In this chapter, we outline some key research topics, and sample studies, associated with the various issues explored in Parts 1 and 2. In the next chapter, we explore the steps involved in carrying out a research project, and discuss the ways in which cultural factors need to be taken into consideration in relation to each of them.

Our aim in this chapter is to help aspiring researchers gain an overview of the range of issues that can be investigated within the broad field of intercultural interaction, and of the varying approaches and methods that can be used to research these issues. For each of the topic areas, we identify the main themes that have been investigated by researchers from different disciplinary backgrounds and we list some sample studies that have been conducted on these themes. We discuss the data collection methods used in these studies, and key issues that need to be considered when researching these topics.

When selecting the studies we have attempted to satisfy a number of criteria. Firstly, while not neglecting culture-comparative studies, we have given priority to culture-interactional studies. The need for a move away from culture-comparative insights towards more culture-interactional studies has been a central belief that has guided the writing of this book. Secondly, we have selected studies from a variety of disciplines. Our belief that the study of intercultural interaction must be informed and underpinned by research priorities, insights and methods derived from diverse areas is clear in the sub-title we have chosen for the book and is also evident in the literature we have reviewed in the book. Thirdly, we chose the studies so that as wide a range of approaches and methods as possible are illustrated.

10.1 Researching intercultural interaction competence (cf. Chapters 3 and 8)

Research into intercultural interaction competence (ICIC) covers a range of different themes, as Research Studies 10.1 indicates. Nearly all of the studies, and all those we present here, have their origins in the fields of psychology, communication studies or management studies, because applied linguists and language education specialists have rarely researched this topic. On the few occasions when they have done so, they have usually worked on its conceptualization (e.g. Byram 1997) or else they have contributed to a hybrid framework for its assessment (e.g. the INCA project). The empirical studies on ICIC (see Chapter 3) either generated knowledge about the nature of ICIC, which was then subsequently used to conceptualize it, or else examined assumed individual components of ICIC, which contributed to supporting (or not) certain posited conceptualizations of ICIC.

Research Studies 10.1 Examples of topics of research associated with intercultural interaction competence (and data collection methods)

Conceptualizations and components of ICIC

- A conceptualization of ICIC which attempts to construct a multidimensional understanding of ICIC which reduces the influences of cultural biases (Arasaratnam and Doerfel 2005) [interviews]; (Arasaratnam 2006) [questionnaire].
- A four-stage model of how cultural sensitivity develops in international business relationships. (Shapiro, Ozanne and Saatcioglu 2008) [observation and interviews].

- The relationship between ICIC and empathy (Arasaratnam 2006) [questionnaires].
- The relationship between ICIC (in the healthcare context) and empathy, intercultural experience and bilingualism (Gibson and Zhong 2005) [questionnaires].
- The effect of anxiety and uncertainty on the perceived effectiveness of communication in two relationships and two cultures (Gudykunst and Nishida 2001) thus contributing to the testing of Gudykunst's AUM theory of intercultural communication (1993, 1995) [questionnaire].

The relationships between ICIC and broader measures of adjustment and success

- The relationship between psychological adjustment and ICIC among members of immigrant families (Lee and Chen 2000) [questionnaires].
- The effect of ICIC on the success of student expatriates and the development of a multiple success measure linked to various components of intercultural competence (Gelbrich 2004) [questionnaire].
- The relationship of ICIC to success measured in terms of the performance of multicultural teams (Matveev and Nelson 2004) [questionnaires].

The significance of ICIC for professional contexts

- Cross-cultural variations in the perceived importance of the ICIC of tour guides (Leclerc and Martin 2004) [questionnaire].
- The perceived ICIC of medical providers, including patient perceptions of their ability to communicate with a diverse patient population (Gibson and Zhong 2005) [questionnaire].
- Impact of intercultural competence on negotiation style and whether it can override the impact of national and organizational culture (Chaisrakeo and Speece 2004) [interviews and questionnaires].

The relationship between ICIC and membership of a particular cultural group

- Comparison of the 'rhetorical sensitivity' (which emphasizes relational aspects over pragmatic goal-seeking) of students from two cultures (Knutson et al. 2003) [questionnaire].
- Effects of the national cultural orientations of team members on their perceptions of ICIC (Matveev and Nelson 2004) [questionnaires].

Where the studies are not concerned with models and constituents of ICIC, some have aimed rather at underlining the value of ICIC for social cohesion, education abroad and international business purposes. Especially in the latter case, intercultural developers are often required to attempt to make the business case for intercultural development interventions, and such studies can supply much-needed evidence to aid the transfer of research insights into practice. This link to practice is obvious in those studies aimed at investigating the significance of ICIC for a variety of professional contexts. Again this is a topic of great relevance for practitioners and development professionals who are increasingly being requested to help promote the ICIC of specific groups for specific purposes. Development interventions can be more effective and more efficient if we know which particular aspects of ICIC are salient for particular groups. Gibson and Zhong (2005) make a number of proposals in this direction which may be especially interesting to applied linguists; for example, investigating links between L2 competence and ICIC, and examining links between non-verbal communication and ICIC. A final strand of recent research concerns the relationship between perceived ICIC and membership of a particular cultural group.

One consequence of this topic being investigated primarily by experts in psychology, communication studies or management studies is that these disciplines tend to adopt a survey approach using psychometric questionnaires (rather than using qualitative methods such as interviews). Sometimes these questionnaires are devised by the authors of the studies themselves as in Gudykunst and Nishida (2001). This is also the case with Matveev and Nelson (2004), who used the Cross-Cultural Communication Competence (CCC) questionnaire, which was based on previous work by Matveev, Rao and Milter (2001). Other studies use questionnaires which are in the public domain and have been shown to be sound, such as the Self-Perceived Communication Competency scale (McCroskey and McCroskey 1988) and the Personal Report of Intercultural Communication Apprehension (PRICA) (Neuliep and McCroskey 1997), both of which are available free of charge on the Internet.[1] Still others use hybrid forms derived from other questionnaires, or modified forms – sometimes shortened – of already existing questionnaires. For example, Matveev and Nelson (2004) collected data by using the modified seven-point, 45-item High-Performance Team questionnaire (Wheelan 1990, 1994). Leclerc and Martin's (2004) questionnaire was adapted from two inventories (Martin, Hammer and Bradford 1994; and Pavitt and Haight 1986), both based on the Behavioral Expectations Model.

Qualitative methods have also been used in recent studies when it is a matter of exploring broader issues connected with the conceptualization of ICIC. Arasaratnam and Doerfel (2005), for example, used open-ended interviews with participants from 15 countries in their attempt to develop a culture-free conceptualization of ICIC. Shapiro, Ozanne and Saatcioglu (2008) used three phases of interviews over a number of years: 28 informal interviews and participant observations spread over a 26-month period were followed by in-depth, open-ended interviews with a subset of 12 informants. An analysis of the data collected in this phase led to the generation of further questions used in telephone interviews. Chaisrakeo and Speece (2004) employed semi-structured interviews supplemented by questionnaires, amongst them the Organizational Culture Index (Oliver and Anderson 1994) and the Intercultural Effectiveness Scale (Hammer, Gudykunst and Wiseman 1978).

Such interview methods may appeal particularly to the applied linguist used to working qualitatively with restricted amounts of real-life language data and perhaps lacking a mastery of the statistical methods necessary for the analysis of quantitative data. However, a quantitative approach provides the opportunity for using existing and tried-and-tested instruments (such as those presented here and in Sections 8.2 and 8.3 of Chapter 8), and it is often valuable to combine the two approaches. For example, as we have mentioned previously, research evidence indicates that intercultural interaction may be improved significantly by using message communication competencies (see Concept 4.1), for example, by using active listening and linguistic accommodation to negotiate meaning, repair communicative disturbances and to create understanding. To test this proposition that such message communication competencies are indeed a component of ICIC, such quantitative assessments of ICIC could be combined with a qualitative investigation of real-life language data to explore whether the skills co-occur with a high degree of ICIC.

10.2   Researching understanding and rapport in intercultural interaction (cf. Chapters 4 and 5)

Research in this area can be roughly divided into four broad areas, as shown in Research Studies 10.2. As indicated by the studies listed, there is a certain amount of research that explicitly focuses on the construction of (mis)understanding and/or rapport in intercultural interaction, but there is a far greater amount of research that explores aspects of communication or interaction that may have an impact on it.

Research Studies 10.2   Examples of topics of research associated with understanding and rapport in intercultural interaction (and data collection methods)

The study of (mis)understanding/rapport in intercultural interaction

- Misunderstandings in healthcare consultations in multilingual settings (Roberts et al. 2005) [video].

- Service encounters between Korean shopkeepers and African-American customers: problematic (Bailey 2000); friendly (Ryoo 2005) [video; observation; post-event interview].
- Rapport management in Chinese–British business interactions (Spencer-Oatey and Xing 2004) [video; observation; interview].
- (Im)politeness in New Zealand workplaces (Schnurr, Marra and Holmes 2007) [selection from corpus of audio recordings].
- Topical talk in initial encounters between Japanese and American students (Mori 2003) [video].
- Conflicts in online intercultural dialogue (Schneider and von der Emde 2005) [online record; participant post-event reflection].
- Rapport promotion in service encounters and the impact of cultural values (Chan et al. 2004) [questionnaire].

The (comparative) study of specific features of language use

- Expressing refusals in Korean and in American English (Kwon 2004) [DCT questionnaire].
- Backchannel behaviour in German and English monolinguals and bilinguals (Heinz 2003) [audio]
- Silence in intercultural communication in university seminars (Nakane 2006) [interview, questionnaire, video, audio, observation].
- Humour in business meetings (Rogerson-Revell 2007) [audio].
- Latino/Anglo-American differences in attributions to situations involving touch and silence (Albert and Ha 2004) [critical incident questionnaire].

The study of communication styles and preferences

- Communication styles in English and German (House 2006) [multiple collections of linguistic data].
- Communication style and relationship satisfaction between international and host students (Shigemasu and Ikeda 2006) [questionnaire].
- Values, self-construals and communication style (Kapoor et al. 2003) [questionnaire].
- Societal preferences for conflict mediation in Gambia (Davidheiser 2005) [archival sources, interview, questionnaire, observation, audio, panel discussion].

The study of communication networks and modes of communication

- Intercultural contact and interaction among multicultural university students (Halualani et al. 2004) [questionnaire].
- Students' media choice to communicate with professors in Japan and America (Richardson and Smith 2007) [questionnaire].
- Global virtual team dynamics and effectiveness (Maznevski and Chudoba 2000) [interview, observation, communication log, questionnaire, company documentation].

The study of the co-construction of (mis)understanding and rapport in intercultural interaction is almost exclusively carried out by applied linguists and discourse analysts. It normally requires a detailed analysis of the unfolding of meaning within an interchange, and access to the exact verbal and non-verbal behaviour that is used is essential for this. For oral interaction, this requires the collection of audio or video data, and for online text interaction, it requires the digital saving of the exchanges. For oral interaction, there is a growing preference for the use of video data since this provides non-verbal information that can inform the verbal analysis, and can also allow a multimodal analysis to be carried out, if required. If there is a need to understand the participants' evaluative judgements, as is often the case in studies of rapport, then the discourse data needs to be supplemented with post-event playback/interview data (e.g., Spencer-Oatey and Xing 2004; Ryoo 2005). Such data can provide very illuminating insights into the perceptions of the participants of the interaction, often demonstrating how different these can be. Very occasionally, a completely different approach is taken. For example, a study by Chan and colleagues (2004), which was a collaboration between three psychologists and an applied linguist, used a questionnaire which included Schwartz's PVQ (see Section 11.1.2). They investigated people's interactional concerns (including rapport) in selected contexts, and explored whether their concerns were correlated with the values they held.

Up to now, there have been relatively few studies that have focused on (mis)understanding and rapport in authentic intercultural interaction; far more studies focus on the analysis of specific features of language use. A large proportion of these studies are culture-comparative in nature, and a few (e.g., Heinz 2003) are both culture-comparative and culture-interactional in scope. As we mentioned in Chapter 1, when analysing intercultural interaction it is very helpful to have 'baseline data' about the languages/cultures of the participants, and comparative studies are helpful in so far as they can provide that information. However, it cannot be assumed that linguistic/cultural conventions will necessarily be transferred to intercultural contexts of use, so any such information needs to be used primarily for explanatory rather than predictive purposes.

Studies of specific features of language use also require access to discourse data if the focus is on the productive use of such features. Again this means the collection of video, audio or online digital data. However, it may be difficult to predict when certain features of language use will occur naturalistically, and in such cases, linguists have frequently used a type of questionnaire that comprises simple scenarios with brief, partially completed interactions. (For further details see Section 11.2.3.) The scenarios are designed in such a way as to elicit the language features being researched, while controlling the contextual variables that could influence how they are operationalized. Traditionally, the respondents complete the interactions on paper, but a major concern over using this self-report data is that it may differ significantly from people's actual use. There is thus a growing preference among linguists to collect authentic discourse data; however, a valuable alternative is to use role play or simulation (see Section 11.2.3; see also Kasper 2008 for a very helpful critical account of different methods for collecting linguistic data).

If a researcher's focus is on how people react to the use of specific features of verbal or non-verbal behaviour, then playback/interview and/or questionnaire data needs to be collected. The design of the questionnaire can often be complex, requiring several stages for its development. Albert and Ha (2004), for example, developed a critical incident questionnaire (see Concept 9.1) and explain the different steps that were involved.

Linguistic studies of the productive use of language provide large amounts of very detailed descriptions and these can provide rich insights into specific interactions and/or people's use of specific linguistic features. However, for non-linguist professionals or for intercultural developers, such studies can be too detailed or too idiosyncratic for application to real-life. There is a great need for linguists to consider the practical applications of their analyses, to cooperate with non-linguist experts and professionals in their research, and to present them in ways that are meaningful to non-linguistic audiences. Roberts and colleagues (2005) is an excellent but relatively rare example of this being done, although it is more common in relation to discrimination (see the next section).

Perhaps because of this concern for generalizable findings, some research (especially in psychology and communication studies) focuses on general patterns of language use, such as communication styles and communication networks. Research into communication styles requires access to large amounts of data in order that macro patterns (or absence of them) can be detected. House (2006), for example, draws on eight different collections of German–English discourse data in order to ascertain whether there are any differences in German and English macro-communication styles. For psychologists, it is particularly common not to study people's communication style preferences *per se*, but rather to investigate what individual or cultural factors influence them (e.g., Kapoor et al. 2003). Questionnaire data is usually collected for this, often using scales that have been developed and validated by previous research.

A fourth focus of research is on communication networks and modes of communication. This area of research can be of major practical relevance, especially to those interested in intercultural communities, such as university students, residents of certain urban districts or members of international projects. Once again, questionnaires are frequently used for collecting data for this type of research, but research into the communication networks and communication modes of international teams can be particularly challenging. Maznevski and Chudoba (2000), for example, report the following data sources: semi-structured interviews (within team and around team), unstructured interviews, observation of face-to-face meetings, observation of conference calls, communication logs, questionnaires and company documentation.

10.3   Researching disadvantage and domination in intercultural interaction (cf. Chapter 6)

Research on disadvantage and domination can be roughly divided into four broad areas, as shown in Research Studies 10.3. The areas are often closely interlinked, in that disadvantage, racism and domination can stem from cross-cultural differences in impression formation as well as from the stereotypes that people may hold, so some studies cover multiple elements.

Research Studies 10.3   Examples of topics of research associated with disadvantage and domination in intercultural interaction (and data collection methods)

The study of impressions and impression management

- British and Chinese evaluative reactions to different types of responses to compliments (Spencer-Oatey, Ng and Dong 2008) [questionnaires].
- A lawyer's use of impression management in a closing argument at a trial (Hobbs 2003) [recording of an authentic court trial, broadcast on TV].
- Impression management in 'intercultural' German job interviews (Birkner and Kern 2008) [recordings of job interviews, recordings of interview panels evaluating candidates, interviews with company staff].
- Impression management in a Hong Kong workplace (Bilbow 1997) [recordings of naturally occurring conversations, playback to participants and members of other cultural groups].

The study of disadvantage

- Migration, ethnicity and competing discourses (institutional and personal) in job interviews (Campbell and Roberts 2007) [video recording of job interviews, post-event video feedback sessions, post-event interviews].
- Perceived discrimination, social support networks, and psychological well-being among three immigrant groups (Jasinskaja-Lahti et al. 2006) [questionnaire].
- Labour market discrimination via white- or black-sounding names on resumes (Bertrand and Mullainathan 2003) [field 'experiment'].

The study of stereotypes

- Use of Asian American stereotypes as resources in conversations among Asian Americans (Reyes 2004) [video recording of conversations].
- Dynamic stereotypes about women and men in Latin America and the United States (Diekman et al. 2005) [questionnaire].
- Restaurant servers' stereotyping and social categorization of members of other social groups (Mallinson and Brewster 2005) [interviews].

The study of prejudice, racism and domination

- Deflecting responsibility in employer talk about race discrimination (Tilbury and Colic-Peisker 2006) [in-depth interviews].
- Racial insults and reported speech in neighbour complaints and police interrogations (Stokoe and Edwards 2007) [recordings of neighbour dispute interactions, including recordings of telephone calls to mediation centres and of police interrogation of suspects].

Theories about impression formation and impression management (cf. Section 6.1) have been developed within social psychology, sociology and business, but there are comparatively few studies that have researched it empirically in relation to intercultural interaction. There is a need, therefore, for many more studies in this area. Key issues that need to be researched include:

- Cross-cultural and intercultural perspectives on people's evaluative judgements/perceptions of certain features of behaviour/language use.
- The discourse strategies that people use to try to manage the impressions they convey to others.
- The impact that differing evaluative judgements of certain features of behaviour/language use can have in relation to disadvantage.

One way of finding out the impressions that people form of others when they act in certain ways or use certain language patterns is to present them with different options/examples in given contexts and to ask them to evaluate them. The sample items can be presented in a questionnaire with brief scenarios and answered individually (as, for example, in Spencer-Oatey, Ng and Dong 2008); alternatively, they can be presented more dynamically, such as with audio or video clips, and evaluated either individually or in small groups.

Using questionnaires can be appropriate in cross-cultural studies when the aim is to find out how, generally speaking, members of two or more ethnolinguistic groups evaluate certain types of behaviour or language use. As with all comparative studies, it provides useful general background information. However, it is equally important, if not more so, to investigate the reactions of the actual participants in a particular intercultural interaction to the language and behaviour used. For this, two types of data are needed: recordings of the discourse of the interaction plus the participants' post-event evaluative comments. To obtain the latter, the most common way is to interview the participants, asking them to describe their reactions and evaluations. In doing this, it can be especially useful to play back the recording of the interaction, asking each participant (or small group of them) to stop it at points where they had a strong reaction (positive or negative) to something that was said or done (cf. Spencer-Oatey and Xing 2004, 2008). An advantage of this procedure is that people's reactions and judgements can often be linked to specific features of language use or behaviour. Unfortunately, however, there can be practical problems associated with this, in that the interactions may be too long to play back in full (e.g., it would be completely impracticable to play back three days of meetings in real-time) or else some of the participants may need to leave immediately after the interaction (e.g., overseas visitors may need to leave immediately for the airport). An alternative is to select shorter stretches for playback, but of course if that is done, it is important to ensure that the extracts are selected on a principled basis.

Another possibility is just to talk to the participants, without playback. This is what Birkner and Kern (2008) did in their study of job interviews, and they were still able to link many of the comments to features of language use. For some types of interactions, there may also be other sources of relevant information, such as the deliberations of an interview panel in studies of job interviews; again, Birkner and Kern collected this type of data.

Gathering information on people's evaluative reactions to interactions is, of course, just one aspect of the research. If those reactions are to be linked with people's specific language use and/or behaviour, it is also vital to collect and analyse discourse/behavioural data. The most comprehensive way of doing this is to video record the interactions. Then, sections or features can be selected for transcription and analysis. Advances in technology allow this to be done in very sophisticated and unobtrusive ways nowadays. Which features of language use and/or behaviour are selected for analysis is highly dependent on the data itself. For example, Hobbs (2003) and Birkner and Kern (2008) each focus on very different linguistic features, because the precise details of the interactions they are analysing are very different.

Some research studies focus directly on disadvantage, and here the range of approaches is much greater. Some take a discourse approach, and collect multiple sources of interactional data as described above (video recordings of interactions, post-event video feedback sessions, post-event interviews). They then analyse the discourse in great detail, expounding the linguistic factors that underlie the disadvantage that some participants experience. Campbell and Roberts (2007) is good example of such a research method. Needless to say, this type of approach is particularly common among applied linguists and discourse analysts. Research on disadvantage by cross-cultural psychologists is very different in design. These researchers typically use psychometric measures to explore statistically the factors that influence disadvantage. For instance, Jasinskaja-Lahti and colleagues (2006) collected questionnaire data from over 2000 immigrants in Finland and examined whether the frequency with which they felt they were being discriminated against was related to their sense of psychological well-being. Occasionally, a very different method is used. For example, the business economists Bertrand and Mullainathan (2003) carried out a 'field experiment' in which they responded to 'help-wanted' advertisements in local newspapers. They submitted multiple resumes which were equivalent except for the name: half had African-American-sounding names and the other half had white-sounding names. They then measured the number of call-backs each resume received for interviews, and found a statistically highly significant difference between the rate for the African-American-sounding names and the white-sounding names.

Other research focuses on stereotypes, and again there are very different approaches in the way this is done. In linguistics, a common approach is to examine the ways in which people orient in their interaction to widely held stereotypes or (co-)construct the discourse in terms of them. Reyes (2004), for example, examines the ways in which circulating stereotypes of Asian Americans emerge as resources in conversations among Asian Americans, and how they reappropriate them to accomplish meaningful social actions. Similarly, Mallinson and Brewster (2005) examine semi-structured interviews with restaurant staff to explore how they categorize customers by drawing on racial stereotypes or regional stereotypes. Needless to say, discourse data is essential for these types of studies. Psychological studies of stereotypes, on the other hand, typically take a very different approach. Large-scale surveys are the most typical method of data collection, and rather than analysing how stereotypes are constructed, such researchers typically try to identify the stereotypes that people hold, and to examine the extent to which they are accurate, dynamic, positive or negative, and so on (e.g., cf. Diekman et al. 2005).

Yet other research focuses on racism and domination. Once again, discourse analysts conduct a significant proportion of this type of research. Of course, it is not easy to collect naturally occurring, unsolicited discourse data that exhibits racism and domination because the occurrence of such language cannot easily be predicted. So one possibility is to interview people about their experiences of racism, or to interview people such as employers who need to address such matters. This is the approach that Tilbury and Colic-Peisker (2006) took – they interviewed employers and then analysed the various strategies that these employers used to discuss racial, ethnic and religious issues in relation to an employment situation. However, as Stokoe and Edwards (2007: 342) point out, interviews can tell us little or nothing about how racism *actually occurs* in everyday life, and so they collected naturally occurring data where they anticipated it would occur. They built up a data set of neighbour dispute interaction, gathering it in regions where there were large minority ethnic communities. They then analysed it in three ways: the placement of racial insults, the design and composition of the insults, and the responses of people in authority to reports of those insults.

10.4   Researching adaptation to unfamiliar cultures (cf. Chapter 7)

Research on adaptation to unfamiliar cultures covers four main issues, as shown in Research Studies 10.4. However, the strands are closely interconnected, so some research covers more than one issue.

Research Studies 10.4   Examples of topics of research associated with adaptation to unfamiliar cultures (and data collection methods)

The study of personal reactions to experiencing unfamiliar cultures

- Chinese students' psychological and sociocultural adjustments to Britain (Spencer-Oatey and Xiong 2006) [questionnaire; semi-structured interviews].
- Domestic relocation within Indonesia and experience of stress (Hutchings and Ratnasari 2006) [semi-structured telephone interviews with managers who were relocated to different areas of Indonesia].
- Narratives of migration and settlement by Moroccan economic migrants (Baynham 2006) [narrative interviews with Moroccan economic migrants in London].

The study of factors affecting the adaptation process

- The relative importance of antecedents (individual variables, job variables and non-work variables) to cross-cultural adjustment (Palthe 2004) [questionnaires completed by US business executives in Japan, South Korea and the Netherlands].
- The impact of different types of motivation for studying abroad on the adaptation of international students (Chirkov et al. 2007) [questionnaires completed by Chinese international students in Belgium and Canada].
- The influence of international students' social networks (local host, co-national and co-international) on their acculturation to Australia. (Kashima and Loh 2006) [questionnaires completed by Asian international students in Australia].
- The influence of emotion recognition and emotion regulation on intercultural adjustment (Yoo et al. 2006) [questionnaires completed by international students in the USA].

The study of strategies for coping with unfamiliar cultures

- The impact of different acculturation strategies on psychological and sociocultural adaptation, and the intervening effect of flexibility in self-presentation (Kosic, Mannetti and Sam 2006) [questionnaires completed by Polish immigrants in Italy].
- The adaptation and survival strategies that Albanian immigrants develop in relation to settling in Italy (Kosic and Triandafyllidou 2003) [unstructured interviews with Albanian immigrants to Italy].

The study of personal growth and change

- The effect of a period abroad on people's beliefs in their own capabilities (Milstein 2005) [questionnaires completed by participants in the Japan Exchange and Teaching Programme].

- The use of a 'culture learning journal' to promote and evidence personal growth. (Berwick and Whalley 2000) [twice-weekly journal entries by Canadian students during a 3-month visit to Japan].
- Pre-immigrants' narratives on language and identity (Barkhuizen and de Klerk 2006) [in-depth narrative interviews].

The study of multiple aspects of adaptation

- Using critical incidents to investigate cross-cultural transitions (perceived stressors, ways of coping, view of self) (Arthur 2001) [open-ended questions about critical incidents that students participating in international development had experienced. Questions were answered six different times during the 2-month (approx.) period of international involvement].

One important theme within adaptation is the ways that people react to unfamiliar cultures; for example, how different they find their experiences, how difficult they find it to adjust, the ways in which they react psychologically (e.g., the amount of stress they feel), and how they make sense of their experiences. There are two main ways of obtaining such information: through a questionnaire and/or through an in-depth interview. If the aim is to measure quantitatively the degree to which people have adjusted to an unfamiliar culture, it is best to use a standard measuring instrument that has been validated for cross-cultural use. This helps ensure that the questionnaire items operate equally effectively in different cultural contexts, and that the results are reliable and valid. The results also need to be checked statistically, such as by factor analysis and scale reliability testing, to ensure that the scales have operated in the way intended. Spencer-Oatey and Xiong (2006) is an example of this type of approach. They used Zung's (1965) Self-Rating Depression Scale and a modification of Ward and Kennedy's (1999) Sociocultural Adaptation Scale (see Section 11.2.2) as standard measuring instruments, and they conducted a range of statistical tests on the questionnaire results in order to check that the instruments were operating as intended.

If the aim is to obtain rich and descriptive data about people's experiences, then interviews (e.g., semi-structured or narrative) can be used. Hutchings and Ratnasari (2006), for example, used semi-structured interviews to investigate the non-work stresses experienced by Indonesian financial managers when they were transferred to culturally very different regions of Indonesia. Baynham (2006) elicited narrative data by asking broad questions, such as 'What made you decide to come to England?'. In analysing and reporting such data, researchers with a more realist epistemological stance tend to present their findings in terms of the dominant viewpoint or experience, using phrases such as 'the majority of interviewees said [...]' (cf. Hutchings and Ratnasari 2006). In contrast, researchers who hold a more radical epistemological stance may not even report how many people they interviewed; rather, they select extracts from their interview data to illustrate the series of points they wish to make (cf. Baynham 2006).

A second important theme in relation to adaptation is the factors that influence how well people adapt to an unfamiliar culture. Studies of this issue are particularly common within the disciplines of psychology and communication studies. The factors investigated are extremely broad ranging, as illustrated by the following small sample: level of self-determined motivation and content of goals (Chirkov et al. 2007); social ties (international, conational and local) and need for closure (Kashima and Loh 2006); emotion recognition and emotion regulation (Yoo et al. 2006). All such studies take a quantitative approach. Researchers typically use a long questionnaire comprising a number of component scales that, on the one hand, measure the various factors that could influence adjustment, and that, on the other hand, measure outcome variables such as psychological and/or sociocultural adjustment. The data are analysed statistically, using techniques such as confirmatory factor analysis, correlation and regression, and the results are presented in terms of whether there is a link between a given factor and level of adjustment.

A third theme is the strategies that people use to help them cope with their adjustment to an unfamiliar culture. One approach, which is especially widely used in psychology and communication studies, is to explore it quantitatively, using a questionnaire to identify the level of adaptation attained and the strategies used to achieve this. In analysing the data, statistical tests are used to explore whether given strategies affect adaptation and if so, in what way. Alternatively, the theme can be researched from a qualitative perspective.[2] For example, in-depth interview data can offer deep insights into the complexities of migrants' experiences, as Kosic and Triandafyllidou's (2003) study shows.

A fourth theme for research is the personal growth and change that can take place through the adaptation process. This can be researched in a variety of ways. One possibility is to use questionnaires that probe self-perceived change; Milstein (2005) is an example of this. Alternatively, the topic can be researched in much more qualitative ways. Narrative interviews are one possibility. Barkhuizen and de Klerk (2006), for instance, interviewed Afrikaans-speaking South Africans who planned to emigrate to New Zealand. They report several major narrative threads in participants' stories, two of which were the process of change and their imagined identity changes. Another possible method is to use learning journals. Berwick and Whalley (2000), for example, asked Canadian high school students to keep a culture learning journal in which they recorded and reflected on their experiences during a study abroad period in Japan.

As explained at the beginning of this section, some studies cover multiple issues. Arthur (2001), for example, collected data from Canadian students in Vietnam on the experiences they found stressful, the strategies they used to cope, their use of social support, and their shifting views of self. Arthur used a critical incident methodology for this, in which she posed open-ended questions on the above issues and asked people to respond in relation to a specific incident or event that they had experienced that week. Data collected from the critical incidents were then subjected to a thematic content analysis by three trained raters.

10.5 Researching intercultural interaction competence development (cf. Chapter 9)

As mentioned in Section 9.3.4, a relatively frequent topic for research is the effectiveness of aspects of development interventions in educational and/or professional contexts. Recent studies have examined the effectiveness of their design, the methods and materials employed, and also the learning preferences of the participants. These topics are exemplified in Research Studies 10.5.

Research Studies 10.5   Examples of topics of research associated with ICIC development (and data collection methods)

*The effectiveness of development interventions in the **educational** context*

- The hypothesis that the period of time spent in an international school would be positively correlated with the pupils' intercultural sensitivity (Straffon 2003) [questionnaire, interviews].
- Changes in students' attitudes toward cultural difference while participating in a university event celebrating cultural diversity (Klak and Martin 2003) [questionnaire].
- The extent to which a short-term, staff-led study abroad programme can affect the intercultural sensitivity of student participants (Anderson and Lawton 2006) [questionnaire].

*The nature and effectiveness of development interventions in the **professional** development context*

- Attitude change in medical trainees after cultural competency training (Altshuler, Sussman and Kachur 2003) [questionnaire].
- Kinds of pre-departure development interventions US executives experienced before living and working in Mexico, the most frequently used and the most effective training methods (Celaya and Swift 2006) [questionnaire, scenarios].
- The hypothesis that intercultural experience and development interventions positively affect a manager's choice of behaviours to make them appropriate to the local environment (a case we mentioned in Chapter 9) and thus his/her effectiveness (Glick 2002) [questionnaires].
- The usefulness of ICIC development interventions by investigating the results of foreign assignments associated with giving or not giving expatriate managers pre-departure, post-arrival and sequential training (Selmer 2002) [questionnaire].

The effectiveness of development design, methods and materials

- The contribution of a host-country workforce in order to improve the outcomes of development interventions for expatriate managers being prepared for that particular culture (Vance and Ensher 2002) [interviews].
- Investigation of whether the addition of a skills-based sociocultural competency module to a general communication skills course at undergraduate level would lead to social benefits for those taking part (Mak and Buckingham 2007) [questionnaires].
- The development a Hawaiian Intercultural Sensitizer (see Section 9.3.3) to train non-Hawaiian university personnel, including measures to ensure its effectiveness (Dela Cruz et al. 2006) [questionnaires].
- The validity of 21 critical incidents (see Section 9.3.3) designed for development purposes in three Western immigrant countries (Herfst, van Oudenhoven and Timmerman 2008) [questionnaires, lay and expert assessment].
- The best uses of moving pictures to develop intercultural sensitivity in late adolescents and adults (Wilkinson 2007) [Delphi approach].

The learning preferences of participants

- Differences in learning styles of over 300 students in business administration from three different cultures (Barmeyer 2004) [questionnaire].
- Culturally based learning preferences of participants in development interventions (Fischer and Kopp 2007) [questionnaire].

Of key significance for practitioners is evidence that development interventions which use the insights generated by intercultural research are actually effective and lead to more successful intercultural interaction. No matter how much practitioners may or may not find intercultural research interesting and worthwhile in itself, the question of usefulness is of overriding importance in organizations when it comes to the allocation of scarce resources for development purposes. For these reasons, effectiveness research of the kind reported on here is of critical importance in the transfer and acceptance of research insights from less application-oriented research in the intercultural field.

Probably for practical reasons, all of the studies of development effectiveness in the *educational* context investigate changes in attitudes or sensitivity immediately after the intervention. All three studies listed in Research Studies 10.5 do so by using the Intercultural Development Inventory (IDI) (see Section 11.2.2) measure of intercultural competence that was developed by Mitchell R. Hammer and Milton Bennett and was based on the Development Model of Intercultural Sensitivity (DMIS) proposed by Bennett (1986, 1993) (see Section 7.2.1). Straffon (2003) supplements it with structured interviews with highest and lowest scoring students in order to add depth and context to the findings.

A more critical question than that of changes in attitudes and sensitivity is whether interventions actually lead to a change in interactional behaviour. This is the question which only Glick (2002) and Selmer (2002) have set out to answer in the *professional development* context. Other studies concentrate on attitude change. Here, the IDI does not dominate to the same extent as in the educational context, with only Altshuler and colleagues (2003) using it. Selmer (2002), in an exploratory study, devised a pencil-and-paper questionnaire; Celaya and Swift (2006) used their own online questionnaire, supplemented by 30 intercultural scenarios with the request to respondents to suggest appropriate responses in order to measure cultural understanding. Glick's (2002) more complex study of US foreign service staff necessitated the use of questionnaires from the management field, namely the Leader Behaviour Description Questionnaire (Hemphill and Coons 1957) to measure perceived leader behaviours and the Minnesota Satisfaction Questionnaire (Weiss et al. 1967) to measure employee satisfaction with superiors.

A striking omission in recent effectiveness research in both *professional development* and *educational contexts* is the longitudinal investigation of the relationship between development interventions and longer-term changes in attitudes and behaviour (cf. Section 9.2.2) captured months or years after the intervention. This is something which, in spite of the obvious difficulties, some of the researchers represented here (Anderson et al. 2006; Glick 2002; Selmer 2002) as well as below (Mak and Buckingham 2007; and Herfst, van Oudenhoven and Timmerman

2008) also see a need for. The latter underline the need in development effectiveness research to assess post-development behaviours, either in simulated intercultural roles plays or in real-life, the assessment being carried out by peers, subordinates or superiors or in 360 degree fashion.

Of particular interest to applied linguists may be the implications that the authors of two of the studies see as a result of their work. Celaya and Swift (2006) suggest investigating not only the contribution of training to ICIC but also, amongst other things, that of language competency. Altshuler, Sussman and Kachur (2003) recommend that further research should tackle the interrelationships between ICIC and communication skills. Both these suggestions underline the possible backwash effect of effectiveness research on the conceptualization of ICIC itself.

The other major topic of research in the development of ICIC concerns the *effectiveness of development design, methods and materials*. Section 9.3.1 emphasizes the crucial role that needs analysis can play in the design of more effective interventions, and this is an area with considerable scope for further research, as Vance and Ensher (2002) demonstrate. Intercultural development has developed a canon of frequently used methods (cf. Section 9.3.3) and key among them are critical incidents (e.g., investigated by Herfst, van Oudenhoven and Timmerman 2008) and intercultural sensitizers (e.g., examined by Dela Cruz et al. 2006) (see Section 9.3.3 for explanations of these methods). It is appropriate that these and other methods (cf. Mak and Buckingham 2007; Wilkinson 2007), as well as the materials used in the interventions, should be subject to serious investigation – this is something that would again add credibility to the intercultural profession in the eyes of the practitioner.

When it comes to the instruments used in the investigation of the effectiveness of development design, methods and materials, other tools rather than the IDI are used in the studies presented above. Mak and Buckingham (2007) use the Interpersonal Skills Checklist (Ishiyama 1996) and an interculturally adapted version of Fan and Mak's (1998) social self-efficacy scale for students.

Herfst, van Oudenhoven and Timmerman (2008) demonstrate the validity of using critical incidents by relating: (a) lay respondents' personal competencies – measured by completing the Multicultural Personality Questionnaire (Van der Zee and Van Oudenhoven 2001); and (b) their self-reported intercultural behaviour to their performance on the critical incidents. Dela Cruz and colleagues (2006), following Salzman's (1990) procedure for constructing Intercultural Sensitizers, applied the Ethnocultural Identity Behavioral Index (Horvath 1997) and the Multigroup Ethnic Identity Measure (Phinney 1992) in their study.

In the qualitative studies of development design, methods and materials, Vance and Ensher (2002) collected data through open-ended, exploratory field interviews lasting 30–60 minutes and Wilkinson (2007) did so by applying what is known as the Delphi approach (Linstone and Turoff 1975). Twenty-four experts were selected to form a panel of participants who were sent a series of questions to be answered in rounds. Responses generated in one round were shared, usually anonymously, with the participants in the next round, who then reacted to the responses of their fellow panel members. This procedure allows a synthesis of expert assessment to be created.

The effectiveness of development design, methods and materials may ultimately depend on the learners themselves and their culturally influenced *learning preferences*. Recent research on intercultural development has tended to leave this essential factor out of the equation. Barmeyer's study (2004), which uses Kolb's (1985) Learning Style Inventory (LSI) , and Fischer and Kopp (2007), are exceptions and reminders of the need for more insights into learners' preferences and of how this knowledge may lead to improved development interventions.

10.6 Concluding comments

We have aimed in this chapter to illustrate the wide range of research topics that can be explored in relation to intercultural interaction. If you are interested in conducting research for yourself in this field but have little or no experience to date, we recommend that you choose an issue that interests you and then read the studies we have listed for that topic. This will help you consider the different research approaches that can be taken and to choose one for yourself. In the next chapter, we consider the steps involved in carrying out a research project, focusing particularly on the ways in which culture needs to be taken into account.

Notes

1. Available respectively at: http://www.jamescmccroskey.com/measures/communication_competence.htm and: http://www.jamescmccroskey.com/measures/prica.htm (both accessed 22 Nov. 2008).
2. Some researchers may use both approaches; see, for example, the two studies by Kosic and colleagues listed in Research Studies 10.4.

11
Culture and the Research Process

Cross-cultural research is not for the fainthearted.
Teagarden et al. 1995: 1262

Chapter outline

11.1   Culture and initial planning
11.2   Culture and data collection
11.3   Culture and data analysis and interpretation
11.4   Culture and research ethics

This chapter discusses the various steps involved in carrying out a research project, focusing primarily on the impact that cultural factors can have on this process. For general guidance on research methodology, we recommend readers look at books such as Denscombe (2007) or Frankfort-Nachmias and Nachmias (1996).

11.1   Culture and initial planning

11.1.1   Culture-comparative or culture-interactional research

In planning any research into intercultural interaction, a fundamental question is whether the research will be culture-comparative or culture-interactional in approach. In a culture-comparative approach, data is obtained independently from two or more different cultural groups and is compared for its similarities and differences. Culture-interactional research, on the other hand, investigates what happens when members of two different cultural groups interact with each other. For instance, Kwon's (2004) study of the expression of refusals in Korean and American English is a culture-comparative study, whereas Bailey's study of service encounters between Korean shopkeepers and African-American customers is a culture-interactional study. (See Section 10.2 for more examples of studies taking these differing approaches.)

Both approaches are useful, and in large studies can be combined. Culture-comparative research provides valuable baseline data about the values, beliefs, behavioural conventions and so on of a given cultural group. Such data is interesting in its own right and, as we explain in Section 11.3, it is also important for data analysis and interpretation, as it can help explain intercultural interaction phenomena. However, it cannot be assumed that linguistic/cultural values, beliefs and conventions will necessarily be transferred to intercultural contexts of use or that they will impact significantly on the interaction itself. This is because participants co-construct their interaction, and cultural factors can influence this to varying degrees. Culture-interactional research is particularly important for our understanding of intercultural interaction, and relatively speaking, there has been much less culture-interactional than culture-comparative research. There is thus a great need for more research that explores the dynamics of intercultural interaction.

11.1.2 'Handling' culture in research

A second fundamental question is how culture will be 'treated' within the research. There are noticeable disciplinary differences in this respect. In much research in applied linguistics and discourse analysis, as well as in business and management, people of different nationalities, people from different organizations, professional groups or religious groups, or speakers of different languages, are simply assumed to be from different cultures by virtue of their membership. There is usually no attempt to measure culture independently; members of the two social groups are simply researched for certain features, either comparatively or interactionally.

In cross-cultural psychology, on the other hand, it is typically regarded as extremely important to investigate empirically the cultural characteristics of the participants of a study, so that any inferences about the impact of culture on behaviour are not based on the norms of the group as a whole, but on the cultural characteristics of these particular respondents (see also Section 11.3.1). This is a very important component to include in quantitative studies that aim to explore the impact of certain cultural characteristics on certain behaviour. So if this is to be done, there needs to be a way of operationalizing the culture. As explained in Chapter 2, in terms of national culture, by far the most frequent way of operationalizing it (which is usually only done in cross-cultural psychology research or in communication studies research) is in terms of individuals' fundamental values. For example, when Kapoor and colleagues (2003) compared communication styles in India and the United States, they incorporated measures of individualism – collectivism and of self-construals in order to examine whether these factors influenced people's communication style preferences. They used items based partly on Schwartz's conceptualization of values (see Section 2.2.1). Similarly, Chan and colleagues (2004) used Schwartz's Portrait Values Questionnaire (Instrument 11.1) to examine how fundamental values might influence people's interactional concerns in service encounters. (For information on other instruments for measuring values, see Matsumoto et al. 1997; Triandis, Chen and Chan 1998; Hofstede 2001.)

Instrument 11.1   The Schwartz Value Survey (SVS) and Schwartz's Portrait Value Questionnaire (PVQ)

Described in Chapter 2, Schwartz's framework has received empirical underpinning through the use of two main instruments: the Schwartz Value Survey (SVS) (the original questionnaire) and the Portrait Values Questionnaire (PVQ). Both were devised by Schwartz and his colleagues and are reported on in numerous publications. The PVQ is less abstract and less cognitively demanding than the SVS.

According to Schwartz et al. (2001: 523) the PVQ contains: 'short verbal portraits of 29 different people [...] Each one describes a person's goals, aspirations, or wishes that point implicitly to the importance of a value. For example, "Thinking up new ideas and being creative is important to him. He likes to do things in his own original way" describes a person for whom self-direction values are important.'

For each such description, the respondent answers the question 'How much like you is this person?'. They tick a box on a six-point scale ranging from 'very much like me' to 'not like me at all'.

It is important that the PVQ asks respondents to compare the description of the person to themselves and not vice versa as 'comparing other to self directs attention only to aspects of the other that are portrayed, so the similarity judgement is also likely to focus on these value-relevant aspects' (Schwartz et al. 2001: 523).

Schwartz et al. (2001: 524) claim that the questionnaire can be completed in ten minutes, exists in decentred (see Concept 11.2; also Section 11.1) Hebrew and English and in male and female versions, and can be understood by 11-year-olds in three continents.

When other types of cultural groups are being researched, it is rare for instruments to be used to measure the values held by the members.

There are a few exceptions (e.g., Wang 2001), but usually membership alone is taken as 'proof' of the research participants' cultural characteristics.

Another key question is which cultural groups to investigate. More often than not, researchers select them on the basis of convenience; for example, they themselves may be from that cultural group and/or they may have good contacts among members of it. These are important practical considerations, especially since proficiency in the language(s) of the other cultural group(s) is so important (see Section 11.2.2). However, for some researchers such practical reasons are inadequate; cross-cultural psychologists, for instance, typically expect a theoretical justification for the choices, and they usually conceive of this in terms of degree of similarity/difference in fundamental values between the selected groups, and the impact this may have on the behavioural feature(s) to be researched.

11.1.3   The challenge of decentring

Since scientific investigation is itself a cultural artefact, one of the biggest challenges in conducting culture-comparative and culture-interactional research is overcoming the potentially biasing effect of one's own cultural background. This can occur in the research questions asked, in the theoretical frameworks used in the research, in the data collection process and in the analysis of the data. We need to endeavour continually to decentre – to move away from our own cultural perspective and to give equal weight to the perspectives of all the cultural groups involved (Concept 11.1; see also Concept 11.2). This is not easy, but is of vital importance, and so it is a theme that we return to frequently in this chapter.

Concept 11.1   Decentring

In cross-cultural and intercultural research, there is a high risk that data collection and analysis is conducted from the cultural viewpoint of the researcher and hence may be culturally biased. The term 'decentring' refers to the process of moving away from the researcher's perspective so that more equal weight is given to various cultural perspectives. The term was originally used by Brislin (1970) in relation to the development of cross-culturally equivalent research instruments. During the backtranslation process, it may emerge that certain concepts or meanings have no close linguistic or cultural equivalents in the target language/culture. The original instrument is thus adjusted, and so 'decentred' away from the original language/culture in which it was conceptualized.

(Spencer-Oatey 2008a: 328)

Steers, Bischoff and Higgins (1992) illustrate the problem with an analogy: what is the best way of learning about the nature and essence of water – to talk with a fish (assuming the fish can speak!) or with a fisherman? Each informant can provide helpful insights, but neither is complete or accurate on its own. Both perspectives are needed. In relation to our own cultural biases, we are often like a fish swimming in water – we are so embedded in our own culture that we have difficulty 'stepping outside' and realizing that others may view it very differently. Yet when we look at someone else's culture, we may be like the fisherman – we may fail to grasp the affordances and constraints of the water for those who are actually living in it. So the 'key to progress here is for the fish and the fisherman to team up and share experiences, viewpoints, and expertise to achieve the best possible answer to the question' (Steers, Bischoff and Higgins 1992: 329).

What, then, are the implications of this for the theoretical frameworks we may use in our research? Let us suppose we want to investigate how gratitude is expressed in given contexts in English and Hindi. We could compare the frequency with which performative phrases such as 'Thank you' (and its equivalent in Hindi) are used in the chosen situation, and then draw conclusions on the basis of the data we collect. However, if gratitude is expressed non-verbally much more frequently in Hindi than in English, and if we only collect verbal data on 'thank you', our results will be biased and our conclusions invalid.

It is essential, therefore, at the very beginning of a culture-comparative or culture-interactional project, to reflect critically on whether the theoretical framework you propose to use is relevant and applicable to all the cultural groups you intend to study. If you have extensive experience of both/all groups, you may be able to reflect meaningfully on this on your own. If you do not, however, it will be wise to consider working collaboratively with someone from the other cultural group(s) as Steers, Bischoff and Higgins (1992) imply. Many of the studies listed in Chapter 10 illustrate this type of research team composition (e.g., Spencer-Oatey and Xing 2004 – different national group membership; Roberts et al. 2005 – different professional group membership). As we explain in the next sections of this chapter, there are clear practical benefits for such a composition, and so we recommend that research team membership is given very careful thought.

In line with this, it is often extremely helpful if the researchers can reflect on the ways in which their own interests, values, identities etc. may influence or bias their research, and question themselves on how they may need to change, as people and as researchers, as a result of the research.

11.2   Culture and data collection

In view of the constraints on the length of this book, it is not feasible to provide a detailed account of different methods for data collection and their relative strengths and weaknesses. Here we just explain and discuss those methods and issues that are particularly pertinent to culture-comparative and culture-interactional research. We refer readers to relevant studies (either analysed in Part 1 of the book or listed in Chapter 10) for more detailed information.

Three main types of data are collected for intercultural interaction research: authentic interaction data; self-report/survey data; and (semi-) experimental data. We consider each of these in turn.

11.2.1   Collecting authentic interaction data

The collection of real-life interaction data includes (but is not limited to):

- Video-/audio-recording of authentic interactions.
- Non-participant observation of the contexts in which the authentic interactions take place.

These types of data can provide in-depth, rich insights into specific interactions and their contexts, and are vital for any analyses that require detailed information about the language, behaviour and context of particular types of interaction. Chapters 4–7 report the kinds of insights that can emerge from analyses of this type of data, and Chapter 10 lists further studies that used this approach (e.g., Bailey 2000; Campbell and Roberts 2007; Mori 2003; Roberts et al. 2005; Spencer-Oatey and Xing 2004). There is a relative paucity of research that gathers this type of data, and so there is a pressing need for more studies of this kind. It should be borne in mind, though, that it can often be difficult to negotiate access to this kind of data, especially to acquire permission to record potentially sensitive interactions. Moreover, handling the data can be a challenge: the choice or development of a transcription method which yields the appropriate amount and kind of detail is very challenging (see Quote 11.1) and the amount of time needed to transcribe the data should not be underestimated. For an introduction to transcribing spoken discourse, see Cameron (2001: 31–44); for examples of transcribed discourse see any of the studies listed in this paragraph; Mori (2003) incorporates video images.

> ## Quote 11.1   Transcribing talk
>
> All transcription is representation, and there is no natural or objective way in which talk can be written. [...] Inevitably, the more complex the data, for example, video as opposed to audio recording, the more reduction is going on and the more decisions transcribers have to make about fixing sound and vision on the page.
>
> Transcribers, therefore, have to use or develop a transcription system that can best represent the interactions they have recorded, and this means managing the tension between accuracy, readability, and what Mehan (1993) calls *the politics of representation*.
>
> (Roberts 1997: 168)

11.2.2   Collecting self-report data: generic issues

Self-report methods can be used to collect data on a very wide range of topics and issues. They vary considerably in procedure, and include (but are not limited to) diaries, interviews, questionnaires and psychometric tests. In this section we explore a number of generic issues that apply to these various methods; in the next section we give two examples of standard instruments.

Self-reports of authentic incidents

Some types of self-report data are somewhat akin to authentic interaction data in that they deal with real-life incidents that the respondents experienced. One very useful technique, particularly for investigating the achievement of understanding and rapport, is to combine the collection of self-report data with the recording of authentic interaction data, by interviewing participants soon after a particular event or incident. Birkner and Kern (2008); Campbell and Roberts (2007) and Spencer-Oatey and Xing (2004, 2008) all used this technique.

However, it can also be very useful to collect independent self-report accounts of critical incidents (see Concept 9.1). It is typically difficult (although not always completely impossible) to predict when such incidents will occur, so the most feasible way of collecting large amounts of this type of data is to use diaries/journals or open-ended questionnaires. People are usually asked to keep records of any incidents or experiences that were noticeable to them in some way, either negatively (e.g., made them feel particularly stressed, embarrassed or annoyed, or struck them as particularly ineffective for the activity concerned) or positively (e.g., made them feel particularly happy, proud or self-satisfied, or struck them as particularly effective for the activity concerned). Participants are asked to describe this incident and to provide some additional information, such as the following:

- Where the incident took place
- Who else was involved (the other person's gender, age, national or ethno-linguistic culture, organization, and relationship to the respondent)
- The respondent's emotional reactions to what happened
- How they dealt with what happened
- Their reflections on the incident several days later.

Studies that have used this approach include Arthur (2001), Berwick and Whalley (2000), and Spencer-Oatey (2002). As we noted in Section 2.3, Thomas (1996a) used critical incident data to explore the 'culture standards' that underlie them.

Designing questions

Designing questions is a fundamental requirement for the collection of self-report data and is particularly important for (semi-)structured interviews and questionnaires. In fact, if the research topic lends itself best to the use of a questionnaire, the researcher may have the option of using an existing instrument (see Section 11.2.3 and Chapter 12) or of adapting one (e.g., Ward and Kennedy, 1999, maintain that their Sociocultural Adaptation Scale is a flexible instrument that can easily be modified – see Section 11.2.3). However, this does not remove the need to make sure that the questions are suitable for use with respondents from different cultural backgrounds. It is vital to ensure that the questions are conceptually meaningful to all groups of respondents, otherwise the results will be invalid. Decentring (Concept 11.1) is fundamental to this process. Consider, for example, the following scenario from a questionnaire by Chan and colleagues (2004) that was used to investigate some aspects of service encounters:

> You are studying in one of the computer rooms at your university. Your computer has crashed twice, and when it crashes a third time, you go to a technician to ask for help because it is wasting you a lot of time. He simply says, 'Sorry, this happens all the time. I can't do anything'.

This scenario assumes that universities have computer rooms for student use and that there is a technical help-desk which is responsible for dealing with any technical problems that may occur. Clearly, if this scenario was to be used with a range of respondents, some of whose university did not provide that service and some of whose did, the questionnaire (or at least this item) would not yield valid results. The researchers would need to decentre away from their own conceptions of common service situations and find ones that are equally realistic for all the groups of respondents. Often there is no way of judging that *a priori*; the only option is to conduct a pilot which asks people from all of the target groups whether the items are realistic for them.

Another aspect of question design, that applies to questionnaires, is the format they are presented in. One very common format is Likert-type scales in which respondents are asked to rate items on 5-, 6- or 7-point scales (or similar). This format is used when the researcher: (a) wants to find out people's attitude to something or people's assessment of the frequency with which a given behaviour/situation occurs, and (b) when their responses are likely to be on a continuum. This format is extremely flexible and useful, and is very widely used in all types of research, including culture-related studies. Schwartz's PVQ questionnaire (Instrument 11.1), for instance, uses a Likert-type scale. However, care needs to be taken in analysing and interpreting the data from this format, as we discuss in Section 11.3.1. (For examples of culture-related studies using Likert-type scales, see many of the studies listed in Chapter 10, including Spencer-Oatey and Xiong 2006; Kapoor et al. 2003. For a general research methodology discussion of Likert-type scales, see Frankfort-Nachmias and Nachmias 1996 or Denscombe 2007).

Dealing with language: translation

Closely associated with the problem of designing questions that are similarly meaningful to all the groups of respondents is the question of choice of language for the research. This is of fundamental significance. Firstly, it is vital to be aware that even in the same language, the same words can mean significantly different things to different people. Spencer-Oatey and Tang (2007: 166), for example, report how a group of British staff who were developing e-learning materials had to spend considerable time at the beginning of their project reaching agreement on the exact meaning of words such as 'module', 'unit' and 'activity'. Across languages equivalence of meaning is even more complex, as the connotation of words can be so different (see Quote 11.2).

Quote 11.2   Linguistic non-equivalence: the meaning of *home*

The concept of *home* is highly variable from one culture to another, as it carries with it connotations of family units, the composition of which differs significantly from one culture to another, and can also be laden with culturally-dependent political undertones, as in the current debate in the United States about same-sex couples making a 'home' together. There are also global political connotations; the United States now has a Department of 'Homeland Security' to protect the American 'homeland,' which should probably be taken to refer to the concept of a national 'home' that separates the American 'us' from the foreign 'other.'

(Creech 2006)

If you want to carry out a comparative study, you may need to collect data in different languages and you will then need to ensure that your research instruments are as linguistically equivalent as possible. Even if you are fluent in both languages, it would be wise to involve at least one other person in order to help achieve this.

One of the most common ways of increasing linguistic equivalence is to use backtranslation. This involves the following steps: (i) one person translates the research instrument into the target language; (ii) another person translates the target language version back into the original language; (iii) the two versions are compared, and if there are no discrepancies (which in practice is unlikely to happen), the two instruments are regarded as equivalent. If some differences are found, the language of both versions is fine-tuned and the procedure is repeated until all discrepancies are eradicated. (See Concept 11.2).

A second approach to improving linguistic equivalence is to use a 'committee approach'. In this, several bilingual people work together to translate a research instrument into a target language. While doing this, they discuss their preferences for different words and phrases, and finally agree on a version that represents their shared consensus.

Whichever approach is used, it is very common to find that certain concepts or meanings have no close linguistic or cultural equivalents in the target language/culture. When this happens, decentring (Brislin 1970, 2000) needs to occur. In other words, the original instrument needs to be decentred or adjusted away from the original language/culture in which it was conceptualized (Concept 11.1). Some examples of this process are given in Concept 11.2.

Concept 11.2   Linguistic equivalence, backtranslation and decentring

David Dixon (personal communication) wanted to develop a questionnaire in Chinese and English to compare British and Chinese students' attitudes towards learner autonomy. For one of the items, the original version was: 'In the last 4 months I have disagreed with something a teacher told the class.' This was translated into Chinese as: 在过去的4个月里，我曾对课堂上老师说的东西表示不同意见, and then backtranslated as: 'During the last four months, I have voiced different opinions for the teachers' utterance.' This backtranslation brought out the ambivalence of the word 'disagree' in English – that it can refer to either vocalized or non-vocalized disagreement. He then discussed this with the translators and decided he really wanted to convey internal disagreement. So he changed the English to: 'In the last 4 months, I have thought that something a teacher told the class was wrong' and used the following Chinese translation: 在过去的4个月里，我曾认为老师说的有些东西不正确。 He then discussed this with two more translators who agreed that this was closer to what he was aiming at.

Spencer-Oatey (1992: 154) needed a linguistically equivalent questionnaire in Chinese and English. She reports: 'I asked a Chinese lecturer to translate the bank of items and questionnaire instructions into Chinese. I checked his translation personally, and found numerous places where the Chinese and English versions were not completely equivalent. For example, the Chinese version of the English scale label *extremely unlikely* could be interpreted as *completely impossible*, because in Chinese there is only one word which corresponds to the two English words *likely* and *possible*. And the Chinese version of the English scale label *strongly agree* could be interpreted as *totally agree*. Clearly these were crucial lack of equivalences that could have seriously undermined the reliability of the research if they had not been rectified.

The translator and I went through the English and Chinese versions line by line, and item by item, talking through lack of equivalences, and modifying either the English or Chinese versions or both. In this and the rest of the translation process we used the principle of *decentring* [...] For example, item 33 in the questionnaire (*Provide PG students with regular opportunities for consulting with the tutor*) was produced in the following way. Originally the item was worded as follows: *Arrange regular office hours during which PG students can come for help if they wish.* When this was translated into Chinese, it literally meant *Periodically set aside time for tutoring PG students who need help.* Clearly, there were several aspects in which the items were non-equivalent: regular – periodic; arrange – set aside; office hours – (not translated); want help – need help; (not in original) – tutoring. Part of the problem was the non-existence of office hours in Chinese universities. If students want to see their tutors, they can simply turn up at their office or even their home. So the next English version was as follows: *Be available at regular times for PG students to come for help if they wish.* However, the phrase *Be available* was extremely difficult to translate into natural Chinese, so the wording was changed yet again. Finally, we came up with a version that was acceptable in both languages and cultures, and was included as item 33 in the final version of the questionnaire: *Provide PG students with regular opportunities for consulting with the tutor.*

Dealing with language: using interpreters

If you wish to collect interview or discourse data from members of another cultural group and you do not speak their language, it is best to include in your research team a person from that target group or a speaker of their language. If you do not, and you decide to use an interpreter, you need to be aware of the kinds of research-related difficulties that you may encounter. Kamler and Threadgold (2003), for example, provide a helpfully frank account of the problems they faced in conducting narrative workshops with Australian Vietnamese women. Taking feminist and poststructuralist positions, these researchers wanted to encourage older Vietnamese women to produce verbal and visual stories of their lives, with a view to 'opening up spaces for alternative voices and discourses, previously marginalised narratives and new interpretations, meanings and values' (2003: 139). However, they soon encountered some serious problems:

> Somewhat naively, we really imagined that the interpreter would provide a bridge between our two realities that would be straightforward to work with in linguistic terms. [...] When we saw the first full English translation of one of the recorded workshops, however, we realised that the interpreter was constantly re-interpreting our questions, or not quite understanding us. She also tended at times to rework the women's responses for our ears. [...] those scholars who regularly work in cross-cultural contexts will recognise the need for appointing a translator who is not part of the group. We had not conducted research in cross-cultural contexts before and willingly accepted the translator Minh, because she was suggested by the Australian Vietnamese Women's Association. There were, moreover, several good reasons for doing so, all of which have more to do with building an ethical research practice, and making initial contact with a new community, than with attending to the complexities of translation. [...] What we had not bargained for sufficiently was the interpreter's agenda, her concern for the welfare of the community and her concern to mediate our perceptions of that community.
>
> (Kamler and Threadgold 2003: 141–2)

Kamler and Threadgold found that they needed to employ an independent translator to transcribe and translate everything that was said during the narrative workshops. When they became aware of the extent to which the interpreter was mediating what was said, not only linguistically but also in terms of the self-representations of the women, they decided to employ a second interpreter. Her brief was to let the researchers know when translation problems were occurring. So as Kamler and Threadgold explain, the translations within their data were 'dense and very complex, very much a struggle for power and for the right to define what was being represented to the research team' (2003: 146).

Gaining access/finding respondents

Gaining access to data collection opportunities and finding respondents can be challenging for all researchers, but in culture-comparative and culture-interactional research it can be even more difficult, especially when comparable datasets are required. Good contacts are vital, and a research team comprising members from the different cultural groups can help provide this. Even so, data collection may not go according to plan, as Easterby-Smith and Malina report in relation to their UK–China management research (see Quote 11.3).

Quote 11.3   Easterby-Smith and Malina on gaining research access

Expecting at the outset that access to Chinese organizations would prove very difficult, the UK researchers were most surprised to discover that this was not the case. A key factor in gaining access was that the senior Chinese researchers worked in prestigious universities and had therefore developed excellent networks that included former students who were by now senior managers in the target companies. Because of these personal links, the project was not reliant on the official gatekeepers who normally allow access for foreign researchers only to showcase organizations [...], and this advantage enabled the team to reach areas that would not normally be accessible. Access to UK companies proved much more difficult, and three of the four companies named in the original research proposal were unable to confirm their provisional commitments. These were eventually replaced by three other companies with characteristics slightly different from those originally planned, and the Chinese team members then had to find new companies at their end that would provide good matches.

(Easterby-Smith and Malina 1999: 79)

Conducting interviews

Even when access has been successfully negotiated, the actual carrying out of the interviews can be equally challenging. Attention needs to be paid to the ethnicity of the researcher and the interviewees (Quote 11.4), and if the interviews are to be conducted by different researchers or research teams, very careful advanced preparation and briefing is needed. Even so, unexpected issues can arise, as both Usunier (1998) and Easterby-Smith and Malina (1999) report (Quotes 11.4 and 11.5).

Quote 11.4   Usunier on interview planning

The objective and process of the interview must often be explained at the beginning. When briefing native interviewers (management students) in Mauritania, I was asked the following question: 'What do you want us to tell the interviewee to answer?' It was necessary to explain to the interviewers that interviewing was a distanced and objective process, where interviewees had complete freedom of response. [...] Furthermore, among the Mauritanian interviewers, the Maures of Arabic descent clearly explained that they would not interview Black Africans. Fortunately, there were some Black Africans who were potential interviewers for their own ethnic group. Strong ingroup orientation implies that group membership has to be shared between interviewer and interviewee for the process to take place.

(Usunier 1998: 119–20)

Quote 11.5   Easterby-Smith and Malina on cross-cultural differences in conducting interviews

Fieldwork relied on interviews with key decision makers at the participating companies, supported by examination of documents and informal discussions with additional personnel. At least two researchers, including one from each of the national groups, were involved in each interview. The interviews in China were conducted in Mandarin, without the use of interpreters. Despite the whole team's having discussed and agreed on the methods to be used in the project, all the researchers were surprised at differences that emerged in the way fieldwork interviews had to be conducted in the two countries. The Chinese team members were surprised at the informality and short duration of the interviews in the UK companies (normally, 1–2 hours). The UK researchers were surprised that interviews in China were more like lectures, with managers reading from prepared reports in day-long meetings attended by at least three other members of the company. Questions were not usually allowed until after each speech was finished. During informal discussions with these managers later on, they explained that a spontaneous exchange of ideas would have led to ill-prepared answers. As one of the Chinese academics explained further, 'How can they answer questions if they have not prepared the answers?' This was one of the first indications that the two national groups might have different ontological orientations: it seemed that the Chinese people were looking for accurate data and factual information, whereas the UK people were more interested in perceptions and interpretations. [...]

[...] a reflexive insight is that observing the approach of the Chinese colleagues to data collection revealed how much the UK team members' expectations about fieldwork were conditioned by their own experiences in the United Kingdom.

(Easterby-Smith and Malina 1999: 80)

Sampling issues

Stening and Zhang (2007: 127–8) comment as follows: 'Sampling [...] is a non-trivial aspect of any empirical research study. However, the problems are multiplied many times over in cross-cultural research, especially in relation to the possibility that we may be choosing unrepresentative samples.' Some fundamental concerns are as follows:

- Are the samples equivalent in terms of demographic variables such as age, sex, religion and so on?
- To what extent can the samples be taken as representatives of the cultural groups being studied?

There are no easy solutions to either of these issues. For more details of sampling in cross-cultural research, see Stening and Zhang (2007); for a general discussion of sampling, see Frankfort-Nachmias and Nachmias (1996) or Denscombe (2007).

11.2.3   Collecting self-report data: using standard instruments

If ICIC is understood as the ability to interact across cultures effectively and appropriately, it is clearly of interest to researchers to investigate what, if any, features of intercultural interaction correlate with a high degree of interactional effectiveness and appropriateness. For example, does the interculturally competent interactant intervene on the meta-level to repair disturbances in the communication and create understanding more often than the only averagely competent interactant, and how?

In order to carry out such research, there is a need for instruments that can provide measures of ICIC. Here, we present two instruments that have been used for research into intercultural interaction. The first is widely used by social psychologists to investigate people's degree of adaptation to an unfamiliar culture. The second, which is more controversial, is used by some interculturalists to measure degree of intercultural sensitivity.

Sociocultural Adaptation Scale (SCAS)

In Chapter 3 we noted how flexibility in affect, behaviour and cognition is a key feature of successful ICIC, and Chapter 7 examined in greater detail aspects of the adaptation process that can result from flexibility and which may be necessary for successful intercultural interaction, such as dealing with culture shock, sensitivity to cultural difference, and the need and opportunity for personal growth and its relationship to identity.

Ward and colleagues have distinguished in various publications (e.g., Ward and Kennedy 1993; Ward and Kennedy 1999) between two types of cross-cultural adaptation: psychological (emotional/affective) and sociocultural (behavioural) adaptation. One instrument which attempts to assess the kind of sociocultural adaptation demanded by intercultural interaction is the Sociocultural Adaptation Scale (SCAS). It asks respondents to rate on a five-point scale the amount of difficulty they are experiencing in various situations (e.g., going shopping, talking about yourself with others) as a resident in an unfamiliar culture. Higher scores reflect greater sociocultural adaptation problems.

Instrument 11.1   Extract from Ward and Kennedy's (1999) Sociocultural Adaptation Scale

Please indicate how much difficulty you experience in each of these areas in [name of host country].
Use the following 1 to 5 scale:

1 = no difficulty
2 = slight difficulty
3 = moderate difficulty
4 = great difficulty
5 = extreme difficulty

1. Making friends
2. Using the transport system
3. Making yourself understood
4. Getting used to the pace of life
5. Going shopping
6. Going to social events/gatherings/functions
7. Worshipping in your usual way
8. Talking about yourself with others
9. Understanding jokes and humor
10. Dealing with someone who is unpleasant/cross/aggressive
11. Dealing with people in authority
12. Accepting/understanding the local political system
13. Understanding the locals' world view
14. Being able to see two sides of an intercultural issue

(Ward and Kennedy 1999: 663)

Ward and Kennedy (1999: 662) describe it as a flexible instrument, generally containing 20–23 items, which can easily be modified according to the sample under investigation. Whereas most items are behavioural in nature, recent versions have included items of a more cognitive nature (e.g., 12, 13 and 14 in Instrument 11.1). Ward and Kennedy's analysis of a number of different studies indicate the scale has a high degree of reliability and satisfactory construct validity.

Ward and Kennedy (1999: 673–4) conclude the SCAS 'can assist with the development of theory and research on social skills acquisition across cultures, intercultural effectiveness and culture learning. [...] The SCAS may also prove useful to practitioners for training programs and evaluations'. Indeed, with its focus on difficulties encountered, it resembles aspects of needs analysis (see Chapter 9), which ideally provides a starting point for measures to develop ICIC. This clear focus on difficulty also reminds us of the largely unsatisfied need in research and development contexts also to consider success factors in intercultural interaction.

The Intercultural Development Inventory

Although primarily devised for developmental purposes, The Intercultural Development Inventory (IDS) is claimed by its developers also to be suitable for research purposes.

Based on the Development Model of Intercultural Sensitivity (DMIS) proposed by Bennett (1986, 1993) and described in Section 7.2.1, the Intercultural Development Inventory (IDI) is a measure of intercultural competence developed by Mitchell R. Hammer and Milton Bennett which assesses respondents by assigning them to one of six developmental stages.

Instrument 11.2   The Intercultural Development Inventory (IDI)

This instrument consists of a 50-item, paper-and-pencil questionnaire that assesses the major stages of intercultural competence as conceptualized in DMIS theory.

Describing it as both valid and reliable, the website[1] of one of the originators of the IDI suggests it can be used for a wide variety of purposes, including: '(1) individual assessment in coaching, counselling situations, (2) group analysis in teambuilding efforts, (3) organizational-wide needs assessment for training design, (4) programme evaluation to assess effectiveness of various interventions, and (5) research [...] It can generate a graphic profile of an individual's or a group's predominant stage of intercultural development and textual interpretation of that stage and associated transition issues'.

According to the DMIS (Bennett 1993: 29–65), these six stages represent various steps in the development of intercultural sensitivity observed amongst individuals who are faced with cultural difference.

The instrument consists of statements reflecting the different DMIS stages, and respondents are required to express agreement or disagreement using a five-point Likert-like scale. Examples would be 'Technology is creating a single world-wide culture', 'I like people from different cultures' and 'People are fundamentally the same despite apparent differences in cultures'. The website[2] of another of the originators of the instrument claims it measures 'an individual's (or group's) fundamental worldview orientation to cultural difference, and thus the individual's or group's capacity for intercultural competence'. A sample IDI profile and a comprehensive list of research publications relating to the DMIS and the IDI are also to be found on the website.

The IDI is different from intercultural competence assessment tools which are criterion-referenced, that is which assess how closely respondents correspond to a set of behaviours or features which are believed to be related to intercultural competence.

As with many of the self-assessment instruments originating in the United States, a few of the items are perhaps more susceptible than others to the perverting effects of social desirability, that is the bias which arises when respondents give an answer that aims more at being acceptable to other people, such as the scorer or trainer, than genuine. It is easy to understand that regardless of what respondents really think, few would want to be seen to be agreeing totally with a statement such as 'People from other cultures are generally lazier compared to people from my culture'. Interestingly, though, Hammer, Bennett and Wiseman (2003: 439), and Paige and colleagues (2003) report that their testing showed that the IDI scores were not significantly affected by socially desirable responses.

The IDI has been thoroughly investigated and Hammer, Bennett and Wiseman (2003) have claimed it to be reliable and valid. They conclude that 'the DMIS model is largely supported by testing associated with the development of the IDI. Thus we feel that the final, 50-item IDI can be used with confidence as a measurement of the five dimensions of the DMIS identified in this research' (2003: 441). Paige and colleagues (2003: 467) conclude that the IDI 'is a reliable measure that has little or no social desirability bias and reasonably, although not exactly, approximates the developmental model of intercultural sensitivity'.

However, Greenholtz (2005: 88), in his study of data obtained using a Japanese translation of the IDI, raises 'strong doubts about the cross-cultural transferability of [...] the IDI and raised some doubts about the DMIS as a model for understanding world views with respect to difference, in cultures other than US American. [...] These results indicate that the IDI should still be considered to be work in progress, at least in a cross-linguistic environment, rather than a "reliable and valid instrument" ready to pull off the shelf for all research contexts. A lot of room remains for further research in non-US American cultures, using subject utterances in languages other than English.' This is an example of culture-centredness in intercultural interaction research (see Section 11.1.3).

11.2.4   Collecting semi-experimental data

A third category of data collection methods that is relatively common in culture-comparative and culture-interactional research takes a semi-experimental approach. It includes (but is not limited to) discourse completion tasks, simulated negotiation, and role plays.

Discourse completion

In linguistics, if the research topic focuses on the productive use of specific features of language use, discourse data is needed, and ideally this means the collection of video, audio or online digital data. However, as we have noted already, it may be difficult to predict when certain features of language use will occur naturalistically, and in such cases, linguists have frequently devised a written or oral task known as a 'Discourse Completion Task' (DCT). Each item in a DCT starts with a situational description followed by a brief dialogue that has one turn as an open slot; the context given in the scenario is designed to constrain the open turn so that it elicits the desired communicative act (e.g., a request or an apology). (See Kwon 2004 and Kasper 2008 for examples.)

DCTs are also particularly useful if the researcher is interested in the impact of certain variables such as power or distance on language use, because such variables cannot easily be controlled in natural contexts. However, a major concern over using this method is that the language that people use or report in this non-authentic situation may differ significantly from their actual use. Tran (2006) proposes a 'naturalized role play' to help address this issue, but there is a growing preference among applied linguists for using authentic discourse data. (See Kasper 2008 for a very helpful critical account of different methods for collecting linguistic data.)

Simulated negotiations

The use of simulated negotiations is a long established method of data-collection in the field of organizational psychology and management and has been used in both culture-comparative and culture-interactional investigations of negotiation. One well-known simulation game is the

Kelley game (Kelley 1966). This is a simple bargaining negotiation about the prices of three types of goods that generates about half an hour of interaction. In the analysis of the recorded interaction, the occurrence of specific features (e.g., periods of silence, frequency of interruption, timing of first offers) can be correlated with other measured variables such as transactional effectiveness in terms of individual gains and joint gains resulting from the negotiation, perceived satisfaction, similarity to or attractiveness of the other party, as well as culture (which is generally, not individually, measured). The Kelley game has been used in both culture-comparative (e.g., Graham 1983; Campbell et al. 1988; Adler, Brahm and Graham 1992) and culture-interactional studies (e.g., Adler and Graham 1989). A more recent simulated negotiation game, *Cartoon* (Brett and Okumura, n.d.) has also been used in both types of study (e.g., Adair 2003; Adair and Brett 2005; Adair, Weingart and Brett 2007). *Bolter Turbines Negotiation Simulation*, described by Graham (1984) is another simulation that has been used for research purposes (e.g., Lee, Yang and Graham 2006). Simulated negotiations may be a useful way of generating in a short time data which is predictable in nature.

Role play

Role play as a means of eliciting data differs from simulated negotiations in that those taking part may be required not only to conduct a specified activity but also to take on and act out a specified or imagined identity or to recall and act out specific authentic interactions. A thorough discussion of the full range of role play types and their use in pragmatics research is to be found in Kasper (2008) and is useful too when considering how to collect culture-comparative or culture-interactional data.

11.2.5 The researcher–participant relationship

On a number of occasions in this chapter, we have hinted at the importance in culture-comparative and culture-interactional research of managing effectively the relationship between the researcher and those being researched. This is vital both for gaining access to a research site and/or participants and for maximizing the quality of the data obtained from them. It is also important from a research ethics point of view – an issue that we return to in Section 11.4.

We have already discussed the importance of managing language issues in designing research questions. Language also needs to be considered with regard to the researcher–participant relationship. If the researcher can communicate in the participant's language, this helps to establish a good rapport between them and to pave the way for effective data collection. If interviews are being used, it is best to conduct them in the participants' native language whenever possible, because the participants are likely to be able to express themselves more accurately and convey more complex ideas in their mother tongue. If the researcher is fluent enough to do this him/herself, that is ideal because, as we saw in Section 11.2.2, using an interpreter raises a number of difficulties.

In addition to language, a range of other features of the researcher's identity need to be taken into account, including gender, age, and level of seniority. For example, Mulder and colleagues (2000) report that in their Bolivian health-related project, the principal researcher, who was a youthful-looking outsider to the rural community being studied, was constructed by the local respondents as 'weak' and 'incapable', and as a result, the locals tried to keep her in a subordinate and marginal position. In contrast, Easterby-Smith and Malina (1999) report that a young female British researcher, who was often ignored by interviewees when working with an older male in the United Kingdom, experienced the complete opposite in China – she was treated with exaggerated importance because of her foreign status. So in planning data collection, very careful thought needs to be given to the identity characteristics of the researcher(s) and the impact such characteristics may have on the participants' willingness to cooperate.

Another important consideration is the nature of the relationship between the researcher and the participant. Marra (2008) reports that in the 'Language in the Workplace' research that she, Holmes and colleagues conducted, a 'respectful relationship' was noticeably different in the two types of ethnic workplaces they were researching, Māori and Pākehā (indigenous and European-based New Zealander). In the latter, the researchers needed to avoid imposing on busy participants whereas in the former they needed to build warm sociable relations (see also Section 11.4). (For further examples of the impact that the researcher–participant relationship can have on the research process, see Garner, Raschka and Sercombe 2006.)

11.3   Culture and data analysis and interpretation

11.3.1   Analysing quantitative data

As explained above (Section 11.2.2, Designing questions), many researchers use Likert-type scales in their questionnaires, and in culture-comparative research, the typical goal is to ascertain whether the respondents from the different cultural groups have similar or different viewpoints. However, if the mean ratings of the different groups are significantly different from a statistical point of view, it is important to be aware that we should not simply conclude that there is necessarily a genuine culturally-based difference in viewpoint. This is because of the potential impact of 'cultural response sets' – the tendency for members of given cultures to have a preference for using certain parts of the scale when responding, irrespective of the content of the particular items. For example, members of some cultural groups may hesitate to use the extreme endpoints of a scale, whereas members of other groups may be happy to do so.

As a result of this, any differences in the means should not be taken at face value. Fortunately, there are statistical procedures for handling this. First, the data need to be checked statistically to assess whether cultural response sets may be operating, and if they are, further procedures for adjusting the results statistically should be used. Matsumoto and Juang (2008) provide helpful information about this.

A further consideration in the analysis and interpretation of quantitative data is the 'meaningfulness' of a statistically significant difference. Sometimes the probability of obtaining a given result is very low (i.e. it is statistically significant), but the effect size is small; that is the mean values do not reflect meaningful differences among individuals. Again, there are statistical procedures for checking this, and these need to be reported along with the probability statistics. Matsumoto and Juang (2008) again provide helpful information about this.

If differences across cultural groups genuinely emerge from the statistical analyses, 'interpreting their cause' is another danger to be wary of. Sometimes, if a specific difference is found between, say, respondents from Britain and Malaysia, it could be tempting to explain the difference by referring to the mean fundamental values that people such as Hofstede (2001) have reported for the two countries (e.g., differences in Individualism–Collectivism, or in Power Distance; see Concept 2.4). However, we cannot be sure that the respondents in our sample necessarily hold the same values as the country-level means reported by Hofstede or others. So as Matsumoto and Juang (2008) explain, unless the researchers have: (a) incorporated actual measures of these values within their study (as discussed in Section 11.1.2), (b) have found that the two groups differ as individuals on these measures, and (c) have shown that the value differences can account for the other behavioural difference being researched, such an interpretation is not necessarily warranted. Psychologists pay much greater attention to these matters than linguists do. It is very rare, in fact, for linguists to include these additional measures (e.g., cf. Bjørge 2007), and this is something that they need to consider more carefully when conducting quantitative studies.

11.3.2   Interpreting the 'meaning' of qualitative data

Near the beginning of this chapter (Section 11.1.3), we noted the importance of decentring, not only in initial planning and data collection, but also in data analysis, mentioning the value of both 'insider' and 'outsider' perspectives in interpreting data. Why then is it important to have both 'insider' and 'outsider' perspectives when analysing and interpreting data?

We suggest that there are three main contributions that insiders can make to this process (cf. Louis and Bartunek 1992: 107). They can:

- provide factual information and/or correct factual errors;
- help identify implicit meanings and feelings;
- offer rationales for behaviour that is difficult to interpret.

Outsiders, on the other hand, are often in a better position to:

- notice behaviour that insiders simply 'take for granted';
- challenge assumptions.

So there are clearly several advantages to having a mixed-culture team, yet in practice this is not always possible. When that is the case, an alternative is to use the respondents themselves as 'insider' contributors. Marra (2008) reports that this is the procedure they used in the *Language in the Workplace* project with Māori organizations (when the members of the research team were all Pākehā) and that it worked extremely well (see Quote 11.6).

Quote 11.6   Marra on insider perspectives in data analysis

Whereas in Pākehā organizations, the first official feedback session is a time for us to present our 'expert' analysis of the data, and that is precisely what the organization expects, in the Māori organizations the sessions typically become interactive workshops where the research participants and workplace participants negotiate understandings and knowledge-sharing occurs. For example, instead of making claims about what constitutes an effective Māori workplace based on data analysis, our most satisfying interactions have been those where the discussion has been built around asking workplace participants about what they consider important, and also asking if possible interpretations we can postulate based on the discourse are credible or even possible. This practice recognizes the various types of information and skills that we all bring to the table. The results are a richer and more culturally sensitive set of interpretations.

(Marra 2008: 313)

11.3.3 Interpreting intercultural interaction data

One of the major challenges in analysing intercultural interaction data is the difficulty of distinguishing the influence of cultural factors on the interaction from the various other factors that could have had an influence, including idiosyncratic personal factors. Post-event explanatory comments are useful here, in that the participants may be able to contribute valuable insights on this. Another useful source is comparative data. As we noted in Section 11.1.1, culture-comparative studies can provide useful baseline data about the norms and conventions in the countries concerned. Such baseline data cannot (or should not!) be used to predict how an intercultural interaction will necessarily take place – interaction is far too dynamic for that. Nevertheless, there will almost inevitably be elements of pragmatic transfer in intercultural interactions, and culture-comparative research findings can be useful in helping identify these (see Žegarac and Pennington 2008).

11.3.4 Epistemological positions and data analysis

Despite the advantages of mixed-culture teams discussed in Section 11.3.2, working in large-scale insider–outsider (i.e. intercultural) research teams can sometimes be very challenging. Differing viewpoints and perspectives can lead to conflicts, and people need to be able to handle these effectively. Moreover, different interests, foci and epistemological positions may all emerge at this point. Easterby-Smith and Malina (1999), for example, report that they experienced these in their UK–China research team (see Quote 11.7). (For more examples of the impact of different professional viewpoints in international collaborations, see Section 4 of Spencer-Oatey 2007b.)

Quote 11.7   Data analysis and epistemological positions

Although the team agreed quickly on the need to write up separate cases for each company, it took a long time to reach consensus on how to make sense of the data. [...] It became evident that the UK team members were most interested in differences, whether these were between accounts of the same decision in one company or between accounts of similar decisions in different companies, whereas the Chinese team members were more interested in the similarities between the practices of companies and were therefore most concerned to ensure that observations were accurate and that the 'facts' were right. [...] [It soon emerged that] the two teams held different ontological positions regarding the object of inquiry and different epistemological positions about methods of inquiry.

(Easterby-Smith and Malina 1999: 81)

11.4   Culture and research ethics

All research needs to be conducted ethically and most professional organizations offer 'good practice' guidelines to help with this. For example, the British Psychological Society has a 'Code of ethics and conduct' which comprises four ethical principles (respect, competence, responsibility, integrity) and a set of standards for each of the principles (e.g., Standard of privacy and confidentiality, Standard of informed consent). Similarly, most universities require that the research planned by their staff and students is given ethical approval before it is started. In this section, we consider the question of research ethics from an intercultural perspective.

11.4.1   Differing perspectives on ethical procedures

As indicated above, guidelines on ethically responsible research frequently highlight the importance of being respectful, of gaining the informed consent of the participants, and of being particularly careful about the power relations between the researcher and the participants. However, as Marra explains (see Quote 11.8), although such guidelines seem on the surface to be perfectly reasonable and obvious, they can in fact require very different types of operationalization in different contexts. For further discussion of some complexities in implementing ethical guidelines in different cultural contexts, see Mulder and colleagues (2000).

Quote 11.8   Reflections on 'being respectful'

[...] these guidelines, which largely advocate respect and engagement, appear to be reasonable and obvious goals for any ethical researcher. [...] [T]o show respect in our Pākehā organizations, we aimed to be unobtrusive [...]. Our goal was always to avoid imposing on busy participants; we aimed to be

> practically invisible in the data collection phase, following our sociolinguistic assumptions regarding the importance of minimizing observer effects. In [...] Māori research, however, this behaviour could be considered disrespectful. To show respect we need to [...] make efforts to build solidarity with our workplace colleagues. This meant 'fronting up' in the organizations to show our commitment to the research goals of benefiting Māori, by being visible and available, being involved, as well as accepting hospitality and reciprocating in turn.
>
> (Marra 2008: 309, 312)

11.4.2 Representation of groups

Finally, we return very briefly to the notion of representation. We noted in Section 11.2.2 that participants may want to represent themselves to the researcher(s) in certain ways and that this can influence the data collection process. This also works in the reverse. Researchers need to ensure that any descriptions of cultural groups that emerge from their findings do not misrepresent the groups or oversimplify them. This can sometimes happen inadvertently, so one of the best ways of avoiding this problem is to ensure that the research team is culturally mixed and comprises members of the cultural groups being studied. If this is not practicable (or even if it is), then working closely with the informants not only in the data analysis and interpretation stage (as illustrated in Section 11.3.2 with respect to the *Language in the Workplace* project), but also in the dissemination stage, is a process that we highly recommend.

Notes

1. http://www.idiinventory.com/about.php/ (accessed 23 Sept. 2008).
2. http://www.intercultural.org/idi_theidi.php/ (accessed 23 Sept. 2008).

Suggestions for further reading

Denscombe, M. (2007) *The Good Research Guide for Small-Scale Social Research Projects*, 3rd edn. Buckingham: Open University Press. This accessible book is useful for those who want to learn more about research methods in general. It provides a comprehensive introduction to the main approaches to social research and the methods most commonly used by researchers in the social sciences.

Easterby-Smith, M. and Malina, D. (1999) Cross-cultural collaborative research: Toward reflectivity. *The Academy of Management Journal*, 42 (1): 76–86. This article provides fascinating insights into the challenges experienced by a Chinese–UK research team during a collaborative research project.

Kasper, G. (2008) Data collection in pragmatics research. In H. Spencer-Oatey (ed.) *Culturally Speaking: Culture, Communication and Politeness Theory*, 2nd edn, pp. 279–303. London: Continuum. This chapter provides an excellent overview and critical discussion of many different types of methods for the collection of culture-comparative and culture-interactional data.

Marra, M. (2008) Recording and analysing talk across cultures. In H. Spencer-Oatey (ed.) *Culturally Speaking: Culture, Communication and Politeness Theory*, 2nd edn, pp. 304–21. London: Continuum. This chapter provides an insightful account of the issues faced by researchers when collecting and analysing data from culturally different communities.

Matsumoto, D. and Juang, L. (2008) *Culture and Psychology*, 4th edn. Belmont, CA: Thomson Higher Education. Chapter 2 of this book, 'Cross-cultural research methods', provides an excellent introduction to the features of research design that need to be taken into account in cross-cultural research.

Part 4
Resources

12
Resources

Gather in your resources, rally all your faculties, marshal all your energies, focus all your capacities upon mastery of at least one field of endeavor.

John Haggai

Chapter outline

12.1   Books
12.2   Journals
12.3   Associations and conferences
12.4   Websites
12.5   Assessment instruments
12.6   Resources for developing intercultural interaction competence
         Books
         Games and simulations
         Internet resources
         Videos, DVDs and hybrid materials
         Publishers of videos, DVDs and hybrid materials

The list of resources below is necessarily not comprehensive. It represents a personal selection rather than a choice made according to certain objective criteria. In the category 'Books', however, titles are also included which meet the criteria of 'significance for the area' or 'overview character' or 'collection of key readings'.

Within the categories numbered 12.1–12.5, the resources are listed under broad disciplinary areas in keeping with the multidisciplinary approach of the book. The areas are:

- applied linguistics / language education / education;
- psychology (social, cross-cultural) / communication studies;

- international business and management studies;
- anthropology;
- multidisciplinary.

Text in quotation marks is taken, unless otherwise indicated, from descriptions made by the publishers, authors, etc. of the media in question and placed on the Internet.

12.1   Books

The years given indicate the year of the latest edition or printing of the book in question.

Applied linguistics / language education / education

Alfred, G., Byram, M. and Fleming, M. (eds) (2003). *Intercultural Experience and Education*. Clevedon: Multilingual Matters.

Byram, M. (1989). *Cultural Studies in Foreign Language Education*. Clevedon: Multilingual Matters.

Byram, M. (1997). *Teaching and Assessing Intercultural Communicative Competence*. Clevedon: Multilingual Matters.

Candlin, C. N. and Gotti, M. (eds) (2004). *Intercultural Aspects of Specialized Communication*. Bern: Peter Lang.

Corbett, J. (2003). *An Intercultural Approach to English Language Teaching*. Clevedon: Multilingual Matters.

Hall, B. J. (2007). *Among Cultures: Challenge of Communication*. Fort Worth, TX: Wadsworth (3rd edn).

Hall, J. K. (2002). *Teaching and Researching Language and Culture*. Harlow, Essex: Pearson Education.

Holliday, A., Kullman, J. and Hyde, M. (2004). *Intercultural Communication: An Advanced Resource Book*. London: Routledge.

Kiesling, S. F. and Paulston, C. B. (eds) (2005). *Intercultural Discourse and Communication: The Essential Readings*. Oxford: Blackwell.

Kotthoff, H and Spencer-Oatey, H. (2007). *Handbook of Applied Linguistics, Volume 7: Intercultural Communication*. Berlin: Mouton de Gruyter.

Lange, D. L. and Paige, R. M. (2003). *Culture as the Core: Perspective on Culture in Second Language Education*. Charlotte, NC: Information Age Publishing.

Sercu, L., Bandura, E., Castro, P., Davcheva, L., Laskaridou, C., Lundgren, U., Méndez Garcia, M.d.C. and Ryan, P. (2005). *Foreign Language Teachers and Intercultural Competence*. Clevedon: Multilingual Matters.

Muskens, G., Ager, D. E. and Wright, S. (1993). *Language Education for Intercultural Communication*. Clevedon: Multilingual Matters.

O'Dowd, R. (ed.) (2007). *Online Intercultural Exchange: An Introduction for Foreign Language Teachers*. Clevedon: Multilingual Matters.

Paige, R. M. (ed.) (2001). *Education for the Intercultural Experience*. Yarmouth, ME: Intercultural Press (2nd edn).

Risager, K. (2006). *Language and Culture: Global Flows and Local Complexity*. Clevedon: Multilingual Matters.

Shaules, J. (2007). *Deep Culture: The Hidden Challenges of Global Living*. Clevedon: Multilingual Matters.

Spencer-Oatey, H. (2008). *Culturally Speaking: Managing Rapport through Talk across Cultures*. London: Continuum (2nd edn).

Wierzbicka, A. (2003). *Cross-Cultural Pragmatics*. Berlin: Mouton de Gruyter.

Psychology (social, cross-cultural, cultural) / communications studies

Adler, L. L. and Gielen, U. P. (eds) (2001). *Cross-Cultural Topics in Psychology*. Westport: Praeger (2nd edn).

Bennett, M. J. (1998). *Basic Concepts of Intercultural Communication*. Yarmouth, ME: Intercultural Press.

Berry, J. W., Poortinga, Y. H., Segall, M. H. and Dasen, P. R. (2002). *Cross-Cultural Psychology: Research and Applications*. Cambridge: Cambridge University Press (2nd edn).

Berry, J.W., Poortinga, Y. H. and Pandey, J. (eds) (1997). *Handbook of Cross-Cultural Psychology: Theory and Method*. Volume 1. Boston: Allyn & Bacon (2nd edn).

Berry, J. W., Dasen, P. R. and Saraswathi, T. S. (eds) (1997). *Handbook of Cross-Cultural Psychology: Basic Processes and Human Development*. Volume 2. Boston: Allyn & Bacon (2nd edn).

Berry, J.W., Segall, M. H. and Kâğıtçıbaşı, Ç. (eds) (1997). *Handbook of Cross-Cultural Psychology: Social Behavior and Applications*. Volume 3. Boston: Allyn & Bacon (2nd edn).

Brislin, R. (2000). *Understanding Culture's Influence on Behavior*. Orlando, FL: Harcourt College Publishers.

Chen, G.-M. and Starosta, W. J. (2005). *Foundations of Intercultural Communication*. Lanham, MD: University Press of America.

Chryssochoou, X. (2004). *Cultural Diversity: Its Social Psychology*. Malden, MA: Blackwell.

Gudykunst, W. B. (2003). *Cross-Cultural and Intercultural Communication*. Thousand Oaks, CA: Sage.

Gudykunst, W. B. (2004). *Bridging Differences: Effective Intergroup Communication*. Thousand Oaks, CA: Sage (4th edn).

Gudykunst, W. B. (ed.) (2005). *Theorizing about Intercultural Communication*. Thousand Oaks, CA: Sage.

Gudykunst, W. B. and Mody, B. (eds) (2003). *Handbook of International and Intercultural Communication*. Thousand Oaks, CA: Sage (2nd edn).

Gudykunst, W. B. and Kim, Y. Y. (2003). *Communicating with Strangers: An Approach to Intercultural Communication*. New York: McGraw-Hill (4th edn).

Harkness, J. A., Van de Vijver, F. J. R. and Mohler, P. P. (2003). *Cross-Cultural Survey Methods*. New Jersey: Wiley.

Jandt, F. E. (2003). *Intercultural Communication: A Global Reader*. Thousand Oaks, CA: Sage.

Jandt, F. E. (2007). *An Introduction to Intercultural Communication: Identities in a Global Community*. Thousand Oaks, CA: Sage (5th edn).

Kim, Y. Y. (2001). *Becoming Intercultural: An Integrative Theory of Communication and Cross-Cultural Adaptation*. Thousand Oaks, CA: Sage.

Lustig, M. W. and Koester, J. (2006). *Intercultural Competence: Interpersonal Communication Across Culture*. Boston: Allyn & Bacon (5th edn).

Matsumoto, D. (2007). *Culture and Psychology*. Belmont, CA: Wadsworth Publishing (4th edn).

Ratner, C. (2002). *Cultural Psychology: Theory and Method*. New York: Kluwer Academic/Plenum.

Sam, D. L. and Berry, J. W. (2006). *The Cambridge Handbook of Acculturation Psychology*. Cambridge: Cambridge University Press.

Samovar, L., Porter, R. and McDaniel, E. (2006). *Intercultural Communication: A Reader*. Belmont: Wadsworth (11th edn).

Saphiere, D. H., Mikk, B. K. and DeVries, B. I. (2005). *Communication Highwire: Leveraging the Power of Diverse Communication Styles*. London: Intercultural Press.

Segall, M., Dasen, P., Berry J. and Poortinga, Y. (2002). *Human Behavior in Global Perspective: An Introduction to Cross-Cultural Psychology*. Boston: Allyn & Bacon (rev. 2nd edn).

Smith, P. B. and Bond, M. H. (1998). *Social Psychology across Cultures*. London: Prentice Hall Europe (2nd edn).

Smith, P. B., Bond, M. H. and Kağıtçıbası, Ç. (2006). *Understanding Social Psychology across Cultures. Living and Working in a Changing World*. London: Sage.

Straub, J., Weidemann, A. and Weidemann, D. (eds) (2007). *Handbuch interkulturelle Kommunikation und Kompetenz: Grundbegriffe, Theorien, Anwendungsfelder. (Handbook of Intercultural Communication and Competence: Basic Concept, Theories, Fields of Application)*. Stuttgart: Metzler.

Thomas, A. (ed.) (2003). *Psychologie interkulturellen Handelns (Psychology of Intercultural Action)*. Göttingen: Hogrefe (2nd edn).

Thomas, A., Kinast, E.-U. and Schroll-Machl, S. (eds) (2005). *Handbuch Interkulturelle Kommunikation und Kooperation. Band 1: Grundlagen und Praxisfelder (Handbook of Intercultural Communication and Cooperation. Volume 1: Principles and Practice)*. Göttingen: Vandenhoeck & Ruprecht (rev. 2nd edn).

Thomas, A., Kammhuber, S. and Schroll-Machl, S. (eds) (2007). *Handbuch Interkulturelle Kommunikation und Kooperation. Band 2: Länder, Kulturen und Interkulturelle Berufstätigkeit (Handbook of Intercultural Communication and Cooperation. Volume 2: Countries, Cultures and Intercultural Professions)*. Göttingen: Vandenhoeck & Ruprecht (rev. 2nd edn).

Ting-Toomey, S. and Chung, L. C (2007). *Understanding Intercultural Communication*. Belmont, CA: Wadsworth Roxbury Publishing Company (2nd edn).

Ting-Toomey, S. (1999). *Communicating across Cultures*. New York: The Guilford Press.

Triandis, H. C. (1995). *Individualism and Collectivism*. Boulder, CO: Westview Press.

Triandis, H. C. (1994). *Culture and Social Behaviour*. New York: McGraw Hill.

Varner, I. and Beamer, L. (2004). *Intercultural Communication in the Global Workplace*. Boston, MA: Irwin/McGraw-Hill.

Ward, C., Bocher, S. and Furnham, A. (2001). *The Psychology of Culture Shock*. London: Routledge.

Wiseman, R. L. (1995). *Intercultural Communication Theory*. Thousand Oaks, CA: Sage.

Wiseman, R. L. and Koester, J. (1993). *Intercultural Communication Competence*. Thousand Oaks, CA: Sage.

International business and management studies

Adler, N. (2007). *International Dimensions of Organizational Behavior*. Cincinnati: South-Western College Publishing (5th edn).

Brake, T., Walker, D. M. and Walker, T. (2003). *Doing Business Internationally: The Guide to Cross-Cultural Success.* New York: McGraw Hill (2nd edn).

Canney-Davison, S. and Ward, K. (1999). *Leading International Teams.* London: McGraw Hill.

Carté, P. and Fox, C. (2004). *Bridging the Culture Gap: A Practical Guide to International Business Communication.* London: Kogan Page.

Comfort, J. and Franklin, P. (2008). *The Mindful International Manager: Competences for Working Effectively Across Cultures.* York: York Associates.

Ferraro, G. P. (2005). *The Cultural Dimension of International Business.* Upper Saddle River, NJ: Prentice Hall (5th edn).

Ghauri, P. and Usunier, J.-C. (2003). *International Business Negotiations.* Oxford: Elsevier Science Ltd (2nd edn).

Guirdham, M. (2005). *Communicating across Cultures at Work.* Basingstoke: Palgrave.

Hampden-Turner, C. and Trompenaars, F. (2000). *Building Cross-Cultural Competence-How to Create Wealth from Conflicting Values.* West Sussex, England: John Wiley & Sons.

Harris, P., Moran, R. T. and Moran, S. V. (2007). *Managing Cultural Differences: Global Leadership Strategies for the 21st Century.* Amsterdam and Boston: Elsevier/Butterworth-Heinemann (7th edn).

Hofstede, G. (2001). *Culture's Consequences: Comparing Values, Behaviors, Institutions, and Organizations Across Nations.* Thousand Oaks, CA: Sage (2nd edn).

Hofstede, G. and Hofstede, G. J. (2005). *Cultures and Organizations: Software of the Mind. Intercultural Cooperation and Its Importance for Survival.* New York: McGraw-Hill (2nd edn).

Holden, N. J. (2002). *Cross-Cultural Management: A Knowledge Management Perspective.* Harlow: Pearson Education.

House, R. J., Hanges, P. J., Javidan, M., Dorfman, P. W. and Gupta, V. (eds) (2004). *Culture, Leadership, and Organizations: The GLOBE Study of 62 Societies.* London: Sage.

Jackson, T. (2002). *International HRM: A Cross-Cultural Approach.* London: Sage.

Lane, H. W., DiStefano, J. J. and Maznevski, M. L. (2006). *International Management Behavior: Text, Readings and Cases.* Malden, MA: Blackwell (5th edn).

Lane, H. W., Maznevski, M. L., Mendenhall, M. E. and McNett, J. (eds) (2004). *The Blackwell Handbook of Global Management: A Guide to Managing Complexity.* Malden, MA: Blackwell.

Marx, E. (2001). *Breaking through Culture Shock.* London: Nicholas Brealey (new edn).

Mead, R. (2005). *International Management: Cross-Cultural Dimensions.* Oxford: Blackwell (3rd edn).

Schneider, S. C. and Barsoux, J.-L. (2003). *Managing across Cultures.* London: Pearson Education (2nd edn).

Simons, G. F. (ed.) (2002). *EuroDiversity: A Business Guide to Managing Difference.* Boston: Butterworth-Heinemann.

Thomas, D. C. and Inkson, K. (2003). *Cultural Intelligence: People Skills for Global Business.* San Francisco: Berret-Koehler.

Thomas, D. C. (2002). *Essentials of International Management: A Cross-Cultural Perspective.* Thousand Oaks, CA: Sage.

Thomas, D. C. (2003). *Readings and Cases in International Management: A Cross-Cultural Perspective*. London: Sage.

Trompenaars, F. and Hampden-Turner, C. (2004). *Managing People Across Culture*. Chichester, West Sussex: Capstone.

Trompenaars, F. and Hampden-Turner, C. (1997). *Riding the Waves of Culture: Understanding Diversity in Global Business*. London: Nicholas Brealey (2nd edn).

Trompenaars, F. and Woolliams, P. (2003). *Business across Cultures*. Chichester: Capstone.

Trompenaars, F. and Woolliams, P. (2004). *Marketing Across Culture*. Chichester: Capstone.

Usunier, J.-C. (1998). *International and Cross-Cultural Management Research*. London: Sage.

Usunier, J.-C. (2005). *Marketing across Cultures*. Harlow: Pearson Educational (4th edn).

Anthropology

Barnard, A. (2002). *Encyclopedia of Social and Cultural Anthropology*. New York: Routledge.

Ember, C. R. and Ember, M. (eds) (2006). *Cultural Anthropology*. Upper Saddle River, NJ: Prentice Hall (12th edn).

Geertz, C. (2005). *The Interpretation of Cultures*. New York: Basic Books (new edn).

Hall, E. T. (1959). *The Silent Language*. New York: Double Day.

Hall, E. T. (1966). *The Hidden Dimension*. New York: Double Day.

Hall, E. T. (1976). *Beyond Culture*. Garden City, NY: Anchor Press.

Hannerz, U. (1992). *Cultural Complexity. Studies in the Social Organization of Meaning*. New York: Columbia University Press.

Haviland, W. A., Prins, H. E. L., Walrath, D. and McBride, B. (2004). *Cultural Anthropology: The Human Challenge*. Belmont, CA: Wadsworth Publishing (11th edn).

Herzfeld, M. (2001). *Anthropology: Theoretical Practice in Culture and Society*. Oxford: Blackwell.

Kluckhohn, F. R. and Strodtbeck, F. L. (1973). *Variations in Value Orientations*. Westport, CT: Greenwood Press (reprinted).

Kottak, C. P. (2003). *Cultural Anthropology*. New York: McGraw-Hill (10th edn).

McKinney, C. V. (2000). *Globe Trotting in Sandals: A Field Guide to Cultural Research*. Dallas, TX: SIL International.

Spradley, J. P. and McCurdy, D. W. (2006). *Conformity and Conflict: Readings in Cultural Anthropology*. Boston: Allyn & Bacon (12th edn).

12.2 Journals

Applied linguistics / language education / education

Annual Review of Applied Linguistics
http://journals.cambridge.org/action/displayJournal?jid=APL

Applied Linguistics
http://www.oxfordjournals.org/applij/about.html

Intercultural Pragmatics
http://www.degruyter.com/rs/384_7078_ENU_h.htm

Journal of Language and Intercultural Communication
http://www.ialic.arts.gla.ac.uk/journal.html

Journal of Pragmatics
http://www.elsevier.com/wps/find/journaldescription.cws_home/
505593/description

Language and Intercultural Communication
http://www.multilingual-matters.net/laic/

Language, Culture and Curriculum
http://www.multilingual-matters.net/lcc/

Linguistics and Education
http://www.elsevier.com/wps/find/journaldescription.cws_home/
620373/description#description

Multilingua – Journal of Cross-Cultural and Interlanguage Communication
http://www.degruyter.de/rs/384_400_DEU_h.htm

Pragmatics
http://ipra.ua.ac.be/main.aspx?c=*HOME&n=1268

Research on Language and Social Interaction
http://rolsi.uiowa.edu/

TESOL Quarterly
http://www.tesol.org/s_tesol/seccss.asp?CID=632&DID=2461

Psychology (social, cross-cultural, cultural) / communication studies

Applied Psychology: An International Review
http://www.blackwellpublishing.com/journal.asp?ref=0269–994X

Communication Monographs
http://www.tandf.co.uk/journals/titles/03637751.asp

Cross-Cultural Psychology Bulletin
http://www.iaccp.org/bulletin/index.php

Culture and Psychology
http://cap.sagepub.com/

Human Communication Research
http://www.blackwellpublishing.com/journal.asp?ref=0360–3989

International Journal of Psychology
http://www.tandf.co.uk/journals/titles/00207594.asp

Journal of Applied Psychology
http://www.apa.org/journals/apl/

Journal of Cross-Cultural Psychology
http://jcc.sagepub.com/

Journal of Intercultural Communication
http://www.immi.se/intercultural/

Journal of Intercultural Communication Research
http://www.tandf.co.uk/journals/titles/17475749.asp

Journal of Social Psychology
http://www.heldref.org/jsp.php

Personnel Psychology
http://www.blackwellpublishing.com/journal.asp?ref=0031–5826&site=1

International business studies and management science

Business Communication Quarterly
http://www.sagepub.com/journalsProdDesc.nav?prodId=Journal201670

Cross Cultural Management: An International Journal
http://www.emeraldinsight.com/Insight/viewContainer.do?container
Type=Issue&containerId=23494

Human Resource Management Review
http://www.elsevier.com/wps/find/journaldescription.cws_home/
620229/description#description

International Business Review
http://www.sciencedirect.com/science/journal/09695931

International Journal of Cross-Cultural Management
http://ccm.sagepub.com/

International Journal of Human Resource Management
http://www.informaworld.com/smpp/title~content=t713702518~db=jour

International Studies of Management and Organization
http://www.mesharpe.com/mall/results1.asp?ACR=imo

Journal of Business Communication
http://job.sagepub.com/

Journal of Cross-Cultural Competence and Management
http://www.iko-verlag.de/IKO-Webshop/index.html?target=dept_87.html

Journal of International Business Studies
http://www.jibs.net/

Journal of International Management
http://www.elsevier.com/wps/find/journaldescription.cws_home/601266/
description#description

Journal of Management Studies
http://www.blackwellpublishing.com/aims.asp?ref=0022–2380&site=1

Journal of Organizational Behavior
http://www3.interscience.wiley.com/cgi-bin/jhome/4691

Management International Review
http://www.bwl.uni-kiel.de/mir/

Thunderbird International Business Review
http://www.thunderbird.edu/knowledge_network/journals/index.htm

Anthropology

Annual Review of Anthropology
http://arjournals.annualreviews.org/loi/anthro?cookieSet=1

Anthropology Today
http://www.blackwellpublishing.com/journal.asp?ref=0268–540X

Cultural Anthropology
http://www.culanth.org/

Current Anthropology
http://www.journals.uchicago.edu/CA/home.html

Ethnography
http://www.sagepub.co.uk/journalsProdDesc.nav?prodId=Journal200906

Journal of Contemporary Ethnography
http://jce.sagepub.com/

Multidisciplinary

Crosscultural Research
http://www.sagepub.com/journalsProdDesc.nav?prodId=Journal200972

Intercultural Education
http://www.tandf.co.uk/journals/carfax/14675986.html

International Journal of Intercultural Relations
http://www.elsevier.com/wps/find/journaldescription.cws_home/535/
description#description

Journal of Intercultural Studies
http://www.tandf.co.uk/journals/titles/07256868.asp

12.3   Associations and conferences

Applied linguistics / language education / education

American Association for Applied Linguistics AAAL
http://www.aaal.org
AAAL organizes an annual conference.

Association International de Linguistique Appliquée / International Association of Applied Linguistics AILA
http://www.aila.info
AILA organizes the triennial AILA World Congress.

International Association for Languages and Intercultural Communication
http://www3.unileon.es/grupos/ialic/
IALIC organizes an annual conference.

International Pragmatics Association
http://ipra.ua.ac.be
IPrA organizes biennial international conferences.

International Society for Language Studies
http://www.isls-inc.org/
ISLS organizes a biennial conference.

Teachers of English to Speakers of Other Languages, Inc. (TESOL)
http://www.tesol.org
TESOL organizes an annual conference.

Psychology (social, cross-cultural, cultural) / communication studies

American Psychology Association
http://www.apa.org
The APA organizes an annual convention.

International Association for Cross-Cultural Psychology
http://www.iaccp.org/
IACCP holds a biennial international congress and regional conferences in most years.

International Association of Applied Psychology
http://www.iaapsy.org/
The IAAP sponsors or cosponsors various conferences.

International Communication Association
http://www.icahdq.org/
The International Communication Association regularly organizes conferences and publishes *Human Communication Research, Communication Theory,* the *Journal of Communication,* and the *Journal of Computer-Mediated Communication.*

International Union of Psychological Science
http://www.am.org/iupsys/mtg.html
International listing of congresses and conferences in psychology.

National Communication Association (NCA)
www.natcom.org
The NCA organizes an annual convention.

World Communication Association
http://facstaff.uww.edu/wca/
WCA organizes various conferences and publishes *Journal of Intercultural Communication* and *Journal of Intercultural Communication Research.*

International business and management studies

Academy of International Business
http://aib.msu.edu/
AIB holds an annual international meeting, an annual conference on emerging research frontiers in international business studies and individual chapter meetings around the world.

Association for Business Communication (ABC)
http://www.businesscommunication.org/
The ABC organizes numerous conferences and conventions worldwide.

British Academy of Management
http://www.bam.ac.uk/

EGOS – European Group for Organizational Studies
http://www.egosnet.org
EGOS holds an annual conferences and annual colloquia.

European International Business Academy
http://www.eiba-online.org

IACCM – International Association of Cross-Cultural Competence and Management
http://iaccm.wu-wien.ac.at

Society for Human Resource Management
http://www.shrm.org

Anthropology

American Anthropological Association (AAA)
http://www.aaanet.org
AAA organizes an annual meeting.

American Ethnological Society
http://www.aesonline.org
A section of the American Anthropological Association (AAA), which organizes an annual meeting.

The Royal Anthropological Institute
http://www.therai.org.uk/
Organizes conferences.

Multidisciplinary

IAIE – International Association for Intercultural Education
http://www.iaie.org
IAIE organizes workshops, seminars and conferences and publishes the academic journal *Intercultural Education*.

International Academy for Intercultural Research (IAIR)
http://www.interculturalacademy.org/
The IAIR organizes conferences.

SIETAR – Society for Intercultural Education, Training and Research
http://www.sietar.org
Co-organizes SIETAR Global Conferences.
There are numerous SIETARs at national level such as those in France, India, the Netherlands and the United Kingdom. They organize national and international conferences.

SIETAR UK (Society for Intercultural Education, Training and Research)
http://www.sietar.org.uk
Organizes various conferences and events.

SIETAR Europa (Society for Intercultural Education, Training and Research)
http://www.sietar-europa.org
SIETAR Europa organizes conferences.

SIETAR USA (Society for Intercultural Education, Training and Research)
http://www.sietarusa.com/
SIETAR USA organizes an annual conference and has local groups.

Society for Cross-Cultural Research (SCCR)
http://www.sccr.org/
Holds an annual meeting, sponsors the quarterly journal *Cross-Cultural Research*, published by Sage Publications, and publishes the *SCCR Annual Meeting*.

12.4 Websites

Web resources are ephemeral in the extreme and for that reason we include only those that have existed over the years that this book has taken to write.

Applied linguistics / language education / education

Linguistic Bibliography / Bibliographie Linguistique
http://www.blonline.nl/
This bibliography 'provides bibliographical references to scholarly publications on all branches of linguistics and all the languages of the world, with the emphasis on non-Indo-European languages and lesser known Indo-European languages. As regards the place of publication, we focus particularly on linguistic works published outside Western Europe and North-America.'

Subject Centre for Languages, Linguistics and Area Studies
http://www.llas.ac.uk/index.aspx
'A publicly funded service, providing UK-wide support and services for higher education in Languages, Linguistics and Area Studies.'

Psychology (social, cross-cultural, cultural) / communication studies

Acculturation Research Bibliography
By Floyd W. Rudmin
http://ispp.org/bibliographies/RudminAcculturationResearchBibliography.pdf.
Includes publications up to 2007, often with linked abstract.

Communication Institute for Online Scholarship (CIOS)
http://www.cios.org/
'The Communication Institute for Online Scholarship is a [...] not-for-profit organization supporting the use of computer technologies in the service of communication scholarship and education.' 'CIOS online services provide access to thousands of files in the resource library as well as dozens of scholarly conferences enrolling over 4000 professionals and students. Also available is the online journals index database indexing more than 36,500 bibliographic references from 78 communication journals and

electronic white pages for more than 5000 professionals and students in the communications field' (Hall 2002: 209).

European Resources for Intercultural Communication
http://www.fh-koeln.de/ERIC/Englisch/index_engl.html
'The ERIC network is implementing a database featuring various kinds of documents and sources – textual, multimedia. film etc. They all refer to culture-forming factors in virtually every European country. Resources of this kind as well as information on current activities in the field of intercultural communication will be made accessible through an internet portal. Intercultural seminars on the web are also part of the agenda of ERIC."

International business and management studies

Anne-Wil Harzing's website
http://www.harzing.com/
A truly amazing compendium of information and publications useful in research in international and cross-cultural management put together by Prof. Anne-Wil Harzing.

dialogin.com – The Delta Intercultural Academy
http://www.dialogin.com/
dialogin The Delta Intercultural Academy is a not-for-profit knowledge and learning community for all those professionally interested or involved in intercultural business and management communication. Edited by Peter Franklin.

Emerald
http://www.emeraldinsight.com/
An electronic publisher of over 180 journals providing a wide range of online services. Some content is free of charge.

Geert Hofstede's website
http://feweb.uvt.nl/center/hofstede/index.htm
This is not to be confused with ...

ITIM
http://www.geert-hofstede.com/
... which also offers much information about Hofstede's dimensions.

International Management/Business, Comparative and Cross-Cultural Management
http://www.harzing.com/litbase.htm

A free downloadable 'database containing thousands of literature references in the area of International Management/Business, Comparative and Cross-cultural Management' provided by Prof. Anne-Weil Harzing.

Trompenaars-Hampden-Turner's website
http://www.7d-culture.nl/welcome/index.htm

Anthropology

AnthroBase
http://www.anthrobase.com/
Searchable, multilingual database of texts on social and cultural anthropology.

Anthropology and Related Links
http://academic.pg.cc.md.us/~ahabermr/anthrolinks.html

Anthropology Resources on the Internet
http://www.aaanet.org/resources/
Provided by the American Anthropological Association, this site contains lists/discussion groups, literature and libraries, news and media, organizations and institutes, resources for teachers/professors, applied/practicing anthropology, funding opportunities, general resources.

AnthroSource
http://www.anthrosource.net/
'Premier online resource serving the research, teaching, and professional needs of anthropologists. Developed by the American Anthropological Association (AAA), AnthroSource brings 100 years of anthropological material online to scholars and the public.'

SocioSite: Social and Cultural Anthropology
http://www.sociosite.net/topics/anthropo.php
A large directory of anthropology related websites from all over the world.

Multidisciplinary

Culture Source Bibliography of Intercultural Communication
http://www.culture-source.de
Bibliography of more than 2100 intercultural communications publications in English and German. Searchable by keywords.

Global People
http://www.globalpeople.org.uk

A set of resources for promoting intercultural effectiveness in international partnerships, developed by staff at the University of Warwick. The resources include a Life Cycle Model, a Competency Framework and a Learning Process Model for intercultural effectiveness, as well as various articles. There are numerous authentic case examples.

Intercultural Insights (Yahoo Group)
http://finance.groups.yahoo.com/group/interculturalinsights/
'A members-only resource exchange and professional development discussion group on intercultural and cross-cultural business, training, education, research and consulting topics for experienced intercultural professionals.'

Intercultural U (formerly InterculturalRelations.com)
http://cms.interculturalu.com/
'Online community of people from around the world who are interested in intercultural relations. [...] Topics covered on this site include: racism, prejudice, stereotypes, hate crimes, culture, diversity, multiculturalism, race, ethnicity, linguistics, intercultural and diversity training/consulting, culture shock, ethnocentrism, nonverbal communication, intercultural communication, cross cultural psychology, cultural anthropology and race relations.' With blogs, forum, library.

SIETAR Europa Online Documentation Centre
http://www.sietar.de/SIETARproject/index.html
'Our aim is the creation of a multilingual intercultural online knowledge management system that is totally browser accessible, to be permanently a part of the SIETAR website, a regularly updated source for information on intercultural research, publications, tools and other professional intercultural resources for SIETAR members and guests.'

Social Science Research Network (SSRN)
http://www.ssrn.com
'Social Science Research Network (SSRN) is devoted to the rapid worldwide dissemination of social science research and is composed of a number of specialized research networks in each of the social sciences.' The downloading articles and membership are free.

World Values Survey
http://www.worldvaluessurvey.org/
'This is a place to learn more about values and cultural changes in societies all over the world.'

12.5   Assessment instruments

The list of assessment instruments that follows is a conflation of those instruments listed in four sources:

1. Fantini, A. E. (2006). *Exploring and Assessing Intercultural Competence.* Brattleboro, VT: Federation of The Experiment in International Living, 87–94.
2. Paige, R. M. (2004). Instrumentation in intercultural training. D. Landis, J. M. Bennett and M. J. Bennett (eds), *Handbook of Intercultural Training*, Volume 3. Thousand Oaks, CA: Sage, 85–128.
3. SIETAR Europe: www.sietar-europa.org/SIETARproject/index.html (accessed on 28 Sept. 2008.
4. Chapter 8 of the current volume.

The categorisation adopted here is that used by Paige (2004: 94).

The names of the assessment instruments are followed by a symbol indicating the sources in which they are to be found: Paige: ∗; SIETAR: □; Fantini: ●; Chapter 8: ▼. Where the instrument's source is a company, it is followed by the name and place of that company in brackets. However, its source does not appear in the bibliography at the end of this section.

Organizational assessment and development

A   Organizational culture

1. Organizational Climate Inventory ∗ (Cooke and Lafferty 1983; Cooke and Szumal 1993)
2. Culture for Diversity Inventory ∗ ▼ (Human Synergistics/Center for Applied Research 2001; Cooke and Lafferty 1995)
3. Assessing Diversity Climate ∗ ▼ (Kossek and Zonia 1993)

B   Equal opportunity climate

1. Military Equal Opportunity Climate Survey ∗ (Dansby et al. 2001, Landis 1990)
2. University Equal Opportunity Climate Survey ∗ ▼ (Landis et al. 1996)

Personal assessment and development

A   Intercultural development

1. Intercultural Development Inventory (IDI) ∗ □ ● ▼ (Hammer 1999; Hammer and Bennett 2001a, 2001b)
2. The Global Team Process Questionnaire □ ● (GTPQ) (ITAP International Inc., Newtown)

3. Intercultural Readiness Check (IRC) □ ● (IBI Intercultural Business Improvement, Laren NL)
4. Personal Cultural Perspective Profile (PCPP) □ ● (Ramsey 1994)
5. Foreign Assignment Success Test (FAST) □ ● (Black 1988)
6. The International Mobility Assessment (IMA) □ ● (Tucker International LLC., Boulder, CO)

B   *Cultural values and value orientation*

1. Intercultural Sensitivity Inventory (ICSI) * □ ● ▼ (Bhawuk and Brislin 1992)
2. Horizontal and Vertical Individualism and Collectivism * (Gelfand and Holcombe 1998; Singelis et al. 1995)
3. Self-Construal Scale * (Singelis 1994)
4. Value Orientations Survey (VOS) * ▼ (Kluckhohn and Strodtbeck 1961)
5. Four-Value Orientation Inventory * (Casse 1982)
6. Intercultural Conflict Style Inventory * □ ● (Hammer 2003)
7. Cross-Cultural Sensitivity Scale (CCSS) □ ● (Pruegger and Rogers 1993)
8. The Cultural Orientations Indicator (COI) □ ● ▼ (TMC, Princeton)
9. Test of Intercultural Sensitivity (TICS) □ ● (Weldon et al. 1975)
10. Insights Discovery System □ ● (Insights Learning and Development Ltd., Dundee)
11. Multicultural Counseling Awareness Scale (MCAS) □ ● (Ponterotto et al. 1990)
12. Beliefs, Events, and Values Inventory (BEVI) ● (Shealy 2004)
13. Schwartz Value Survey (SVS) ● ▼ (IMO, Göttingen)
14. Portrait Value Questionnaire (PVQ) ▼ (Schwartz et al. 2001)
15. Worldprism Profiler ▼ (TMA, www.tmaworld.com)

C   *Cultural identity*

1. Bicultural Involvement Questionnaire * (Szapocznik et al. 1980)
2. Multigroup Ethic Identity Measure * (Phinney 1992)
3. Multi-Index Ethnocultural Identity Scale * (Horvath 1997; Yamada 1998)
4. Personal Dimensions of Difference * (Dunbar 1997)
5. Black Racial Identity Scale * (Helms and Parham 1990, 1996)
6. Cross Racial Identity Scale * (Cross and Vandiver 2001; Worrell et al. 2001)
7. White Racial Identity Attitudes Scale * (Helms 1984; Helms and Carter 1990)

8. Acculturation Rating Scale for Mexican Americans-II * (Cuellar et al. 1995)
9. Suinn-Lew Asian Self-Identity Acculturation Scale * (Suinn et al. 1987)
10. Third Culture Adolescent Questionnaire * (Gerner et al. 1992)
11. The Culture in the Workplace Questionnaire □ ● (ITAP International Inc., Newtown)
12. Trompenaar's Seven Dimensions of Culture and Corporate Culture Profiles □ ● (Trompenaars Hampden-Turner, Amsterdam)
13. Personal Orientation Inventory (POI) □ ● (Uhes and Shybut 1971)
14. Peterson Cultural Style Indicator □ ● (Across Cultures Inc., Saint Paul, MN)
15. Intercultural Perspective Taking Instrument ● (Steglitz 1993)

D   *Learning styles*

1. Learning Styles Inventory * (Kolb 1993, 1999)
2. Sociocultural Checklist (SC) ● (CCDES, 2002, Ferndale, WA)

E   *Global awareness and worldmindedness*

1. Cross-Cultural World-Mindedness Scale * (Der-Karabetian and Metzer 1993)
2. GAP Test: Global Awareness Profile * □ ● (Corbitt 1998)
3. Intercultural Awareness Profiler (IAP) ▼ (Trompenaars Hampden-Turner, Amsterdam)
4. Peterson Cultural Awareness Test □ ● (Across Cultures Inc., Saint Paul, MN)
5. Global Mindedness Scale ● (Hett 1993)
6. Worldmindedness Scale ● (Sampson and Smith 1957)

F   *Cultural adjustment, culture shock, and cultural adaptation*

1. Cross-Cultural Adaptability Inventory (CCAI) * □ ● ▼ (Kelley and Meyers 1999)
2. Culture Shock Inventory * (Reddin 1994)
3. Overseas Assignment Inventory (OAI) * □ ● (Tucker 1999)
4. Sociocultural Adaptation Scale (SCAS) * ▼ (Searle and Ward 1990; Ward and Kennedy, 1999)
5. Living and Working Overseas Predeparture Questionnaire □ ● (Kealey 1988)
6. The Evaluation of Expatriate Development (EED) □ ● (Tucker International LLC., Boulder, CO)
7. Supervisory Evaluation of Expatriate Development (SEED) □ ● (Tucker International LLC., Boulder, CO)

G   *Personality characteristics*

1. Myers-Briggs Type Indicator ∗ (Brown and Knight 1999)
2. Singer-Loomis Type Deployment Inventory ∗ (Singer et al. 1996)
3. Hogan Personality Inventory □ ● (Hogan Assessment Systems, Tusla, Oklahoma)
4. Intercultural Personality Test (IPT) ▼ (ICUnet AG, Passau)

H   *Intercultural and multicultural competence*

1. Multicultural Awareness-Knowledge-Skills Survey ∗ (D'Andrea et al. 1991)
2. Cultural General Assimilator ∗ (Cushner and Brislin 1996)
3. Behavioral Assessment Scale for Intercultural Communication (BASIC) □ ● (Olebe and Koester 1989)
4. Multicultural Counseling Inventory (MCI) □ ● (Sodowsky et al. 1994)
5. Cultural Competence Self-Assessment Questionnaire (CCSAQ) □ ● (Mason 1995)
6. Expatriate Profile (EP) □ ● (Park Li Group, New York, 1996)
7. The Intercultural Competence Assessment (INCA) Project □ ● ▼ (www.incaproject.org)
8. Intercultural Competency Scale □ ● (Elmer 1987)
9. Prospector □ ● (Spreitzer et al. 1997)
10. The SAGE (The Self-Assessment for Global Endeavors) □ ● (Caligiuri and Associates, New Brunswick, NJ)
11. The International Profiler ▼ (Worldwork Ltd., London)
12. Global View 360 ▼ (Worldwork Ltd., London)
13. Cross-Cultural Counseling Inventory □ ● (LaFrombroise et al. 1991)
14. Objective Job Quotient System (OJQ) □ ● (Global Interface Pty Ltd., Drummoyne)
15. Intercultural Sensitivity Survey □ ● (Towers 1991)
16. The International Candidate Evaluation (ICE) □ ● (Tucker International LLC., Boulder, CO)
17. Assessment of Intercultural Competence ● (AIC) (Fantini 2000)
18. Intercultural Sensitivity Index ● (Olson and Kroeger 2001)
19. Internationslism Scale ● (Lutzker 1960)
20. Model of Intercultural Communication Competence ● (Arasaratnam 2006)
21. Global Team Player ▼ (ICUnet AG, Passau)
22. Test of Intercultural Sensitivity (TIS) ▼ (ICUnet AG, Passau)

I Prejudice and racism

1. Color-Blind Racial Attitudes Scale * (Neville et al. 2000)
2. Attitudinal and Behavioral Openness Scale * (Caligiuri et al. 2000)
3. Radicalism-Conservatism Scale ● (Nettler and Huffman 1957)
4. Bogardus Social Distance Scale ● (Bogardus 1959)
5. Teaching Tolerance – Bias Test and Tips □ ● (http://www.tolerance. org/hidden_bias/index.html)

Bibliography of the assessment instruments listed above

Arasaratnam, L. A. (2006). Further testing of a new model of intercultural communication competence. *Communication Research Reports*, 23 (2): 93–9.

Bhawuk, D. P. S. and Brislin, R. W. (1992). The measurement of intercultural sensitivity using the concepts of individualism and collectivism. *International Journal of Intercultural Relations*, 16(4): 413–36.

Black, J. S. (1988). Work role transitions: A study of American expatriate managers in Japan. *Journal of International Business Studies*, 19(2): 277–94.

Bogardus, E. S. (1959). Social Distance Scale. *Sociology and Social Research*, 17, 265–71.

Brown, C. and Knight, K. (1999). Introduction to self-awareness inventories. In S. M. Fowler and M. G. Mumford (eds), *Intercultural Sourcebook: Cross-Cultural Training Methods*, Vol. 2, pp. 19–30. Yarmouth, ME: Intercultural Press:

Caligiuri, P. M., Jacobs, R. R. and Farr, J.L. (2000). The Attitudinal and Behavioral Openness Scale: Scale development and construct validation. *International Journal of Intercultural Relations*, 24(1): 27–46.

Casse, P. (1982). *Training for the Multicultural Manager*. Washington: SIETAR.

Cooke, R. A. and Lafferty, J. C. (1983). *The Organizational Culture Inventory*. Plymouth, MI: Human Synergistics.

Cooke, R. A. and Lafferty, J. C. (1995). *Culture for Diversity Inventory*. Arlington Heights.

Cooke, R. A. and Szumal, J. L. (1993). Measuring normative beliefs and shared behavioral expectations in organizations: The reliability and validity of the Organizational Culture Inventory. *Psychological Reports*, 72, 1299–330.

Corbitt, J. N. (1998). *Global Awareness Profile*. Yarmouth, ME: Intercultural Press.

Cross, W. E. and Vandiver, B. J. (2001). Nigrescence theory and measurement: Introducing the Cross Racial Identity Scale (CRIS). In J. G. Ponterotto, J. M. Casas, L. A. Suzuki and C. M. Alexander (eds), *Handbook of Multicultural Counseling*, pp. 371–93. Thousand Oaks, CA: Sage.

Cuellar, A., Arnold, B. and Maldonado R. (1995). Acculturation Rating Scale for Mexican Americans-II: A revision of the original ARSMA scale. *Hispanic Journal of Behavioral Sciences*, 17: 275–304.

Cushner, K. and Brislin, R. W. (1996). *Intercultural Interactions: A Practical Guide*. Thousand Oaks, CA: Sage (2nd edn).

D'Andrea, M., Daniels, J. and Heck, R. (1991). Evaluating the impact of multicultural counseling training. *Journal of Counseling and Development*, 70: 143–50.

Dansby, M. R., Stewart, J. B. and Webb, S. C. (eds) (2001). *Managing Diversity in the Military*. New Brunswick, NJ: Transaction.

Der-Karabetian, A. and Metzger, J. (1993). The Cross-Cultural World-Mindedness Scale and political party affiliation. *Psychological Reports*, 72: 1069–70.

Dunbar, E. (1997). The Personal Dimensions of Difference Scale: Measuring multi-group identity with four ethnic groups. *International Journal of Intercultural Relations*, 21 (1): 1–28.

Elmer, M. I. (1987). *Intercultural Effectiveness: Development of an Intercultural Competency Scale*. Unpublished Doctoral Dissertation. Michigan, MI: Michigan State University.

Fantini, A. E. (2000). A central concern: Developing intercultural competence. In A. E. Fantini (ed.), *SIT Occasional Papers Series: Inaugural issue – about our institution*, pp. 23–42, Brattleboro, VT: School for International Training.

Gelfand, M. J. and Holcombe, K. M. (1998). Behavioral patterns of horizontal and vertical individualism and collectivism. In T. M. Singelis, *Teaching about Culture, Ethnicity, and Diversity: Exercises and Planned Activities*, pp. 121–31. Thousand Oaks, CA: Sage.

Gerner, M., Perry, F., Moselle, M. A. and Archbold, M. (1992). Characteristics of internationally mobile adolescents. *Journal of Social Psychology*, 30: 197–214.

Hammer, M. R. (1999). A measure of intercultural sensitivity: The Intercultural Development Inventory. In S. M. Fowler and M. G. Mumford, *Intercultural Sourcebook: Cross-Cultural Training Methods*, vol. 2, pp. 61–72. Yarmouth, ME: Intercultural Press.

Hammer, M. R. (2003). *The Intercultural Conflict Style Inventory*. North Potomac, MD: Hammer Consulting Group.

Hammer, M. R. and Bennett, M. J. (2001a). *The Intercultural Development Inventory: Instrument*. Portland: Intercultural Communication Institute.

Hammer, M. R. and Bennett, M. J. (2001b). *The Intercultural Development Inventory: Manual*. Portland: Intercultural Communication Institute.

Helms, J. E. (1984). Toward a theoretical explanation of the effects of race on counseling: A Black and White model. *The Counseling Psychologist*, 17: 227–52.

Helms, J. E. and Carter, R. T. (1990). White Racial Identity Attitude Scale (Form WRIAS). In J. E. Helms, *Black and White Racial Identity: Theory, Research and Practice*, pp. 249–51. New York: Greenwood Press.

Helms, J. E. and Parham, T. A. (1990). Black Racial Identity Attitude Scale (Form RIAS-B). In J. E. Helms, *Black and White Racial Identity: Theory, Research and Practice*, pp. 245–7. New York: Greenwood Press.

Helms, J. E. and Parham, T. A. (1996). The development of the Racial Identity Attitude Scale. In R. L. Jones, *Handbook of Tests and Measurements for Black Populations*, vol. 2. Hampton, VA: Cobb & Henry.

Hett, J. E. (1993). The development of an instrument to measure global-mindedness, Thesis (Ed. D.), University of San Diego.

Horvath, A. M. (1997). Ethnocultural identification and the complexities of ethnicity. In K. Cushner and R. W. Brislin, *Improving Intercultural Interactions: Modules for Cross-Cultural Training Programs*, vol. 2, pp. 165–83. Thousand Oaks, CA: Sage.

Kealey, D. J. (1988). *Explaining and Predicting Cross-Cultural Adjustment and Effectiveness: A Study of Canadian Technical Advisers Overseas*. Hull and Quebec: Canadian International Development Agency.

Kelley, C. and Meyers, J. (1999). The cross-cultural adaptability inventory. In S. M. Fowler and M. G. Mumford, *Intercultural Sourcebook: Cross-Cultural Training Methods*, vol. 2, pp. 53–60. Yarmouth, ME: Intercultural Press.

Kluckhohn, F. R. and F. L. Strodtbeck (1961). *Variations in Value Orientations*. Evanston, IL: Row, Peterson.

Kolb, D. A. (1993). *Learning-Style Iventory: Self-Scoring Inventory and Interpretation Booklet (Version LSI-IIa)*. Boston: HayGroup.

Kolb, D. A. (1999). *The Kolb Learning Style Inventory: Version 3*. Boston: HayGroup.

Kossek, E. and Zonia, S. (1993). Assessing diversity climate: A field study of reactions to employer efforts to promote diversity. *Journal of Organizational Behaviour*, 14: 61–81.

LaFromboise, T. D., Coleman, H. L. K., and Hernandez, A. (1991). Development and factor structure of the Cross-Cultural Counseling Inventory – Revised. *Professional Psychology: Research and Practice*, 22: 380–8.

Landis, D. (1990). *Military Equal Opportunity Cimate Survey: Reliability, Construct Validity and Preliminary Field Test*. Oxford, MS: University of Mississippi Center for Applied Research and Evaluation.

Landis, D., Dansby, M. R. and Tallarigo, R. S. (1996). The use of Equal Opportunity Climate in intercultural training. In D. Landis and R. S. Bhagat, *Handbook of Intercultural Training*, pp. 244–63. Thousand Oaks, CA: Sage.

Lutzker, D. R. (1960). Internationalism as a predictor of cooperative behavior. *Journal of Conflict Resolution*, 4 (4): 426–30.

Mason, J. L. (1995). *Cultural Competence Self-Assessment Questionnaire: A Manual for Users*. Portland, Research and Training Center on Family Support and Children's Mental Health.

Nettler, G. Y. and Huffman, J. (1957). Political opinion and personal security. *Sociometry*, 20: 51–66.

Neville, H. A., Lilly, R. L., Duran, G., Lee, R. M. and Browne, L. (2000). Construction and initial validation of the Color-Blind Racial Attitudes Scale (CoBRAS). *Journal of Counseling Psychology*, 47: 59–70.

Olebe, M. and Koester, J. (1989). Exploring the cross-cultural equivalence of the Behavioral Assessment Scale for intercultural communication. *International Journal of Intercultural Relations*, 13 (3): 333–47.

Olson, C. L. and Kroeger, K. R. (2001). Global competency and intercultural sensitivity. *Journal of Studies in International Education*, 5 (2): 116–37.

Paige, R. M. (2004). Instrumentation in intercultural training. In D. Landis, J. M. Bennett and M.J. Bennett, *Handbook of Intercultural Training*, pp. 85–128. Thousand Oaks, CA: Sage.

Phinney, J. S. (1992). The Multigroup Ethnic Identity Measure: A new scale for use with diverse groups. *Journal of Adolescent Research*, 7: 156–76.

Ponterotto, J. G., Sanchez, C. M. and Magids, D. M. (1990). *The Multicultural Counseling Awareness Scale (MCAS): Form B, Revised Self-Assessment*. New York: Fordham University.

Pruegger, V. J. and Rogers, T. B. (1993). Development of a scale to measure cross-cultural sensitivity in the Canadian context. *Canadian Journal of Behavioural Science*, 25 (4): 615–21.

Ramsey, M. (1994). Use of a Personal Cultural Perspective Profile (PCPP) in developing counsellor multicultural competence. *International Journal for the Advancement of Counselling*, 17 (4): 283–90.

Reddin, W. J. (1994). *Using Tests to Improve Training: The Complete Guide to Selecting, Developing and Using Training Instruments*. Englewood Cliffs, NJ: Prentice Hall.

Sampson, D. L. and Smith, H. P. (1957). A scale to measure world-minded attitudes. *Journal of Social Psychology*, 45: 99–106.

Schwartz, S. H., Melech, G., Lehmann, A., Burgess, S., Harris, M. and Owens, V. (2001). Extending the cross-cultural validity of the theory of basic human values with a different method of measurement. *Journal of Cross-Cultural Psychology*, 32 (5): 519–42.

Searle, W. and Ward, C. (1990). The prediction of psychological and sociocultural adjustment during cross-cultural transitions. *International Journal of Intercultural Relations*, 14: 449–64.

Shealy, C. N. (2004). A model and method for 'making' a combined-integrated psychologist: Equilintegration (EI) Theory and the Beliefs, Events, and Values Inventory (BEVI). *Journal of Clinical Psychology*, 60 (10): 1065–90.

SIETAR (2003). *Online Documentation Centre*: http://www.sietar-europa.org/SIETARproject/index.html (accessed 28 Sept. 2008).

Singelis, T. M. (1994). The measurement of independent and interdependent self-construals. *Personality and Social Psychology Bulletin*, 20: 580–91.

Singelis, T. M., Triandis, H. C., Bhawuk, D. and Gelfand, M. J. (1995). Horizontal and vertical dimensions of individualism and collectivism: A theoretical and measurement refinement. *Cross-Cultural Research*, 29: 240–75.

Singer, J., Loomis, M., Kirkhart, E. and Kirkhart, L. (1996). *The Singer-Loomis Type Deployment Inventory – Version 4.1*. Gresham: Moving Boundaries.

Sodowsky, G. R., Taffe, R. C., Gutkin, T. B., and Wise, S. (1994). Development of the Multicultural Counseling Inventory (MCI): A self-report measure of multicultural competencies. *Journal of Counseling Psychology*, 41 (2): 137–48.

Spreitzer, G. M., McCall, M. W. and J. D. Mahoney. (1997). Early identification of international executive potential. *Journal of Applied Psychology*, 82 (1): 6–29.

Steglitz, I. (1993). Intercultural perspective-taking: The impact of study abroad, Thesis (PhD), University of Minnesota.

Suinn, R. M., Rickard-Figueroa, K., Lew, S. and Vigil, P. (1987). The Suinn-Lew Asian Self-identity Acculturation Scale: An initial report. *Educational and Psychological Measurement*, 47: 401–7.

Szapocznik, J., Kurintes W. and Fernandez, T. (1980). Bicultural involvement and adjustment in Hispanic-Americans. *International Journal of Intercultural Relations*, 4 (3): 353–65.

Towers, K. L. (1991). *Intercultural Sensitivity Survey: Construction and Initial Validation*. Unpublished doctoral dissertation. University of Iowa.

Tucker, M. F. (1999). Self-awareness and development using the Overseas Assignment Inventory. In S. M. Fowler and M. G. Mumford, *Intercultural Sourcebook: Cross-Cultural Training Methods*, vol. 2, pp. 45–52. Yarmouth, ME: Intercultural Press.

Uhes, M. J. and Shybut, J. (1971). Personal orientation inventory as a predictor of success in Peace Corps training. *Journal of Applied Psychology*, 55 (5): 498–9.

Ward, C. and Kennedy A. (1999). The measurement of sociocultural adaptation. *International Journal of Psychology*, 23 (6): 659–77.

Weldon, D. E., Carlson, D. E., Rissman, A. K., Slobodin, L. and Triandis, H. C. (1975). A laboratory test of effects of culture assimilator training. *Journal of Psychology and Social Psychology*, 32 (2): 300–10.

Worrell, F. C., Cross, W. E., Jr. and Vandiver, B. J. (2001). Nigrescence theory: Current status and challenges for the future. *Journal of Multicultural Counseling and Development*, 29: 201–13.

Yamada, A.-M. (1998). Multidimensional identification. In T. M. Singelis, *Teaching about Culture, Ethnicity and Diversity: Exercises and Planned Activities*, pp. 141–5. Thousand Oaks, CA: Sage.

12.6 Resources for developing intercultural interaction competence

Books

Batchelder, D. and Warner, E. G. (eds) (1977). *Beyond Experience: The Experiential Approach to Cross-Cultural Education*. Brattleboro, VT: Experiment Press.

Bernaus, M., Andrade, A. I., Kervran, M., Murkowska, A. and Sáez, F. T. (2007). *Plurilingual and Pluricultural Awareness in Language Teacher Education: A Training Kit*. Strasbourg: Council of Europe Publishing.

Brislin, R. W. and Yoshida, T. (1994). *Intercultural Communication Training: An Introduction*. Thousand Oaks, CA: Sage.

Brislin, R. W. and Yoshida, T. (eds) (1994). *Improving Intercultural Interactions: Modules for Cross-Cultural Training Programs*. Thousand Oaks, CA: Sage.

Byram, M., Nichols, A. and Stevens, D. (2001). *Developing Intercultural Competence in Practice*. Clevedon: Multilingual Matters.

Comfort, J. and Franklin, P. (2008). *The Mindful International Manager: Competences for Working Effectively Across Cultures*. York: York Associates.

Cushner, K. and Brislin, R. W. (2000). *Intercultural Interactions: A Practical Guide*. Thousand Oaks, CA: Sage (2nd edn).

Cushner, K. and. Brislin, R. W (eds) (1997). *Improving Intercultural Interactions: Modules for Cross-Cultural Training Programs. Multicultural Aspects of Counseling*, vol. 2. Thousand Oaks, CA: Sage.

Fowler, S. M. and Mumford, M. G. (1995). *Intercultural Sourcebook: Cross-Cultural Training Methods*, vol. 1. Yarmouth, ME: Intercultural Press.

Fowler, S. M. and Mumford, M. G. (1999). *Intercultural Sourcebook: Cross-Cultural Training Methods*, vol. 2. Yarmouth, ME: Intercultural Press.

Gardenswartz, L., Rowe, A., Digh, P. and Bennett M. F. (2003). *The Global Diversity Desk Reference: Managing an International Workforce*. San Franciso: Pfeiffer.

Gibson, R. (2002). *Intercultural Business Communication*. Oxford: Oxford University Press.

Grove, Cornelius (1989). *Beyond Experience: The Experiential Approach to Cross-Cultural Education*. Yarmouth, ME: Intercultural Press (2nd edn).

Hofstede, G. J., Pedersen, P. B. and Hofstede, G. (2007). *Exploring Culture: Exercises, Stories and Synthetic Cultures*. Yarmouth, ME: Intercultural Press.

Kohls, L. R. and Knight, J. M. (1994). *Developing Intercultural Awareness*. Yarmouth, ME: Intercultural Press (2nd edn).

Kohls, L. R. and Brussow, H. L. (1995). *Training Know-How for Cross Cultural and Diversity Trainers*. Duncanville: Adult Learning Systems Inc.

Landis, D. and Brislin, R. (eds) (1983). *Handbook of Intercultural Training*, vol. 1. New York: Pergamon.

Landis, D. and Bhagat, R. S. (eds) (1996). *Handbook of Intercultural Training*, Thousand Oaks, CA: Sage.

Landis, D., Bennett, J. M. and Bennett, M. J. (eds) (2004). *Handbook of Intercultural Training*, Thousand Oaks, CA: Sage.

Peace Corps (1997). *Culture Matters: The Peace Corps Cross-Cultural Workbook.* Washington: Peace Corps Information Collection and Exchange. Downloadable at: http://www.peacecorps.gov/wws/publications/culture/pdf/ workbook.pdf (accessed 16 Nov. 2008).

Seelye, N. H. (ed.) (1996). *Experiential Activities for Intercultural Learning.* Yarmouth, ME: Intercultural Press.

Singelis, T. M. (ed.) *Teaching About Culture, Ethnicity, and Diversity: Exercises and Planned Actvities.* Thousand Oaks, CA: Sage.

Storti, Craig (2001). *The Art of Crossing Cultures.* Yarmouth, MA: Intercultural Press.

Storti, Craig (2001). *Old World, New World: Bridging Cultural Differences: Britain, France, Germany and the U.S.* Yarmouth, ME: Intercultural Press.

Storti, Craig (1994). *Cross-Cultural Dialogues.* Yarmouth, MA: Intercultural Press.

Storti, Craig (1997). *The Art of Coming Home.* Yarmouth, MA: Intercultural Press.

Storti, Craig (1999). *Figuring Foreigners Out: A Practical Guide.* Yarmouth, MA: Intercultural Press.

Stringer, D. M. and Cassiday, P. A. (2002). *Fifty-Two Activities for Exploring Values Differences.* Yarmouth, ME: Intercultural Press.

Tomalin, B. and Stempleski, S. (1994). *Cultural Awareness.* Oxford: Oxford University Press.

Utley, Derek (2004). *Intercultural Resource Pack.* Cambridge: Cambridge University Press.

Verluyten, S. P. (2007). *Cultures: From Observation to Understanding. A Workbook.* Leuven: Acco.

Games and simulations

BaFa' BaFa'
by Garry Shirts
http://www.stsintl.com/business/bafa.html
In *BaFa' BaFa'* 'participants come to understand the powerful effects that culture plays in every person's life. It may be used to help participants prepare for living and working in another culture or to learn how to work with people from other departments, disciplines, genders, races, and ages.'

BARNGA: A Simulation Game on Cultural Clashes
by Sivasailam Thiagarajan and Raja Thiagarajan
http://interculturalpress.com/store/pc/viewPrd.asp?idcategory=74& idproduct=30
'BARNGA is the classic simulation game on cultural clashes. Participants experience the shock of realizing that despite their good intentions and the many similarities amongst themselves, people interpret things differently from one another in profound ways, especially people from

differing cultures. Players learn that they must understand and reconcile these differences if they want to function effectively in a cross-
cultural group.'

Diversophy
by George Simons
http://www.diversophy.com
'An intercultural training instrument in the form of a game for 3 to
8 people in one or several groups playing simultaneously. Players are
tested on facts and appropriate behavioral choices, share their own
background and experiences with diversity or intercultural challenges, get advice about the culture they are exploring, and undergo
the risks of living or working in a new environment or with people
different from themselves. Over twenty culture specific games are
available in up to four languages.' (http://www.sietar.de/SIETARproject/
Games&simulations.html)

Ecotonos: A Unique Simulation for Working across the Cultural Divide
by Nipporica Associates
http://www.nipporica.com/prod.htm
'A powerful and extremely adaptable simulation, Ecotonos breaks the
usual stereotypes and barriers. Participants improve their skills and strategies for making decisions and solving problems in groups with sometimes conflicting priorities. Ecotonos can be used multiple times with
the same people by selecting a new problem and different variables, with
each replay offering new and different cross-cultural perspectives. Eight
to fifty participants form three groups and create their own "cultures".
Participants begin to solve a problem in their monocultural groups, then
mingle to continue problem solving in multicultural groups. The simulation and debriefing require a minimum of three hours.'

*Randömia Balloon Factory: A Unique Simulation for Working across the
Cultural Divide*
by Cornelius Grove and Willa Hallowell
http://interculturalpress.com/store/pc/viewPrd.asp?idcategory=74&
idproduct=5
'Simulates a realistic business-related problem that many Western
managers and trainers experience when they interact with people who
have different value-driven behaviors. It is designed for 15 to 35 participants and takes approximately three hours. One unique feature is
that the Richlanders – composed of some mixture of US American,
Anglo-Canadian, British, Irish, German, Dutch, Belgian, Scandinavian,

Australian, or New Zealander participants – play themselves. They receive no cultural rules, unlike the Randömians, who are given specific rules on how to behave.'

Redundancia: A Foreign Language Simulation
http://www.nipporica.com/prod.htm
'Participants experience speaking a language nonfluently: how it affects one's ability to stay focused and connected with the listener, and one's feelings of competence and confidence. Participants also experience listening to second language speakers: their own tendencies to help or to become distracted. Observers note the speaker's nonverbal communication. Extremely powerful.'

The Albatross
by T. Gochenour. Originally found in D. Batchelder, and E. G. Warner (eds) (1977) *Beyond Experience: The Experiential Approach to Cross-Cultural Education.* Brattleboro, VT: Experiment Press.

Yan-koloba
http://www.yan-koloba.com/
'Imagine a team building game which reaches across all cultural boundaries and engages the players in an exercise that teaches character traits such as respect, trust, responsibility, tolerance, unity and acceptance, all in a FUN and relaxed environment. This team building activity results in raised self-esteem, enhanced leadership skills, and more pronounced appreciation for teamwork!'

Internet resources

Freebies and Goodies
http://www.thiagi.com/freebies-and-goodies.html
A wide selection of games, puzzles, interactive lectures, tips for facilitators, etc. provided free of charge by the originator of Barnga (see above).

Videos, DVDs and hybrid materials
A World of Difference – Working Successfully across Cultures
http://www.worldwork.biz/legacy/www/docs2/world_of_difference.phtml
'A 35-minute video drama (also available in DVD format), with a comprehensive trainer's manual, a self-study workbook, exercises, slides, handouts etc. which can be reproduced. The video training pack is ideal for use whilst giving feedback for the International Profiler, for developing awareness in multi-cultural teams, and for cross-cultural workshops

generally. [...] Detailed training programmes of two days and half a day are included in the trainer's manual. The training programmes and video ensure a sound basis for experienced and inexperienced international professionals to understand the challenges and complexities of working in a world of difference. They will also aid the development of the practical skills and attitudes required to work with differences, rather than against them, in the pursuit of an organisation's international goals.' Developed by the originators of the WorldWork Ltd framework of international competencies.

A World of Differences – Understanding Cross-Cultural Communication
http://www.diversityrx.org/HTML/MOCPT7.htm
'This video examines fourteen different ways – both verbal and nonverbal – that people from two different cultures can experience communication failures and conflict. Examples in the video include mis-translation, the difficulty of understanding idioms from another culture, cultural differences in personal space, patterns of touch, etiquette and ritual, the expression of emotions, ideas about food, gestures, courtship differences, and parent-child interactions. The video illuminates and brings to life important concepts like cross-cultural communication, culture, communication failures, and "culture shock". The video also comes with a detailed Instructor's Guide.'

Cultural Detective
http://www.culturaldetective.com/
A sophisticated package of training materials developed by a large team of well-known intercultural trainers. 'Complete Cultural Detective® Packages include three things:

1. A Series Guide, with complete instructions on how to facilitate a Cultural Detective learning event, including definitions of culture, intercultural communication, and intercultural competence.
2. Participant Materials, which is what you will print for your participants. This usually includes an introduction to the culture, a Values Lens, explanations of the values and their negative perceptions, proverbs or sayings that illustrate the values, a minimum of five critical incidents, a list of best practices for bridging cultures, and a bibliography.
3. Facilitator Manual, which includes a story to introduce the Cultural Detective Method, examples of the values and their negative perceptions in action, sample debriefs of the critical incidents, and a list of music that you might play during a learning event.

Often, additional material is included in the package.'

Going International
http://www.griggs.com/videos/giser.shtml
'Each title in this series deals with specific aspects of international adjustment. Through examples of real life experiences, video drama, practical suggestions, and theoretical discussion, the films provide comprehensive guidelines for making a successful adjustment to living and doing business abroad.'

Not My Type: Valuing Diversity
http://www.videoarts.com/productDetails.do?no=NMT1&cat=DIVERSITY
Training materials by George Simons and Walt Hopkins including DVD, course leader's guide, delegate worksheets on disk, PowerPoint slides / OHPs on disk, self-study workbook on disk. 'Innovative video that challenges individuals to become aware of their own thinking processes and question their misleading assumptions about other people. [...] The programme encourages managers and team members to become aware of their own thinking processes and question their assumptions of other people. It helps them to see others as individuals and demonstrates how to benefit from a rich diversity of backgrounds and experience.'

Publishers of videos, DVDs and hybrid materials

Griggs Productions
http://www.griggs.com/
Produced *Going International*, *Valuing Diversity*, and *Valuing Relationships*.

Intercultural Press
http://www.interculturalpress.com
Publishes *Cultural Diversity*, *At the Heart of the Bull*, *Aliens*, and *Cold Water*. 'Videos and DVDs from Intercultural Press help make sense of the often challenging experience of interacting with people from other cultures or working and studying abroad. Perfect for use in international exchange orientations, corporate training workshops, business schools, and more, these programs will help students and professionals alike understand and reap the rewards of cultural diversity.'

Intercultural Resource Cooperation (ICR)
http://www.irc-international.com/
Produced *The Cross-Cultural Conference Room*; *Telling it Like it is: Reflections on Cultural Diversity*; *Better off Together Than A-P-A-R-T: Intercultural Communication / An Overview*; *Chinese Cultural Values: The Other Pole of the Human Mind*; *International Business Practices: Hidden Dimensions*;

A Different Place: The Intercultural Classroom; Cultural Dimensions in International Business: An Interactive Video Seminar.

Jossey-Bass/Pfeiffer
http://www.pfeiffer.com/
Publishes training guides, videos, games and other resources, including *Diversity Bingo*; the *Workplace Diversity* series includes selections on communicating, staffing, team building and tools for valuing diversity.

Simulation Training Systems
http://www.stsintl.com/
Publishes the simulations *BaFá BaFá, RaFá RaFá, Star Power, Pumping the Colors, Where do you Draw the Line?, What is No?* 'We design, produce, deliver and sell experiential training programs (simulations)' both for business customers and schools 'in the areas of cross-cultural relations, diversity, empowerment, team building, the use and abuse of power, ethics or sexual harassment.'

References

Abe, H. and Wiseman, R. L. (1983). A cross-cultural confirmation of the dimension of intercultural effectiveness. *International Journal of Intercultural Relations*, 7: 53–67.

Adair, W. L. (2003). Integrative sequences and negotiation outcome in same- and mixed-culture negotiations. *International Journal of Conflict Management*, 14 (3–4): 273–96.

Adair, W. L. and Brett, J. M. (2005). The negotiation dance: Time, culture, and behavioral sequences in negotiation. *Organization Science*, 16 (1): 33–51.

Adair, W. L., Weingart, L. and Brett, J. (2007). The timing and function of offers in US and Japanese negotiations. *Journal of Applied Psychology*, 92 (4): 1056–68.

Adler, N. (2001). *International Dimensions of Organizational Behavior*, 4th edn. Ohio: South-Western College Publishing.

Adler, N. J. and Graham, J. L. (1989). Cross-cultural interaction: The international comparison fallacy? *Journal of International Business Studies*, Fall: 515–37.

Adler, N. J., Brahm, R. and Graham, J. L. (1992). Strategy implementation: A comparison of face-to-face negotiations in the People's Republic of China and the United States. *Strategic Management Journal*, 13 (6): 449–66.

Alagiah, G. (2006). *A Home from Home: From Immigrant Boy to English Man*. London: Little, Brown.

Albert, R. D. (1983). The intercultural sensitizer or culture assimilator. In D. Landis and R. Brislin (eds), *Handbook of Intercultural Training: Issues in Theory and Design*, vol. 1, pp. 186–217. New York: Pergamon Press.

Albert, R. D. (1995). The Intercultural Sensitizer/Culture Assimilator as a cross-cultural training method. In S. M. Fowler and M. G. Mumford (eds), *Intercultural Sourcebook: Cross-Cultural Training Methods*, vol. 1, pp. 157–68. Yarmouth, ME: Intercultural Press.

Albert, R. D. and Ha, I. A. (2004). Latino/Anglo-American differences in attributions to situations involving touch and silence. *International Journal of Intercultural Relations*, 28 (3–4): 253–80.

Altshuler, L., Sussman, N. M. and Kachur, E. (2003). Assessing changes in intercultural sensitivity among physician trainees using the intercultural development inventory. *International Journal of Intercultural Relations*, 27 (4): 387–401.

Anderson, P. H., Lawton, L., Rexeisen, R. and Hubbard, A. (2006). Short-term study abroad and intercultural sensitivity: A pilot study. *International Journal of Intercultural Relations*, 30 (4): 457–69.

Apte, M. (1994). Language in sociocultural context. In R. E. Asher (ed.), *The Encyclopedia of Language and Linguistics*, vol. 4, pp. 2000–10. Oxford: Pergamon Press.

Arasaratnam, L. A. (2006). Further testing of a new model of intercultural communication competence. *Communication Research Reports*, 23 (2): 93–9.

Arasaratnam, L. A. and Doerfel, M. L. (2005). Intercultural communication competence: Identifying key components from multicultural perspectives. *International Journal of Intercultural Relations*, 29 (2): 137–63.

Arthur, N. (2001). Using critical incidents to investigate cross-cultural transitions. *International Journal of Intercultural Relations*, 25 (1): 41–54.

Arundale, R. B. (2006). Face as relational and interactional: A communication framework for research on face, facework, and politeness. *Journal of Politeness Research: Language, Behaviour, Culture*, 2 (2): 193–216.

Auer, P. (2007). Introduction. In P. Auer (ed.), *Style and Social Identities: Alternative Approaches to Linguistic Heterogeneity*, pp. 1–21. Berlin: Mouton de Gruyter.

Avruch, K. (1998). *Culture and Conflict Resolution*. Washington DC: United States Institute of Peace Press.

Bailey, B. (1997). Communication of respect in interethnic service encounters. *Language in Society*, 26: 327–56.

Bailey, B. (2000). Communicative behavior and conflict between African-American customers and Korean immigrant retailers in Los Angeles. *Discourse and Society*, 11 (1): 86–108.

Bandura, E. and Sercu, L. (2005). Culture teaching practices. In L. Sercu, with E. Bandura, P. Castro, L. Davcheva, C. Laskaridou, U. Lundgren, M. del Carmen, M. García and P. Ryan (eds), *Foreign Language Teachers & Intercultural Communication: An International Investigation*, pp. 75–89. Clevedon: Multilingual Matters.

Barham, K. and Devine, M. (1991). *The Quest for the International Manager: A Survey of Global Human Resource Strategies*. London: Ashridge Management Guide/Economist Intelligence Unit.

Barkhuizen, G. and de Klerk, V. (2006). Imagine identities: Preimmigrants' narratives on language and identity. *International Journal of Bilingualism*, 10 (3): 277–99.

Barmeyer, C. I. (2004). Learning styles and their impact on cross-cultural training: An international comparison in France, Germany and Quebec. *International Journal of Intercultural Relations*, 28 (6): 577–94.

Baynham, M. (2006). Performing self, family and community in Moroccan narratives of migration and settlement. In A. De Fina, D. Schiffrin and M. Bamberg (eds), *Discourse and Identity*, pp. 376–97. Cambridge: Cambridge University Press.

Bennett, J. M. and Bennett, M. J. (2004). Developing intercultural sensitivity: An integrative approach to global and domestic diversity. In D. Landis, J. M. Bennett and M. J. Bennett (eds), *Handbook of Intercultural Training*, 3rd edn, pp. 147–65. Thousand Oaks, CA: Sage.

Bennett, M. J. (1986). A developmental approach to training for intercultural sensitivity. *International Journal of Intercultural Relations*, 10: 179–86.

Bennett, M. J. (1993). Towards ethnorelativism: A developmental model of intercultural sensitivity. In R. M. Paige (ed.), *Education for the Intercultural Experience*, 2nd edn, pp. 21–71. Yarmouth, ME: Intercultural Press.

Bennett, M. J. (1995). Critical incidents in an intercultural conflict-resolution exercise. In S. M. Fowler and M. G. Mumford (eds), *Intercultural Sourcebook: Cross-Cultural Training Methods*, vol. 1, pp. 147–56. Yarmouth, ME: Intercultural Press.

Bennett, M. J. (No date). A developmental model of intercultural sensitivity. http://www.library.wisc.edu/EDVRC/docs/public/pdfs/SEEDReadings/int-CulSens.pdf (accessed 22 Aug. 2008).

Berardo, K. and Simons, G. (2004). *The Intercultural Profession: Its Profile, Practices & Challenges.* Available at: http://www.sietar-europa.org/about_us/ICP_Survey_Report.pdf (accessed 5 Oct. 2008).

Berry, J. (1969). On cross-cultural comparability. *International Journal of Psychology,* 4, 119–128.

Berry, J. W. (2004). Fundamental psychological processes in intercultural relations. In D. Landis, J. M. Bennett and M. J. Bennett (eds), *Handbook of Intercultural Training.* 3rd edn, pp. 166–84. Thousand Oaks, CA: Sage.

Berry, J. W. (2006). Stress perspectives on acculturation. In D. L. Sam and J. W. Berry (eds), *The Cambridge Handbook of Acculturation Psychology,* pp. 43–57. Cambridge: Cambridge University Press.

Berry, J. W. and Sam, D. (1997). Acculturation and adaptation. In J. W. Berry, M. H. Segall and Ç. Kâğitçibaşi (eds), *Handbook of Cross-Cultural Psychology.* Volume 3: *Social Behavior and Applications,* 2nd edn, pp. 291–326. Boston: Allyn & Bacon.

Bertrand, M. and Mullanathan, S. (2003). Are Emily and Greg more employable than Lakisha and Jamal? A field experiment on labor market discrimination. National Bureau of Economic Research, Working Paper 9873. Available at: http://www.nber.org/papers/w9873/ (accessed Apr. 2008).

Berwick, R. F. and Whalley, T. R. (2000). The experiential bases of culture learning: A case study of Canadian high schoolers in Japan. *International Journal of Intercultural Relations,* 24 (3): 325–40.

Bhabha, H. K. (1990). The third space: Interview with Homi Bhabha. In J. Rutherford (ed.), *Identity: Community, Culture, Difference,* pp. 207–21. London: Lawrence & Wishart.

Bhawuk, D. P. S. and Brislin, R. W. (1992). The measurement of intercultural sensitivity using the concepts of individualism and collectivism. *International Journal of Intercultural Relations,* 16 (4): 413–36.

Bhawuk, D. P. S. and Brislin, R. W. (2000). Cross-cultural training: A review. *Applied Psychology: An International Review,* 49 (1): 162–91.

Bilbow, G. T. (1997). Cross-cultural impression management in the multicultural workplace: The special case of Hong Kong. *Journal of Pragmatics,* 28: 461–87.

Birkner, K. and Kern, F. (2008). Impression management in 'intercultural' German job interviews. In H. Spencer-Oatey (ed.), *Culturally Speaking: Culture, Communication and Politeness Theory,* pp. 241–57. London: Continuum.

Bjørge, A. K. (2007). Power distance in English lingua franca email communication. *International Journal of Applied Linguistics,* 17 (1): 60–80.

Blackman, C. (1997). *Negotiating China: Case Studies and Strategies.* St Leonards, Australia: Allen & Unwin.

Blanton, S. (n.d.). http://www.quotationspage.com/quote/34285.html and http://www.blantonpeale.org/ (both accessed 14 Oct. 2008).

Blommaert, J. (1991). How much culture is there in intercultural communication? In J. Blommaert and J. Verschueren (eds), *The Pragmatics of International & Intercultural Communication,* pp. 13–31. Amsterdam: John Benjamins.

Blommaert, J. (1998a). Different approaches to intercultural communication: A critical survey. Plenary lecture, Lernen und Arbeiten in einer international vernetzten und multikulturellen Gesellschaft, Expertentagung Universität Bremen, Institut für Projektmanagement und Witschaftsinformatik (IPMI), 27–28 February 1998. Available at: http://africana.rug.ac.be/texts/research-publications/publications_on-line/Intercultural_Communication.htm   (last accessed 8 Mar. 2005).

Blommaert, J. (1998b). Review of Ben Rampton, 'Crossing: Language and Ethnicity among Adolescents', London: Longman. *Journal of Sociolinguistics,* 2 (1): 119–23.

Bochner, S. (2006). Sojourners. In D. L. Sam and J. W. Berry (eds), *The Cambridge Handbook of Acculturation Psychology,* pp. 181–97. Cambridge: Cambridge University Press.

Bochner, S., McLeo, B. M. and Lin, A. (1977). Friendship patterns of overseas students: A functional model. *International Journal of Psychology,* 12: 277–97.

Bolten, J. (2001). Interkulturelles Coaching, Mediation, Training und Consulting als Aufgaben des Personalmanagements internationaler Unternehmen. In A. Clermont, W. Schmeisser and D. Krimphove (eds), *Stratgisches Personalmanagement in Globalen Unternehemen,* pp. 1–16. München: Vahlen.

Bond, M. H. and Hwang, K.-K. (1986). The social psychology of Chinese people. In M. H. Bond (ed.), *The Psychology of the Chinese People,* pp. 213–66. Hong Kong: Oxford University Press.

Bourdieu, P. (1977). *Outline of a Theory of Practice.* Cambridge: Cambridge University Press.

Breidenbach, J. and Zukrigl, I. (1998). *Tanz der Kulturen. Kulturelle Identität in der globalisierten Welt.* Munich: Kunstmann.

Brett, J. M. and Okumura, T. (n.d.) *Cartoon.* Evanston, IL: Dispute Resolution Center. Available from http://www.kellogg.northwestern.edu/drrc/teaching/cross_cultural.htm (accessed 24 Feb. 2009).

Brislin, R. (2000). *Understanding Culture's Influence on Behavior.* Orlando, FL: Harcourt College Publishers.

Brislin, R. W. (1970). Back translation for cross-cultural research. *Journal of Cross-Cultural Psychology,* 1: 185–216.

Brislin, R. W. (1978). Contributions of cross-cultural orientation programmes and power analysis to translation/interpretation. In D. Gerver and H. W. Sinaiko (eds), *Language, Interpretation and Communication.* New York: Plenum Press. Proceedings of the NATO Symposium on Language and Communication 26 Sept. to 1 Oct. 1977.

Brislin, R. W. and Yoshida, T. (eds) (1994). *Improving Intercultural Interactions: Modules for Cross-Cultural Training Programs.* Thousand Oaks, CA: Sage.

Brown, P. and Levinson, S. C. (1987). *Politeness: Some Universals in Language Usage.* Cambridge: Cambridge University Press. Originally published as Universals in language usage: Politeness phenomenon. In Esther Goody (ed.) (1978). *Questions and Politeness: Strategies in Social Interaction.* New York: Cambridge University Press.

Brown, R. and Gilman, A. (1960). Pronouns of power and solidarity. In T. A. Sebeok (ed.), *Style in Language,* pp. 253–76. Cambridge, MA: MIT Press. Reprinted in Pier P. Giglioli (ed.) (1972). *Language and Social Context,* pp. 252–82. Harmondsworth: Penguin Books.

Brueck, F. and Kainzbauer, A. (2003). The Culture Standards Method: a qualitative approach in cross-cultural management research: http://marketing.byu.edu/htmlpages/ccrs/proceedings03 (accessed 20 April 2009).

Bucholtz, M. (2007). Variation in transcription. *Discourse Studies*, 9 (6), 784–808.

Burr, V. (1996). *An Introduction to Social Constructionism*. London: Routledge.

Byram, M. (1997). *Teaching and Assessing Intercultural Communicative Competence*. Clevedon: Multilingual Matters.

Byram, M. and Fleming, M. (eds) (1998). *Language Learning in Intercultural Perspective*. Cambridge: Cambridge University Press.

Byram, M., Nichols, A. and Stevens, D. (2001). *Developing Intercultural Competence in Practice*. Clevedon: Multilingual Matters.

California Healthcare Interpreters Association (2002). California Standards for Healthcare Interpreters. Ethical Principles, Protocols, and Guidance on Roles and Interventions. Available at: http://www.calendow.org/reference/publications/pdf/cultural/TCE0701–2002_California_Sta.pdf (accessed 26 Jan. 2007).

Cameron, D. (2001). *Working with Spoken Discourse*. London: Sage.

Campbell, J. D., Assanand, S. and Di Paula, A. (2000). Structural features of self-concept and adjustment. In A. Tesser, R. B. Felson and J. M. Suls (eds), *Psychological Perspectives on Self and Identity*, pp. 67–87. Washington, DC: American Psychological Association.

Campbell, N. C. G., Graham, J. L., Jolibert, A. and Meissner, H. G. (1988). Marketing negotiations in France, Germany, the United Kingdom, and the United States. *Journal of Marketing*, 52: 49–62.

Campbell, S. and Roberts, C. (2007). Migration, ethnicity and competing discourses in the job interview: Synthesizing the institutional and the personal. *Discourse and Society*, 18 (3): 243–71.

Canale, M. and Swain, M. (1980). Theoretical bases of communicative approaches to second language teaching and testing. *Applied Linguistics*, 1 (1): 1–47.

Carroll, R. (1987). *Cultural Misunderstandings: The French-American Experience*. London: University of Chicago Press.

Carté, P. and Fox, C. (2004). *Bridging the Culture Gap: A Practical Guide to International Business Communication*. London: Kogan Page.

Carver, C. S., Scheier, M. F. and Weintraub, J. K. (1989). Assessing coping strategies: A theoretically based approach. *Journal of Personality and Social Psychology*, 56 (2): 267–83.

Castro, P. and Sercu, L. (2005). Objectives of foreign language teaching and culture teaching time. In L. Sercu, E. with Bandura, P. Castro, L. Davcheva, C. Laskaridou, U. Lundgren, M. del Carmen, M. García and P. Ryan (eds), *Foreign Language Teachers & Intercultural Communication: An International Investigation*, pp. 19–38. Clevedon: Multilingual Matters.

Celaya, L. and Swift, J. S. (2006). Pre-departure cultural training: US managers in Mexico. *Cross Cultural Management: An International Journal*, 13 (3): 230–43.

Chaisrakeo, S. and Speece, M. (2004). Culture, intercultural communication competence, and sales negotiation: A qualitative research approach. *Journal of Business and Industrial Marketing*, 19 (4): 267–82.

Chan, S. K.-C., Bond, M. H., Spencer-Oatey, H. and Rojo-Laurilla, M. (2004). Culture and rapport promotion in service encounters: Protecting the ties that bind. *Journal of Asian Pacific Communication*, 14 (2): 245–60.

Chen, G.-M. and Starosta, W. J. (1996). Intercultural communication competence: A synthesis. *Communication Yearbook*, 19: 353–84.

Chen, G.-M. and Starosta, W. J. (2005). *Foundations of Intercultural Communication*, 2nd edn. Lanham, MD: University Press of America.

Chiles, T. (2007). The construction of an identity as 'mentor' in white collar and academic workplaces: A preliminary analysis. *Journal of Pragmatics*, 39 (4): 730–41.

Chirkov, V., Vansteenkiste, M., Tao, R. and Lynch, M. (2007). The role of self-determined motivation and goals for study abroad in the adaptation of international students. *International Journal of Intercultural Relations*, 31 (2): 199–222.

Chryssochoou, X. (2004). *Cultural Diversity, its Social Psychology*. Oxford: Blackwell.

Comfort, J. and Franklin, P. (2008). *The Mindful International Manager: Competences for Working Effectively Across Cultures*. York: York Associates.

Condon, J. (1984). *With Respect to the Japanese*. Yarmouth, ME: Intercultural Press.

Cooke, R. A. and Lafferty, J. C. (1995). Culture for Diversity Inventory. Available at: http://www.humansynergistics.com/products/cdi.aspx (accessed 22 Nov. 2008).

Corder, S. and Meyerhoff, M. (2007). Communities of practice in the analysis of intercultural communication. In H. Kotthoff and H. Spencer-Oatey (eds), *Handbook of Applied Linguistics (HAL)*. Volume 7: *Intercultural Communication*, pp. 441–61. Berlin: Walter de Gruyter.

Coupland, N., Grainger, K. and Coupland, J. (1988). Politeness in context: Intergenerational issues. *Language in Society*, 17: 253–62.

Crawshaw, R. and Callen, B. (2001). Attesting the self: Narration and identity change during periods of residence abroad. *Language and Intercultural Communication*, 1 (2): 101–19.

Creech, R. (2006). 'Home' is culturally dependent. Posting on the theme: (Non)-equivalence at word level (translation of the word 'home'): http://www.proz.com/forum/linguistics/41171-non_equivalence_at_word_level_translation_of_the_word_%E2%80%98home%E2%80%99.html/ (accessed 28 Aug. 2008).

Cross, S. E. (1995). Self-construals, coping, and stress in cross-cultural adaptation. *Journal of Cross-Cultural Psychology*, 26: 673–97.

Crystal, D. (1997). *English as a Global Language*. Cambridge: Cambridge University Press.

Cui, G. (1989). Intercultural effectiveness: An integrative approach. *35th Annual Conference of the International Communication Association*, San Francisco, CA.

Cui, G. and Awa, N. E. (1992). Measuring intercultural effectiveness: An integrative approach. *International Journal of Intercultural Relations*, 16: 311–28.

Cui, G. and van den Berg, S. (1991). Testing the construct validity of intercultural effectiveness. *International Journal of Intercultural Relations*, 15: 227–41.

Cushner, K. and Brislin, R. W. (1996). *Intercultural Interactions: A Practical Guide*. London: Sage.

Davidheiser, M. (2005). Culture and mediation: A contemporary processual analysis from southwestern Gambia. *International Journal of Intercultural Relations*, 29 (6): 713–38.

Davis, S. L. and Finney, S. J. (2006). A factor analytic study of the Cross-Cultural Adaptability Inventory. *Educational and Psychological Measurement*, 66 (2): 318–30.

Decker, J. S. (1990). Marija Dixon: Building bridges between East and West. *Detroit Marketplace*, December: 20–6.

Dela Cruz, K. C. K., Salzman, M. B., Brislin, R. and Losch, N. (2006). Hawaiian attributional perspectives on intercultural interactions in higher education: Development of an intercultural sensitizer. *International Journal of Intercultural Relations*, 30 (1): 119–40.

Denscombe, M. (2007). *The Good Research Guide for Small-Scale Social Research Projects*. Buckingham: Open University Press.

Devine, P. (1989). Stereotypes and prejudice. *Journal of Personality and Social Psychology*, 56: 5–18.

Diekman, A. B., Eagly, A. H., Mladinic, A. and Ferreira, M. C. (2005). Dynamic stereotypes about women and men in Latin America and the United States. *Journal of Cross-Cultural Psychology*, 36 (2): 209–26.

Dinges, N. G. and Baldwin, K. D. (1996). Intercultural competence. A research perspective. In D. Landis and R. S. Bhagat (eds), *Handbook of Intercultural Training*, 2nd edn, pp. 106–23. Thousands Oaks, CA: Sage.

Doyle, J. (1989). Cultures can be bridged. *Observer and Eccentric*, p. 17. Birmingham.

Eades, D. (1992). *Aboriginal English and the Law: Communicating with Aboriginal English Speaking Clients: A Handbook for Legal Practitioners*. Brisbane: Queensland Law Society.

Eades, D. (2002). Evidence given in unequivocal terms: Gaining consent of Aboriginal kids in court. In J. Cotterill (ed.), *Language in the Legal Process*, pp. 162–79. Basingstoke: Palgrave Macmillan.

Eades, D. (2007). Understanding aboriginal silence in legal contexts. In H. Kotthoff and H. Spencer-Oatey (eds), *Handbook of Applied Linguistics*. Volume 7: *Intercultural Communication*, pp. 285–301. Berlin: Mouton de Gruyter.

Easterby-Smith, M. and Malina, D. (1999). Cross-cultural collaborative research: Toward reflexivity. *The Academy of Management Journal*, 42 (1): 76–86.

Eggins, S. and Slade, D. (1997). *Analysing Casual Conversation*. London: Cassell.

Europublic (2007). LACE – The Intercultural Competences developed in Compulsory Foreign Languages Education in the European Union. Brussels: Directorate General Education and Culture of the European Commission. Report available at: http://ec.europa.eu/education/policies/lang/key/studies_en.html/ Research data available at: http://www.lace2007.eu/ (both accessed 5 Oct. 2008).

Ewington, N. and Trickey, D. (2003). *A World of Difference: Working Successfully across Cultures. Self-Study Workbook*. London: Capita Learning and Development.

Fan, C. and Mak, A. S. (1998). Measuring social self-efficacy in a culturally diverse student population. *Social Behavior and Personality*, 26: 131–44.

Ferraro, G. (2005). *The Cultural Dimension of International Business*, 5th edn. Upper Saddle River, NJ: Prentice Hall.

Fiedler, F. E., Mitchell, T. and Triandis, H. C. (1971). The Culture Assimilator: An approach to cross-cultural training. *Journal of Applied Psychology*, 55: 95–102.

Fischer, B. and Kopp, B. (2007). Evaluation of a Western training concept for further education in China. *Interculture Journal*, 4: 57–75).

Fiske, A. P. (1992). The four elementary forms of sociality: Framework for a unified theory of social relations. *Psychological Review*, 99 (4): 689–723.

FitzGerald, H. (2003). *How Different are We? Spoken Discourse in Intercultural Communication*. Clevedon: Multilingual Matters.

Foucault, M. (1986). Of other spaces. *Diacritics*, 16 (1): 22–7. Available at: http://foucault.info/documents/heteroTopia/foucault.heteroTopia.en.html (last accessed 24 Mar. 2006).

Fougère, M. (2008). Identity in intercultural contexts. In H. Spencer-Oatey (ed.), *Culturally Speaking: Culture, Communication and Politeness*, pp. 187–203. London: Continuum.

Fowler, S. M. and Blohm, J. M. (2004). An analysis of methods for intercultural training. In D. Landis, J. M. Bennett and M. J. Bennett (eds), *Handbook of Intercultural Training*, pp. 37–84. Thousands Oaks, CA: Sage.

Frankfort-Nachmias, C. and Nachmias, D. (1996). *Research Methods in the Social Sciences*, 5th edn. London: Arnold.

Franklin, P. (2006). *Communicating and Cooperating with German Business People: A Guide for the British*. CD-ROM. Konstanz: KIeM Institute for Intercultural Management, Values and Communication.

Franklin, P. (2007). Differences and difficulties in intercultural management interaction. In H. Kotthoff and H. Spencer-Oatey (eds), *Handbook of Intercultural Communication*, pp. 263–84. Berlin: Mouton de Gruyter.

Freeman, M., Miller, C. and Ross, N. (2000). The impact of individual philosophies of teamwork on multi-professional practice and the implications for education. *Journal of Interprofessional Care*, 14 (3): 237–47.

Freeth, D., Hammick, M., Reeves, S., Koppel, I. and Barr, H. (2005). *Effective Interprofessional Education: Development, Delivery and Evaluation (Promoting Partnership for Health)*. Oxford: Blackwell.

Friedman, R., Chi, S.-C. and Liu, L. A. (2006). An expectancy model of Chinese-American differences in conflict-avoiding. *Journal of International Business Studies*, 37: 76–91.

Gallagher, T. J. (2000). Value orientations and conflict resolution: Using the Kluckhohn Value Orientations Model. In K. W. Russo (ed.), *Finding the Middle Ground: Insight and Applications of the Value Orientation Method*, pp. 185–94. Yarmouth, ME: Intercultural Press.

Gallois, C., Ogay, T. and Giles, H. (2005). Communication accommodation theory. In W. B. Gudykunst (ed.), *Theorizing about Intercultural Communication*, pp. 121–48. Thousand Oaks, CA: Sage.

Gardenswartz, L., Rowe, A., Digh, P. and Bennett, M. (2003). *The Global Diversity Desk Reference: Managing an International Workforce*. San Francisco: Pfeiffer.

Garner, M., Raschka, C. and Sercombe, P. (2006). Sociolinguistic minorities, research, and social relationships. *Journal of Multilingual and Multicultural Development*, 27 (1): 61–78.

Geertz, C. (1973). *The Interpretation of Cultures*. London: Hutchinson.

Gelbrich, K. (2004). The relationship between intercultural competence and expatriate success: A structural equation model. *Die Unternehmung*, 58 (3–4): 261–77.

Gibson, D. W. and Zhong, M. (2005). Intercultural communication competence in the healthcare context. *International Journal of Intercultural Relations*, 29 (5): 621–34.

Gibson, R.(2000). *Intercultural Business Communication*. Berlin and Oxford: Cornelsen.

Gibson, R. (2002). *Intercultural Business Communication*. Oxford: Oxford University Press.

Glick, N. D. (2002). The relationship between cross-cultural experience and training, and leader effectiveness in the US Foreign Service. *International Journal of Cross-Cultural Management*, 2 (3): 339–56.

Goffman, E. (1959). *The Presentation of Self in Everyday Life*. New York: Anchor Books.

Goffman, E. (1967). *Interaction Ritual: Essays on Face-to-Face Behaviour*. New York: Pantheon.

Goodwin, C. (2000). Action and embodiment within situated human interaction. *Journal of Pragmatics*, 32: 1489–522.

Graddol, D. (1997). *The Future of English?* London: British Council.

Graham, J. L. (1983). Brazilian, Japanese, and American Business negotiations. *Journal of International Business Studies*, 14 (1): 47–61.

Graham, J. L. (1984). Bolter Turbines, Inc. negotiation simulation. *Journal of Marketing Education*, 4: 28–36.

Greenholtz, J. F. (2005). Does intercultural sensitivity cross cultures? Validity issues in porting instruments across languages and cultures. *International Journal of Intercultural Relations*, 29 (1): 73–89.

Grosjean, F. (1982). *Life with Two Languages*. Cambridge, MA: Harvard University Press.

Gudykunst, W. B. (1993). Toward a theory of effective interpersonal and intergroup communication: An anxiety/uncertainty management perspective. In R. L. Wiseman and J. Koester (eds.), *Intercultural Communication Competence*, pp. 33–71. Newbury Park, CA: Sage.

Gudykunst, W. B. (1995). Anxiety/uncertainty management (AUM) theory: Current status. In R. L. Wiseman (ed.), *Intercultural Communication Theory*, pp. 8–58. Thousand Oaks, CA: Sage.

Gudykunst, W. B. (2004). *Bridging Differences: Effective Intergroup Communication*, 4th edn. London: Sage.

Gudykunst, W. B. and Hammer, M. R. (1983). Basic training design: Approaches to intercultural training. In D. Landis and R. W. Brislin (eds), *Handbook of Intercultural Training*. Volume 1: *Issues in Theory and Design*, pp. 118–54. New York: Pergamon Press.

Gudykunst, W. B. and Nishida, T. (2001). Anxiety, uncertainty, and perceived effectiveness of communication across relationships and cultures. *International Journal of Intercultural Relations*, 25 (1): 55–71.

Gudykunst, W. B., Guzley, R. M. and Hammer, M. R. (1996). Designing intercultural training. In D. Landis and R. S. Bhagat (eds), *Handbook of Intercultural Training*, 2nd edn, pp. 61–80. Thousand Oaks, CA: Sage.

Gumperz, J. J. (1982). *Discourse Strategies*. Cambridge: Cambridge University Press.

Gumperz, J. J. (1992). Contextualization and understanding. In A. Duranti and C. Goodwin (eds), *Rethinking Context: Language as an Interactive Phenomenon*, pp. 229–52. Cambridge: Cambridge University Press.

Gumperz, J. J. and Roberts, C. (1980). *Developing Awareness Skills for Interethnic Communication. Occasional Papers No. 12.* Singapore: Seamo Regional Language Centre.

Gumperz, J. J. and Roberts, C. (1991). Understanding in intercultural encounters. In J. Blommaert and J. Verschueren (eds), *The Pragmatics of International and Intercultural Communication*, pp. 51–90. Amsterdam: John Benjamins.

Günthner, S. (2007). Intercultural communication and the relevance of cultural specific repertoires of communicative genres. In H. Kotthoff and H. Spencer-Oatey (eds), *Handbook of Intercultural Communication*, pp. 127–51. Berlin: Mouton de Gruyter.

Gutt, E.-A. (2000). *Translation and Relevance*. Manchester: St Jerome Publishers.

Hale, S. (2007). *Community Interpreting*. Basingstoke: Palgrave Macmillan.

Hall, B. J. (2002). *Among Cultures: The Challenge of Communication*. Fort Worth, TX: Harcourt College.

Hall, E. T. (1959). *The Silent Language*. Garden City, NY: Doubleday.

Hall, E. T. (1966). *The Hidden Dimension*. New York: Doubleday.

Hall, E. T. (1976). *Beyond Culture*. New York: Doubleday.

Hall, E. T. (1983). *The Dance of Life*. New York: Doubleday.

Hall, E. T. and Hall, M. R. (1990). *Understanding Cultural Differences: Germans, French and Americans*. Yarmouth, ME: Intercultural Press.

Halualani, R. T., Chitgopekar, A., Thi, J. H., Morrison, A. and Dodge, P. S.-W. (2004). Who's interacting? And what are they talking about? – intercultural contact and interaction among multicultural university students. *International Journal of Intercultural Relations*, 28 (5): 353–72.

Hamilton, D. L. (1979). A cognitive-attributional analysis of stereotyping. In L. Berkowitz (ed.), *Advances in Experimental Social Psychology*, vol. 12, pp. 53–84. New York: Academic Press.

Hamilton, D. L., Sherman, S. J. and Ruvolo, C. M. (1990). Stereotype-based expectancies: Effects on information processing and social behavior. *Journal of Social Issues*, 46 (2): 35–60.

Hammer, M. R. (1989). Intercultural communication competence. In M. R. Asante, W. B. Gudykunst and E. Newmark (eds), *Handbook of International and Intercultural Communication*, pp. 247–60. Newbury Park: Sage.

Hammer, M. R., Bennett, M. J. and Wiseman, R. (2003). Measuring intercultural sensitivity: The Intercultural Development Inventory. *International Journal of Intercultural Relations*, 27 (4): 421–43.

Hammer, M. R., Gudykunst, W. B. and Wiseman, R. L. (1978). Dimensions of intercultural effectiveness: An exploratory study. *International Journal of Intercultural Relations*, 2: 382–93.

Hampden-Turner, C. and Trompenaars, F. (2000). *Building Cross-Cultural Competence: How to Create Wealth from Conflicting Values*. Chichester: John Wiley.

Handy, C. R. (1976). *Understanding Organizations*. London: Penguin.

Hannerz, U. (1992). *Cultural Complexity: Studies in the Social Organization of Meaning*. New York: Columbia University Press.

Heine, S. J., Lehman, D. R., Markus, H. R. and Kitayama, S. (1999). Is there a universal need for positive self-regard? *Psychological Review*, 106: 766–94.

Heinz, B. (2003). Backchannel responses as strategic responses in bilingual speakers' conversations. *Journal of Pragmatics*, 35: 1113–42.

Hemphill, J. K. and Coons, A. E. (1957). Development of the Leader Behavior Description Questionnaire. In R. M. Stogdill and A. E. Coons (eds), *Leader Behavior: Its Description and Measurement*, pp. 6–38. Columbus: Ohio State University, Bureau of Business Research.

Henley, A. and Schott, J. (1999). *Culture, Religion and Patient Care in a Multi-Ethnic Society.* London: Age Concern.

Herfst, S. L., van Oudenhoven, J. P. and Timmerman, M. E. (2008). Intercultural effectiveness training in three Western immigrant countries: A cross-cultural evaluation of critical incidents. *International Journal of Intercultural Relations,* 32: 67–80.

Hewstone, M. and Giles, H. (1986). Social groups and social stereotypes in inter-group communication: A review and model of intergroup communication breakdown. In W. B. Gudykunst (ed.), *Intergroup Communication,* pp. 10–26. London: Edward Arnold.

Hill, J. (2005). *What Has Christianity Ever Done for Us? Its Role in Shaping the World Today.* Oxford: Lion Hudson.

Hinton, P. (2000). *Stereotypes, Cognition and Culture.* Hove: Psychology Press.

Hobbs, P. (2003). 'Is *that* what we're here about?': A lawyer's use of impression management in a closing argument at trial. *Discourse and Society,* 14 (3): 273–90.

Hofstede, G. (1991). *Cultures and Organizations: Software of the Mind.* London: HarperCollinsBusiness.

Hofstede, G. (1996). Riding the waves of commerce: A test of Trompenaars' 'model' of national culture differences. *International Journal of Intercultural Relations,* 20 (2): 189–98.

Hofstede, G. (2001). *Culture's Consequences: Comparing Values, Behaviors, Institutions, and Organizations Across Nations.* Thousand Oaks, CA: Sage. (First edn published in 1980).

Hofstede, G. J., Pedersen, P. B. and Hofstede, G. (2002). *Exploring Culture: Exercises, Stories, and Synthetic Cultures.* Yarmouth, ME: Intercultural Press.

Holliday, A., Hyde, M. and Kullman, J. (2004). *Intercultural Communication: An Advanced Resource Book.* London: Routledge.

Holmes, J. and Stubbe, M. (2003). *Power and Politeness in the Workplace.* London: Longman.

Horvath, A. M. (1997). Ethnocultural identification and the complexities of ethnicity. In K. Cushner and R. W. Brislin (eds), *Improving Intercultural Interactions: Modules for Cross-Cultural Training Programs,* vol. 2, pp. 165–83. Thousand Oaks, CA: Sage.

House, J. (2003). Misunderstanding in intercultural university encounters. In J. House, G. Kasper and S. Ross (eds), *Misunderstanding in Social Life: Discourse Approaches to Problematic Talk,* pp. 22–56. London: Longman.

House, J. (2006). Communicative styles in English and German. *European Journal of English Studies,* 10 (3): 249–67.

House, R. J., Hanges, P. J., Javidan, M., Dorfman, P. W. and Gupta, V. (eds) (2004). *Culture, Leadership, and Organizations: The GLOBE Study of 62 Societies.* London: Sage.

Hutchings, K. and Ratnasari, S. W. (2006). Cross-cultural non-work transition stresses: Domestic transferees in Indonesia. *Cross Cultural Management: An International Journal,* 13 (2): 114–31.

Ingulsrud, J. E., Kai, K., Kadowaki, S., Kurabane, S. and Shiobara, M. (2002). The assessment of cross-cultural experience: Measuring awareness through critical text analysis. *International Journal of Intercultural Relations*, 26 (5), 473–92.

Ishiyama, F. I. (1996). Development and validation of the Interpersonal Skills Checklist. Unpublished manuscript. Vancouver: University of British Columbia.

Jackson, T. (2002). *International HRM: A Cross-Cultural Approach*. Thousand Oaks, CA: Sage.

Jacobson, W., Sleicher, D. and Burke, M. (1999). Portfolio assessment of intercultural competence. *International Journal of Intercultural Relations*, 23 (3): 467–92.

Jasinskaja-Lahti, I., Liebkind, K., Jaakkola, M. and Reuter, A. (2006). Perceived discrimination, social support networks, and psychological well-being among three immigrant groups. *Journal of Cross-Cultural Psychology*, 37 (3): 293–311.

Jenkins, R. (2004). *Social Identity*, 2nd edn. London: Routledge.

Jones, M. (1997). *Prejudice and Racism*, 2nd edn. New York: McGraw Hill.

Jones, M. (2002). *Social Psychology of Prejudice*. Upper Saddle River, NJ: Pearson Education.

Kamler, B. and Threadgold, T. (2003). Translating difference: Questions of representation in cross-cultural research encounters. *Journal of Intercultural Studies*, 24 (2): 137–51.

Kapoor, S., Hughes, P. C., Baldwin, J. R. and Blue, J. (2003). The relationship of individualism–collectivism and self-construals to communication styles in India and the United States. *International Journal of Intercultural Relations*, 27 (6): 683–700.

Kashima, E. S. and Loh, E. (2006). International students' acculturation: Effects of international, conational, and local ties and need for closure. *International Journal of Intercultural Relations*, 30 (4): 471–86.

Kasper, G. (2008). Data collection in pragmatics research. In H. Spencer-Oatey (ed.), *Culturally Speaking: Culture, Communication and Politeness Theory*, pp. 279–303. London: Continuum.

Kaufert, J. M. (1999). Cultural mediation in cancer diagnosis and end of life decision-making: The experience of Aboriginal patients in Canada. *Anthropology and Medicine*, 6 (3): 405–21.

Kealey, D. J. (1989). A study of cross-cultural effectiveness: Theoretical issues, practical applications. *International Journal of Intercultural Relations*, 13: 387–428.

Kelley, C. and Meyers, J. E. (1993). *The Cross-Cultural Adaptability Inventory*. Yarmouth, ME: Intercultural Press.

Kelley, H. H. (1966). A class-room study of the dilemmas in interpersonal negotiation. In K. Archibald (ed.), *Strategic Interaction and Conflict*, pp. 49–73. Berkley: Berkley Institute of International Studies, University of California.

Kerekes, J. A. (2004). Preparing ESL learners for self-presentation in insitutional settings outside the classroom. *Prospect*, 19 (1), 22–46. Available at: http://www.ameprc.mq.edu.au/docs/prospect_journal/volume_19_no_1/19_1_2_Kerekes.pdf/ (accessed 1st Apr. 2008).

Kim, Y. Y. (2001). *Becoming Intercultural: An Integrative Theory of Communication and Cross-Cultural Adaptation*. Thousand Oaks, CA: Sage.

Kim, Y. Y. (2005) Adapting to a new culture: An integrative communication theory. In W. B. Gudykunst (ed.), *Theorizing about Intercultural Communication*, pp. 375–400. London: Sage.

Kim, Y. Y. and Korzenny, F. (1991). Intercultural communication competence: A systems-theoretic view. In S. Ting-Toomey and F. Korzenny (eds), *Cross-Cultural Interpersonal Communication (International and Intercultural Communication Annual*, vol. 15, pp. 259–75. London: Sage.

Kimmel, P. R. (1995). Facilitating the Contrast-Culture Method. In S. M. Fowler and M. G. Mumford (eds), *Intercultural Sourcebook: Cross-Cultural Training Methods*, vol. 1, pp. 69–80. Yarmouth, ME: Intercultural Press.

King, A. (1993). From sage on the stage to guide on the side. *College Teaching*, 41 (1): 30–5.

Klak, T. and Martin, P. (2003). Do university-sponsored international cultural events help students to appreciate 'difference'? *International Journal of Intercultural Relations*, 27 (4): 445–65.

Kluckhohn, F. R. and Strodtbeck, F. L. (1961/1973). *Variations in Value Orientations*. New York: Harper & Row.

Knapp, K. and Knapp-Potthof, A. (1990). Interkulturelle Kommunikation. *Zeitschrift für Fremdsprachenforschung*, 1: 62–93.

Knapp-Potthoff, A. and Knapp, K. (1987a). The man (or woman) in the middle: Discoursal aspects of non-professional interpreting. In K. Knapp, W. Enninger and A. Knapp-Potthoff (eds), *Analyzing Intercultural Communication*, pp. 181–211. Berlin: Mouton de Gruyter.

Knapp-Potthoff, A. and Knapp, K. (1987b). Interweaving two discourses – the difficult task of the non-professional interpreter. In J. House and S. Blum-Kulka (eds), *Interlingual and Intercultural Communication*, pp. 151–68. Tübingen: Gunter Narr.

Knutson, T. J., Komolsevin, R. K., Chatiketu, P. and Smith, V. R. (2003). A cross-cultural comparison of Thai and US American rhetorical sensitivity: Implications for intercultural communication effectiveness. *International Journal of Intercultural Relations*, 27 (1): 63–78.

Kohls, R. and Brussow, H. L. (1995). *Training Know-How for Cross-Cultural and Diversity Trainers*. Duncanville, TX: Adult Learning Systems.

Kolb, D. A. (1985). *LSI – Learning Style Inventory: Self-Scoring Inventory and Interpretation Booklet*. Boston: McBer Publishing.

Kondo, M., Tebble, H., Alexieva, B., v. Dam, H., Katan, D., Mizuno, A., Setton, R. and Zalka, I. (1997). Intercultural communication, negotiation and interpreting. In Y. Gambier, D. Gile and C. Taylor (eds), *Conference Interpreting: Current Trends in Research (Proceedings of the International Conference on Interpreting: What do we know and how? Turku, August 25–27, 1994)*. Amsterdam: John Benjamins.

Kosic, A. and Triandafyllidou, A. (2003). Albanian immigrants in Italy: Migration plans, coping strategies and identity issues. *Journal of Ethnic and Migration Studies*, 29 (6): 997–1014.

Kosic, A., Mannetti, L. and Sam, D. L. (2006). Self-monitoring: A moderating role between acculturation strategies and adaptation of immigrants. *International Journal of Intercultural Relations*, 30 (2): 141–58.

Kossek, E. and Zonia, S. (1993). Assessing Diversity Climate: A field study of reactions to employer efforts to promote diversity. *Journal of Organizational Behaviour*, 14: 61–81.

Kraemer, A. J. (1999). A method for developing deep cultural self-awareness through intensive practice: A retrospective. In S. M. Fowler and M. G. Mumford (eds), *Intercultural Sourcebook: Cross-Cultural Training Methods*, vol. 2, pp. 225–40. Yarmouth, ME: Intercultural Press.

Kramsch, C. (1998). *Language and Culture*. Oxford: Oxford University Press.

Kroeber, A. and Kluckhohn, C. (1952). *Culture: A Critical Review of Concepts and Definitions* (Papers of the Peabody Museum, vol. 47, no. 1). Cambridge, MA: Peabody Museum.

Kühlmann, T. and Stahl, G. (1998). Diagnose interkultureller Kompetenz: Entwicklung und Evaluierung eines Assessment-Centers. In C. Barmeyer and J. Bolten (eds), *Interkulturelle Personalorganisation (Intercultural Personnel Management)*, pp. 213–24. Sternenfels: Verlag für Wissenschaft und Praxis.

Kwantes, C. T., Bergeron, S. and Kaushal, R. (2005). Applying social psychology to diversity. In F. W. Schneider, J. A. Gruman and L. M. Coutts (eds), *Applied Social Psychology: Understanding and Addressing Social and Practical Problems*, pp. 331–54. Thousand Oaks, CA: Sage.

Kwon, J. (2004). Expressing refusals in Korean and in American English. *Multilingua*, 23: 339–64.

LACE (2007). The LACE (Languages and Cultures in Europe) Report: The Intercultural Competences Developed in Compulsory Foreign Languages Education in the European Union. The European Commission: DG Education, Training, Culture and Multilingualism. Available in English, German and French at: http://ec.europa.eu/education/policies/lang/key/studies_en.html (accessed 11 Oct. 2008).

Landis, D. and Brislin, R. W. (eds) (1983). *Handbook of Intercultural Training*. Volume 1: *Issues in Theory and Design*. New York: Pergamon Press.

Landis, D., Bennett, J. M. and Bennett, M. J. (eds) (2004). *Handbook of Intercultural Training*, 3rd edn. Thousand Oaks, CA: Sage.

Landis, D., Dansby, M. R. and Tallarigo, R. S. (1996). The use of Equal Opportunity Climate in intercultural training. In D. Landis and R. S. Bhagat (eds), *Handbook of Intercultural Training*, 2nd edn, pp. 244–63. Thousand Oaks, CA: Sage.

Lane, H. W., Distefano, J. J. and Maznevski, M. L. (2006). *International Management Behavior*. Oxford: Blackwell.

Langer, E. J. (1989). *Mindfulness*. Cambridge, MA: Perseus Books.

Leary, M. R. (1995). *Self-Presentation: Impression Management and Interpersonal Behavior*. Boulder, CO: Westview Press.

Leary, M. R. (2007). Motivational and emotional aspects of the self. *Annual Review of Psychology*, 58: 317–44.

Leclerc, D. and Martin, J. N. (2004). Tour guide communication competence: French, German and American tourists' perceptions. *International Journal of Intercultural Relations*, 28 (3–4): 181–200.

Lee, B. K. and Chen, L. (2000). Cultural communication competence and psychological adjustment. *Communication Research Reports*, 27: 764–92.

Lee, K., Yang, G. and Graham, J. L. (2006). Tension and trust in international business negotiations: American executives negotiating with Chinese executives. *Journal of International Business Studies*, 37: 623–41.

Leech, G. (1983). *Principles of Pragmatics*. London: Longman.

Leech, G. (2005). Politeness: Is there an East–West divide? *Journal of Foreign Languages*, 6. Available at: http://www.ling.lancs.ac.uk/staff/geoff/leech2006-politeness.pdf (accessed 15 Feb. 2007).

Leech, G. (2007). Politeness: Is there an East–West divide? *Journal of Politeness Research: Language, Behaviour, Culture*, 3 (2): 167–206.

Leslie, J. B., Dalton, M., Ernst, C. and Deal, J. (eds) (2002). *Managerial Effectiveness in a Global Context: A Working Model of Predictors*. Greensboro, NC: Centre for Creative Leadership.

Leung, T. and Yeung, L. L. (1995). Negotiation in the People's Republic of China: Results of a survey of small business in Hong Kong. *Journal of Small Business Management*, 33 (1): 70–7.

Levinson, S. C. (1979). Activity types and language. *Linguistics*, 17: 365–99.

Liberman, K. (1981). Understanding Aborigines in Australian courts of law. *Human Organization*, 40: 247–55.

Liedke, M., Redder, A. and Scheidter, S. (1999). Interkulturelles Handeln lehren – ein diskursanalytischer Trainingsansatz. In G. Brünner, R. Fiehler and W. Kindt (eds), *Angewandte Diskursforschung – Methoden und Anwendungsbereiche*, vol. 2, pp. 148–79. Opladen: Westdeutscher Verlag.

Lim, T.-S. (1994). Facework and interpersonal relationships. In S. Ting-Toomey (ed.), *The Challenge of Facework: Cross-Cultural and Interpersonal Issues*, pp. 209–29. New York: State University of New York Press.

Linstone, H. A. and Turoff, M. (eds) (1975). *The Delphi Method: Techniques and Applications*. Reading, MA: Addison-Wesley.

Littlewood, W. (1981). *Communicative Language Teaching: An Introduction*. Cambridge: Cambridge University Press.

Long, M. (1983). Linguistic and conversational adjustments to non-native speakers. *Studies in Second Language Acquisition*, 5 (2): 177–93.

Louis, M. R. and Bartunek, J. M. (1992). Insider/outsider research teams: Collaboration across diverse perspectives. *Journal of Management Inquiry*, 1 (2): 101–10.

MacIsaac, D. and Jackson, L. (1994). Assessment processes and outcomes: Portfolio construction. *New Directions for Adult and Continuing Education*, 62: 63–72.

Mackie, M. (1973). Arriving at 'truth' by definition: The case of stereotype inaccuracy. *Social Problems*, 20: 431–47.

Mak, A. S. and Buckingham, K. (2007). Beyond communication courses: Are there benefits in adding skills-based ExcelL™ sociocultural training? *International Journal of Intercultural Relations*, 31 (3): 277–91.

Malin, N. (ed.) (2000). *Professionalism, Boundaries and the Workplace*. Oxford: Blackwell.

Mallinson, C. and Brewster, Z. W. (2005). 'Blacks and bubbas': Stereotypes, ideology, and categorization process in restaurant servers' discourse. *Discourse and Society*, 16 (6): 787–807.

Markus, H. R. and Kitayama, S. (1991). Culture and the self: Implications for cognition, emotion, and motivation. *Psychological Review*, 98 (2): 224–53.

Marra, M. (2008). Recording and analysing talk across cultures. In H. Spencer-Oatey (ed.), *Culturally Speaking: Culture, Communication and Politeness Theory*, pp. 304–21. London: Continuum.

Marriott, H. E. (1990). Intercultural business negotiations: The problem of norm discrepancy. *ARAL Series S*, 7: 33–65.

Martin, J. N., Hammer, M. R. and Bradford, L. (1994). The influence of cultural and situational contexts on Hispanic and non-Hispanic communication competence behaviors. *Communication Quarterly*, 2: 160–79.

Marx, E. (2001). *Breaking through Culture Shock*. London: Nicholas Brealey.

Matsumoto, D. (1996). *Culture and Psychology*. Pacific Grove, CA: Brooks/Cole.

Matsumoto, D. and Juang, L. (2008). *Culture and Psychology*, 4th edn. Belmont, CA: Thomson Higher Education.

Matsumoto, D., Yoo, S. H. and LeRoux, J. A. (2007). Emotion and intercultural adjustment. In H. Kotthoff and H. Spencer-Oatey (eds), *Handbook of Intercultural Communication*, pp. 77–97. Berlin: Mouton de Gruyter.

Matsumoto, D., Weissman, M., Preston, K., Brown, B. and Kupperbusch, S. (1997). Context-specific measurement of individualism-collectivism on the individual level: The IC Interpersonal Assessment Inventory (ICIAI). *Journal of Cross-Cultural Psychology*, 28: 743–67.

Matsumoto, Y. (1988). Reexamination of the universality of face: Politeness phenomena in Japanese. *Journal of Pragmatics*, 12, 403–26.

Matveev, A. V. and Nelson, P. E. (2004). Cross-cultural communication competence and multicultural team performance: Perceptions of American and Russian managers. *International Journal of Cross Cultural Management*, 4: 253–70.

Matveev, A. V., Rao, N. and Milter, R. G. (2001). *Developing a Scale to Measure Intercultural Communication Competence: A Pilot Study in Multicultural Organizations*. Atlanta, GA: International and Intercultural Communication Division of the National Communication Association.

Maznevski, M. and Chudoba, K. (2000). Bridging space over time: Global virtual team dynamics and effectiveness. *Organization Science*, 11 (5): 473–92.

McCroskey, J. C. and McCroskey, L. L. (1988). Self-report as an approach to measuring communication competence. *Communication Research Reports*, 5: 108–13.

McSweeney, B. (2002). Hofstede's model of national cultural differences and their consequences: A triumph of faith – a failure of analysis. *Human Relations*, 55 (1): 89–118.

Mehan, H. (1993). Beneath the skin and between the ears: A case study in the politics of representation. In S. Chaiklin and J. Lave (eds), *Understanding Practice*, pp. 241–68. Cambridge: Cambridge University Press.

Mifflin, L. (1996). ABC sends a young point of view into the field: Up and coming Anderson Cooper. *New York Times*, 11 February. Available at: http://query.nytimes.com/gst/fullpage.html?res9506E4DB1539F932A25751C0A96095826 0&partnerrssnyt&emcrss (accessed 22 Aug. 2008).

Mills, J. (2004). Mothers and mother tongue: Perspectives on self-construction by mothers of Pakistani heritage. In A. Pavlenko and A. Blackledge (eds), *Negotiation of Identities in Multilingual Contexts*, pp. 161–91. Clevedon, Avon: Multilingual Matters.

Milstein, T. (2005). Transformation abroad: Sojourning and the perceived enhancement of self-efficacy. *International Journal of Intercultural Relations, 29* (2): 217–38.

Moghaddam, F. M. (1998). *Social Psychology: Exploring Universals across Cultures.* New York: Freeman.

Moore, D. R. and Dainty, A. R. J. (2001). Intra-team boundaries as inhibitors of performance improvement in UK design and build projects: A call for change. *Construction Management and Economics, 19,* 559–62.

Moore, E. (2004). Sociolinguistic style: A multidimensional resource for shared identity creation. *Canadian Journal of Linguistics/Revue canadienne de linguistique,* 49 (3–4): 375–96.

Mori, J. (2003). The construction of interculturality: A study of initial encounters between Japanese and American students. *Research on Language and Social Interaction,* 36 (2): 143–84.

Morris, D., Collett, P., Marsh, P. and O'Shaughnessy, M. (1979). *Gestures: Their Origins and Distribution.* New York: Stein & Day.

Morris, M. W., Williams, K. Y., Leung, K., Larrick, R., Mendoza, M. T., Bhatnagar, D., Li, J., Kondo, M., Luo, J.-L. and Hu, J.-C. (1998). Conflict management style: Accounting for cross-national differences. *Journal of International Business Studies,* 29 (4): 729–48.

Mulder, S. S., Rance, S., Suárez, M. S. and Condori, M. C. (2000). Unethical ethics? Reflections on intercultural research practices. *Reproductive Health Matters,* 8 (15): 104–12.

Müller-Jacquier, B. (2000). Linguistic awareness of cultures: Grundlagen eines Trainingsmoduls. In J. Bolten (ed.), *Studien zur internationalen Unternehmenskommunikation,* pp. 18–48. Leipzig: H. Popp.

Nahavandi, A. and Malekzadeh, A. R. (1988). Acculturation in mergers and acquisitions. *Academy of Management Review,* 13: 79–90.

Nakane, I. (2006). Silence and politeness in intercultural communication in university seminars. *Journal of Pragmatics,* 38: 1811–35.

Nees, G. (2000). *Germany: Unravelling an Enigma.* Yarmouth, ME: Intercultural Press.

Neuliep, J. W. and McCroskey, J. C. (1997). The development of intercultural and interethnic communication apprehension scale. *Communication Research Reports,* 14: 385–98.

Nipporica (1997). *ECOTONOS: A Multicultural Problem-Solving Simulation.* Yarmouth, ME: Intercultural Press.

Oberg, K. (1960). Culture shock: Adjustment to new cultural environments. *Practical Anthropology,* 7: 177–82.

Office of Ethnic Affairs Te Tari Matawaka (1995). Let's Talk. Guidelines for Government Agencies Hiring Interpreters. Available at: http://www. ethnicaffairs.govt.nz/oeawebsite.nsf/wpg_URL/Resources-Ethnic-Affairs-Publications-Lets-Talk-Guidelines-For-Government-Agencies-Hiring-Interpreters?OpenDocument&ExpandView (accessed 2 April 2009).

Ohbuchi, K.-I. and Takahashi, Y. (1994). Cultural styles of conflict management in Japanese and Americans: Passivity, covertness, and effectiveness of strategies. *Journal of Applied Social Psychology,* 24 (15): 1345–66.

Okabe, R. (1983). Cultural assumptions of East and West: Japan and the United States. In W. B. Gudykunst (ed.), *Intercultural Communication Theory: Current Perspectives,* pp. 21–44. Beverly Hills, CA: Sage.

Oliver, R. L. and Anderson, E. (1994). An empirical test of the consequences of behavior-and-outcome-based sales control systems. *Journal of Marketing*, 58: 53–67.

Ortuno, M. M. (1991). Cross-cultural awareness in a foreign language class: The Kluckhohn Model. *The Modern Language Journal*, 75 (4): 449–59.

Ortuno, M. M. (2000). Value orientations and foreign language study. In K. W. Russo (ed.), *Finding the Middle Ground: Insight and Applications of the Value Orientations Method*, pp. 151–62. Yarmouth, ME: Intercultural Press.

Paige, R. M. (1993). *Education for the Intercultural Experience*, 2nd edn. Yarmouth, ME: Intercultural Press.

Paige, R. M. (2004). Instrumentation in intercultural training. In D. Landis, J. M. Bennett and M. J. Bennett (eds), *Handbook of Intercultural Training*, 3rd edn, pp. 85–128. Thousand Oaks, CA: Sage.

Paige, R. M., Jacobs-Cassuto, M., Yershova, Y. A. and DeJaeghere, J. (2003). Assessing intercultural sensitivity: An empirical analysis of the Hammer and Bennett Intercultural Development Inventory. *International Journal of Intercultural Relations*, 27 (4): 467–86.

Palthe, J. (2004). The relative importance of antecedents to cross-cultural adjustment: Implications for managing a global workforce. *International Journal of Intercultural Relations*, 28 (1): 37–60.

Parsons, T. and Shils, E. A. (1951). *Toward a General Theory of Action*. Cambridge, MA: Harvard University Press.

Pavitt, C. and Haight, L. (1986). Implicit theories of communicative competence: Situational and competence level differences in judgments of prototype and target. *Communication Monograph*, 53: 221–35.

Pennington, D. C. (1986). *Essential Social Psychology*. London: Edward Arnold.

Pennycook, A. (1994). *The Cultural Politics of English as an International Language*. London: Longman.

Peter, L. J. (1969). *The Peter Principle: Why Things Go Wrong*. New York: Morrow.

Phillips, T. (2004). Dealing with difference through integration. Speech given at the *Multicultural Futures* Conference, Monash Prato Centre, Tuscany, Italy, 22–23 September. Extracts from speech available at: http://www.cre.gov.uk/Default.aspx.LocID-0hgnew00s.RefLocID-0hg00900c001002.Lang-EN.htm (accessed 19 Feb. 2007).

Phillipson, R. (1992). *Linguistic Imperialism*. Oxford: Oxford University Press.

Phinney, J. S. (1992). The Multigroup Ethnic Identity Measure: A new scale for use with diverse groups. *Journal of Adolescent Research*, 7: 156–76.

Pike, K. L. (1954). *Language in Relation to a Unified Theory of the Structure of Human Behavior, Part 1*. Glendale, CA: Summer Institute of Linguistics.

Pöchhacker, F. (2004). *Introducing Interpreting Studies*. London: Routledge.

Pölzl, U. (2005). *Exploring the Third Space: Negotiating Culture in English as a Lingua Franca*. Unpublished PhD thesis, University of Vienna.

Prechtl, E. and Davidson-Lund, A. (2007). Intercultural competence and assessment: perspectives from the INCA project. In H. Kotthoff and H. Spencer-Oatey (eds), *Handbook of Intercultural Communication*, pp. 467–90. Berlin: Mouton de Gruyter.

Pye, L. W. (1995). Factions and the politics of *Guanxi*: Paradoxes in Chinese administrative and political behaviour. *The China Journal*, 34 (July): 35–53.

Rackham, N. and Carlisle, J. (1978). The effective negotiator – Part I. The behaviour of successful negotiators. *Journal of European Industrial Training*, 2 (6): 6–11.

Rampton, B. (1995). *Crossing: Language and Ethnicity among Adolescents*. London: Longman.

Relph, E. (1976). *Place and Placelessness*. London: Pion.

Reyes, A. (2004). Asian American stereotypes as circulating resource. *Pragmatics*, 14 (2–3): 173–92.

Richardson, R. M. and Smith, S. W. (2007). The influence of high/low-context culture and power distance on choice of communication media: Students' media choice to communicate with Professors in Japan and America. *International Journal of Intercultural Relations*, 31 (4): 479–502.

Risager, K. (1998). Language teaching and the process of European integration. In M. Byram and M. Fleming (eds), *Language Learning in Intercultural Perspective*, pp. 242–54. Cambridge: Cambridge University Press.

Roberts, C. (1997). The politics of transcription. Transcribing talk: Issues of representation. *TESOL Quarterly*, 31 (1): 167–72.

Roberts, C. (1998). Awareness in intercultural communication. *Language Awareness*, 7 (2–3): 109–27. Available at: http://www.multilingual-matters.net/la/007/0109/la0070109.pdf (accessed 18 Feb. 2007).

Roberts, C., Byram, M., Barro, A., Jordan, S. and Street, B. (2001). *Language Learners as Ethnographers*. Clevedon: Multilingual Matters.

Roberts, C., Davies, E. and Jupp, T. (1992). *Language and Discrimination*. London: Longman.

Roberts, C., Moss, B., Wass, V., Sarangi, S. and Jones, R. (2005). Misunderstandings: A qualitative study of primary care consultations in multilingual settings, and educational implications. *Medical Education*, 39, 465–75.

Rogerson-Revell, P. (2007). Humour in business: A double-edged sword. A study of humour and style shifting in intercultural business meetings. *Journal of Pragmatics*, 39: 4–28.

Rosch, E. (1978). Principles of categorization. In E. Rosch and B. B. Lloyd (eds), *Cognition and Categorization*, pp. 27–48. Hillsdale, NJ: LEA.

Rosenfeld, P., Giacalone, R. A. and Riordan, C. (2002). *Impression Management: Building and Enhancing Reputations at Work*. London: Thomson Learning.

Rost-Roth, M. (2007). Intercultural training. In H. Kotthoff and H. Spencer-Oatey (eds), *Handbook of Intercultural Communication*, pp. 491–518. Berlin: Mouton de Gruyter.

Ruben, B. D. (1989). The study of cross-cultural competence: Traditions and contemporary issues. *International Journal of Organizational Behaviour*, 13: 229–40.

Runnymede Trust (Commission on the Future of Multi-Ethnic Britain) (2000). *The Future of Multi-Ethnic Britain (The Parekh Report)*. London: Profile Books.

Russo, K. W. (ed.) (2000a). *Finding the Middle Ground: Insight and Applications of the Value Orientations Method*. Yarmouth, ME: Intercultural Press.

Russo, K. W. (2000b). Value orientations method: The conceptual framework. In K. W. Russo (ed.), *Finding the Middle Ground: Insight and Applications of the Value Orientations Method*, pp. 3–20. Yarmouth, ME: Intercultural Press.

Ryoo, H.-K. (2005). Achieving friendly interactions: A study of service encounters between Korean shopkeepers and African-American customers. *Discourse and Society*, 16 (1): 79–105.

Salzman, M. B. (1990). The construction of an intercultural sensitizer for training non-Navajo personnel. *Journal of American Indian Education*, 309 (1): 25–33.

Schäfer, B. (1994). Stereotype und Vorurteile als Voraussetzungen und Barrieren gesellschaftlicher Kommunikation. In W. K. F. and F. Naumann (eds), *Kommunikation und Humanontogenese*, pp. 460–70. Bielefeld: Kleine Verlag.

Schneider, D. J. (2004). *The Psychology of Stereotyping.* London: Guilford Press.

Schneider, J. and von der Emde, S. (2006). Conflicts in cyberspace: From communication breakdown to intercultural dialogue in online collaborations. In J. Belz and S. L. Thorne (eds), *Internet-Mediated Intercultural Foreign Language Education*, pp. 178–206. Boston: Thomson Higher Education.

Schneider, S. C. and Barsoux, J.-L. (2003). *Managing across Cultures*, 2nd edn. London: Prentice Hall.

Schnurr, S., Marra, M. and Holmes, J. (2007). Being (im)polite in New Zealand workplaces: Māori and Pākehā leaders. *Journal of Pragmatics*, 39, 712–29.

Schroll-Machl, S. (2002). *Doing Business with Germans: Their Perception, Our Perception.* Göttingen: Vandenhoeck & Ruprecht.

Schwartz, S. H. (1992). Universals in the content and structure of values: Theoretical advances and empirical tests in 20 countries. In M. P. Zanna (ed.), *Advances in Experimental Social Psychology*, vol. 25, pp. 1–65. San Diego, CA: Academic Press.

Schwartz, S. H. (1999). A theory of cultural values and some implications for work. *Applied Psychology: An International Review*, 48 (1): 23–47.

Schwartz, S. H. and Bardi, A. (2001). Value hierarchies across cultures. *Journal of Cross-Cultural Psychology*, 32 (3): 268–90.

Schwartz, S. H., Melech, G., Lehmann, A., Burgess, S., Harris, M. and Owens, V. (2001). Extending the cross-cultural validity of the theory of basic human values with a different method of measurement. *Journal of Cross-Cultural Psychology*, 32 (5): 519–42.

Schwartz, T. (1992). Anthropology and psychology: an unrequited relationship. In T. Schwartz, G. M. White & C. A. Lutz (eds), *New Directions in Psychological Anthropology*, pp. 324–49. Cambridge: Cambridge University Press.

Scollon, R. and Scollon, S. W. (1981). *Narrative, Literacy, and Face in Interethnic Communication.* New Jersey: Ablex.

Scollon, R. and Scollon, S. W. (1995). *Intercultural Communication.* Oxford: Blackwell.

Secord, P. F. and Backman, C. W. (1964). *Social Psychology.* New York: McGraw Hill.

Sedikides, C., Gaertner, L. and Toguchi, Y. (2003). Pancultural self-enhancement. *Journal of Personality and Social Psychology*, 89: 539–51.

Selmer, J. (2002). To train or not to train? European expatriate managers in China. *International Journal of Cross Cultural Management*, 2 (1): 37–51.

Sercu, L. (2005a). Teaching foreign languages in an intercultural world. In L. Sercu, with E. Bandura, P. Castro, L. Davcheva, C. Laskaridou, U. Lundgren,

M. del Carmen, M. García and P. Ryan (eds), *Foreign Language Teachers & Intercultural Communication: An International Investigation*, pp. 1–18. Clevedon: Multilingual Matters.

Sercu, L. (2005b). The foreign language and intercultural competence teacher. In L. Sercu, with E. Bandura, P. Castro, L. Davcheva, C. Laskaridou, U. Lundgren, M. del Carmen, M. García and P. Ryan (eds), *Foreign Language Teachers & Intercultural Communication: An International Investigation*, pp. 130–59. Clevedon: Multilingual Matters.

Shapiro, J. M., Ozanne, J. L. and Saatcioglu, B. (2008). An interpretive examination of the development of cultural sensitivity in international business. *Journal of International Business Studies*, 39: 71–87.

Shigemasu, E. and Ikeda, K. i. (2006). Face threatening act avoidance and relationship satisfaction between international students and Japanese host students. *International Journal of Intercultural Relations*, 30 (4): 439–56.

Shirts, R. G. (1974/1995). *BaFa BaFa: A Cross Culture Simulation*. Del Mar, CA: Simile II, Simulation Training Systems.

Shirts, R. G. (1976). *RaFa RaFa: A Cross Culture Simulation*. Del Mar, CA: Simile II.

SIETAR Europa Online Documentation Centre: http://www.sietar.de/SIETAR project/index.html (accessed 4 Oct. 2008).

Simon, B. (2004). *Identity in Modern Society: A Social Psychological Perspective*. Oxford: Blackwell.

Simpson, D. T. (1977a). Handling group and organizational conflict. In J. E. Jones and J. W. Pfeiffer (eds), *Annual Handbook for Group Facilitators*, pp. 120–2. San Diego, CA: University Associates.

Simpson, D. T. (1977b). Conflict styles: Organizational decision making. In J. E. Jones and J. W. Pfeiffer (eds), *Annual Handbook for Group Facilitators*, pp. 15–19. San Diego, CA: University Associates.

Singelis, T. M. (1998). *Teaching about Culture, Ethnicity and Diversity: Exercises and Planned Activities*. Thousand Oaks, CA: Sage.

Smith, E. R. and Zárate, M. A. (1992). Exemplar-based model of social judgment. *Psychological Review*, 99: 3–21.

Smith, L. E. (1993). English as an international auxiliary language. In L. E. Smith (ed.), *Readings in English as an International Language*. Oxford: Pergamon.

Smith, P. B. and Bond, M. H. (1998). *Social Psychology across Cultures*. London: Prentice Hall Europe.

Smith, P. B., Bond, M. H. and Kağıtçıbası, Ç. (2006). *Understanding Social Psychology across Cultures: Living and Working in a Changing World*. London: Sage.

Smith, P. B., Peterson, M. F. and Schwartz, S. H. (2002). Cultural values, sources of guidance, and their relevance to managerial behavior: A 47-nation study. *Journal of Cross-Cultural Psychology*, 33: 2.

Soja, E. W. (1989). *Postmodern Geographies – The Reassertion of Space in Critical Social Theory*. London: Verso Books.

Sparrow, L. M. (2000). Beyond multicultural man: Complexities of identity. *International Journal of Intercultural Relations*, 24 (2): 173–201.

Spector, P. E., Cooper, C. L. and Sparks, K. (2001). An international study of the psychometric properties of the Hofstede values survey module 1994: A comparison of individual and country/province level results. *Applied Psychology: An International Review*, 50 (2): 269–81.

Spencer, L. M. and Spencer, S. M. (1993). *Competence at Work: Models for Superior Performance*. New York: John Wiley & Sons.

Spencer-Oatey, H. (1992). *Cross-Cultural Politeness: British and Chinese Conceptions of the Tutor–Student Relationship*. Unpublished PhD thesis, Lancaster University.

Spencer-Oatey, H. (1996). Reconsidering power and distance. *Journal of Pragmatics*, 26 (1): 1–24.

Spencer-Oatey, H. (2002). Managing rapport in talk: Using rapport sensitive incidents to explore the motivational concerns underlying the management of relations. *Journal of Pragmatics*, 34: 529–45.

Spencer-Oatey, H. (2005). Rapport management theory and culture. *Intercultural Pragmatics*, 2–3: 335–46.

Spencer-Oatey, H. (2007a). Theories of identity and the analysis of face. *Journal of Pragmatics*, 39: 639–56.

Spencer-Oatey, H. (ed.) (2007b). *e-Learning Initiatives in China: Pedagogy, Policy and Culture*. Hong Kong: Hong Kong University Press.

Spencer-Oatey, H. (ed.) (2008a). *Culturally Speaking: Culture, Communication and Politeness Theory*, 2nd edn. London: Continuum.

Spencer-Oatey, H. (2008b). Introduction. In H. Spencer-Oatey (ed.), *Culturally Speaking: Culture, Communication and Politeness Theory*, 2nd edn, pp. 1–8. London: Continuum.

Spencer-Oatey, H. (2008c). Face, (im)politeness and rapport. In H. Spencer-Oatey (ed.), *Culturally Speaking: Culture, Communication and Politeness Theory*, 2nd edn, pp. 11–47. London: Continuum.

Spencer-Oatey, H. and Jiang, W. (2003). Explaining cross-cultural pragmatic findings: Moving from politeness maxims to sociopragmatic interactional principles (SIPs). *Journal of Pragmatics*, 35: 1633–50.

Spencer-Oatey, H. and Stadler, S. (2009). *The Global People Competency Framework. Competencies for Effective Intercultural Interaction*. Warwick Occasional Papers in Applied Linguistics #3. Available at: http://www.globalpeople.org.uk/

Spencer-Oatey, H. and Tang, M. (2007). Managing the collaborative process in international projects: Programme management perspectives. In H. Spencer-Oatey (ed.), *e-Learning Initiatives in China: Pedagogy, Policy and Culture*, pp. 159–73. Hong Kong: Hong Kong University Press.

Spencer-Oatey, H. and Xing, J. (2003). Managing rapport in intercultural business interactions: A comparison of two Chinese-British welcome meetings. *Journal of Intercultural Studies*, 24 (1): 33–46.

Spencer-Oatey, H. and Xing, J. (2004). Rapport management problems in Chinese–British business interactions: A case study. In J. House and J. Rehbein (eds), *Multilingual Communication*, pp. 197–221. Amsterdam: John Benjamins.

Spencer-Oatey, H. and Xing, J. (2005). Managing talk and non-talk in intercultural interactions: insights from two Chinese–British business meetings. *Multilingua*, 24: 55–74.

Spencer-Oatey, H. and Xing, J. (2007). The impact of culture on interpreter behaviour. In H. Kotthoff and H. Spencer-Oatey (eds), *Handbook of Intercultural Communication*, pp. 219–36. Berlin: Walter de Gruyter.

Spencer-Oatey, H. and Xing, J. (2008). A problematic Chinese business visit to Britain: Issues of face. In H. Spencer-Oatey (ed.), *Culturally Speaking: Culture, Communication and Politeness Theory*, 2nd edn, pp. 258–73. London: Continuum.

Spencer-Oatey, H. and Xiong, Z. (2006). Chinese students' psychological and sociocultural adjustments to Britain: An empirical study. *Language, Culture and Curriculum*, 19 (1): 37–53.

Spencer-Oatey, H., Ng, P. and Dong, L. (2008). British and Chinese reactions to compliment responses. In H. Spencer-Oatey (ed.), *Culturally Speaking: Culture, Communication and Politeness Theory*, pp. 95–117. London: Continuum.

Spiegel, J. P. and Papajohn, J. (2000). Training program in ethnicity and mental health. In K. W. Russo (ed.), *Finding the Middle Ground: Insight and Applications of the Value Orientations Method*, pp. 77–99. Yarmouth, ME: Intercultural Press.

Spitzberg, B. H. (1988). Communication competence: Measures of perceived effectiveness. In C. Tardy (ed.), *A Handbook for the Study of Human Communication*, pp. 67–105. Norwood: Ablex.

Spitzberg, B. H. (1989). Issues in the development of a theory of interpersonal competence in the intercultural context. *International Journal of Intercultural Relations*, 13: 241–68.

Stahl, G. (2001). Using assessment centers as tools for global leadership development: An exploratory study. In M. Mendenhall, T. Kühlmann and G. Stahl (eds), *Developing Global Business Leaders: Policies, Processes and Innovations*, pp. 197–210. Westport, CT: Quorum Books.

Steers, R. M., Bischoff, S. J. and Higgins, L. H. (1992). Cross-cultural management research: The fish and the fisherman. *Journal of Management Inquiry*, 1 (4): 321–30.

Stening, B. W. and Zhang, M. Y. (2007). Methodological challenges confronted when conducting management research in China. *International Journal of Cross-Cultural Management*, 7 (1): 121–42.

Stewart, E. C. (1995). Contrast-culture training. In S. M. Fowler and M. G. Mumford (eds), *Intercultural Sourcebook: Cross-Cultural Training Methods*, vol. 1, pp. 47–58. Yarmouth, ME: Intercultural Press.

Stokoe, E. and Edwards, D. (2007). 'Black this, black that': Racial insults and reported speech in neighbour complaints and police interrogations. *Discourse and Society*, 18 (3): 337–72.

Storti, C. (1999). Cross-cultural dialogues. In S. M. Fowler and M. G. Mumford (eds), *Intercultural Sourcebook: Cross-Cultural Training Methods*, vol, 2, pp. 203–10. Yarmouth, ME: Intercultural Press.

Straffon, D. A. (2003). Assessing the intercultural sensitivity of high school students attending an international school. *International Journal of Intercultural Relations*, 27 (4): 487–501.

Tarakeshwar, N., Stanton, J. and Pargament, K. I. (2003). Religion: An overlooked dimension in cross-cultural psychology. *Journal of Cross-Cultural Psychology*, 34 (4): 377–94.

Teagarden, M. B., Von Glinow, M. A., Bowen, D. E., Frayne, C. A., Nason, S., Huo, Y. P., Milliman, J., Arias, M. E., Butler, M. C., Geringer, J. M., Kim, N.-H., Scullion, H., Lowe, K. B. and Drost, E. A. (1995). Toward a theory of comparative management research: An idiographic case study of the best international human resources management project. *The Academy of Management Journal*, 38 (5): 1261–87.

Ten Thije, J. D. (2001). Ein diskursanalytisches Konzept zum interkulturellen Kommunikationstraining. In J. Bolten and K. Schröter (eds), *Im Netzwerk interkulturellen Handelns: Theoretische und praktische Perspektiven der interkulturellen Kommunikationsforschung*, pp. 176–204. Sternenfels: Wissenschaft und Praxis.

Thiagaran, S. and Steinwachs, B. (1990). *Barnga: A Simulation Game on Cultural Clashes*. Yarmouth, ME: Intercultural Press.

Thomas, A. (1988). Untersuchung zur Entwicklung eines interkulturellen Handlungstrainings in der Managerausbildung (Research for developing intercultural action training as part of managerial training). *Psychologische Beiträge*, 30 (1–2): 147–65.

Thomas, A. (1989). Interkulturelles Handlungstraining in der Managerausbildung (Intercultural action training in management education) *Wirtschafts wissenschaftliches Studium*, 6: 281–6.

Thomas, A. (1996a). Analyse der Handlungswirksamkeit von Kulturstandards (Analysis of the effectiveness of culture standards). In A. Thomas (ed.), *Psychologie interkulturellen Handelns (Psychology of Intercultural Action)*, pp. 107–35. Göttingen: Hofgrefe-Verlag.

Thomas, A. (1996b). *Psychologie interkulturellen Handelns (Psychology of Intercultural Action)*. Göttingen: Hogrefe-Verlag.

Thomas, A. (2003a). Interkulturelle Kompetenz: Grundlagen, Probleme, Konzepte (Intercultural competence: Principles, problems, concepts). *Erwägen, Wissen, Ethik*, 14 (1): 137–50.

Thomas, A. (2003b). Kultur und Kulturstandards (Culture and culture standards). In A. Thomas, E.-U. Kinast and S. Schroll-Machl (eds), *Handbuch Interkulturelle Kommunikation und Kooperation. Band 1: Grundlagen und Praxisfelder (Handbook of Intercultural Communication and Cooperation. Volume 1: Principles and Fields of Application)*, pp. 19–31. Göttingen: Vandenhoeck and Ruprecht.

Thomas, J. (1983). Cross-cultural pragmatic failure. *Applied Linguistics*, 4 (2): 91–112.

Thomas, J. (1995). *Meaning in Interaction: An Introduction to Pragmatics*. London: Longman.

Thomas, K. (1976). Conflict and conflict management. In M. Dunnette (ed.), *The Handbook of Industrial and Organizational Psychology*, pp. 889–935. Chicago: Rand McNally.

Tilbury, F. and Colic-Peisker, V. (2006). Deflecting responsibility in employer talk about race discrimination. *Discourse and Society*, 17 (5): 651–76.

Ting-Toomey, S. (1999). *Communicating across Cultures*. New York: The Guilford Press.

Ting-Toomey, S. and Chung, L. C. (2005). *Understanding Intercultural Communication*. Los Angeles: Roxbury.

Ting-Toomey, S. and Kurogi, A. (1998). Facework competence in intercultural conflict: An updated face-negotiation theory. *International Journal of Intercultural Relations*, 22 (2): 187–225.

Tomalin, B. and Stempleski, S. (1993). *Cultural Awareness*. Oxford: Oxford University Press.

Tran, G. Q. (2006). The naturalized role-play: An innovative methodology in cross-cultural and interlanguage pragmatics research. *Reflections on English Language Teaching*, 5 (2): 1–24.

Triandis, H. C. (1989). The self and social behavior in differing cultural contexts. *Psychological Review*, 96: 506–20.

Triandis, H. C. (1994). *Culture and Social Behavior.* New York: McGraw Hill.

Triandis, H. C. (1995). Culture-specific assimilators. In S. M. Fowler and M. G. Mumford (eds), *Intercultural Sourcebook: Cross-Cultural Training Methods,* vol. 1, pp. 179–86. Yarmouth, ME: Intercultural Press.

Triandis, H. C., Chen, X. P. and Chan, D. K.-S. (1998). Scenarios for the measurement of collectivism and individualism. *Journal of Cross-Cultural Psychology,* 29 (2): 275–89.

Trompenaars, F. (1993). *Riding the Waves of Culture.* Burr Ridge, IL: Irwin.

Trompenaars, F. and Hampden-Turner, C. (1997). *Riding the Waves of Culture: Understanding Cultural Diversity in Business,* 2nd edn. London: Nicholas Brealey.

Trubinsky, P., Ting-Toomey, S. and Lin, S.-L. (1991). The influence of individualism-collectivism and self-monitoring on conflict styles. *International Journal of Intercultural Relations,* 15: 65–84.

Tsang, E. W. K. (1998). Inside story: Mind your identity when conducting cross-national research. *Organization Studies,* 19: 511–15.

Tung, R. L. (1987). Expatriate assignments. Enhancing success and minimizing failure. *Academy of Management Executive,* 1 (2): 117–26.

Tversky, A. and Kahnemann, D. (1983). Extensional versus intuitive resoning: The conjunction fallacy in probability judgement. *Psychological Review,* 90: 293–315.

Twitchin, J. and Roberts, C. (1992). *Crosstalk at Work.* London: BBC.

Tyler, A. (1995). The coconstruction of cross-cultural miscommunication. *Studies in Second Language Acquisition,* 17 (2): 129–52.

UNESCO Cultural Diversity Lens website: http://www.unescobkk.org/index.php?id2529 (accessed 22 Aug. 2008).

Usunier, J.-C. (1998). *International and Cross-Cultural Management Research.* London: Sage.

Van der Zee, K. I. and Van Oudenhoven, J. P. (2001). The multicultural personality questionnaire: Reliability and validity of self- and other ratings of multicultural effectiveness. *Journal of Research in Personality,* 35: 278–88.

Van Ek, J. A. (1986). *Objectives for Foreign Language Learning.* Volume I: *Scope*; Volume II: *Levels.* Straßburg: Council of Europe.

Vance, C. M. and Ensher, E. A. (2002). The voice of the host country workforce: A key source for improving the effectiveness of expatriate training and performance. *International Journal of Intercultural Relations,* 26 (4): 447–61.

Victor, D. A. (1992). *International Business Communication.* London: HarperCollins.

Wadensjö, C. (1998). *Interpreting as Interaction.* London: Longman.

Wang, X. (2001). Dimensions and current status of project management culture. *Project Management Journal,* 32 (4): 4–17.

Ward, C. and Kennedy, A. (1993) Psychological and sociocultural adjustment during cross-cultural transitions: A comparison of secondary students at home and abroad. *International Journal of Psychology,* 28: 129–47.

Ward, C. and Kennedy, A. (1999). The measurement of sociocultural adaptation. *International Journal of Intercultural Relations,* 23 (4): 659–77.

Ward, C. and Kennedy, A. (2001). Coping with cross-cultural transition. *Journal of Cross-Cultural Psychology,* 32 (5): 636–42.

Ward, C., Berno, T. and Main, A. (2002). Can the Cross-cultural Adaptability Inventory predict sojourner adjustment? In P. Boski, F. J. R. van deVijver and

A. M. Chodnicka (eds), *New Directions in Cross-Cultural Psychology*, pp. 409–23. Warsaw: Polish Psychological Association.

Ward, C., Bochner, S. and Furnham, A. (2001). *The Psychology of Culture Shock*. Cambridge: Cambridge University Press.

Ward, C., Masgore, A. M., Berno, T. and Ong, A. S. J. (2002). Can the Cross-Cultural Adaptability Inventory predict sojourner adjustment? In P. Boski, F. J. R. van de Vijver and A. M. Chodynicka (eds), *New Directions in Cross-Cultural Psychology: Selected Papers from the Fifteenth International Congress of the International Association for Cross-Cultural Psychology*, pp. 410–23. Warszawa: Wydawn. Inst. Psychologii Pan.

Watson, O. M. and Graves, T. D. (1966). Quantitative research in proxemic behavior. *American Anthropologist*, 68: 971–85.

Weiss, D. J., Davis, R. V., England, G. W. and Lofquist, L. H. (1967). *Manual for the Minnesota Satisfaction Questionnaire*. Minneapolis: University of Minnesota.

Wenger, E. (1998). *Communities of Practice: Learning, Meaning, and Identity*. Cambridge: Cambridge University Press.

Wheelan, S. A. (1990). *Facilitating Training Groups: A Guide to Leadership and Verbal Intervention Skills*. New York: Praeger.

Wheelan, S. A. (1994). *Group Processes: A Developmental Perspective*. Needham Heights, MA: Allyn & Bacon.

White, R. (1993). Saying please: Pragmalinguistic failure in English interaction. *ELT Journal*, 47 (3): 193–202.

White, R. (1997). Going round in circles: English as an international language, and cross-cultural capability. Available at: http://www.rdg.ac.uk/app_ling/circles.htm and http://host.uniroma3.it/docenti/boylan/text/white01.htm (accessed 22 Nov. 2008).

Wight, A. R. (1995). The critical incident as a training tool. In S. M. Fowler and M. G. Mumford (eds), *Intercultural Sourcebook: Cross-Cultural Training Methods*, vol. 1, pp. 127–40. Yarmouth, ME: Intercultural Press.

Wilkinson, L. C. (2007). A developmental approach to uses of moving pictures in intercultural education. *International Journal of Intercultural Relations*, 31 (1): 1–27.

WorldWork (no date). Description of International competencies. Available at: http://www.worldwork.biz/legacy/www/docs2/tip_downloads.phtml (accessed 23 May 2009).

Xiong, Z. (2005). *Cross-Cultural Adaptation and Academic Performance: Overseas Chinese Students on an International Foundation Course at a British University*. Luton: Unpublished PhD Thesis, University of Luton.

Yau, O. H. M. and You, H. (1994). *Consumer Behaviour in China: Customer Satisfaction and Cultural Values*. London: Routledge.

Ylänne-McEwen, V. (2008). Communication accommodation theory. In H. Spencer-Oatey (ed.), *Culturally Speaking: Culture, Communication and Politeness Theory*, 2nd edn, pp. 164–86. London: Continuum.

Yoo, S. H., Matsumoto, D., LeRoux, J. A. and Liu, S. (2006). The influence of emotion recognition and emotion regulation on intercultural adjustment. *International Journal of Intercultural Relations*, 30 (3): 345–64.

Yum, J. O. (1988). The impact of Confucianism on interpersonal relationships and communication patterns in East Asia. *Communication Monographs*, 55: 374–88.

Žegarac, V. (2007). A cognitive pragmatic perspective on communication and culture. In H. Kotthoff and H. Spencer-Oatey (eds), *Handbook of Intercultural Communication*, pp. 31–53. Berlin: Mouton de Gruyter.

Žegarac, V. and Pennington, M. (2008). Pragmatic transfer. In H. Spencer-Oatey (ed.), *Culturally Speaking: Culture, Communication and Politeness Theory*, 2nd edn, pp. 141–63. London: Continuum.

Ziegenfuss, D. E. and Singhapakdi, A. (1994). Professional values and the ethical perceptions of internal auditors. *Managerial Auditing Journal,* 9 (1): 34–44.

Zung, W. W. E. (1965). A self-rating depression scale. *Archives of General Psychiatry,* 12: 63–70.

Index